Rethinking Revolutionary Change in Europe

Rethinking Revolutionary Change in Europe

A Neostructuralist Approach

Bailey Stone

ROWMAN & LITTLEFIELD
Lanham • Boulder • New York • London

Published by Rowman & Littlefield
An imprint of The Rowman & Littlefield Publishing Group, Inc.
4501 Forbes Boulevard, Suite 200, Lanham, Maryland 20706
https://rowman.com

6 Tinworth Street, London SE11 5AL, United Kingdom

Copyright © 2020 by The Rowman & Littlefield Publishing Group, Inc.

All rights reserved. No part of this book may be reproduced in any form or by any electronic or mechanical means, including information storage and retrieval systems, without written permission from the publisher, except by a reviewer who may quote passages in a review.

British Library Cataloguing in Publication Information Available

Library of Congress Cataloging-in-Publication Data

Names: Stone, Bailey, 1946- author.
Title: Rethinking revolutionary change in Europe : a neostructuralist approach / Bailey Stone.
Description: Lanham : Rowman & Littlefield, [2020] | Includes bibliographical references and index. | Summary: "Reconsidering the English, French, and Russian revolutions, this book offers an important approach to the theoretical and comparative study of revolutions. Stone proposes an innovative 'neostructuralist' synthesis of competing structuralist and postmodernist theory that marks a critical advance in our understanding of revolution"-- Provided by publisher.
Identifiers: LCCN 2019038980 (print) | LCCN 2019038981 (ebook) | ISBN 9781538131374 (cloth) | ISBN 9781538131381 (epub)
ISBN 9781538163870 (pbk)
Subjects: LCSH: Revolutions--Europe--Case studies. | Revolutions--Philosophy. | Great Britain--History--Puritan Revolution, 1642-1660. | France--History--Revolution, 1789-1799. | Soviet Union--History--Revolution, 1917-1921.
Classification: LCC JC491 .S795 2020 (print) | LCC JC491 (ebook) | DDC 303.6/4094--dc23
LC record available at https://lccn.loc.gov/2019038980
LC ebook record available at https://lccn.loc.gov/2019038981

Contents

Acknowledgments		vii
Introduction: Structuralism, Postmodernism, and—Neostructuralism?		ix
1	Modernizers versus Traditionalists in the European Revolutions	1
2	In Search of the Elusive *Ancien Régime* Bourgeoisie	41
3	To Kill a Monarch: From Proceduralism to Revolutionary *Raison d'État*	75
4	Circumstances versus Ideas in the Revolutionary "Furies"	113
5	Crises of Revolutionary Legitimacy: Thermidorian Outcomes	155
Conclusion: Neostructuralism and the Postrevolutionary State as Historical Problem		197
Suggestions for Further Reading		205
Notes		233
Index		279

Acknowledgments

Thanks must go here to a few of those individuals without whose personal support, professional advice, and/or contributions to revolutionary studies I could not possibly have written this book.

Recognition is first of all due to Jack Goldstone, sociologist in the Schar School of Policy and Government at George Mason University. From the inception of this study, Professor Goldstone was ready at all times to encourage my writing and, at the same time, to criticize my interpretations of European revolutionary change in countless ways that proved to be essential. I owe him an enormous debt of gratitude.

I also received encouragement in my work from other prominent scholars, certainly not least among them Emeritus Professor Thomas E. Kaiser (now successfully relocated from the University of Arkansas to academic pursuits on the East Coast); Professor Michel Gueldry at the Middlebury Institute of International Studies in Monterey, California; Professors Abdel Razzaq Takriti and Sarah Fishman at the University of Houston, Texas; and many others as well. Special thanks go in addition to David Carrithers of the Department of Political Science at the University of Tennessee at Chattanooga, who invited me in 2006 to contribute to a symposium on "Liberty, Monarchy, and Regicide: The Trial and Execution of Charles I" held in Cleveland, Ohio, in October 2007. (I hope that some of the insights I acquired at that symposium are reflected in this book's chapter on revolutionary regicides.)

I am grateful as well for the critical reactions to my work offered on several occasions over the past two years in the Five Colleges International Relations Seminar at the University of Massachusetts Amherst. Special thanks to Political Science Emeritus Professor Eric Einhorn for inviting me to attend the sessions of that seminar. Collegial and specialist commentary can be so beneficial (in so many ways) when one is engaged in writing a major work of reconceptualization and reinterpretation.

Many thanks go as well to Susan McEachern, senior executive editor for History, International Studies, and Geography at Rowman & Littlefield Publishers in Boulder, Colorado, and to her editorial associates, for helping me to prepare my latest manuscript for publication. I certainly anticipate as a result a long and fruitful working relationship with Rowman & Littlefield.

Last but surely not least, acknowledgment is due once again to certain very special individuals in the private corridors of my life. As always in the past, so now, they know who they are.

Introduction

Structuralism, Postmodernism, and—Neostructuralism?

There was a time when European historians and other social scientists laboring in the vineyards of comparative revolutionary analysis *thought* that they had things largely figured out. Taking their cue from imposing figures in English and French revolutionary studies such as Christopher Hill and Georges Lefebvre—not to mention earlier luminaries such as Karl Marx and Friedrich Engels—these specialists saw the upheavals of 1640 to 1660 in England and 1789 to 1799 in France as having resulted fundamentally from struggles between economically regressive or "feudal" aristocracies and economically progressive or "capitalist" gentry and/or "bourgeois" *élites*. In both cases, so the narrative held, the entrepreneurial élitists, coveting both a greater degree of status recognition and a more influential role in public affairs, and profiting from the support of humble folk of city and/or countryside, won out over their aristocratic antagonists *and* over absolute monarchies that were insolvent in their finances, inefficient in their bureaucratic procedures, and superannuated in their vision of society. Needless to add, this venerable paradigm also informed what social scientists in the postwar Union of Soviet Socialist Republics had to say about Russia: for them, the October 1917 upheaval remained the inevitable result of class confrontation between "capitalists" and workers—a confrontation in which Lenin's selfless Bolsheviks, the very incarnation of revolutionary vanguardism, had unerringly blazed the way to the world's first truly socialist society.[1]

But how times have changed! Due in part to the archival labors of younger historians, in part to the theorizing of postwar social scientists, and in part to a "real-world" context of shifting post–Cold War East-West relations, new interpretations of the great European revolutions have arisen to challenge old orthodoxies on this contentious subject. First came classic revisionists in the United Kingdom and the United States such as Alfred Cobban, George V. Taylor, and Conrad Russell (dubbed, unsurprisingly, "Anglo-Saxons" by their French colleagues), who, from the mid-1950s on, deemphasized long-term revolutionary causation and regarded European revolutions as originating in fortuitous convergences of short-term factors and also continuing on the basis of unpredictable contingencies.[2] More recently, however, learned commentary on the English, French, and Russian Revolutions seems increasingly characterized by complex and often polemical exchanges between "postmodernists" celebrating personal "agency"; textual *deconstruction*; the explanatory power of revolutionary discourse and ideology; and "structuralists" playing up the importance of state formation, state/class interactions, and international politics. My primary objective in this book is to identify *five specific issues in the English, French, and Russian Revolutions* and to show how, taken together, they are most effectively interpreted through an innovative "neostructuralist" synthesis of postmodernist and structuralist perspectives. But it would probably make the most sense to begin here by discussing structuralism and postmodernism in generalized, theoretical terms. We can then hope that such a discussion will leave us with the framework we require for our ensuing analysis of the five specific revolutionary issues.

Before proceeding to a reappraisal of structuralism and postmodernism, however, we should briefly acknowledge four prestructuralist approaches to revolutionary analysis that were popular among certain social scientists of early and mid-twentieth-century vintage. One prominent group of historians "attempted to chart the *natural history of revolutions* from their earliest stirrings to the consolidation of the new regime."[3] Although Crane Brinton's *The Anatomy of Revolution* is by far and away the most frequently cited work in this genre, it has had to share the stage over the years with studies by Lyford P. Edwards, George S. Pettee, Rex D. Hopper, and others.[4] Then, again, "structural/functional" theorists—most famously, Chalmers Johnson—argued that revolutions in general have occurred when supposedly "disequilibrated" social systems, weighed down by accumulating "multiple dysfunctions," and further destabilized by their intransigent and incompetent ruling élites, have been propelled toward terminal breakdowns by precipitants of various types—factors such as defeats in war, the emergence of truly revolutionary parties, the rise to prominence of charismatic leaders, and so forth.[5] Finally, two other groups of prestructuralist scholars found various ways to prioritize *psychological* dynamics, focusing either on the discontents, politicization, and public roles of *individual leaders* in revolutionary situations or on what sociologist Michael S. Kimmel has called "the *aggre-*

gate social psychology of mass discontent that leads to revolutionary mobilization."[6]

To one extent or another, of course, all of these earlier specialists reacted to, and derived some of their analytical insights from, the historical literature on the major European (and other) revolutions. And so have those theorists writing much more recently in what they themselves have quite frequently identified as structuralist or postmodernist veins. We will first endeavor here to develop a theoretical definition of structuralism *as well as review its tendency to "split" into two principal subfields*; then, we will explain how the postmodernist tendency *has managed to follow an analogous trajectory*.

Michael Kimmel, whose *Revolution: A Sociological Interpretation* remains one of the very best introductions to basic sociological writings on revolution, has identified the "three structural elements that compose a theory of revolution" as the "international context," "class struggle," and the "state." He goes on to contend that "the decisive importance of capitalist industrialization and state-building" provides the "center-piece for structural theories of revolution in the social sciences." Revolutions are, "at their core, *about* capitalist industrialization and state centralization, and these processes provide the framework for structural theories." At the same time, we note with interest Kimmel's *Weberian* rather than *Marxian* "take" on the entity that is so central to structuralist revolutionary theory today: namely, *the state*. "Paying attention to the state as an active agent in revolutionary struggles," he says, "means treating [it] as an analytically distinct category from either the class structure upon which it is based or the social values that it may embody."[7] Accepting this final assertion means endorsing Kimmel's overall formulation that the "state," although never standing "entirely above society," preserves at all times a certain irreducible measure of autonomy from both socioeconomic interests *and* societal values.

Michael Kimmel's emphasis upon both "capitalist industrialization" *and* "state centralization" in his initial discussion of structural theories of revolution also reflects what has become a very significant "split" within the structuralist family—between what I shall call Marxist/Leninist "capitalism-centered structuralism" and Weberian/Hintzian "state-centered structuralism." We will not be detained too long here by the former of these two tendencies: it is probably fair to say that most sociologists and other social scientists writing theoretically on revolution over the past several decades have gravitated to state-centered rather than to capitalism-centered structuralism. Still, we certainly should acknowledge that *some* modern theorists of revolution—most impressively, Immanuel Wallerstein—*have* premised their theories upon the Marxist assumption that "the affairs of state and of capitalism are inextricably interrelated, that they are only two sides, or aspects, of . . . the same historical development," and that, consequently, statist interests in history have *ultimately* been reflective of, and hence largely reducible to, interests of international economic development.[8] Wallerstein—to revisit his case briefly—has over the years posited the primary importance of a "capitalist world system" developing since early modern times and deeply conditioning both the contours of interstate competition (i.e., geopolitics) and the likelihood for localized outbreaks of revolution. For Wallerstein, revolutions have historically been most characteristic of regions on the "periphery" or "semiperiphery" of the capitalist world system, subject to the tug-and-pull of competing state-imperialist interests.[9] It is undeniable that capitalism-centered structuralism has left a mark upon the historiography of, specifically, the English, French, and Russian Revolutions. Furthermore, we may find later on that it also contributes at times to a *neostructuralist* interpretation of specific issues embedded in these revolutions.

This having been said, we must concern ourselves here primarily with the state-centered strain of structuralism, which has figured so prominently in revolutionary writing of recent times. As we noted earlier, the theoretical roots of this approach to revolution lie largely in the seminal works of German sociologist Max Weber and his compatriot, historian Otto Hintze. Unlike Marx and Lenin, who conceived the state largely through the prism of socioeconomic class struggle, Weber and Hintze saw in the state, and especially in its *administrative* and *bureaucratic* aspects, "processes that cannot be reduced to class analysis and that [nonetheless] are directly relevant to the study of revolution."[10] A "compulsory political organization with continuous operations will be called a state," Weber wrote, "insofar as it successfully upholds the claim to the *monopoly* of the *legitimate* use of physical force in the enforcement of its order."[11] Thus, for Weber, revolutions were quite logically to be seen as events largely brought on by breakdowns in the state's ability to administer the means of such "physical force," both *internally* (with police repression of domestic opposition) and *externally* (with a sustained military capacity to defeat foreign adversaries). In other words, we can already begin to divine, with Weber, a theoretical linkage of *statist* analysis with *revolutionary* analysis. Such a theoretical linkage was then taken even farther with Otto Hintze. As Michael Kimmel has observed, the "kernel of Hintze's theory of revolution" lay in the fact that it "describes how political opposition is first set in motion by autonomous states pursuing distinctly political interests in the global arena."[12] And undeniably such "political opposition," once "set in motion," *can* lead to genuine revolution. Thus, Max Weber and (even more explicitly) Otto Hintze—reconceptualizing the state as a semiautonomous *geopolitical* as well as *sociopolitical* entity, and associating issues of state formation with issues of international politics and revolutionary causation, process, and consequences. In all of this, they were clearly anticipating subsequent state-centered structuralist explanations of revolution.

Of all those explanations, the most influential—if, at the same time, controversial—has surely been Theda Skocpol's 1979 synthesis entitled *States and Social Revolutions*. In this work, the erstwhile student of Barrington Moore, Jr., sharing something of her mentor's preoccupation with peasant class formation and state development in a global context of comparative modernization, set out what she called a "comparative historical analysis" of the French, Russian, and Chinese Revolutions. Essentially, she maintained, full-blown "social-revolutionary transformations" of all three countries occurred when resounding failures in state foreign and internal policies dialectically interacted and then *explosively converged*. The inability of Bourbon France, Romanov Russia, and Qing China to compete militarily (and, secondarily, economically) with Britain, Germany, and Japan, respectively, not only undermined the international prestige and security of these old regime states but also subverted their control over their "home" societies by compromising the status of "dominant class" feudal/landholding interests facing increasingly restive peasant elements in the countryside. Loss of control over the rurally oriented class structures *within* these countries, reinforcing as it did a failure of geostrategic/economic outreach abroad, permitted what Skocpol referred to as "societal political crises" in all three cases to blossom unexpectedly into full-scale sociopolitical upheavals: the French, Russian, and Chinese states, in other words, could no longer adequately control the evolution of public affairs. Furthermore, in all three revolutionary situations—it is of related interest to add here—Skocpol saw *postrevolutionary states* eventually emerging which proved to be notably more successful than the *ancien régime* states had been at carrying out foreign and domestic policies on the basis of administrative, bureaucratic, and, in some measure, economic reforms.[13]

To observe that *States and Social Revolutions*, perhaps more than any other state-centered structuralist exegesis of revolution, has elicited favorable and unfavorable reactions from theorists of both structuralist *and* postmodernist persuasion, would be to restate the obvious. I myself have dealt with this matter in considerable detail elsewhere.[14] It would serve our purposes best at this point to suggest how even those scholars continuing to work (more or less) within the limits of state-centered structuralism have still attempted to modify and thereby move beyond what they have seen as Theda Skocpol's thought-provoking but too *exclusionary*, too *mechanically applied* brand of structuralism.

Efforts to "improve upon" (if not, assuredly, reject altogether) the analytic schema advanced in *States and Social Revolutions* usually have involved placing a greater emphasis upon human motivation, social/demographic change, and the roles of ideas/ideologies in the outbreak (and subsequent *process*) of revolutions. Hence, for instance, the late sociologist Charles Tilly contributed substantially to this discussion by bringing into his structuralist account of revolution a healthy admixture of what Skocpol had largely dismissed as "voluntarism." In other words, he played up the issue of *personal agency*, of the roles of "contenders, or coalitions of contenders" with "competing claims to control of the state" in revolutionary times.[15] Then, again, sociologist Jack Goldstone, writing several years ago about France's 1789 revolution, cited "underlying demographic and economic trends" in the eighteenth century that, in combination with "conflicts over religion and shifts in public opinion," helped to produce a conjuncture of forces capable of toppling the Bourbon *ancien régime*. Goldstone, in this connection, was especially intrigued by *demographic dynamics*, including overall population growth and changes in the *distribution* of population "across cities and the countryside, across age groups, across social and economic and legal divisions, and across regions."[16] As for the question of the *ideological/cultural* roots of revolution, it has drawn a very interesting reaction from Goldstone's colleague Timothy P. Wickham-Crowley, who has suggested that a prospective division of labor might best have structural theorists focusing upon the long-term and immediate *origins* of revolution, and cultural analysts concerning themselves with "what the revolutionaries do to society once in power." After all—so, in any case, this particular specialist has concluded—the "powers of ideology to remake the social order seem greatest when disorder reigns and both [revolutionary] state and society are *already* in flux or chaos."[17] Still, after all is said and done, the same Charles Tilly who so usefully added to Skocpolian structuralism an element of *voluntarism* in effect *reaffirmed* Skocpol's emphasis on the *international/domestic* nexus in revolutionary analysis by insisting that "to know which states are liable to revolution we must examine not only their domestic politics, but also their locations in the prevailing set of relations among states."[18] State-centered structuralism, as modified and as *complicated* along the lines adduced previously, will—even more than capitalism-centered structuralism, perhaps—inform a neostructuralist perspective on the great European revolutions.

Moreover, contrary to what some of structuralism's postmodernist detractors have claimed, the impulse toward this perspective on revolution has lost nothing of its vigor in recent years. Even scholars otherwise inclined toward ideological/cultural analysis have sometimes yielded to the impulse. In 2006, for example, the late comparativist historian Martin Malia—for all of his withering criticism of Skocpol's version of structuralism—admitted that for a "general revolution" to occur "there must first exist the framework of a *unitary state* to focus all political, social, and other forms of protest in a single set of institutions." And "this focus on the transformation of state structures, and the concomitant challenge to existing state legitimacy," he added, "is what gives to a general revolution both its explosive character and its political-ideological nature."[19] Six years later, another historian deeply committed to culturalism, Dan Edelstein, nonetheless owned up to "the basic fact that revolutions are first and foremost political affairs." While they undoubtedly possess "broad cultural and social ramifications," Edelstein went on, "without this political thrust [revolutions] would not be revolutions."[20] Again, as recently as 2014, two scholars long addicted to confronting these kinds of issues—namely, Jack Goldstone and I—brought out books revalorizing, if from somewhat different angles, a structuralist slant on comparative revolutionary analysis. In *Revolutions: A Very Short Introduction*, Goldstone, trying as ever to refine his position on this contentious subject, differentiated carefully between "structural causes" of revolution, that is, "long-term and large-scale trends that undermine existing social institutions and relationships," and "transient causes," that is, "contingent events, or actions by particular individuals or groups, that reveal the impact of longer term trends and often galvanize revolutionary oppositions to take further action." As was to be expected, *demographic change* loomed as large as ever in Goldstone's analysis, which continued also to stress *processual* issues.[21] As for my *Anatomy of Revolution Revisited*, it advanced what I called at that time "a *modified*, nuanced structuralism" applicable at least to the English, French, and Russian Revolutions—a structuralism that had states in all three situations of upheaval reacting "not only to long-term exogenous imperatives of a geostrategic nature, but also to endogenous pressures reflecting the 'objective' needs, anxieties, and cosmologies of 'ordinary' men and women (as well as, admittedly, the demands of intra-*élite* 'special interests')."[22]

Thus, structuralism—in one form or another—marches on in the realm of revolutionary theory. But what about the *other* side of this coin? That is, what about postmodernist theorizing of revolution? Here, we should likely avoid being too easily discouraged by anthropologist Ernest Gellner's complaint that it is "almost impossible to give a coherent definition or account of postmodernism."[23] After all, there *are*, surely, canonical reference points here in the earlier works of Michel Foucault and Jacques Derrida,[24] and, as we will see later, other scholars have also enlarged upon the subject. The first point to make here is that postmodernist writing on revolution, much like the structuralist literature on the subject, has tended to "split" into two strains. Modern German historian Richard J. Evans, notably, has explained this bifurcation as a distinction forged between relatively "moderate" postmodernism and something altogether more "extreme." In its "more moderate guise," Evans allowed, postmodernism "has encouraged historians to take the irrational in the past more seriously, to pay more attention to ideas, beliefs and culture as influences in their own right, to devote more effort to framing our work in literary terms, to put individuals, often humble individuals, back into history, [and] to emancipate ourselves from . . . a . . . straitjacket of social-science approaches, quantification, and socioeconomic determinism."[25] *Radical* postmodernism, on the other hand, Evans argued, is less defensible: it "takes its cue from another post, post-structuralism, roughly speaking the idea that language is arbitrarily constructed, and represents nothing but itself, so that whenever we read something, the meaning we put into it is necessarily our own and nobody else's, except of course insofar as our own way of reading is part of a wider discourse or set of beliefs."[26] For Evans, such a *discursive* kind of postmodernism has a corrosive impact on the historical discipline: it forecloses any possibility that scholars could ever agree on what historical documents and/or artifacts actually *mean*, and therefore makes commonly shared interpretative findings all but unattainable.

Richard Evans's arraignment of what he called radical postmodernism—or poststructuralism—has, predictably, drawn heavy fire from advanced postmodernist authors. Exemplifying this tendency, British postmodernist Beverley Southgate saw Evans as hypocritical: "having acknowledged the force of postmodernism," Southgate opined, "Richard Evans continues to write against it and in defiance of it." He followed this up with a laundry list of analytical sins that Evans had (supposedly) committed in his feckless defense of what Southgate disparaged as "modernist" history.[27] We will soon have to return to Southgate's advocacy of radical postmodernism. Yet, in all fairness to Richard Evans, we should first point out that others in academia have also differentiated between "moderate" and "radical" strains of postmodernist analysis. For example, the respected political scientist Pauline Marie Rosenau held that "post-structuralists remain uncompromisingly antiempirical whereas the post-modernists focus on the concrete in the form of . . . daily life, as an alternative to theory." Beyond this, Rosenau maintained that what she termed "skeptical" poststructuralism all too often offered "a pessimistic, gloomy, negative assessment" of life, and that it viewed the "post-modern age" as "one of fragmentation, disintegration, malaise, meaninglessness . . . and societal chaos." Yet we should note *at the same time* that Rosenau, like Evans and other scholars, readily conceded the *usefulness* of moderate or (to use her term) *affirmative* postmodernism, which "often provides fascinating insights across a wide range of topics because it focuses on what is nonobvious, left out, and generally forgotten in a text and examines what is unsaid, overlooked, understated, and never overtly recognized." The insights derived from *this* postmodernism, Rosenau was consequently quick to reiterate, are "innovative and stimulating."[28]

Alas, however, radical postmodernists would regard such fine points of exposition with disdain. For confirmation of this, we return once again to Beverley Southgate. Not for him, the temporizing statements and cautionary definitions hazarded by "faint-hearts" such as Ernest Gellner, Richard Evans, and Pauline Marie Rosenau. For Southgate—and in this he spoke for many another postmodernist as well—history should have a deliberately "destabilizing" and "decentering" function:

postmodern history's function becomes to *destabilize*—endlessly to question certainties, reveal alternatives, and provoke reassessments. . . . In a situation where . . . certainties of meaning are deliberately "shaken," and where that "shaking" itself is seen as a positive virtue, and as a legitimate aim for history, there can be no going back to [the] confident modernist belief in history as "a search for truth and the construction of *knowledge* about the past," built on a core of "factual information."

The "prospect of such finalities and closures," insisted Southgate, "has been lost in postmodernity."[29] It can therefore scarcely astonish us that, in announcing and championing *this kind* of approach to history, Southgate not only "deconstructed" such classic building blocks of structuralist analysis as Marxian class economics, the state, and interstate relations, but also interrogated feminist/gendered and postcolonial narratives in provocative ways. It was not merely a question of challenging patriarchy by advocating for "women's studies" and of challenging privileged imperialist/metropolitan perspectives by empathizing with indigenous viewpoints, contended Southgate; the *very terms of analysis* in such situations must *themselves* be fundamentally rethought:

> Even the central roles—whether of male/female or imperialist/colonist—need to be historicized and their contingency and heterogeneity recognized. For just as definitions of men and women have been applied, or imposed, in relation to each other and in accordance with prevailing power structures, so too have identities in the context of colonial and post-colonial historical narratives. As the supposed fixity of such identities is questioned, so the centres of our histories are once more destabilized.[30]

In this reading, then, history *as a discipline* retreated "from being a truthful representation of a single reality to being a problematic, multi-layered . . . textuality, having at best a tenuous connection with the elusive actuality that it purport[ed] to describe."[31]

This radical postmodernist description of history as "a problematic, multi-layered . . . textuality" is critical, for it takes us back to Jacques Derrida's stress upon *texts* and *deconstruction* in the "processing" of history. And for "texts," why not substitute "scripts"? This is precisely what Keith M. Baker essayed in relation to the French Revolution in an article nearly thirty years ago,[32] and recently (in collaboration with Dan Edelstein) he has suggested extending this kind of radical textual approach to "comparative revolutions" *in general*. Perhaps we should let Baker and Edelstein speak here for themselves:

> In politics, as in the theater or on the screen, scripts generate events. They do so in the obvious sense that a script suggests positions to be taken, actions to be carried out, incidents to be anticipated. They do so, less obviously, in the

sense that positions that have been taken, actions that have been carried out, or incidents that have occurred are necessarily configured (or reconfigured) to give them meaning within a script—or within competing scripts. . . . Competition to impose a script, or to control a script that has been imposed, is a fundamental fact of politics, though perhaps never more . . . than in a situation that has been declared revolutionary.[33]

"Scripts generate events," we suspect, is, in essence, the old radical postmodernist or poststructuralist wine poured into superficially "new" bottles. Although the essays presented in this anthology make for marvelously stimulating reading, they leave us with the unresolved tension between structuralist and postmodernist—especially, radical postmodernist—approaches to revolution. As David Bell summed it up in the afterword to this anthology, this remains "the tension between seeing revolution in terms of impersonal structural change, and seeing it in terms of conscious political will."[34]

Whether or not we persist in going a bit beyond this by regarding the postmodernist approach to history as "split," somewhat like the structuralist approach, into two discrete strains—in this case, moderate (affirmative) and radical (skeptical) strains—there is no question that theorists inspired by postmodernism *tout court* have had useful things to say about revolutionary causes and process. Eric Selbin, for instance, contributing to an anthology of articles on revolutionary theory, stated bluntly that "structural theories alone will never allow us to ascertain whether a social revolution occurred in any particular instance. We must . . . bring people back in. . . . Revolutions do not come, they are made." For Selbin, leaders *and* the citizens they lead incessantly impress upon us the importance of agency in all revolutions.[35] Selbin's colleague John Foran, for his part, also conjured up agency in the revolutionary process. "Political culture . . . spans and links culture with discourse and ideology," he opined, "and puts us on the path to understanding agency as carried by social forces."[36] Then, again, Iranian-American feminist Valentine Moghadam, contributing to the same anthology, argued persuasively that "feminist studies have revealed the significance of gender dynamics and their links to political, economic, and ideological processes, including constructions of national identity, in times of social transformation." Moghadam reminded her readers, too, that "research should also attempt to situate gender issues . . . in the various stages of a revolution, including the prerevolutionary conditions, proximate causes, the course of the revolution, and its short-term and long-term outcomes."[37] We need not necessarily go so far, theoretically speaking, as, for example, a Beverley Southgate or a Keith Baker to be able to acknowledge and applaud the value, in revolutionary studies, of such postmodernist observations.

By the same token, however, structuralists of one stamp or another will be—in fact, *should be*—insistent as well on emphasizing certain serious limitations of postmodernism in revolutionary analysis. To begin with, there is the problematic tendency of even some relatively moderate postmodernists to *decontextualize* political culture unduly in a revolutionary situation. John Foran addressed this issue when he insisted that "culture must [always] be rigorously linked to social structure and imaginatively synthesized with political economy and international contexts."[38] Interestingly, historian Gary Wilder made much the same point in an *American Historical Review* "Forum" of 2012. Historians, he warned, cannot afford to underestimate "the analytic and political costs of a wholesale turn away from structural analysis, societal explanation, long-term processes and large-scale transformations . . . [and] dialogue with the social sciences."[39] Furthermore, however fashionable the postmodernist "turn" may remain today in certain quarters, it has *not* managed to "deconstruct away" basic elements of structuralist analysis such as socioeconomic class and the state. Pauline Marie Rosenau, for example, has noted that, for "orthodox Marxists, materialist Marxists, and Marxist-Leninists," postmodernism's "narrow focus" on language, discourse, and culture makes it "frivolous," "anti-political," and all too likely to shield from accountability those individuals responsible for class exploitation in society.[40] As for statist analysis, it remains as durable today as does Weber's bureaucratically conceived state itself. "We should bear in mind," political scientist Noel S. Parker has observed, "that, to date, the increase of visible constraints upon the nation-state as a place of collective autonomy seems not . . . to have removed that element of the revolutionary narrative."[41] Parker's comment here could easily be taken to reaffirm Max Weber's structuralist prophecy issued back in 1918, that year of universal warfare and upheaval: namely, that revolutions will all too often be likely to result in newly-rejuvenated, ever-more-coercive states.

Significantly, some aficionados of revolution have for years been identifying as an indispensable goal in this field the elaboration of a "fourth generation" of revolutionary theory that might somehow accommodate and reconcile the most reasonable elements of both structuralism *and* postmodernism. John Foran raised this issue on the pages of *Sociological Theory* in 1993,[42] and Jack Goldstone enlarged upon the same subject in the *Annual Review of Political Science* eight years later.[43] I tried at least to *begin* to "bridge the gap" between these warring perspectives in 2014 in *The Anatomy of Revolution Revisited*; still, it should be evident by now that, with the present book, I hope to take this project much farther. But to "transition" from the realm of *general theory* to the *specific domain* of the three classic European revolutions requires, first of all, that we gain a much more specific sense of how the boundary between structuralism and postmodernism has in recent times run through the ever more voluminous historiographies on the English, French, and Russian Revolutions.

It might be best to start here with France, and with François Furet, who, in his landmark *Pensée la Révolution française* (1978), heralded postmodernism in revolutionary literature. In this work, Furet offered an interpretation of the old regime and of 1789 to 1799 keying on the notion of an absolutist political culture that demanded national consensus and demonized (and eventually guillotined) those deemed to have deviated from that national consensus.[44] Moreover, Furet and some of his allies profited from the 1989 bicentennial to repeat their call for a *cultural* exegesis of revolutionary change in France.[45] More recently, postmodernism has meant a "colonial/post-colonial" effort to *retheorize* the revolutions in the eighteenth century as "transAtlantic" in nature. Although the "Atlantic theme" here looks back to the works of R. R. Palmer and Jacques Godechot in the mid-twentieth century,[46] it patently takes on new dimensions in the work of scholars like David Armitage, Wim Klooster, Laurent Dubois, Paul Cheney, and Pierre Serna.[47] Thus, for instance, Dubois, long a student of the late-eighteenth-century Haitian Revolution, has reconceptualized the French and Haitian Revolutions as, basically, but two individual "moments" in a much larger and fully integrated process of "macrohistorical transformation" agitating the wider Atlantic world of the times.[48] Such an argument, Gary Wilder has noted, amounts to saying that "revolutionary republicanism and republican universalism" must be "dissociated" from the "French metropolitan territory or ethnicity," and that historians thus must see in republican France an "imperial formation" rather than a "national state."[49] Paul Cheney, for his part, synthesizing the histories of the Enlightenment, Atlantic civilizations, and the French Revolution, has portrayed the requirements and risks of international commerce as helping to induce and radicalize revolutionary change in France.[50] In their own individual ways, Armitage, Klooster, and Serna have been similarly eager to recast the "wave" of late-eighteenth-century Atlantic revolutions in a comparative/analytic fashion.[51]

Yet this recent postmodernist thrust in revolutionary historiography has provoked a vigorous counterthrust. To begin with, not every expert on Atlantic affairs has endorsed Dubois's summons to write a new kind of history that is "at once local and Atlantic, at once French and Caribbean."[52] Jeremy Popkin is one of many historians steeped in Haitian revolutionary affairs of the late eighteenth century who still feel it best to pursue as *separate* (if, indeed, at times *interacting*) the trajectories of French and Haitian history. True, Popkin has been quick to remind us that debates about colonial rights and slavery "were an integral part of the events leading to the [French] Revolution, particularly during the period of the 'pre-revolution' in 1787-89," and he has been equally quick to postulate an "imperial" or "colonial" dimension to the events in France during the turbulent 1790s. There was, to be sure, a certain measure of interaction between this "metropolitan" power and the drama unfolding simultaneously in the French Caribbean.[53] Yet in no way has Popkin, like Dubois, abandoned a fundamental identification with France. And there are very good reasons for this. Dubois's notion (for example) that "the Atlantic economy and the transformation of social and economic life that it propelled . . . actually drove the [French] revolution" must be seen, like a number of his other observations, as magnifying the "imperial/colonial" element in the French upheaval out of all proportion.[54] Palpably, the old regime *and* revolutionary French were maneuvering within, and reacting to, a larger world embracing West-Eurasian as well as American (and in general, overseas) regions. The foreign policies of Choiseul, Vergennes, and their successors in the 1790s remind us of that basic fact. Indeed, in that connection, a structuralist counterargument has just as undeniably reasserted itself in recent decades. It has included unflagging efforts by Peter McPhee, Henry Heller, and other capitalism-centered structuralists to reinject a Marxian viewpoint into debates over the *ancien régime* and revolution.[55] It has also included state-centered works by T. C. W. Blanning, Thomas E. Kaiser, and the present author emphasizing the undiminished necessity to situate the origins, process, and results of the French Revolution in a context at least partly geostrategic in nature.[56]

We see a similar situation developing (if a bit later on) in English revolutionary historiography. Leading the postmodernist charge in this case was David Underdown's *Revel, Riot, and Rebellion*.[57] One of Underdown's admirers, Kevin Sharpe, was also one of radical postmodernism's most articulate early champions, arguing, for example, that "historians have not yet faced up to a postmodernist reading of their own discipline," which entailed defining the past as a "representation constructed by the historian from his own cultural vision as well as from the various representations that contemporaries created to discern meaning for themselves."[58] Susan Amussen, Mark Kishlansky, and David Zaret (among others) have enthusiastically followed in these postmodernist footsteps.[59] And here, too, as in the French case, we find a colonial/postcolonial theme in the literature. Carla Pestana and John Donoghue have led the way in this respect. In her 2004 study *The English Atlantic in an Age of Revolution, 1640–1661*, Pestana held that a transAtlantic "English world" arose in the revolutionary 1640s; as a result, events of that era on both sides of the Atlantic became caught up in a grand dialectic affecting those English remaining behind in England as well as colonists (and, obviously, indigenous people) in the New World.[60] Pestana's attempt to chart "the two-way impact of colonies and metropolis on the unfolding of events in these two decades" may not altogether negate the primarily English nature of the 1640 to 1661 upheaval; still, it is commendable for the way it casts new light on the jarring contradictions inevitably generated between the English Revolution's loftiest religious (and, to some extent, secular) ideals and the biting evils of indentured, transported, and enslaved labor. For his part, John Donoghue in *Fire Under the Ashes: An*

Atlantic History of the English Revolution (2013) lauded Pestana's "invaluable survey of colonial politics, religion, and economic life during the Revolutionary era," all the while insisting that *his* book would discuss "the European aspects of the period's Atlantic history in much more detail than does Professor Pestana's work."[61] At the same time, the author assured his readers, in radical postmodernist fashion, that his work would help to "move the study of the [English] Revolution beyond [a] European context as well as [beyond] the limiting confines of the national paradigm of historical analysis."[62]

Yet we may want to query whether Donoghue's approach to issues in the seventeenth-century "English Atlantic" has any more successfully decentered the English Revolution than had Carla Pestana's earlier study. Pestana herself, in reviewing Donoghue's monograph, suggested pointedly that his most important contribution to the field was "not in explaining the origins or course of the English Revolution but in confronting readers with the injustice upon which the Atlantic world rested."[63] This would seem to be the verdict of others as well: Ian K. Steele, for instance, complimented Donoghue for documenting "an intense, evolving, reciprocal relationship between a cluster of radical revolutionaries on both sides of the Atlantic" without in any way "replacing" Pestana's survey, whereas Steele's colleague John Coffee in his review painted Donoghue as essentially an Americanist less familiar with English and European than with American realities.[64] Our reaction to this "Atlanticist" scholarship must be that if it surely enriches our knowledge about interactions between the English and Atlantic colonial worlds in Stuart and early revolutionary times, it does so without altogether displacing the English Revolution beyond British (and European) shores. Moreover, in this field as in French studies, postmodernism has increasingly had to share the limelight not only with a persisting Marxian interest in issues of economic change—see, for this, the brouhaha over the "Brenner thesis"—but also with structuralist concerns about state formation and the nexus between international and domestic affairs. Significantly, in this connection, Jonathan Scott has analyzed Stuart English "instability" in a "European" context, whereas, in different ways, James S. Wheeler, David Cressy, and Geoffrey Parker have all situated the English Revolution in a "global" or even "world-historical" framework.[65] In addition, the recent tendency to see a three-pronged "British" rather than just an English crisis under Charles I, Oliver Cromwell, and the later Stuarts may in some ways have reinforced the state-centered structuralist argument in English revolutionary historiography.

In the ever-more-fertile field of Russian revolutionary historiography, we find the same thrusts and counterthrusts of moderate/radical postmodernism and structuralism. Steve A. Smith, prominent social historian of 1917 (and, more recently, revolutionary China), was among those leading the charge back in the 1990s for postmodernism in Russian studies. In reflections published in 1994, Smith decried "the general distrust of theory and explicit conceptualization that is evident among so many historians of Russia," and also faulted those scholars for "a certain blinkeredness, a tendency to shy away from big questions about 'what it all meant.'" Smith went on to praise postmodernism's tendency "to subvert the grounds on which knowledge claims are secured," and predicted confidently (and, as it turned out, accurately) that "over the next 20 years . . . much of the most challenging work will come from historians who are trying to face up to the discursivity of history as a discipline, [and] its subordination to the effects of language and writing."[66] Although Smith's warm embrace of postmodernist "discursivity" in scholarship on the 1917 Revolution has sparked much controversy among his professional peers, there can be little doubt that numerous historians endorsing moderate and/or radical postmodernism have recently responded to this call. Hence, practitioners of the linguistic/cultural turn such as Christopher Read, Orlando Figes, Boris Kolonitskii, Lynn Mally, and Sheila Fitzpatrick have provided us with some fascinating insights into the many articulations between politics, society, and culture in revolutionary times.[67] Still, even among such specialists, a certain state-centered structuralist leaning has persisted. Thus Orlando Figes has conceded that, in prerevolutionary Russia, "everything depended on the tsarist regime's willingness to introduce reforms," and that Russia's involvement in the First World War must essentially be regarded as "a gigantic test of the modern state."[68] And thus William G. Rosenberg, for all his clarion calls to fellow-Russianists to investigate the processes of cultural change in revolutionary times, has allowed that "the task of state reconstruction" in the wake of 1917 was—correctly—seen by both triumphant Bolsheviks *and* their civil war adversaries as a "political imperative."[69] In effect, such reflective postmodernists were citing chapter and verse from Theodore H. Von Laue's classic *Why Lenin? Why Stalin? Why Gorbachev?*—a work that, in successive editions over the past several decades, has habituated its readers to placing Imperial and revolutionary Russia in the unforgiving—and, incidentally, highly structuralist—context of Eurasian and global power politics.[70]

This general theoretical and Euro-specific discussion of capitalism-centered and state-centered structuralism and moderate and radical postmodernism should provide us with the framework we need for our analysis of *five specific issues* that we will follow through the three classic European revolutions. It must be clear by now that we find the *first three* of the four structuralist/postmodernist approaches to revolutionary analysis to be useful in the study of such issues. In other words, this book will reject only the *extreme discursivity*, the subordination of sociopolitical reality to linguistic analysis associated today with radical or "skeptical" postmodernism (or poststructuralism). Perhaps, at this point, then, it might be helpful to introduce the five specific issues alluded to previously and then suggest how interpreting them will help us come up with a truly innovative neostructuralist synthesis of the most sensible structuralist and postmodernist approaches to revolutionary analysis.

CHAPTER 1: MODERNIZERS VERSUS TRADITIONALISTS IN THE EUROPEAN REVOLUTIONS

This chapter takes on Steve Pincus, a respected historian of seventeenth-century England, who argues that true revolutions occur only after regimes have *irrevocably decided* "to initiate ambitious modernization programs. Revolutions, then, pit different groups of modernizers against one another."[71] In setting out this argument, Pincus differentiates between England's Charles I, whom he (largely correctly) regards as a genuine "traditionalist," and later monarchs, such as James II and France's Louis XVI (and also, at least implicitly, Russia's Nicholas II) whom he *incorrectly* portrays as unambiguous "modernizers." Departing from this provocative—if, I think, largely untenable—argument, as well as from the ideas of prominent modernization theorists such as Samuel Huntington and S. N. Eisenstadt (with even a backward nod to Alexis de Tocqueville), I hope to show here that the English, French, and Russian Revolutions *all* featured bitter struggles, in their origins and in their development, between modernizers of one type or another and traditionalists committed to defending and/or restoring their respective *anciens régimes*.

CHAPTER 2: IN SEARCH OF THE ELUSIVE *ANCIEN RÉGIME* BOURGEOISIE

There has undeniably been a major rediscovery of conflictual social dynamics in capitalism-centered structuralist writing on the European revolutions. Chapter 2 addresses this issue by posing a series of deceptively simple yet in reality *complicated* questions. What, precisely, *was* the "bourgeoisie" in late *ancien régime* England, France, and Russia? If it actually existed, did it have to share the limelight with other socioeconomic classes? And, if so, did it, on a case-by-case basis, play a central, merely supportive, or largely negligible role in state collapse and in the onset of full-blown revolution? Starting with France, then pivoting back to that pioneering, purportedly "capitalist" revolution in England, and finally shifting forward to Russia's unprecedented experimentation with massive, state-sponsored "postcapitalist" modernization, we will see how successful we can be in reappraising the posited "bourgeoisies" of three European countries on the threshold (and in the early stages) of violent sociopolitical change.

CHAPTER 3: TO KILL A MONARCH: FROM PROCEDURALISM TO REVOLUTIONARY *RAISON D'ÉTAT*

Chapter 3 will review the issues that framed the decisions, in revolutionary England, France, and Russia, to do away with Charles I, Louis XVI, and Nicholas II, respectively. The contrast here is usually drawn between England and France, on the one hand, as countries in which the rule of law was sufficiently established to ensure that monarchs, even in revolutionary times, would be dispatched *only* on the basis of formal legal procedure, and Russia, on the other hand, as a country in which, given the lack of an entrenched, Western-style rule of law, a sudden, *unceremonious* decision by revolutionaries to have a deposed monarch killed had a certain hard logic. Less well known, however, is the ultra-leftist effort unsuccessfully mounted in the French case to *theorize* revolution—as would later happen in Russia—to the extent of denying *any* due process to the monarch so as *not* to call the legitimacy of revolution *as such* into question. By retracing the "execution question" from England (1648–1649) to France (1792–1793) to Russia (1917–1918), this chapter explores the growing tension, in the European revolutionary tradition, between principles of formal procedural justice and arbitrary acts of state violence.

CHAPTER 4: CIRCUMSTANCES VERSUS IDEAS IN THE REVOLUTIONARY "FURIES"

As the title of this chapter suggests, it intends to reexamine the roles played by circumstances, on the one hand, and by ideas/ideologies, on the other hand, in the most dangerous, "terroristic" phases of the revolutions in England, France, and Russia. This question was first reexamined in some (but by no means all) of its myriad complexities in the late 1970s and 1980s by François Furet and other practitioners of the new political-cultural (early postmodernist) history in connection with French revolutionary developments (and in anticipation of scholarly bicentennial celebrations planned for 1989 at Paris and elsewhere). Predictably, the heated debates to which Furet-style analysis has given rise among historians of the tumultuous 1790s in France have found a resonant echo in subsequent disputation among English and Russian specialists who have inevitably had to confront their own countries' revolutionary campaigns of terror. Chapter 4 revisits these debates, thereby reevaluating the relative roles played by events and by cultural forces in the most advanced stages of these three upheavals.

CHAPTER 5: CRISES OF REVOLUTIONARY LEGITIMACY: THERMIDORIAN OUTCOMES

This chapter sets out to reevaluate the most recent—as well as much of the older—historiography on the efforts of late revolutionary leaders to secure legitimacy for post-terrorist regimes in England, France, and Russia. In the case of England, it analyzes the constitutional tensions between Oliver and Richard Cromwell and their parliaments (representing English society's "natural rulers") in the Protectorate of 1653 to 1659, and, in the case of France, the somewhat similar tensions between the Directory and the sundry bourgeois and other élitist interests in the French society of the late 1790s. In the Russian case, it scrutinizes the very problematic state of relations between a new Soviet government anchored in urban/proletarian society and the radically different, rural world of the Russian peasantry, as well as analyzing the tensions (in the transitional New Economic Policy society of the 1920s) between the notion of "estates" (*sosloviia*) inherited from the old regime and the Leninist concept of socioeconomic classes. Chapter 5 therefore seeks to explain *why* the Thermidorian efforts to achieve state legitimacy failed in England and France—and *why* they succeeded—at least for the time being—in Russia.

These, then, are the five specific issues around which this study is organized. Again, our purpose here is to employ a mode of revolutionary analysis that meshes the insights of state-centered and (when relevant) capitalism-centered structuralism with postmodernism's emphasis on political culture, ideas, and agency. Thus, for example, chapter 1 combines state-oriented structuralism with postmodernism to show how warring ideological forces helped to thwart urgently needed campaigns of modernization in late *ancien régime* England, France, and Russia. Chapter 2 takes up capitalism-centered structuralist concerns about old regime bourgeois class formation and politicization even as it also underscores the state-centered nature of recent scholarship on the prerevolutionary bourgeoisies in all three countries. Chapter 3, in taking on the grim question of revolutionary regicide, caters to moderate postmodernism by placing all three regicides in *political-cultural* contexts even as it also stresses (in structuralist fashion) the dire *circumstances* in which these drastic actions became possible. Chapter 4 reviews (and tries to mediate between) opposing *circumstantial* and *ideological* explanations of state terror in revolutionary France, Russia, and England. Finally, chapter 5 seeks to explain the *crises of revolutionary legitimacy* in Thermidorian England, France, and Russia by showing how polarized political cultures gained influence in specific geostrategic contexts. In sum, the book valorizes a neo-structuralist approach to (European) revolutionary analysis that appropriates the best from all reasonable theoretical perspectives.

Having said all this, we are left in the end thinking that the *role of the state* lies at (or very near) the heart of European revolutionary analysis (more on this in the conclusion). That this should be the case is, in a way, logical. After all, the revolutions studied in this book broke out in countries recognized for centuries as sovereign polities untrammeled by any kind of colonial dependency on greater powers, and endeavored to modernize those polities through similarly sequenced phases of change. Moreover, all three upheavals unfolded within (or on the edges of) a fiercely competitive system of autonomous states struggling for security, prestige, and (at times) hegemony. Given such realities, we may well ask, how could a state-centered perspective *not* be significant for any thoroughly updated neostructuralist approach to violent transformative change in war-scarred Europe?

Chapter One

Modernizers versus Traditionalists in the European Revolutions

"The Revolution of 1688-89," Steve Pincus has held, "like all modern revolutions, was a struggle ultimately waged between two competing groups of modernizers. The revolution did not pit defenders of traditional society against advocates of modernity. Both Whigs and Jacobites were modernizers."[1] Spelling out one implication of this thesis, Pincus went on to differentiate between England's Charles I, defeated (and eventually executed) in the civil warfare of the mid-seventeenth century, and monarchs in later revolutionary struggles. Though Charles I, "for all of his political ineptitude, was fundamentally willing . . . to defend the traditional society and the traditional polity," Pincus wrote, "James II, in contrast to his father, chose to cast himself as a modernizer." As for Louis XVI, who fell afoul of revolutionaries in late eighteenth-century France: "Far from being a reactionary, [he] was a determined reformer . . . a modernizer" in an upheaval that was essentially "the violent working out of competing modernization programs."[2] Given Pincus's likening of the 1688 to 1689 events to "all modern revolutions," we can justly assume in this chapter that his characterization of James II and Louis XVI as modernizers would extend as well to Russia's ill-omened early twentieth-century tsar, Nicholas II.

Steve Pincus is a respected historian of seventeenth-century England.[3] Therefore it is hardly surprising that his latest book should have almost immediately elicited a wide variety of reactions from his fellow specialists. Most of them have naturally enough been concerned primarily to dwell upon his reinterpretation of the causes, process, and results of the "Glorious Revolution," and have found his recasting of those issues in England's past to be imposing in some respects but problematic in others.[4] While I share their mixed reactions to *1688: The First Modern Revolution*, I want above all—for

1

reasons of theory—to challenge Pincus's idea that revolutions "do not pit modernizers against defenders of an old regime," but happen "when the political nation is convinced of the need for political modernization but there are profound disagreements on the proper course of state innovation."[5] Drawing on a wealth of historical writing, chiefly on the *causes* but also (secondarily) on the *process* of the English Revolution of 1640 to 1660, the French Revolution of 1789 to 1799, and the Russian Revolution of 1917 to 1929, I will show that such major events most assuredly *do* "pit modernizers against defenders of an old regime." Inevitably, therefore, this chapter *from the very start* rejects Pincus's effort to "cut" the mid-seventeenth-century English Revolution "down to size."[6] But, in the *larger theoretical terms* of this study, chapter 1 will be especially concerned to portray three ill-fated old regime monarchs—Charles I, Louis XVI, and Nicholas II—as driven, on the one hand, by the *structural demands of governance* to modernize state and society, even as (on the other hand) they *held themselves back* from state modernization due to their embrace of traditionalism in state and society. Thus chapter 1 deals in both *state-centered structuralism*—the imperative need for modernization—and in *moderate postmodernism*—the divisive ideological forces supporting or opposing such reform at all levels, from monarch on down.

MODERNIZERS VERSUS TRADITIONALISTS: THE ENGLISH CASE

Because chapter 1 has adopted as its *point de départ* a critical stance toward Steve Pincus's *1688: The First Modern Revolution*, it would only be fair for us to begin by reflecting briefly on how Pincus—and other English historians—have handled the concept of modernization as it may (or may not) apply to the Stuart era. We can then turn from *theory* to *reality*—seeking, that is, to analyze the tensions we have posited in our introduction between structuralist issues of state modernization and postmodernist issues of ideological conflict in old regime and early revolutionary England.

We might begin here, therefore, by noting that a scholarly preoccupation with state-associated modernization as a chief cause of revolution, tracing its origins in some respects all the way back to the nineteenth-century ruminations of French statesman and author Alexis de Tocqueville, assumed more sophisticated theoretical trappings in the sociological literature of the post–World War II era.[7] That literature, which included, prominently, Samuel P. Huntington's *Political Order in Changing Societies* and S. N. Eisenstadt's *Revolution and the Transformation of Societies*, spoke of how social and economic changes such as urbanization, industrialization, advances in literacy and education, and mass media expansion tend to undermine state institutions and sources of authority in traditional societies, and thus help (in certain instances) to prepare the way for revolutionary upheavals.[8] Granted, such analyses did *not*, in the 1970s and thereafter, lack their critics: without denying that modernization, however it be defined, had figured in many narratives of statist development, such individuals often questioned the tendency of the Huntingtons and Eisenstadts to associate modernization too closely *in theoretical terms* with outbreaks of sociopolitical revolution. A celebrated example of this was Charles Tilly, who insisted that the historical record reveals "no direct relationship [between] the pace of structural change" and revolution, and that, in reality, "there is no reliable and regular sense in which modernization breeds revolution."[9] Tilly's critique of many applications of modernization theory to revolutionary situations, moreover, has been taken up and further developed by sociologists such as Michael S. Kimmel and Jeff Goodwin.[10] Nonetheless, such arguments have never deterred historians from discussing modernization theory and debating its relative merits and demerits as a tool of inquiry in their own fields of research—such as (in this case) early modern England.

Of course, for English historians, as for others, modernization is a phenomenon that can be about many kinds (or, alternatively, *one* specific kind) of historical change. Peter Lake, on the one hand, contributing in the mid-1990s to a major scholarly reassessment of Charles I's "right-hand man" Thomas Wentworth, (eventually) Earl of Strafford, saw post–World War II historical writing on Stuart England as sanctioning a view of "modernity . . . defined institutionally in terms of the secular state and parliament, . . . culturally in terms of the emergence of a recognizably modern, rational and thoroughly individualist and disenchanted view of the world . . . and socio-economically in terms of the emergence of capitalism and of a socio-political world organised around the means of production and divisions between classes."[11] Such an all-embracing historiographical slant on seventeenth-century English affairs, assuming as it did what Lake refers to as "the benefits of modernity, the controllability of the historical process, [and] the benign capacity of the state to intervene and shape the economic and social development of the nation," struck him as syntonic with many of the optimistic assumptions defining post–World War II England.[12] Yet, for Lake at least, this "modernization paradigm," all-encompassing as it was, and giving rise to scholarship on early modern England by the likes of Geoffrey Elton, Keith Thomas, Lawrence Stone, and Christopher Hill, was destined no less to lose much of its legitimacy in the 1970s era of British "national decline" and "economic crisis," and to be replaced accordingly by "revisionist" and, later, "post-revisionist" schools of inquiry into the seventeenth-century past.

Steve Pincus, on the other hand, as already noted, has taken up the cudgels for a particular *kind* of modernization—that is, *state* modernization—as an explanatory key to *all* revolutions, starting with that of 1688 to 1689 in

England. Put another way: modernization, if defined more narrowly in Pincus's lexicon than in that of Peter Lake, is (at least for Pincus) still very much alive in the early twenty-first-century historian's repertoire of terms of analytical inquiry. And what, exactly, does Pincus *mean* by state modernization? Here, we should probably in all fairness allow him again to speak for himself:

> State modernization will usually include an effort to centralize and bureaucratize political authority, an initiative to transform the military using the most up-to-date techniques, a program to accelerate economic growth and shape the contours of society using the tools of the state, and the deployment of techniques allowing the state to gather information about and potentially suppress social and political activities taking place in a wide range of social levels and geographical locales within the polity.[13]

State modernization in specific countries, viewed this way, assumes some degree of prior *socioeconomic* modernization; still, the transition from socioeconomic modernization to full-blown *state* modernization remains (for Pincus, at least) essential in the gestation of any truly revolutionary situation.

But even if recent historians of seventeenth-century England have not repudiated all talk of modernization as generally as Peter Lake claims they have, reservations about it have no less persisted in scholarly circles.[14] Certainly Steve Pincus's colleagues in British studies have been willing enough to criticize *his* emphasis on the modernity of the 1688 to 1689 revolution. Jeremy Black, for instance, writing in the *American Historical Review*, has questioned Pincus's conception of "Catholic modernity" as a driving force behind James II's policies in the late 1680s: "To argue . . . that the choice [for James II] in foreign policy was 'between a modern Catholic foreign policy and a modern multi-confessional policy' begs the question why the foreign policy of James II should be seen as a modern Catholic one. . . . Some may find 'Catholic modernity' a problematic idea in this context."[15] Without explicitly invoking at this point the issue of James II's Catholicism, Scott Sowerby, too, has found fault with Pincus's reliance on the idea of modernization in his work, speaking here in more *theoretical* terms: "Many different kinds of ideologies can cause revolutions: they can be backward-looking or forward-looking, centralizing or fissiparous. They do not have to be modernizing."[16] Theoretical considerations have in similar fashion given rise to Lionel K. J. Glassey's more elaborate strictures about the argument that "James must have embarked on a 'modernization' programme." True, he "increased the size of the army and the navy, but it is not clear that the discipline, training, equipment, organization or infrastructure of the armed forces underwent substantial change." Again, James II's ministers' methods of surveillance, gathering of intelligence, and press censorship "do not seem markedly different from those employed by the ministers of Elizabeth I,

Oliver Cromwell or Charles II." Furthermore, Glassey has written, the "assertion that 'James's effort to catholicize every level of government was impressive for its thoroughness and efficiency' does not really convince."[17] It would seem, then, from such criticism, that interpretations of *late* seventeenth-century Britain inspired by modernization theory have run into as much heavy weather among revisionist and post-revisionist specialists as—at least according to Peter Lake—have similarly inspired interpretations of Charles I's, Wentworth/Strafford's, and Archbishop Laud's *early* seventeenth-century Britain.

Yet is it possible that Steve Pincus erred, not so much in *finding signs* of modernity in 1688 to 1689, as in *not locating* them primarily *in the "Whiggish" and popular opposition to James II*? Historians of 1688 and 1689 might usefully ponder this possibility. For us, however, *1688: The First Modern Revolution* is lacking primarily in that (1) it ignores in its discussion of trends in revolutionary theory/historiography the current debates between postmodernists stressing ideologies and political culture and structuralists stressing state-centered analysis in domestic and international affairs; and (2) it greatly underrates the world-historical import of England's mid-seventeenth-century upheaval, applying revolutionary analysis *exclusively to the later, "Glorious" events of 1688 to 1689*.

I have no intention here of returning to the former issue: I have already discussed it at length via the introduction to my 2014 study *The Anatomy of Revolution Revisited*.[18] I do, however, wish to engage the latter issue by reasserting a central contention undergirding that 2014 synthesis: namely, that the 1640 to 1660 English Revolution *should be* likened in many ways to the sociopolitical cataclysms in late eighteenth-century France and early twentieth-century Russia. I hence turn now to reevaluating some of the tensions and eventual clashes between modernizers (who *did not* always include Charles I) and traditionalists in old regime and revolutionary England. Here, as in the later French and Russian situations, we will discern the even larger incompatibility between the structuralist need to maintain a powerful state in a dangerous international environment and what moderate postmodernists would correctly identify and analyze as a polarized, indeed, schizoid political culture.

One of the most prominent historians in the postwar generation to wrestle with this issue was Lawrence Stone: he did so in his synoptic, tightly organized essay of 1972 on the origins of the English Revolution. In reviewing the comprehensive domestic policy of "Thorough" that was associated in late prerevolutionary England (not to mention in Scotland and Ireland) with Charles I's two most influential ministers, Thomas Wentworth, the future Earl of Strafford, and William Laud, Archbishop of Canterbury, Stone got right to the matter of the tension between progressive and reactionary forces. After noting that "the objective of 'Thorough' was a deferential, strictly hierarchical, socially stable, paternalist absolutism based on a close union of Church and Crown," Stone characterized the implementation of these policies—in some ways traditionalist, in some ways modernizing—in these terms:

> the governing élites began to split apart, so that the [government's] reaction had to be carried out by a regime already half at war with itself. In the administration, the new advocates of efficiency, austerity, and discipline—self-styled "Thorough"—fought the older, easy-going, routinely venal bureaucrats, whom they dubbed "Lady Mora."[19]

In hence describing a regime on the threshold of revolution, and "already half at war with itself" over conflicting, irreconcilable policies and *values*, Stone was beginning to get at the kinds of tensions *within* the English state that, as we shall see later on, seem in hindsight to have been present as well, and every bit as incendiary, in prerevolutionary and revolutionary France and Russia.

There is an extensive historiography on what Wentworth and Laud were actually attempting to do during the Personal Rule of Charles I (1629–1640). S. R. Gardiner approvingly described Thorough in the late nineteenth century as the "resolute determination . . . of disregarding and overriding the interested delays and evasions of those who made the public service an excuse for enriching themselves at the public expense, or the dry, technical arguments of the lawyers which would hinder the accomplishment of schemes for the public good."[20] Up to a point, this portrayal of a strong yet at the same time benign style of governance was endorsed by constitutionalist J. R. Tanner in lectures he delivered at Cambridge in 1926 to 1927. "In days when politicians were bent only on self-aggrandisement," he affirmed, the authors of Thorough set before themselves "great public objects and pursued them with energy and devotion. The King's measures were planned by them, and the whole frame of government was permeated by their spirit." Yet Tanner also anticipated something of the later scholarly consensus on Charles I's two greatest supporters when he turned to the troubling *constitutional* implications of their rule in Scotland, Ireland, and England. Statesmen inspired by the spirit of Thorough, and "chafing under the restraints imposed by the delays and technicalities of the lawyers," cautioned J. R. Tanner, "would be likely to draw . . . on absolute power in order to reach their goal of a strong, orderly, and reforming government. 'Thorough' might be good government, but it would certainly be prerogative government, and it might come perilously near to arbitrary government."[21] For the comparative analyst of European revolutions, this might also appear to anticipate (at a distance, to be sure) the "enlightened absolutism" of several of Louis XVI's and Nicholas II's greatest modernizing state servants.

Still, if several more recent historians of Thorough during Charles I's Personal Rule are to be believed, there was hardly a watertight collaboration between the king and his two most powerful ministers, whatever the constitutional implications of their policies. G. E. Aylmer and Anthony Milton, among others, have postulated a certain distance between Wentworth and Laud, on the one hand, and Charles, on the other—thereby further validating Lawrence Stone's depiction of a prerevolutionary regime "already half at war with itself." For his part, Aylmer certainly concurred with earlier scholars in portraying Wentworth and Laud as advocating (in correspondence with each other) the establishment of "a higher standard of [administrative] honesty and efficiency, and sometimes a greater degree of ruthlessness, in order to put the King's affairs on a sounder footing." Yet, for Aylmer, this administrative style inevitably meant a certain amount of discord between these statesmen and Charles:

> "Thorough" related to the means necessary to achieve a "clean-up" of the machinery and personnel of government, more than to their ultimate objectives. In long-term aims the champions of Thorough were probably nearer to Charles than they were in the matter of means. Charles's trouble was that he willed the end without always willing the means to achieve it; he wanted to be an absolute ruler without all of the bother and unpleasantness involved. This was to be disastrous for him.[22]

Because of this clash between "means" and "ends," concluded Aylmer, "it is quite impossible to equate the King's government or its policies with Thorough, as personified by Laud and Wentworth."[23] For *his* part, Anthony Milton, contributing to the mid-1990s symposium on Wentworth that was previously referenced, pointed out that a related difference between the ministers and the king lay in their attitudes toward parliament. "What was central to the parliamentary strategy of Wentworth and others," noted Milton, "was that parliaments should never be held by the king under 'an absolute Necessity.' . . . But unless he was desperate for supply, Charles would not call parliaments in the first place. This simply guaranteed that Charles only met parliaments when he was most likely to fall out with them."[24] No wonder, then, that Gerald Aylmer complained years ago about "confusion" in textbooks on early Stuart England that facilely "equate the policy of Laud and Wentworth with that of Charles and his regime."[25]

For all these reasons, we must be exceedingly careful about likening Thorough as practiced by the Wentworths and the Lauds in old regime England too closely to *Charles I's* policies. Granted, there have been occasional revisionist and post-revisionist attempts in recent years to portray Charles I as supporting policies that we might see today, in comparative terms, as at least faintly adumbrating the more pronounced and ambitious state modernization campaigns of reformist ministers in late *ancien régime* France and

Russia. Perhaps the weightiest of these efforts was that of Kevin Sharpe, whose prodigiously researched biography of Charles I tried stoutly to paint him as the architect of a program boasting "quite definite aims for the reformation of local society and government," among other objectives.[26] J. S. Morrill is another prominent student of this period in English history who has (at least at times) tried to depict the king in positive, modernizing colors.[27] Yet such portrayals, to a large extent, have been rejected by Ann Hughes, Michael Young, Norah Carlin, and other post-revisionists who have reassessed the latest scholarship in this contentious field; or perhaps it would be more exact to say that, in acknowledging the nascent tensions between modernizers and traditionalists in a regime "already half at war with itself" on the eve of 1640, such experts have (much like Lawrence Stone before them) tended to accentuate the durability of those forces *obstructing* desperately needed structuralist change more than the influence of those forces actually *favoring* it.

Ann Hughes, for instance, in revisiting the causes of the English Civil War, has presented Charles I in traditionalist colors all the more convincing in that they sort with our accepted wisdom about linked patriarchal and hierarchical perspectives prevailing throughout early modern England:

> all hierarchical relationships were seen as inextricably connected. The patriarchal authority of fathers over their children and their wives, the rule of kings over their people, and the rule of God the father were all alike in nature, and each type of rule was a model for, and helped to justify, the others. A challenge to monarchy could threaten the authority of landlords and local governors, or disrupt the dominance of fathers in their families. The patriarchal model for authority was a particularly effective guarantee of political and social stability, for men of all social classes were inevitably sensitive about threats to their authority in the household.[28]

As Hughes has commented, these kinds of beliefs, framed here in sociological, almost *anthropological* terms, found expression in the king's well-advertised turn to so-called new counsels in the later 1620s and 1630s. The court's response to any threatened breakdown in society "was to stress the hierarchical, authoritarian elements in political culture: political participation was suspect and politics was to work from the 'top down,' with the king transmitting orders which should be obeyed without question or debate."[29] There was scant indication here of the truly modernizing values, the *advocacy of innovative policies* so typical of future prerevolutionary and revolutionary eras—values and advocacy that, for a host of state-structuralist reasons, Charles I so imperatively needed.

The aforementioned Michael B. Young has arrived at similar conclusions regarding Charles I and his governance in the prerevolutionary years. Although undoubtedly conceding that Wentworth and Archbishop Laud, at least, "used the word 'Thorough' to refer to the thoroughgoing determination and housecleaning that would be necessary to create an efficient system of government," and maintaining as well that "Thorough" was "the closest thing to an articulated reforming ideal at the Caroline court," Young has nevertheless appeared in general to be rather unimpressed by its practical achievements.[30] Yes, Charles I held "a personal vision of good government" that (in conjunction with his urgent need for greater revenue!) led him to charge numerous Privy Council commissions and subcommittees with the praiseworthy task of investigating, and proposing reforms for, various departments of government, but what tangible gains resulted from all these activities? Seemingly very few: Young cites in this connection the administrative research of G. E. Aylmer, who found that, in the early part of the reign, "very little was achieved," and that the governmental reforms of the Personal Rule, too, "must be reckoned meagre."[31] Yes, once again, Charles has sometimes been applauded for promoting more responsible and effective governance in the counties through the issuance of the so-called Book of Orders in 1631; yet, here once more, Michael Young has rendered a less-than-glowing judgment on the matter:

> The object of the Book of Orders was to establish oversight of the local Justices of the Peace in their enforcement of existing laws regarding the poor, vagabonds, idleness, and drunkenness.... Although the plan looked good on paper, it broke down in practice.... The central government simply was not equipped to carry out a project on this scale effectively. The Book of Orders did no harm, and perhaps it accomplished some good in so far as it made JPs feel more accountable for what they did. We might therefore call it [only?] a limited failure.[32]

And, of course, given the breakdown in relations between the regime and subjects lacking parliamentary representation during the Personal Rule, increasing efficiency in government—insofar as it was a reality at all—may have only exacerbated existing constitutional tensions in genteel and "middling" society at large.[33] In any case, Young has concluded that, in broad terms, "the government of the 1630s, rather than spearheading a new royal programme, was simply resurrecting earlier policies and returning to the normal interests of peacetime after several years of wartime interruption."[34]

Norah Carlin has returned a similar "post-revisionist" verdict on Charles I's social philosophy and style of governance. "Though revisionist historians see the personal rule as evidence that Charles I was an innovative and modernizing king, resisted by a backward-looking gentry and nobility," she has noted, "he made no structural changes and created no new institutions of government.... Charles's outlook was explicitly traditional rather than modernizing, looking back to 'an idealized past of social order, harmony, community and respect for authority and law' with the king at the centre."[35]

To be sure, the notion of an old regime in England "already half at war with itself" appears at times in Carlin's work. A striking example of this is her characterization of Charles's policy toward the peerage:

> In the 1630s, Charles I pursued a policy of . . . reinforcing the . . . powers of the aristocracy, seeking to restore their "ancient lustre" and inviting them to "join in the management of the affairs of the commonwealth," as he put it in 1629. He promoted the Renaissance idea of an aristocracy of virtue and public service, while at the same time hankering after traditions of feudal loyalty and even considering a revival of the obsolete homage ceremony.[36]

Here, the "Renaissance idea" of an élite of "virtue and public service," to some extent anticipating for us later meritocratic values in prerevolutionary France and Russia, is joined at the hip with a blatant royal favoritism toward the *traditional* aristocracy and, beyond even that, with the possibility of "reinforcing" rather than abrogating the feudal privileges and procedures of the past. Still, Carlin's overall message (like that of Hughes, Young, and other post-revisionists) is one that underscores what was traditionalist rather than modernizing about this *severely conflicted* Stuart monarch.

The picture that is emerging here of a Stuart monarchy "already half at war with itself" is further validated when, thinking in both state-centered structuralist *and* postmodernist terms, we turn to the overarching nexus between *domestic* and *international* affairs. Whereas in *purely internal* affairs some division appeared to prevail, in certain respects, between what Steve Pincus would call "advocates of modernity" (Thomas Wentworth and Archbishop Laud) and "defenders of traditional society" (meaning, above all, the king himself), larger domestic and geostrategic matters brought ministers and monarch together in common defense of an antimodernist worldview. Ominously, however, that worldview was being ever more challenged by English subjects holding what we might now call modernizing beliefs and anxieties. Because, as Derek Hirst has opined, "anti-catholicism" was "the one genuine religio-political conviction of ordinary people" in this era, it was all too easy for Charles I's critics, responding from the late 1620s on to the pathetic record of Stuart military incompetence in the Thirty Years' War but also to disconcerting signs of the king's "popishly-affected" and arbitrary political attitudes, to assume that they in fact spoke with popular favor when they castigated the crown for both its foreign *and* its domestic policy failures.[37] Because Charles decided, after initial hesitation, to throw all of his weight behind eventual Archbishop of Canterbury William Laud's "proArminian" campaign within the Anglican Church, he played directly into the hands of his detractors. In other words, the government's fateful tendency to designate ministers as "priests," to prefer free will over predestinarian theology, and to celebrate hierarchy, ritual, and liturgical devotions in Sunday services to the detriment of the Puritans' drab but beloved preaching and lecturing, only made it easier for politically attuned individuals to associate the English crown with the papal Antichrist they all so loved to fear and detest.[38]

All of this led to a highly "schizoid" political culture in the English *ancien régime*, if we are to believe a new generation of post-revisionist scholars (and if, for now, we are also to give free reign to a *moderate postmodernist* ideological bent). Whereas sociologically inclined historians like Perez Zagorin, Christopher Hill, and Lawrence Stone dwelled in earlier times on the "court versus country" dichotomy in early Stuart England, historians today have shifted their emphasis to the question of rival "conspiracy theories" tying together religious, constitutional, and state/security matters (as already indicated previously) and prescribing radically different remedies for the kingdom's ills. Post-revisionist Ann Hughes has written of a popular (and, we might suggest, modernist?) conspiracy theory "which explained political conflict in terms of an authoritarian popish plot to undermine English laws and liberties as well as true religion, a plot which had alarming support from evil counselors at court." On the other, traditionalist side, Charles and his closest aides naturally saw such views "as a subversive attempt to undermine his God-given authority: 'popularity,' not popery, was the great threat to the stability of English (and British) subjects." Such conspiracy theories—with all of their associated constitutional, social, religious, and geopolitical baggage—were, Hughes has concluded, "mutually reinforcing."[39] In responding to all of this, we may ask: how, in the end, could such diametrically opposed visions (laden as they were with modernizing or traditionalist implications) have possibly been reconciled, and how could they *not* have redounded ultimately to the peril of Charles I?

Here, at least in hindsight, everything seems to have been stacked against the king. Any effort by the Stuart party to tar its opponents with the brush of popular sabotage, of plebeian rebelliousness jeopardizing the divinely ordained ranks of social hierarchy and prerogatives of monarchy, was likely, in these years, to be trumped in the eyes of most English subjects by opposition tactics tarring Charles I and his adherents with the far more damning brush of "popery." After all, "popery" conjured up for most of the king's contemporaries such traumata in recent history as the Marian persecutions of the 1550s, the treason of Mary Stuart and the Spanish Armada of the 1580s, the "Gunpowder Plot" under James I, and all of the Catholic assassinations and other atrocities martyring Protestants in continental Europe—not to mention the near-success of the Austro-Spanish Habsburgs in rolling back (in the Thirty Years' War) a century of Protestantism in continental theaters of action not *that* distant from England's imperiled shores. Post-revisionist research appears to show convincingly how difficult it would be to overestimate the early seventeenth-century tendency, in *all* ranks of English society, to detect priests and other "papists" under every bed, and to hate and fear Ireland (and even, to some extent, Scotland) as prospective avenues for papist infiltration of encircled, evangelical England.⁴⁰ That, over the years leading up to the explosion in 1640, Charles I was partnered with (and increasingly close to) a foreign *and Catholic* wife, cast his lot irrevocably with a High Anglicanism that struck many as indistinguishable from papism, made peace with ultra-Catholic Spain, and even seemed at times to be favoring pro-papist military interests in Ireland, only added finishing touches to a lurid portrait whose provocative strokes affrighted growing numbers of patriotic Englishmen and Englishwomen.

In sum, we have here the riveting spectacle of an early Stuart England hovering on the brink of revolution, in part because its ruling élite was not only "half at war with itself" but also at daggers drawn with many of Charles I's subjects over dueling visions of state and society. But before moving on from the tensions between modernizing and traditionalist tendencies in old regime England to the analogous phenomenon in prerevolutionary France and Russia, we might—again in structuralist and postmodernist vein—offer here some suggestive if necessarily brief examples of how those tensions, further amplified, were instrumental in fueling the *actual process of revolution* in the England of the 1640s and 1650s.

In the case of revolutionary England, modernizers and traditionalists may have squared off against each other in a somewhat less *mass-mobilizing* fashion than would be true in the two larger upheavals later on; still, signs of this confrontation are there, to be duly noted by the comparative analyst. Outstanding in this regard are two incontrovertible facts: (1) that revolutionaries and their adversaries fought a civil war (actually, *two* civil wars) in the 1640s, and (2) that Charles I emerged from this civil strife defeated but determined, if need be, to die as (in his own view, at least) a martyr to the Good Old Cause of divine-right absolutism, "true" religion, and social hierarchy.⁴¹ Although the tensions between modernizing and traditionalist forces in the English Revolution could not take on all of the political and, above all, *social* dimensions that they would assume in the later upheavals, premonitory indications of such tensions *do* reveal themselves in (for instance) the rival armies of the Civil War. Military historian Ian Gentles has pointed to the contrast between patterns of recruitment to, and promotion within, the parliamentary forces headed by Thomas Fairfax and Oliver Cromwell and those prevailing in the royalist formations led by Prince Rupert of the Palatinate. Early on, Rupert's army was officered exclusively by peers and gentry, and it tolerated *no* promotion-by-merit from noncommissioned officer ranks into commanding posts, whereas the parliament's New Model Army boasted noticeably more *lesser gentry* and even some non-gentry officers and allowed for promotion of deserving noncommissioned officers into commissioned officer ranks. In addition, the cavalry brought by Cromwell from his erstwhile Eastern Association Army to the New Model exhibited considerable religious ferment (Gentles has traced its ties with Independent and Baptist congregations in the greater London area in 1646 to 1647) and could vaunt a full contingent of enthusiastic lay preachers and chaplains. Hence, if Prince Rupert's forces continued to embody some of the characteristic values of the English old regime, the New Model was a sort of "revolution within a revolution," permitting within its ranks (under the momentary pressures of military exigency, to be sure) the discussion and even, to some extent, the practice of meritocracy and religious toleration that we would more readily associate with revolutions of a much later date.[42]

The assumption of many of the New Model Army's apprehensive critics that it might serve—especially in the event of a decisive rout of its royalist foes in the civil strife of the 1640s—as an engine of massive sociopolitical change drastically overshot the mark; as all specialists in the field know well, Cromwell, once having (reluctantly, it seems) endorsed Charles I's execution in January 1649, and once ensconced in power himself in the 1650s, reaffirmed a belief in the traditional social order reflecting his own origins as an East Anglian gentleman. Nonetheless, the English Republic of the 1650s continued to stand for a carefully circumscribed measure of religious toleration and *military* meritocracy that was, arguably, revolutionary by the standards of the day; and the chronic royalist plotting against, first, the Commonwealth, and, then, the Protectorate, along with the relentless counterstrokes of the Republic, recalled the dynamics of civil strife (and the clash of values) in the revolutionary 1640s.[43] Beyond this, it is interesting to note that, as those ruling England in the wake of the regicide attempted to defend their impromptu Republic against a wide array of royalist and continental enemies, their naval forces took on something of the radicalism long associated with the New Model Army. "The navy of the 1650s," so Bernard Capp has noted, "contained very few of the gentlemen-captains prominent in the 1630s and none of the aristocratic captains, appointed on the strength of court connections, to be found after the Restoration." Furthermore, however co-opted it may have been by more conservative tendencies later on, the English Navy of the republican period, "for the first and only time in its history . . . became a stronghold of political and religious radicalism, with ideological commitment figuring prominently in appointments and promotions."[44]

The heroics and religious enthusiasm of William Blake's fleet notwithstanding, we are still left with the impression of a very real (if *socially circumscribed*) confrontation between modernizers and traditionalists in revolutionary as in old regime England. Without any doubt, there were some striking premonitions of modern times in early and mid-seventeenth-century England, ranging from Thomas Wentworth's and William Laud's *Thorough* policy in governance and the bitter Puritan arraignment of Catholicism in the 1630s to parliamentary and Cromwellian reforms in the 1640s and 1650s. Yet we leave this section of chapter 1 haunted, above all, by thoughts of a king caught between the pressures generated by the geostrategic/structural needs of governance and the pressures generated by his own traditionalist orientation in an increasingly polarized political culture.

MODERNIZERS VERSUS TRADITIONALISTS: THE FRENCH CASE

In turning to prerevolutionary/revolutionary France, we will find ourselves stressing three key points: (1) Louis XVI, caught like Charles I between structuralist *raison d'état* and his own traditionalist values, was prepared to throw one modernizing minister after another to the reactionary wolves; (2) a subverting dialectic between modernizing and antimodernist values was nevertheless starting to take hold in provincial and local representative institutions in the late old regime; and (3) the revolutionary process, once fully unleashed in France during and following upon the summer of 1789, tremendously intensified a struggle between modernizers and traditionalists that had already begun to manifest itself in the waning years of the old regime.

Although we have (in large part) agreed with Steve Pincus that Charles I was basically "willing . . . to defend the traditional society and the traditional polity" in seventeenth-century England, we cannot accept his subsequent claim that: "Far from being a reactionary, Louis XVI was a determined reformer . . . a modernizer."[45] Certainly this is *not* the sort of impression that experts on late prerevolutionary French history have gathered from all the available evidence in recent years. Pierrette Girault de Coursac, for example, wrote that the future Louis XVI, known in his youth as the duc de Berri, was instructed by his preceptor the duc de La Vauguyon not only to "know the whole extent both of your authority and of the obedience due to you from your subjects," but also to maintain "all the orders of the State and each of them in particular in its rights, properties, honors, distinctions, and privileges."[46] The studies of Louis XVI published by John Hardman and Munro Price suggest that this credo of absolutism, social inequality, and sacrosanct *privilège*, drummed into this impressionable Bourbon prince from the very start, stayed with him to the scaffold—and, more to our point here, militated fatally against his *sustained acceptance* of modernizing values and policies in the twilight years of the old regime.[47]

The die was cast very early on with the Enlightenment's presumed champion and spokesman in office, A.-R.-J. Turgot. Turgot, a renowned physiocratic advocate of free trade and other liberal policies, and one-time reformist *intendant* in the Limousin, held the ministerial portfolio of finances during the first two years of Louis XVI's reign.[48] In attempting to apply some of his reformist notions on a national scale, however, and in arguing against Foreign Minister Charles Gravier, comte de Vergennes and others determined to bring France into the brewing anti-British insurgency in North

America, Turgot fell afoul of powerful vested interests at court—and, eventually, alienated the king himself. Some of the animus against Turgot undoubtedly had to do with the bruised egos of the other ministers of state (and, even more fatally, with the threatened self-esteem of Louis XVI himself), as the popularly lionized *Contrôleur Géneral des Finances* seemed initially to be moving from strength to strength at Versailles. Indeed, John Hardman quotes the king's celebrated *boutade* to the effect that "M. Turgot wants to be me and I don't want him to be me," and also holds that Turgot, "through wanting 'the cooperation of his equals' and 'colleagues who shared his views' . . . was unconsciously moving in the direction of an English-style prime minister."[49] Yet if Louis's eventual decision to dismiss his brilliant finance minister was actuated in part by *constitutional* considerations, it must also have reflected his deeply rooted commitment to *social inequality*. Especially noteworthy in this connection is the fact that Turgotist tax reforms aroused the furious opposition of the (highly privileged) magistrates in the Paris Parlement, the kingdom's most influential court of law, and they had an ally at Versailles in the person of Keeper of the Seals A.-T. Hue de Miromesnil. Miromesnil did everything in his power to focus the king's attention on parliamentary remonstrances that preached up the aristocratic virtues of "the descendants of those chevaliers of past times who placed or maintained the crown upon the heads of Your Majesty's ancestors," and he may also have shared with Louis XVI these drafted parliamentary sentiments: "Providence did not want all men to be equal, and placed them in different conditions. . . . The order of all political States also depends upon such conditions." The moral for the monarch was obvious: Turgot, by even *thinking* of tampering with the existing tax structure, and by proposing other, equally objectionable reforms, was in effect jeopardizing, along with sacrosanct social inequality, the very foundations of the Bourbon state.[50]

And so Turgot, the shining hope of Voltaire and others in the tribe of the Enlightened in France, was cashiered by the king in the spring of 1776. We know today, of course, that he was but the first in a line of state modernizers whose efforts to doctor an *ancien régime* already on its sickbed only incurred royal displeasure. Next in the line of prominent would-be modernizers was Jacques Necker, who, as a Protestant commoner hailing from the Swiss "republic" of Geneva, was offensive three times over to traditionalist Catholic French nobles (and others) at Versailles.[51] In a sense, Necker's dismissal from the finance ministry in 1781 (only belatedly accorded its due in the historiography on old regime France) was even more damaging than Turgot's downfall, for it occurred *in wartime*, and Necker's complicated strategy for managing the huge costs of French involvement in the American War began to unravel with the disgrace of its author. But, again, tellingly, Louis XVI's abandonment of yet another putative savior of his comfortable *monde* of absolutism and *privilège* appears to have reflected both constitutional *and* social-hierarchical considerations. On the one hand, as John Hardman has emphasized, Necker, whose fiscal and administrative reforms were drawing the wrath of venal *officiers*, aristocratic hangers-on at Versailles, intendants, and parlementaires, eventually complained to the king that he was being dealt with "as a mere *ramasseur d'argent* and denied a say in framing the general policies he was asked to finance." This led him early in 1781 to demand that he be granted the status of *ministre d'état*, formal access to the decision-making *conseil d'état*, and full control over the treasuries of both the naval *and* the war ministries, at least for the duration of the war. Louis XVI found such demands unacceptable. "In fact," John Hardman has concluded, "the king, weary of Necker's demanding conditional marks of confidence like an English minister, did not press Necker to stay, though he blamed him for going."[52]

Yet, once again, more than merely *constitutional* issues were involved here. The same Parisian parlementaires who had chanted their praise of inviolable noble privileges and linked the defense of such privileges (and of social hierarchy in general) with the defense of the Bourbon state during Turgot's abortive financial ministry staged a repeat performance in connection with Necker's promulgation (in November 1778) of a decree systematizing the surveying and assessment of taxable lands throughout the kingdom and projecting a higher return—on nobles' as well as commoners' estates—from so-called *vingtième* or "twentieth" (i.e., 5 percent) impositions. This Neckerite effort to augment state revenue, so the judges predictably claimed, could not be implemented without "striking a direct and lasting blow at the property of all orders of citizens, without violating in particular the original exemption of lands of the Nobility from taxation, and without making the hierarchy of orders disappear."[53] The magistrates' crony at Versailles, Keeper of the Seals Hue de Miromesnil, would have made certain that the king, once again, received the "correct" message: namely, that any *meaningful* financial reforms were socially as well as constitutionally subversive. Given what we have already observed about Louis's youthful indoctrination in traditionalist ways of thinking, such a message must have registered deeply with him. Small wonder, then, that in this latest political crisis, the king (in Hardman's phrasing) "did not press Necker to stay"!

Paradoxically, however, Louis XVI's desertion of the next major modernizing finance minister, Charles-Alexandre de Calonne, would be an action that he undertook only with great reluctance, because Calonne had largely retained his confidence from the time of his appointment in 1783 down to the start of the so-called prerevolutionary crisis of 1787 to 1788.[54] Nevertheless, by August 1786, Calonne, driven to distraction by mounting government debt, was forced to urge upon the king an unprecedented program of fiscal/administrative reforms whose constitutional and social ramifications in time would swamp both the *Contrôleur Général des Finances* and his royal master.⁵⁵ To begin with, Calonne wanted to replace the *vingtièmes* with a permanent *subvention territoriale* of unspecified yield to fall in kind on the lands of *all three* orders, that is, including the (hitherto exempt) clergy. Apportionment of the tax, at least in the *pays d'élections*, regions directly administered by the king's own agents, was to be vested in hierarchies of provincial and subordinate assemblies of landowners deliberating without any regard for social rank and dealing with other administrative matters as well. Calonne also aimed to extend the government's stamp tax; reduce the commoners' basic direct tax, the *taille*; exploit the royal domain more efficiently by leasing it out in fiefholds; enable the Church to liberate itself from its huge debts; negotiate further loans for the royal treasury; and, by various means, stimulate agriculture and trade within the kingdom, thereby increasing the yield from both direct and indirect taxation.

Louis XVI's tragedy was that, in allowing Calonne to submit this barrage of modernizing reforms to a specially convened Assembly of Notables in February 1787, he was detonating a national explosion of hopes, doubts, and fears that in time would expose the limits of his own tolerance of constitutional and social innovation. That, within a few months, Louis XVI would feel constrained to dismiss a finance minister whom he had loyally supported for over three years demonstrated that, when push really came to shove, he would revert to his customary defense of the absolutist and hierarchical principles of the *ancien régime*. John Hardman has aptly identified some of the sociopolitical forces that lay behind the king's eventual decision to drop Calonne:

> Calonne fell because he was appealing from a position of weakness to men who could only lose by the measures they were being asked to endorse. They would have been hurt in their pockets and in their social prestige (being asked to sit next to [commoners] in the proposed provincial assemblies). Moreover, the unquantified, permanent tax which the proposed *impôt territorial* represented and the inevitable decline of *pouvoirs intermédiaires*, such as the clergy (which would lose its corporate existence) and parlements, would have created a modern and truly absolute monarchy, foreshadowing that created by Napoleon.

Hence, in an immediate sense, Calonne was "torn to shreds . . . by a body [i.e., the Assembly of Notables] he had called into being."⁵⁶ But, of course, it was the king to whom the luckless finance minister finally had to answer. When, therefore, in March 1787, Calonne audaciously anticipated a tactic of the coming revolution by appealing *over the heads of his privileged critics in the Notables* to the general citizenry with a vehement indictment of privileges and of all royal administration hitherto shrouded in darkness, this proved to be simply too much for Louis XVI—who, after all, was bound to see in such a spectacular gesture a criticism of himself and of all his regal forebears. And so, once again, this king—like Charles I before him—

revealed himself to be caught between structuralist *raison d'état* in an ever-dangerous Europe and what postmodernists today would rightly call his own traditionalist convictions.

But if the king found the dismissal of his erstwhile favorite Calonne to be an uncongenial duty, he would find things only going from bad to worse over the following months. An eleventh-hour spate of reforms in the prerevolution of 1787 to 1788 associated with the new Finance Minister Etienne-Charles Loménie de Brienne and the new Keeper of the Seals Lamoignon de Basville ran aground on the shoals of an unforeseen fiscal crisis reflecting, in turn, growing doubts about French creditworthiness in the indispensable domestic and international money markets.[57] The king appears to have regarded these developments (at least for the time being) with a wearied detachment. If we are to believe his most recent biographer, "the rejection of his cherished reform programme had wrought a profound change in the king: from this time he began to lose his grip on affairs, increased his hunting and eating and his dependence on the queen, in short became the king that many assume he always was."[58] But brutal geopolitical and fiscal pressures gave Louis XVI's government no rest: soon, Loménie de Brienne (and, with him, his collaborator in modernizing reforms Lamoignon de Basville) made way for a reinstated Jacques Necker. This must have been extremely distasteful to the king, but only this reputed Genevan master of financial wizardry (so it was thought at the time) had the wherewithal to rescue the French state from the woes of financial bankruptcy—and, thus, of impotence in worldly affairs.

Yet once again, and indeed for the last time as a more-or-less free historical agent, Louis XVI reverted to his *true form* by rejecting fundamental sociopolitical change. Come the strategic stalemate between modernizers and traditionalists in the Estates General in June 1789, the king had, finally, to bare his deepest convictions. Not for nothing did Georges Lefebvre once remark that Louis's exposition of those reforms he deemed acceptable for France at the *séance royale* staged in the self-proclaimed National Assembly on June 23, 1789, was "of the utmost interest because it shows clearly what was at stake, not only in the following weeks but in the whole Revolution."[59] Although there has been some disagreement among subsequent scholars such as Robert Harris, John Hardman, and Munro Price as to how, exactly, the king and his chief minister Necker differed in their prescriptions for appropriate social and constitutional reforms in these critical days of June 1789, there can be little doubt that the king's address on the subject reflected the last-minute intervention of Marie Antoinette and her reactionary brother-in-law, the comte d'Artois. Munro Price aptly focused on the *terms* of that fateful intervention—terms which were, in his words,

> drawn up [as] a rejection of Necker's compromise and the substitution of a much harder line. The nobility and the clergy were exhorted, but not com-

manded, to discuss and vote by head on matters of general interest . . . they could stipulate that any decisions reached in this manner could only be carried by a two-thirds majority. These arrangements would apply to the present session of the Estates only. The form of organization of future Estates, the rights of the three orders, feudal and seigneurial properties and the honorific prerogatives of the first two orders, were specifically excluded from discussion in common.[60]

In the future (as Price put it), France was to have "a constitutional monarchy," but it was to be one "in partnership with the privileged orders, not the third estate." Evaluated in a broader historical context, the king's defensive address to the delegates convened at the *séance royale* "ended the era in which the crown, influenced first by Calonne and then by Brienne, had sought the alliance of the third in its assault on the first two estates' tax exemptions. Now, in its alarm at the third estate's claims for a greater share of power, the monarchy had closed ranks with the nobility and clergy in a defense of privilege."[61]

Another way of historicizing the royal position on state modernization at the *séance royale* of June 23, 1789, would be to concentrate briefly on the practical—and crucial—question of *access to military employment* in the new France; this was a question that truly exposed the larger connections between geopolitical, constitutional, and social issues in a country long given to regarding itself as the "arbiter of the Continent."[62] Significantly, Necker had spoken out on behalf of the concept of military meritocracy (always a hallmark of state modernization) in the *Conseil du roi* several days prior to the royal session of June 23—and had been quickly assailed for doing so by his more traditionalist colleagues. In particular, the incensed war minister, the comte de Puységur, had angrily protested "against any measure by which the king's hands should be tied in the appointment of army officers, and the king, much disturbed by this possibility, [had] blamed Necker for having even thought of it."[63] Here were both a constitutional question of *state power*—should the executive continue to monopolize control of the kingdom's armed forces?—and a social question of *defining that kingdom's power élite*—should all Frenchmen qualified to serve their country in its positions of public responsibility be allowed to do so irrespective of their social status? Yet transcending *both* of these questions, arguably, was France's compelling structural need for a modernized army with which to defend French strategic interests and project French power abroad. Louis XVI, at the behest of conservatives in the *Conseil du roi*, chose to veto his principal minister on this pivotal question—thereby choosing not only to swim against the current of sociopolitical evolution in France but also (quite conceivably) to subvert his own state's security needs in the ever-perilous arena of European high politics.

Still, as we all know today, the traditionalist triumph registered so dramatically at the *séance royale* of June 23, 1789, was short-lived: the king was soon forced by his need to retain Necker's financial services to retreat from the unrealistic position he had staked out on that occasion. For sure, he did not neglect to summon the leaders of the clergy and nobility and tearfully assure them "that he would never abandon [them], but that he was forced by circumstances to make great sacrifices for unity." Yet Louis XVI's grandiloquent talk of "great sacrifices" notwithstanding, the events of June 23 (as Munro Price has correctly noted) "opened an irrevocable breach between the king and his people," and marked as well an inauspicious turning point in the king's and queen's relationship with Necker. "From that point on they strongly suspected that he cared more about pleasing the populace than serving them."[64] We can imagine, nonetheless, that for Necker, sensitive as he must have been to the very real (if diplomatically muted) hostility of both Louis and Marie-Antoinette, and ever recalling what had transpired during his earlier ministry of 1776 to 1781, there must have been by now a rejuvenated sense of *déjà vu*. But the king had also, in his own manner, come full circle, from his dismissal of modernizers Turgot and "Necker 1" in the early years of his reign to his subsequent abandonment of his favorite Calonne and then the queen's favorites Loménie de Brienne and Lamoignon de Basville in the prerevolution of 1787 and 1788 to, finally, his sullen acceptance of modernizer "Necker 2" in the initial days of full-blown revolution in France.

To take this story much farther at this point, that is, from the troubled aftermath of the June 23 *séance royale* to the July Days and October Days of 1789 and beyond, would be to advance from the domain of revolutionary *origins* to that of revolutionary *process*, thus unduly anticipating observations we will have to make later on. Suffice it to say at this point that, in retrospectively analyzing the roles of Louis XVI and his ministers (would-be modernizers) in the waning years of the old regime, we seem once again to have before our eyes what Lawrence Stone saw in the case of prerevolutionary England: the spectacle of a regime "already half at war with itself." John Hardman, who has reexamined the French situation as carefully as any scholar in recent times, has painted it in these colors:

> Instability was the hallmark of ministerial politics under Louis XVI—instability and division. Ministerial instability was Miromesnil's excuse for doing nothing: "It takes a king," he told [abbé de] Véri, "and even one of talent and strong character, to produce dramatic changes. The rest of us, . . . unsafe in our jobs, can only prepare modifications and plan obsolescence." Division was not only between robe and sword but also between the various "constituencies" of the ministers, of which first and foremost were the king and the queen. Consequently, it is seldom useful to talk of the policies of "le gouvernement" or "le ministère."[65]

Hardman, we may suspect, gets even more directly to the heart of the matter when he comments that Louis's notorious "lack of trust for his ministers . . .

was innate but was also reinforced by his awareness that many of his ministers no longer believed in the system they were operating."[66] Those ministers, in other words, were increasingly "at war with themselves," torn between their traditionalist monarchist loyalties and their presentiments of a more modernized world-to-come. What have we here, if not the tension between traditionalist and modernizing perspectives that we have already discerned (at least in nascent form) in early Stuart England?[67]

Of course, historical comparisons can sometimes be taken too far: Charles I, who seems largely to have operated in a traditionalist mode during the Personal Rule, was not forced to abandon his most important ministers (Strafford and Laud) until the early days of the English Revolution, whereas Louis XVI fired one would-be reformist minister after another during the late 1770s and 1780s. Then, again, we can point to a much more striking example in France than in England of how the dialectic between modernizing and traditionalist values pervaded administration at the provincial/local level as well as at the center of state power. We know this today thanks to recent research on the provincial assemblies that were initially intended to be mediating regional institutions in late eighteenth-century France.

The twists and turns of the historiography on the administrative bodies of landowners instituted under Jacques Necker in the Berry and the Haute Guyenne in 1778 and 1779 and on the more comprehensive hierarchies of assemblies established in the provinces, districts (*élections*), and parishes almost ten years later testify in their own way to the tensions between modernizing and traditional values in old regime France. To believe Pierre Renouvin and Maurice Bordes, the earliest authorities on this experiment in regional and local governance, the assemblies never had much of a chance: because they aroused the jealousy of both the Paris Parlement in the late 1770s and the Assembly of Notables in 1787, Louis XVI hobbled them by dividing their personnel into "estate" contingents, subjecting them to the *intendants*, and underfunding their activities. As a result, the assemblies proved to be too timid to embark on major reforms or to attempt to expand the bases of their recruitment.[68] On the other hand, Peter M. Jones subsequently painted the provincial assemblies in more positive colors, presenting them as real vehicles of "reforming absolutism" in late eighteenth-century France. These local assemblies, argued Jones, by drawing some of the king's subjects into provincial, district, and urban administration, introduced them to the problems posed by *privilège* and helped make them advocates of a new kind of constitutionalism foreshadowing both political *and* social reform, if not outright revolution.[69]

However, Stephen Miller is now reviewing the whole matter of Louis XVI's provincial assemblies in such a manner as to highlight what William H. Sewell Jr. has called the "split ideological personality" of the *ancien régime* in France.[70] True, Miller agrees with P. M. Jones that the 1787 edict establishing these assemblies throughout the *pays d'élections* enabled villagers who could meet certain proprietary qualifications to elect parish representatives to the *municipalités* at the lowest level. At the same time, however, he also stresses that the same "reform" legislation restricted *social participation* in these new assemblies by stipulating that the *crown* (rather than the proprietors in the *pays d'élections*) was to name the first twenty-four members of the top-level provincial assemblies, and that a "top-down" principle of selection-by-cooptation would apply at both the provincial and the district levels of the new system. "The edict granted the Third Estate half of the seats and provided for voting by head rather than by order," Miller says. "But on the whole," he also notes, "the top-down system of appointments brought together archbishops, abbots, and marquises, and a third estate comprising owners of seigneuries, judges in lordly courts, and tax-exempt knights, squires, and officeholders on the path to ennoblement, all generally beholden to the nobles and bishops of their provinces."[71]

Beyond reviewing the details of this legislation, however, Miller seeks ultimately to understand how an administrative innovation intended initially to stand as a "sweeping reform" could have ended up producing regional bodies that would be little more than "forums for the affirmation of privileges." Why—that is to say—did the prerevolutionary French monarchy *not* establish institutions invested with real power, and why was it so eager to cater to what Pierre Renouvin had once termed "the prejudices and interests of the privileged"?[72] The answer that Miller provides, at least at this early juncture in his research on the subject, is particularly relevant for us insofar as it reinforces our sense of a developing confrontation between modernizing and traditionalist values in this apparently typical old regime.

The answer, essentially, comes to us in the form of two observations. First, much like Lawrence Stone in the case of England, this historian leaves us in the case of France with the sense of a monarchy "almost at war with itself" over its defining values. Miller, in part, writes that:

> Although the monarchy had reformers at its highest levels, it proved incapable of accomplishing substantive change. Powerful nobles with influence at court . . . used the patronage afforded by seigneurial rights to rally factions in the royal council and gain advantages over political rivals. The monarchy faced chronic shortages of funds and continually fell back on privileged groups for infusions of cash. Seigneurial rights and privileges formed part of the logic of customary action, the institutionalized ways of doing things, in the king's court and councils and led their members to assimilate a discourse of an historical constitution inimical to a standardized administration of provincial assemblies and fiscal equality.[73]

Louis XVI's government, that is to say, did *not*, in administrative terms, "form a unitary entity." Its fiscal vulnerabilities, in combination with the inertia of custom, threw it back on "the prejudices and interests of the privileged." The second point to stress here concerns prerevolutionary *links of solidarity* between the *privilégiés* at Versailles and their brethren in the countryside. As Miller observes, anticipating the drama of 1789: "The members of the provincial assemblies clearly shared a political practice and idiom with the great nobles of Versailles. It may be for this reason . . . that provincial nobles elected the highest and most distinguished elements of the traditional aristocracy—princes, dukes, marquises, counts, and barons—to the Estates General and that many of them accepted and voted on the *cahiers de doléances* written by great nobles of the capital."[74] There were, in other words, *social* and *ideological* as well as administrative aspects to this dilemma of a prerevolutionary regime divided against itself.

As we will see later on, this portrayal of an *administrative* old regime in France that was "already half at war with itself" over clashing values both nationally *and locally* could serve as well for Romanov Russia. Before moving on to the Russian situation, however, we need to enlarge a bit on this picture of a *schizoid political culture* in France that (much as in prerevolutionary England) commingled domestic and international issues and put the tensions between modernizing and traditionalist forces very much on display. Stuart England's dueling conspiracy theories of Puritans and High Anglicans found something of a French parallel in the rival ecclesiological and constitutional visions of anti-Papal Gallicans/Jansenists and pro-Papal Jesuits. Originally little more than a strain of thought playing up predestinarian and other austere tendencies within Catholicism, Jansenism in time became a focal point of constitutional debate in the old regime. The effort by both the papacy and the crown to suppress the Jansenists, whom they viewed as subversive, revived in some French subjects' eyes the old bugbear of an ultramontane assault on France's historic Gallican liberties. As Dale Van Kley and others have shown, aroused Jansenists in the Paris Parlement, inveterate champions of those liberties, were, by the 1750s and in subsequent decades, calling for a monarchy "controlled by the parlement and ultimately by the nation exercising almost complete control over a democratically constituted and participatory church," whereas pro-Papal polemicists were advocating "a veritably absolute monarch in relation to his lay subjects, encountering his equal only in . . . a similarly authoritarian and monarchically structured church." Given the polarization between these two competing visions, it was only a matter of time before some Gallican-Jansenist magistrates would begin appealing *directly* to the "nation" and even invoking the moribund Estates General in their radicalized discourse. Insofar as he *had* to associate himself with the pro-Papal and pro-Jesuit disputants in this controversy, Louis XVI eventually found himself (somewhat like Charles I in earlier times) further isolated from many of his most patriotic and forward-looking subjects.[75]

This isolation could only prove more dangerous for the king once the revolution was underway in France. There is no need to revisit here Louis XVI's flat rejection, in June 1789, of Jacques Necker's relatively moderate program of political, social, and military reforms, let alone the more radical reforms soon conjured up by the thoroughly politicized deputies to the self-proclaimed National Assembly; we have already traversed this ground. What we need to emphasize at this point is how the revolutionary process in France, once fully unleashed during and following upon the summer of 1789, tremendously intensified the dialectic between modernizing and traditionalist forces that had already started to manifest itself in the waning years of the *ancien régime*. On the one side of this ideological divide, the men of the National (Constituent) Assembly and subsequent legislatures, resuming, so to speak, the state modernization drive associated earlier with Turgot, Necker, Calonne, Loménie de Brienne, and Lamoignon de Basville, implemented a myriad of political, administrative, military, religious, social, and economic reforms far surpassing anything hitherto envisaged in France.[76] On the other side of this divide, the king (fatefully emulating in this Charles I) abandoned (at least in secret) any semblance of a modernizing role. He reacted to the decrees pushed through the Assembly on the tumultuous night of August 4, decrees curtailing feudal and particularist privileges in the kingdom, by discreetly informing the Archbishop of Arles: "I will never consent to the spoliation of my clergy or of my nobility. I will not sanction decrees by which they are despoiled."[77] Soon after the October Days had forced the removal of the royal family (and the Assembly) from Versailles to Paris, Louis, in a memorandum sent secretly to both his Spanish cousin Charles IV and his Austrian brother-in-law Joseph II, repudiated all innovations "extracted from [him] by force" since the June *séance royale*.[78] From this period forward, Louis XVI (increasingly in league with his wife) committed himself to a perilous "double game," overtly pledging fidelity to the revolution but covertly standing by the constitutional, social, and ecclesiological *ancien régime*, and before very long plotting to flee from Paris. "It is difficult to imagine," observes the latest chronicler of the abortive "Flight to Varennes" of June 1791, "that the king's successful escape would not have . . . ignited a full-scale civil war and probably an international war as well."[79]

"Louis XVI and Marie-Antoinette," then, "were prepared to die for their beliefs, and ultimately did so."[80] The Jacobin Terror of 1793 and 1794, of which they were the most notable victims, represents from our theoretical viewpoint the climactic phase of the dialectic—now become lethal indeed—between modernizing and traditionalist forces in late eighteenth-century France. Still, we should also remember that this dialectic (purged, to be sure, of some of its most murderous intensity) survived into the era of Thermidor and beyond. On the one hand, state modernization marched on in the form of genuinely contestatory politics and post-Terrorist reformism in the National

Convention's final year and under the subsequent Directory.[81] On the other hand, traditionalist extremists found a new standard-bearer in the person of Louis XVI's younger brother the comte de Provence, who, upon the death of his nephew ("Louis XVII") in Parisian captivity in 1795, proclaimed himself "Louis XVIII." This Bourbon prince, just as unyieldingly opposed to basic sociopolitical change as his guillotined elder brother, promptly issued the Declaration of Verona, a manifesto calling defiantly for a complete restoration of the social inequality and *privilège* of the *ancien régime*.[82] Yet, in the end, it was the increasingly polarized—and militarized—*internal* politics of the Directory that, by undermining the legitimacy of this first experiment in French republicanism, most badly damaged its prospects for survival. "Though it was chance that gave power to Bonaparte," Jacques Godechot contended, "the coup d'état of 18 Brumaire was a logical outcome of the Revolution."[83] Some may argue that Godechot overstated the case here; still, the undiminished tug-and-pull between modernizers and traditionalists in post-Terrorist France undeniably helped to pave the way for a unifying, charismatic leader like Napoleon Bonaparte.

It seems as certain in the case of France as in that of England that only by combining the insights of state-centered structuralism with those of moderate postmodernism can we adequately appreciate both prerevolutionary and revolutionary issues. In particular, we are left once again with the spectacle of a monarch (this time, Louis XVI) unable to reconcile the (structuralist) requirements of leadership in a fiercely competitive world with a traditionalist rejection of modernizing values and policies.

MODERNIZERS VERSUS TRADITIONALISTS: THE RUSSIAN CASE

In turning finally to old regime/revolutionary Russia, we will find ourselves making three points eerily similar to those we have made in our analysis of France: (1) Nicholas II, as a badly "conflicted" tsar in late Imperial Russia, sacrificed one modernizing minister after another to his reactionary convictions; (2) a subverting tension between progressive and traditionalist values began nonetheless to take hold in newly instituted provincial and district assemblies (*zemstvos*); and (3) the revolutionary process, once fully unloosed in Russia, only intensified a struggle between modernizers and traditionalists that already held explosive implications for this huge but underdeveloped and strategically imperiled country.

If John Hardman has cited Louis XVI's notorious lack of trust for his ministers as a destabilizing factor in prerevolutionary France, Andrew M. Verner, significantly, has argued along similar lines in his complex psychological portrayal of Imperial Russia's last tsar. "How then," he asks, "are we to explain the brief terms of so many . . . ministers and Nicholas's near-universal reputation as suspicious and distrustful?" Verner answers his own question with a reference to the heavy hand of autocracy and bureaucracy, which bore upon all, including (irony of ironies!) the tsar himself, in old regime Russia:

> That which was perceived as a negative trait of Nicholas's personality was . . . his estrangement from the autocratic role in general and his disenchantment with his bureaucracy in particular. . . . Alienated from his bureaucratic role, Nicholas found the daily government routine onerous, was always glad to escape from it by going on vacation or inspection trips, and inevitably hated to return to it. Yet the conditioning of his youth, a sense of duty, and the security he derived from this detested routine compelled him to abide by it.[84]

Still, in his "principled distrust of ministers," whom he viewed as walling him off from his own subjects, Nicholas revealed a "veritable weakness or affinity for private individuals who seemed untainted by any official associations, although tainted in other respects." Those "private" and supposedly "untainted" individuals were most likely to be members of the ultraprivileged Russian nobility:

> Nicholas's very identification with his nobles rendered him vulnerable to their pleas that he play a more traditional, active role once again. This identification revealed just how much he had distanced himself from the role of the constitutional autocrat. Hence he was more likely to heed the nobles' appeal when it suited him. His inability to internalize a consistent conception of the autocrat's role made such a change probable.[85]

Verner's fellow Russianist Dominic Lieven has voiced doubts about aspects of this psychological reading of Nicholas's character, reminding his readers (for instance) that "there were good down-to-earth reasons" for Nicholas's inability to be "an effective autocrat . . . beginning with the immense difficulty of the job." Still, he *has* agreed with Verner, and with all other scholars who have written on Russia's last tsar, that Nicholas "belonged in his innermost values" to an "old European order" of social hierarchy, aristocratic privilege, and inequality.[86]

And so the stage was set in late prerevolutionary Russia, as it had been over a century before in prerevolutionary France, for confrontations between a traditionalist monarch and a remarkable series of would-be modernizing ministers. In the case of Russia, however, the struggle between traditionalist and modernizing forces arguably assumed even greater urgency than it had in the case of France, given the acute international competitive disadvantages under which the late Romanov regime labored, and given the resultant priority placed by the tsar's most powerful advisers on the need for a campaign of forced, state-sponsored modernization. Four of the ministers of particular note in this connection were Sergei Witte, finance minister from 1892 to 1903; Peter Stolypin, interior minister and chairman of the Council of Ministers from 1906 until his assassination in 1911; Stolypin's successor as chairman of the Council of Ministers, V. I. Kokovtsov; and General (and eventual war minister) Aleksei A. Polivanov.

Sergei Witte, haunted by the specter of Russia falling behind the other Great European Powers in the mad scramble for international security and prestige, sought to address this challenge by initiating what was in effect the world's first campaign of state-directed, crash industrialization. Theodore H. Von Laue has recapitulated the main elements in that historically audacious project:

> [Witte] was to raise the productivity of Russia's economy by an extensive program of railroad construction (including the much-postponed Trans-Siberian line). This would result, he argued, in an expansion of Russia's heavy industries supplying the necessary equipment. The growth of these industries would in turn stimulate the supporting light industries. Through the increased demand and improved transportation, even agriculture would benefit. In the end, the new prosperity would yield more revenue to the government. There still remained the problem of funds for the initial capital investment, but Witte hoped that with the introduction of the gold standard (accomplished in 1897) foreign loans would become cheaper and more plentiful and that, eventually, the boom would feed on its own progress.[87]

"Though the Emperor was capable of overruling his Finance Minister on points of detail," Dominic Lieven has observed, "in the 1890s he gave solid support to the core of Witte's policy. . . . Only after 1900 did the monarch's support begin to waver."[88]

What happened, then, after 1900 to undermine this visionary finance minister's standing with Nicholas? Partly it was a matter of clashing opinions on foreign policy: Witte saw the Russian thrust into East Asian affairs as taking on an unduly military nature, and in this matter he was increasingly at odds with the tsar. Again, the economic recession of the early 1900s appeared to discredit some of Witte's initiatives, jeopardizing the viability of specific industries that his policies had helped to foster; those industries became, in some cases, drains upon the state budget, or, if they were cartels, they artificially heightened prices. More systemic, however, was the rivalry which developed between Witte's Finance Ministry and the other ministries, which (unsurprisingly) resented the Finance Ministry's tight control over their budgets. "Long before Russia's first revolutionary crisis," Andrew Verner has observed, "the signs of government disunity were readily apparent to contemporaries and were blamed by many for its worsening problems." Verner has cited the "interminable bureaucratic infighting" of the era:

"individual bureaucrats seemed more concerned with protecting their own positions and scoring victories over their opponents," he wrote, "than with resolving Russia's problems."[89] We have already seen a similar state of affairs in Charles I's England and Louis XVI's France; now, such bureaucratic infighting (under Witte) looked forward to the utter chaos and disastrous "ministerial leap-frog" of 1916 to 1917 in wartime Russia.

Intragovernmental tensions were likely at their worst, however, between the Finance Ministry and the Interior Ministry, and this points to an even more basic problem for Witte and his modernizing acolytes. Dominic Lieven provides a prosopographical key to this problem, describing as he does the radically differing origins of the officialdom in these two dueling ministries:

> Very few officials in the Ministry of Finance were landowners and most came from what, in the West, would have been described as professional middle-class backgrounds. By contrast, the Ministry of Internal Affairs contained many aristocrats, a large number of whom were big landowners and, often, former Guards officers. Such men did not usually have great sympathy for industrial or financial capitalism and thought . . . in traditional terms of order, paternalism and the need for control over, so it was assumed, an unruly and almost childlike peasantry.

"Serious conflict" between finance and interior officials, according to this analysis, was "inevitable."[90] But if this was so, it was due at least in part to the fears aroused in "Privilege Russia"—both within *and* outside the Interior Ministry—by Finance Ministry reforms that might well imperil social hierarchy and, thus, social order in the Empire's vast rural hinterland. Even Sergei Witte's warmest scholarly admirer has agreed that what the finance minister had initially conceived as "a relatively simple and innocuous economic policy . . . had grown into an ever more unmanageable and complex revolutionary leviathan that respected neither authority nor privilege, neither class interest nor even human dignity."[91] Witte found that industrializing Russia meant recasting society: placing the embryonic business community ahead of the landed gentry (even as Russian entrepreneurs were compelled to compete with foreign capitalists), dissolving the peasants' communes and inculcating private initiative in the peasantry even while burdening it with heavier agricultural and monetary taxation, educating the masses, and so on.[92] Small wonder, then, that many in the gentry (*dvorianstvo*), dreading social upheaval before they could even begin to comprehend Russia's tightly linked security and economic/developmental needs, raged against Witte and those of his ilk for subverting the very foundations of their world. Small wonder that such attitudes also infected the angry reactionary élites surrounding Nicholas II—a monarch, as we have already seen, predisposed in any case to do anything required to preserve strong ties with "his" nobility. In retrospect, the tsar's decision to drop Witte from the Finance Ministry in August 1903 (on the eve, as it turned out, of the calamitous Russo-Japanese War) was all but a foregone conclusion.[93]

The tsar's disapproval of Witte's successor as modernizer-in-chief in Russia, Peter Stolypin, in all likelihood was *also* a foregone conclusion—although at least, in this case, Stolypin's assassination at Kiev in September 1911 relieved Nicholas of the need to dismiss him as he had cashiered Witte. Stolypin is best known for his campaign, in the wake of the 1905 revolution, to unleash an agricultural revolution in the vast countryside by transforming a minority of "strong" and "industrious" peasants into private, profiteering landholders. He also endeavored to manage relations between the state bureaucracy and the new parliament (*Duma*) that emerged out of the 1905 upheaval, and to institute local administrative reforms, most notably by including peasants and other country folk in the rural councils (*zemstvos*) and by broadening social access to civil tribunals throughout Russia.[94] Whether or not the interior minister was at all successful in implementing his signature agrarian reform has led to much learned controversy. Although Stolypin's defenders have insisted that, given St. Petersburg's resort to war in 1914, it is unfair to criticize him (and his immediate successor, V. I. Kokovtsov) for failing to consummate the ambitious reform campaign in the Russian countryside, others have been more equivocal in their appraisals. At best, Abraham Ascher has written, "an unqualified judgment on the effectiveness of Stolypin's agrarian reforms is difficult to make." True, Stolypin rightly stated that his reforms were designed to benefit peasants with average-sized holdings as well as affluent *muzhiki*; still, as Ascher has reasonably enough concluded, "the process of privatization and consolidation would have taken many years to reach even a majority of the peasants . . . [and] the obstacles impeding implementation were immense."[95]

There is also no doubt that this last great imperial modernizer was thwarted from the beginning by a disjunction between liberal goals and authoritarian methods of governance. Stolypin favored the creation of the Imperial Duma yet did little to enable political leaders and parties to gain experience in the arts of responsible government. He supported education at all levels yet inflamed the universities by persecuting student activists. He promoted the rule of law yet violated it when it suited his purposes to do so—most infamously in connection with the field courts martial used to chastise revolutionaries in 1906. He often spoke in the parlance of political compromise, yet, as Ascher has observed, he lacked the attributes of "a leader with flexibility, who could persuade associates and even opponents to accept policies they did not find congenial, and who knew how to compromise."[96]

All of this having been said, however, Stolypin's chief biographer has no doubt as to where the primary blame lay for the frustrations encountered by the iron-willed interior minister and chairman of the Council of Ministers: it lay squarely with a monarch as uncomfortable with modernizing values and policies as, in earlier situations, Charles I and Louis XVI had been:

> The most serious obstacle Stolypin had to overcome in his quest to modernize Russia ... was the tsar's resistance to change. Nicholas had never reconciled himself to the concession that had been wrested from him in ... 1905. Nicholas never accepted the Duma as a genuine partner in governing the country. He still looked upon himself as an autocrat and relied for support on the most reactionary groups in society, such as the United Nobility and the Union of the Russian People. Although not unintelligent, he was short-sighted and full of prejudices.[97]

He was also, apparently, full of resentment toward his modernizing interior minister—as, for example, we can see in his exhibiting next to no emotion when Stolypin was gunned down in Kiev on September 1, 1911.[98] In letters written to his mother in the days immediately following Stolypin's death, Nicholas expressed no regret whatsoever over losing so faithful a servant and failed utterly to acknowledge his services to Russia.[99] More revelatory yet was Empress Alexandra's reaction to the events at Kiev. "You seem to do too much honor to his memory," she remarked acidly to Stolypin's successor, V. I. Kokovtsov in early October, "and ascribe too much importance to his activities and to his personality . . . you must not try to follow blindly the work of your predecessor. . . . Find your support in the confidence of the Tsar—the Lord will help you."[100] Could we hope to cite any more stunning testimony to the gap yawning between modernizing and traditionalist viewpoints at the highest levels in prerevolutionary Russia?

Kokovtsov himself was soon to discover in his unenviable role as Stolypin's successor as prime minister how potent that dialectic remained at St. Petersburg. Because many dignitaries doubted that the new prime minister could lay claim to anything like Stolypin's masterful personality and larger vision, Kokovtsov "considered it advisable to publish a statement of his policies in the semi-official newspaper, *Russiia*, declaring that he planned no fundamental changes in the government's program."[101] Basically that meant continuing a policy of industrialization, agrarian reform, and financial restraint at home, and maintenance of peace abroad. In pursuit of the latter goal, the new prime minister executed a crucial stroke of policy—but at the cost, it would seem, of alienating the tsar. In the First Balkan War (1912), Serbia's insistence on confirming Balkan League victories over Turkey by claiming a port on the Albanian coast of the Adriatic Sea provoked a demand by Austria-Hungary (backed, belatedly, by Germany) that the Serbs withdraw from their advanced positions and that a *state* of Albania be created expressly to block Serbian access to the sea.[102] Plans put forth by the Russian War Ministry and General Staff to support Serbia on this issue with a *partial* military mobilization against Vienna were initially approved by Nicholas II but later reversed at a meeting of the tsar and his senior advisers on November 23, 1912—at the urging of Kokovtsov. He made "an impassioned appeal to the Tsar not to permit the fatal error the consequences of which were immeasurable, since we were not ready for war and our adversaries knew it well." Nicholas reluctantly went along with Kokovtsov, and—if diplomatic historian L. C. F. Turner is to be believed—it is fortunate that he did so: "Russian partial mobilization on the scale envisaged by [War Minister] Sukhomlinov would . . . probably have led to Austrian general mobilization. Under the terms of the Austro-German alliance, Germany would then have been required to order general mobilization."[103] This "last-minute intervention of Kokovtsov had averted a catastrophe," at least for the time being; but what might this intervention (along with other, purely *domestic* factors) signify for the prime minister's long-term standing at court?

What it signified became fully evident a year later, when the tsar's smoldering resentment over the (actually rather mild) constraints on his power established in the wake of the 1905 revolution (and his anger over the slights, real or imagined, to his reactionary cohorts in Privilege Russia) led him to plot a possible coup against both the State Duma *and* Kokovtsov's Council of Ministers. The envisioned coup actually began with intrigues directed against Kokovtsov (then engaged in critical financial negotiations abroad) by the reactionary Interior Minister N. A. Maklakov. Maklakov's machinations, however, failed in the face of opposition from several of Kokovtsov's loyal colleagues; furthermore, upon his return to Russia the prime minister courageously protested to Nicholas about Maklakov's recent scheming against him, and insisted that all ministers (in first instance, in this case, the interior minister) observe principles of collective consultation and decision-making in state affairs. Nicholas backed down at this point, but, alas, the ultimate *dénouement* for Kokovtsov was all too predictable: he was dismissed from both the Council Chairmanship and the Finance Ministry on January 30, 1914. Encouraged in this *démarche* by hardened traditionalists at court, the tsar went on to plan a significant retreat from the constitutional reforms extracted from him in 1905.[104] But European war soon broke out, and, as Andrew Verner has sadly recorded, the war "exposed the bankruptcy of Russian autocracy for all the world to see."[105]

The war brings us to our final example of confrontation between an intractably traditionalist tsar and a would-be modernizing minister. For the tottering Romanov regime, immersion in total war from August 1914 meant a life-or-death premium placed on military reform—reform associated most often today by leading specialists with the imposing if ultimately aborted career of tsarist General (and eleventh-hour War Minister) Aleksei A. Polivanov. In fact, Polivanov was winning plaudits from military men for his institutional reforms even *before* Imperial Russia's fateful plunge into war in the summer of 1914. Orlando Figes has reviewed some of Polivanov's prewar accomplishments (as assistant minister of war) and situated them in a broader domestic-political context:

> The grievances of the military professionals...forced them into politics. The emergence of the Duma after 1905 gave them an organ through which to express their opposition to the court's leadership of the military. Many of the more progressive among them, like A. A. Polivanov, the Assistant Minister of War, joined forces with liberal politicians in the Duma, such as Alexander Guchkov, who, whilst arguing for increased spending on the army and especially the navy, wanted this connected with military reforms, including the transfer of certain controls from the court to the Duma and the government. Slowly but surely, the Tsar was losing his authority over the most talented elements of the military élite.[106]

Nicholas struck back in his usual benighted fashion: he tried to reassert his influence in this critical area by appointing the obsequious and later-to-be-disgraced V. A. Sukhomlinov to the post of war minister late in 1908, excoriated the Duma and various reformers for their alleged "interference" in naval affairs in 1909, and then, in May 1912, unceremoniously fired Assistant Minister of War Polivanov.

Then came the war—and the disastrous defeats inflicted on Russian forces by Germany late in 1914 and through much of 1915. The incompetent Sukhomlinov was replaced by a resurgent Polivanov, who collaborated with General Alexei Brusilov on the Southwestern Front, and with other commanders, to revive Russian fortunes in the war and thus, at least conceivably, save the regime. On these related points, Polivanov was remarkably prescient, arguing that Nicholas II's government desperately needed the support of public opinion if it was to prevail against the Central Powers. In a penetrating and timely diagnosis of the situation, the war minister argued that "the very possibility of victory rests in the union of all forces in the country. . . . But how can one achieve this union . . . when the overwhelming majority is not in sympathy with . . . the course of internal policy, nor with the government called upon to conduct this policy?" Polivanov went on to warn the tsar's hardline cronies in Privilege Russia that the Imperial Army—in effect, their final trump card—might begin to disintegrate under the pressure of a war effort being conducted by a despised and increasingly isolated coterie of "leaders" at Petrograd:

> One should not forget that the army is now quite different from the one which marched forth at the beginning of the war. The regular troops are badly thinned out and have been absorbed into the mass of the armed people, . . . [they are] badly trained and not imbued with the spirit of military discipline . . . the officer corps, being filled up with speeded-up promotions and ensigns from the reserve, is not aloof from politics.[107]

In his insistence on analyzing his country's daunting military challenge in what were ultimately *political* terms, Polivanov (had he but known it) was anticipating an important element in subsequent scholarly commentaries on the antecedents to revolution in wartime Russia.

Unfortunately, however, in doing so the war minister (like so many other modernizers in the twilight years of Romanov Russia) incurred the wrath of Empress Alexandra—and thus of her husband. He did so in addition by seconding A. I. Guchkov's work on the Central War-Industries Committee, by collaborating with Duma politicians to finance urgently needed military upgrades, and (even worse, possibly) by criticizing Prime Minister Boris Stürmer for his corruption and Rasputin for his unwarranted meddling in army affairs. "Oh, how I wish you could get rid of Polivanov," Alexandra wrote furiously to Nicholas II in January 1916. "He is simply a revolutionist."[108] Two months later, she got her wish: A. A. Polivanov went the way of Witte, Kokovtsov, and so many other modernizers who had (in effect) tried to stand between the Romanov regime and its eventual self-destruction. Nicholas fired his war minister, reportedly with the gratuitous reflection that "after Polivanov's removal, I shall sleep in peace."[109] No one else slept peacefully, however, at least not among those aware of Russia's dire wartime situation. British military attaché Alfred Knox, who had earlier described Polivanov as "undoubtedly the ablest military organizer in Russia," called his dismissal "a disaster," and French diplomat Maurice Paléologue would later write of him: "He appeared to be one of the regime's last defenders, a man capable of defending it against both the follies of absolutism and the excesses of revolution."[110] An ironic postscript to this harrowing situation would come four years later when Leon Trotsky, now commanding Bolshevik Russia's Red Army, appointed Polivanov (along with General Brusilov and several other sterling former tsarist generals) to a Special Conference overseeing the Western Front during the 1920 Polish War![111] For A. A. Polivanov, this would be a vindication of sorts that manifestly came much too late to salvage the fortunes of Nicholas II, Alexandra Fedorovna, and Company.

Furthermore, the same dialectic between modernizing and traditionalist forces that bedeviled élitist/governing circles at the center of state power in prerevolutionary Russia dogged them as well at the local level. In this latter connection, we immediately note an analogy between the earlier provincial assemblies in Bourbon France and Romanov Russia's *zemstvos*. The *zemstvos*, representative bodies of affluent landowners at the provincial and district (*uezd*) levels, were established as part of the so-called Great Reforms of the 1860s in the wake of the disastrous Crimean War, and were the great hope of liberals in old regime Russia who spoke of the imperative need for a closer integration of government and the governed, and, *socially*, of those dwelling in Privilege Russia with those subjects (most notably peasants) who were *not* so privileged.[112] Unhappily, however, liberal (i.e., modernizing) hopes in this case, much as in the earlier French case, were destined to run aground on the treacherous reefs of privilege, solidarity between court and country *privilégiés*, and administrative governance "already half at war with itself" over its foundational values and practices.[113]

Tellingly, even the Romanov state's leading ministerial reformers, from Witte and Stolypin on, were themselves somewhat ambivalent on this last issue. "Reformers within the state bureaucracy," as Neil Weissman has put it, "sought to expand participation in local government through decentralization as a means both of improving the capabilities of the imperial administrative apparatus and of integrating newly mobilized groups into the polity. Yet they insisted that decentralization should not undermine the state bureaucracy's overall ability to supervise and ultimately to direct the evolution of tsarist society." It may have been supremely ironic, but under the leadership of such individuals, according to Weissman, "administrative reform became a tool for the continuation of essentially centralizing patterns of control into the era of mass politics." Modernizing ministers and bureaucrats "clearly stood for movement in Russian society," but they did so in ways "quite distinct from liberal or socialist progressives."[114] Aware as we are of the often authoritarian methods of governance employed by modernizing dynamos such as Sergei Witte and Peter Stolypin, we can hardly find this conclusion astonishing.

Yet at least we can still classify Witte and Stolypin among the modernizers in prerevolutionary Russia. But what about their Romanov masters? Responding to his father's assassination in 1881, Tsar Alexander III reverted to some of the most brutal, regressive policies of the benighted Russian past, and his ill-starred son Nicholas II (as we well know) would follow in his footsteps from 1894 on. The import of this for the *zemstvos* and town *dumas*, and hence for social relations in the Russian countryside—not to mention for the legitimacy of the Romanov regime as a whole—could not have been auspicious. As a result of traditionalist measures implemented under Alexander III, the *zemstvos* were subjected to a rigorous hierarchy of provincial governors and "land captains" whose veto power over their personnel, funds, and activities was approved and indeed supervised, ultimately, by the Interior Ministry. Nicholas II (we need hardly add) refused to reverse these retrogressive policies after his father's premature death in 1894. Orlando Figes, summing up the most recent research in this area, has placed this fateful refusal in the larger, unforgiving context of prerevolutionary Russian history:

> The counter-reforms of Alexander . . . set the tsarist regime and Russian society on the path of growing conflict. . . . The autocratic reaction against the zemstvos—like the gentry's reaction against democracy with which it became associated—had both the intention and the effect of excluding the mass of the people from the realm of politics. The liberal dream of the "Men of 1864" . . . was undermined as the court and its allies sought to reassert the old paternal

system, . . . in which the peasants, like children or savages, were deemed too primitive to play an active part.[115]

It goes without saying that much of this, representing the triumph in Russia of patriarchal, traditionalist values and policies over the hopes of well-born liberals and even some state modernizers both at the center of power and in the localities, recalls starkly what we have already encountered in connection with the provincial assemblies in prerevolutionary France.

But in elaborating further on the question of the *zemstvos*, we may perceive behind their many difficulties *even deeper social cleavages and class alienation* than existed in old regime France. Dorothy Atkinson has observed—justifiably—that middle-class as well as peasant interests were "inadequately represented" in the zemstvo, and that a growing industrial labor force of ex-peasants "had no voice at all in the institution."[116] Yet in the final analysis it was above all the attitude of the *peasants still working the land* that was crucial to the success of the *zemstvos* in Russia; and *even before* the passage of the reactionary decrees of Alexander III, Terence Emmons has suggested, these *muzhiki* may have been all but lost to the government's well-intentioned but élitist, socially blinkered reformers:

> It is particularly important to [note] the apparent identification of the zemstvo by the peasantry with a single gentry-bureaucratic "establishment." If, as the historians of the nobility and the bureaucracy tell us, the nobility . . . had been effectively bifurcated into a landless service nobility . . . and a provincial landed gentry, increasingly aware of itself as a separate interest . . . the peasants appear to have been quite oblivious to this distinction. And well they might have been, since the gentry-run zemstvo was . . . the government's main collector of direct taxes after the abolition of the poll tax in the 1880s, and . . . most of the main representatives of government authority in the district with whom the peasants had contact were also local noble landowners.

"The *barin* and the *chinovnik*," Emmons has written, "were often one and the same person, the pillar of the order that taxed [the peasants] and prevented them from taking possession of the gentry's lands, which they believed to be their right as a matter of elementary justice."[117]

For this reason, then, the actual measures promulgated by Alexander III's government, as well as those further emasculating the *zemstvos* in the wake of the 1905 revolution—measures that helped to doom Stolypin's program in rural Russia even before Stolypin himself was violently removed from the scene—may have already been *historically irrelevant* at the time they were passed.[118] One scholar has made a related point: that the "symbiotic bond between the autocracy and the nobility," by enduring to the very end, "imposed serious constraints on the development of local self-government in Russia."[119] Yet is this not just another indication that the chasm yawning between "Privilege Russia" and "peasant Russia" in the countryside was *from the start* even wider than that between lords and peasants in old regime France? If so, this cruel reality may have ensured an eventual revolutionary reckoning in Russia's rural spaces far more radical in its mass-mobilizing aspects and far more leveling in its *societal impact* than anything experienced earlier in revolutionary France.

A final point to make about the dialectic between modernizing and traditionalist forces in old regime Russia is that, much as in old regime England and old regime France, it was a *cultural* as well as a political/administrative phenomenon. If, in the case of England, elements of a *schizoid political culture* included dueling conspiracy theories of High Anglicans and Puritans, and if, in the case of France, such elements included competing ecclesiological and constitutional visions of pro-Papal Jesuits and anti-Papal Gallicans and Jansenists, in the case of Russia those elements took the (probably more secular) form of Westernizing and Slavophile perspectives in the Intelligentsia. Perhaps Nicholas II's *rational* interests should ideally have swayed him to align himself with the Westernizers (among whom, of course, were his greatest reforming ministers); unfortunately, however, the "symbiotic bond between autocracy and nobility" led him to align himself with Slavophile traditionalists at court and in the bureaucracy, army, and Russian Orthodox Church.[120] Hence—as postmodernists would correctly insist—the clash between state modernization and tradition was, for Nicholas II much as for Charles I and Louis XVI, all the more isolating in its impact for being fueled by *cultural* as well as by *institutional* influences.

We are, finally, challenged in the case of Russia, as we were in the earlier cases of England and France, to say something about the way modernizers continued to combat traditionalists throughout the revolutionary years. We know today that the unprecedented tribulations of a seemingly unending World War, superimposed on the preexisting strains of massive, state-sponsored modernization in all sectors of Russian society, unleashed tremendous forces across this vast country that in short order swept away monarchy, orthodoxy, and (by the end of 1918) most nobles and bourgeois of erstwhile Privilege Russia. In the countryside, the changes accompanying this turn of events were especially drastic, as the *dvorianstvo* was swallowed up in an all-devouring peasant upheaval. The "honeymoon" in the Russian Revolution, if it existed at all, was therefore cut much more brutally short than it had been in the English and French Revolutions.

There are, nevertheless, several points along the way where we can discern in retrospect the dialectic between modernizing and traditionalist forces—before, that is, the forces of "reaction" were put ignominiously to flight. Three examples of this dialectic will suffice for our purposes. First, in the realm of European geopolitics, two of Russia's foreign ministers during 1917—Paul Miliukov and M. I. Tereshchenko—attempted to uphold what could only be seen in these circumstances as a traditionalist neo-tsarist policy of secret treaties and overt territorial annexations against their modernizing "liberal" and socialist critics both within and outside the successive "coalition governments" of Russia's abortive revolutionary honeymoon. The Bolsheviks' overthrow of Alexander Kerensky's Third Coalition ministry in October would emphatically terminate *that* policy, as Lenin and his comrades moved quickly to take Russia out of World War I altogether.[121]

Second, in the domain of *domestic* politics, deepening sociopolitical polarization at Petrograd culminated in a supposed rightist coup mounted in August 1917 by troops loyal to General Lavr Kornilov, recently named commander-in-chief by Kerensky. Whether Kornilov's involvement in this affair was in fact from the start unequivocally *counterrevolutionary* in nature or stemmed from a "misunderstanding" between him and the prime minister has occasioned much scholarly debate over the years.[122] What seems fairly clear, however, is that the "Kornilov Affair," whether full-fledged "coup" or not, tended to range those desperately trying to retain some vestiges of the old regime in Russia—for instance, urban industrialists, technical specialists, factory managers, engineers, and fearful, besieged rural gentry—against ever-more-radicalized military and proletarian elements.[123] In any case, the coup (if that is indeed what it was) failed, both because of the unreliability of Kornilov's forces and because of the concerted efforts of Bolshevik partisans, moderate socialists, garrison troops, Kronstadt sailors, Red Guards, and others to defend the capital. The defeat of the Kornilov movement was surely one of the major turning points in the process of radicalization leading ultimately to the October 1917 Bolshevik seizure of state power in revolutionary Russia.

The third example of the confrontation between modernizing and traditionalist forces in the Russian case takes us beyond 1917 and into the incomparably messy civil war of the next several years. No doubt Lenin, once ensconced in power, and determined to shift Soviet foreign policy from its initial obsession with German occupation to a primary concern with Allied interventionism in Russian affairs, found it highly convenient to allege links between outside "imperialist" forces and reactionary domestic "enemies" of the revolutionary cause who were holdovers from benighted tsarist (*and* liberal-socialist) times. Yet such allegations were not altogether untrue. As David Foglesong, for instance, has written, liberal propaganda aimed at securing Western intervention against Russia's new Communist masters "was offset . . . by reports about monarchist coups, terror and pograms in White [that is, traditionalist] territories that stoked Western peoples' fears of contributing to a restoration of tsarist oppression."[124] In a like fashion, Evan Mawdsley has identified as one of "two key developments in the late autumn of 1918" the "domination of the anti-Bolshevik movement gained by the Whites," a development that at the time was potentially dangerous to the new

Soviet regime at Moscow and powerfully personified by rightist military figures like A. I. Deniken, N. N. Iudenich, and A. V. Kolchak. Although the "White" forces were never really able to coordinate actions effectively against the new regime, and often alienated the very Russian and non-Russian ethnic groups over which they briefly held sway, there is little doubt that their activities were endorsed by Orthodox priests, "capitalists," and dispossessed landowners who had deplored the Russian Revolution from the very start.[125] In comparative terms, these latter individuals had every bit as much reason to detest the Leninist revolutionaries installed in power by late 1917 as Stuart loyalists had to execrate Cromwell and his partisans in the 1650s or as Bourbon loyalists had to loathe French Jacobins and/or Directorians in the 1790s.

In concluding chapter 1, let us heartily applaud Steve Pincus for highlighting the issue of state modernization in his impressively researched study of the Glorious Revolution. After all, for us, any effort to achieve a neostructuralist synthesis of structuralism and moderate postmodernism actually *requires* that we take state modernization as seriously as Pincus does. Thus, we find that his definition of state modernization as including an attempt "to centralize and bureaucratize political authority," to "shape the contours of society using the tools of the state," and to utilize techniques "allowing the state to gather information about and potentially suppress social and political activities . . . within the polity" gives us (as theorists *but also* as "concerned citizens") pause for very serious reflection. Orlando Figes voiced a similar concern about the problematic aspects of state modernization in his vivid account of the Russian Revolution: "The state, however big," he intoned, "cannot make people equal or better human beings. All that it can do is to treat its citizens equally, and strive to ensure that their free activities are directed towards the general good." After a century scarred by the "totalitarianisms of Communism and Fascism," he went on, "one can only hope that this lesson has been learned."[126] We find it easy enough—indeed, essential—to endorse such a thoughtful commentary.

Yet, as Orlando Figes and so many other scholars writing as postmodernists would *also* insist, revolutions cannot be summed up as simply "competing groups of modernizers." We always find that they also *do* pit "defenders of traditional society" against "advocates of modernity." Revolutions, that is, are emphatically about *ideas* and *visions of society* as well as about state-building. It is in *this* sense that chapter 2 ("Rethinking Revolutions") in *1688: The First Modern Revolution* is inadequate: it is so obsessed with the modernization issue that it lacks *any* detailed treatment of postmodernism's stance upon *the ideological and cultural origins of revolution*.[127] Without this discussion, we could not fully explain *why*, for example, Charles I's regime was "already half at war with itself" by the 1630s; *why* both Louis XVI and Nicholas II punished one modernizing minister after another for trying to save them from self-destruction; or *why* the forces of revolution, once unleashed in these countries, acquired such a lethal intensity. In all of this, we can discover why a *neostructuralist* approach to revolution is so crucial. Neostructuralists not only ask how the need for state modernization helps to make great revolutions possible; with a bow to postmodernism, they can *also* reassess the confrontations between those in revolutionary crises who idealistically (if quixotically) defend the past and those who are determined (if pushed to it) to sacrifice that past on the bloodstained but unassailable altars of state necessity.

Chapter Two

In Search of the Elusive *Ancien Régime* Bourgeoisie

"Most sociologists and other social scientists writing *theoretically* on revolution over the past several decades," this book observed at the start, "have gravitated to state-centered rather than to capitalism-centered structuralism."[1] One of the best ways to track this major shift of emphasis within neostructuralism from *capitalism-centered* to *state-centered* analysis is to reconsider the issue of the *bourgeoisie* in old regime England, France, and Russia. It is admittedly true that, in the case of France, historian Peter McPhee used a bicentennial forum in the *American Historical Review* thirty years ago to remind his readers of Marxist contributions to our comprehension of socioeconomic class dynamics and the progress of capitalism in eighteenth- and nineteenth-century France, and he has returned to this theme recently in an anthology of articles on the 1789 to 1799 period.[2] Yet even though Marx and Engels themselves famously avowed (in the 1848 *Communist Manifesto*) that "the bourgeoisie, historically, has played a most revolutionary part" in the preparation of major sociopolitical upheavals, they were also inclined to situate "bourgeois" upheavals "in the longer-term context of a transition from feudalism to capitalism in Western Europe which spanned many centuries." By doing so, they may well have been speculating that the social origins of revolution in Europe were *not* exclusively bourgeois in nature.[3] If this was indeed their thinking, they anticipated in this many a modern revolutionary scholar.

If, *as neostructuralists*, we want to gain a specific sense of the basic shift we have noted from capitalism-centered to state-centered analysis, we can do no better than to focus on the issue of the bourgeoisie and, in doing so, pose a series of deceptively simple yet in reality *complicated* questions. What, precisely, was the bourgeoisie in the old regimes of England, France, and Russia? If it actually existed, did it have to share the limelight with other classes? And if so, did it, on a case-by-case basis, play a central, merely supportive, or largely negligible role in state collapse and in the onset of full-scale upheaval? Starting with France (whose radical transformation did so much to inspire Marx and Engels in the first place), then returning to that earlier, capitalist (?) revolution in England, and finally homing in on Russia's historic experiment with massive, state-directed socialist change, we will see how successful we can be in sizing up the much-discussed bourgeoisies of three European countries on the eve (and in the early stages) of revolution. Taking up this task will also show how research on social change in these three countries, even as it has acknowledged the legacy of capitalism-centered structuralism, has at the same time pointed up the growing importance of *state-centered* structuralist inquiry—and of the related insights of moderate postmodernist analysis.

A "REVOLUTIONARY BOURGEOISIE" IN OLD REGIME FRANCE: MYTH OR REALITY?

In the case of eighteenth-century France, the notion of a capitalist bourgeoisie as a *central protagonist* in the unleashing of revolution, once virtually unquestionable in the Marxian explanatory paradigm, has in recent decades been vigorously challenged by "social revisionists" from a variety of angles. Accordingly, this notion would seem today to offer less and less of a satisfactory interpretation of revolutionary *social* origins.

Certainly, there were bourgeois of various stripes in the splendid realm of Louis XV and Louis XVI; furthermore, their numbers were undoubtedly increasing as the years wore on. In his *Origins of the French Revolution*, William Doyle, citing what may be "the most credible recent estimate, commanding confidence through the caution with which it is advanced," hypothesized that the French bourgeoisie increased from 700,000 or 800,000 souls in 1700 to about 2.3 million in 1789. "This means that, over a century in which the number of nobles had remained fairly static, and the population as a whole had only risen by about a quarter, the bourgeoisie had almost trebled in size." Moreover, there were likely *economic* concomitants to this purely demographic trend: whether or not bourgeois appropriation of national wealth increased proportionately in the sectors of landholding, industry, banking, and finance during the eighteenth century, we know that bourgeois subjects predominated in the dynamic (if still secondary) sector of maritime trade, and we can also suggest that they owned most of the capital sunk in the ever-critical annuities (*rentes*) of the bellicose and debt-ridden government.[4]

From sinking bourgeois capital in government *rentes* to investing in the notorious venal offices of the *ancien régime* was, of course, something less than a giant's step, and the now well-documented fact that most if not all such posts and sinecures were *appreciating* rather than declining in value during this period probably reflected swelling *bourgeois* competition for them as well as rising levels of statist fiscal exigency. As Doyle and a host of other analysts have observed, such a rivalry over venal offices in turn testified to a "bourgeoisie expanding in numbers, wealth, education, and ambitions."[5] By the same token, however, many historians have for some time now fastened on the issue of venal administrators and sinecurists in prerevolutionary France to sketch out a social portrait that far transcends specifically "bourgeois" individuals: they have, in other words, viewed bourgeois subjects as making up only one element in a multifarious élite of *notables* that was starting to emerge from the chrysalis of the "society of orders" in communities all over the kingdom.

This intriguing turn in old regime scholarship, with all of its implications for narrowly conceived scenarios positing a bourgeoisie as the chief *social* protagonist in the transition to revolution in France, can be traced back at least to the year 1961. At that time, research for Paris, published by Adeline Daumard and François Furet, and for Orléans, emanating posthumously from that neo-Marxian stalwart Georges Lefebvre, began to hint at a novel formation of "notables" in the ascendancy in the *ancien régime*. In the former case, Daumard's and Furet's careful analysis of notarized marriage registers of 1749 disclosed the ties linking the capital's administrators and sinecurists with lawyers, with mercantile and fiscal agents of the crown—and, perhaps most significantly, with full-fledged noblemen.[6] In the latter case, Lefebvre's research at Orléans yielded this memorable portrayal of an urban oligarchy that was surely *not* to be straitjacketed within any antediluvian schema of three "estates" in France:

> It did not form a compact bloc, but its diverse members shared a certain way of life; they all had the same respect for birth and wealth, the same horror of bad marriages, the same arrogance towards men of little property, and the same contempt for the populace. . . . They all met at the Academy of Sciences and Letters, in the Agricultural Society, in the Masonic Lodges, in the Philanthropic Society, and in the literary societies which were, in effect, their clubs. Lastly, they monopolized the urban administration. . . . These then were the "notables" who were to become the ruling class of France from the Consulate on.[7]

How poorly this sorts, we must note, with Lefebvre's very readable but also markedly less sophisticated account of sequential "class revolutions" in *The Coming of the French Revolution*, written back in the ideologically polarized European world of the late 1930s!

Such analyses, moreover, focusing upon urban *notables* in leadership roles in the French *ancien régime* rather than upon long-premised tensions between so-called feudal aristocrats and capitalist bourgeois, have multiplied over the past three or four decades. Hence, Olwen Hufton, when surveying the "respectable" ranks of society at picturesque Bayeux in Normandy, found a *monde* of "urban nobles of comfortable rather than great means" constituting a group that "partly monopolized the government of the town and the surrounding district, helped the canons run the *bureau de charité*, and directed civic functions." Such urban notables, in Hufton's own summation, "were carrying out useful public functions in the company of the professional sections of the *bourgeoisie* from whom some of them had originally been recruited."[8] Meanwhile, at Troyes and at Reims, lying to the east of Paris, Lynn Hunt has found, "wholesale merchants, lawyers, and doctors" had, by the mid-eighteenth century, "been integrated into the ruling circle of royal officials and noblemen. . . . Ruling linked noble and bourgeois, landowner and merchant. . . . Political interests overshadowed underlying economic and status distinctions."[9] Robert Darnton, for his part, has unearthed strikingly similar realities prevailing at Montpellier in southeastern France in 1768. "A new urban elite," Darnton has concluded, "was forming in opposition to the common people" at Montpellier. This novel élite, battening on government finance as well as on state-promoted commerce, featured the usual mix of *honnêtes gens* making up a world of cultured, affluent nobles and bourgeois, and (likely) could boast the usual number of *officiers* discharging essential public functions.[10] A similar situation has been depicted by Daniel Roche at Dijon, Châlons-sur-Marne, Bordeaux, and a host of other communities boasting provincial academies in the eighteenth century. His painstaking analysis of the recruitment to these cultural institutions has pointed up the privileged role played in the cities and towns hosting them by "an economically and politically influential noblesse" working hand-in-glove, it would seem, with a "bourgeoisie of office, of administration, and of the liberal professions." If we are to believe Roche, we have here, once again, a society of élites prefiguring in many ways the proprietary, multifaceted élite of late-revolutionary and nineteenth-century France.[11]

All of this having been duly recorded, however, we should note that the social revisionists of the 1960s, 1970s, and 1980s did *not* altogether abandon the scholarly distinctions once drawn so regularly between bourgeois subjects and members of the first two estates in prerevolutionary France. It is, after all, one thing to discern signs of the gestation of a modern élite under Louis XV and Louis XVI conjoining the administrative labors, cultural activities, and lifestyles of noble and bourgeois luminaries. It is quite another thing to predict confidently that the much broader "upper crust" of gentility in the old regime—including within its ranks literally thousands of not-so-enlightened rural squires as well as sophisticated urban *notables*—could survive as an identifiable class (however we define this term) under the impact of an unprecedented revolutionary crisis in national governance. Georges

Lefebvre most likely had this conundrum in mind when, in describing his *Orléanais*, he commented that noble *privilège* continued to be a "powerful internal barrier" within society's upper ranks, "dividing men whom so many other bonds united."[12] However much such caution might be attributed by some to Lefebvre's residual Marxism, Daniel Roche sounded equally reserved when characterizing his provincial academicians: "nobles and bourgeois," he wrote, "however unified by the language of Enlightenment," could not ignore and never fundamentally questioned the "barrier of privilege" within their academic societies.[13] Then, yet again, there was the testimony of French historian Marcel Reinhard on the same general point: "The problem of the relations between elite and nobility [as of 1789] was still unresolved," he noted. "The resolution of this capital question was left to those who wanted to regenerate the kingdom."[14]

And, in fact, what we have chosen in this book to call a Marxist-derived "capitalism-centered structuralism" has persisted in work done subsequently on the bourgeoisie in prerevolutionary France. We recall, for instance, how Peter McPhee seized the opportunity, in a 1989 bicentennial forum in the *American Historical Review*, to reject the long-rumored demise of the kind of historical class analysis associated in earlier days with titans such as Georges Lefebvre and Albert Soboul, and poured (some carefully qualified) scorn on latter-day methods of interpreting the French past, such as "revisionism" and "modernization theory."[15] To be sure, McPhee's primary objective in this rather polemical article was to question the assumptions of Alfred Cobban and other early revisionists regarding the allegedly retardative impact of the Revolution on peasant agricultural productivity in nineteenth-century France; still, his approach to questions of revolutionary process and consequences seemed also to herald *more generally* a newly skeptical attitude toward revisionist portrayals of a *société des notables* in the waning years of the *ancien régime*.

Then, just two years after Peter McPhee signaled these historiographical concerns, Colin Jones declared himself "foolhardy enough to suggest that the Revolution did have long-term social origins"—origins that, he went on to insist, "related directly to the development of capitalism" in prerevolutionary France.[16] Hence, for Jones, the need to interrogate revisionism in terms as aggressive as those used by Peter McPhee. "Given the development of commercial capitalism in eighteenth-century France, the spread of a consumer society, the development of professionalization within the service sector of the economy which this helped to spawn, and the appearance of associated forms of civic sociability," wrote Jones, it no longer seemed "realistic to disparage the vitality nor indeed the ideological autonomy of the Old Regime bourgeoisie." After citing an array of sources to document in detail these economic, social, and civic developments in the old regime, Jones felt entitled to posit "a relative 'bourgeoisification' of Old Regime society"—and, thus, to challenge the revisionist idea of a newfangled *société des notables* replacing in France the outdated society of orders. Although not altogether rejecting Alfred Cobban's celebrated conception of a "revolutionary bourgeoisie" consisting of "a mixture of landowners, venal officers, and professional men," Jones undeniably shifted *his* conceptual focus to the role, in bourgeois class formation, of budding consumerism, capitalism, and derivative *civisme*:

> Who, then, were the "revolutionary bourgeoisie"? . . . I have argued here . . . that the professions and indeed a great many venal office-holders . . . were in fact responding to and very much part of the development of capitalism in the Old Regime. These groups were more genuinely bourgeois than ever before, and exuded a new civic professionalism which had its roots in a developing "market-consciousness" and which clashed with the corporative values espoused by many of their fellows. They shared the vision and the reflexes of the commercial bourgeoisie of the Old Regime in a far more direct way than has hitherto been recognized.[17]

The professionalism or "sociability" associated with these developments, Jones wrote, took on a more "material form" among an "increasingly homogeneous bourgeoisie" and its allies "among the liberal aristocracy, even as it contributed to the downfall of the Old Regime by eroding the deferentialism and hierarchical structures of the Society of Orders."[18] Jones, it would appear, was trying to perform a delicate balancing act, accepting on the one hand the revisionist view of evolutionary change in the social-élitist ranks of prerevolutionary French society, yet simultaneously insisting on the crystallization, within that society, of bourgeois "vitality" and "ideological autonomy."

Shortly thereafter, Peter McPhee executed a similar balancing act in a new survey of social and economic developments in modern France. On the one hand, he drew the reader's attention to "the textile factories of Lyon, Abbéville, Elbeuf and Rouen," the "iron foundries and coal mines (such as at Le Creusot in Burgundy, Niederbronn in Alsace and Anzin in Flanders)," and the "economic boom" in the principal Atlantic ports "where a triangular trade linked France with its Caribbean colonies and Africa through commerce in slaves, wines and spirits, sugar, coffee, cotton and indigo"; and he saw all of this as indicative of a "distinctively capitalist bourgeoisie . . . expanding the scale of its enterprises" in the old regime. On the other hand, McPhee conceded (almost as Alfred Cobban might have) that bourgeois in France were as likely to draw their wealth from a combination of legal practice, bureaucratic and other professional pursuits, and investment in secure if low-return annuities, lands, and seigneurial services and dues as from more dynamic yet riskier capitalist ventures in industry and/or commerce.[19]

What is most arresting here, however, is the strategy adopted by McPhee for dealing with the revisionist challenge to Marxian views on the *sociopoli-*

tical transition from old regime to revolution in France. Yes, he acknowledged, revisionist historians had "contested whether there were deep-seated . . . causes of the political friction . . . in 1788, and whether there were class lines of social antagonism." Yes, once again, such specialists had "pointed to the co-existence of nobles and wealthy bourgeois in an élite of notables." But here, McPhee insisted, was the *really critical* point:

> within this bourgeois and noble élite was a ruling class of nobles with inherited titles who dominated the highest echelons of privilege, office, wealth, and status. Social changes since 1750 had aggravated tensions between this élite and the less eminent majority of the privileged orders. . . . The specific provisions for the . . . Estates General were to focus these conflicting images of a regenerated France with remarkable clarity.

In this (rather orthodox) schema, the "challenge to an aristocratic conception of property, hierarchy and social order emanating from a wealthier, larger and socially-frustrated bourgeoisie" was, for McPhee, crucial in explaining "the entrenched hostility of most nobles towards fiscal and social reforms" on the eve of revolution in France, and this challenge would only take on a new edge throughout 1789.[20]

Thus, Peter McPhee—striving, much like Colin Jones before him, to salvage some elements of the old Marxist thesis on the revolutionary bourgeoisie in the case of old regime France. By the time historian Gwynne Lewis decided, in the late 1990s, to reissue Alfred Cobban's 1964 revisionist classic *The Social Interpretation of the French Revolution*, an even *more delicate* balancing act seems to have been in order. In his thoughtful introduction to this second edition of the work, Lewis separated out his issues very carefully in reassessing Cobban's revisionism on the bourgeoisie in prerevolutionary France. Yes, Lewis allowed, wealthy merchants in this class typically settled into low-risk, nonentrepreneurial vocations once they had made their fortunes in the more dynamic world of commerce. When it came to industrialists, however, Lewis argued that Cobban had "too readily dismissed their influence":

> Certainly, eighteenth-century France was not a country of factories, steel mills and coal mines (though she was not devoid of them). However, a number of recent works have indicated that, despite the prevalence of rural, proto-industrial . . . production, there were groups of influential *négociants* (wholesale merchants) and industrialists who were *beginning* to transform France from a country dominated by commercial capital to one in which modern financial and industrial forms of production and exchange could operate successfully.[21]

Overall, Lewis concluded, "the rapidly expanding bourgeoisie involved in trade and industry, although still in a minority when compared with the landed and professional bourgeoisie, *were* increasingly important" and *would* be (Alfred Cobban to the contrary notwithstanding) represented in the ruling assemblies and committees of the revolutionary era-to-come.[22]

But whatever subtlety on this subject was displayed in the 1990s by scholars like Peter McPhee, Colin Jones, and Gwynne Lewis was abandoned in 2006 by Henry Heller. In *The Bourgeois Revolution in France, 1789-1815*, Heller affirmed boldly that "class conflict was the central feature of the Revolution" and (in words recalling Albert Soboul and Claude Mazauric in earlier decades) depicted this upheaval as "led by the bourgeoisie, which was prepared to use popular violence to attack and dismantle the feudal system."[23] However, in developing this argument, Heller tied himself up in self-contradiction. After declaring (in good orthodox fashion) that "capitalism destabilized the *ancien régime* and provided the middle class with the economic strength and cultural confidence to overthrow the traditional nobility," and after topping this off with the observation that "it was the bourgeoisie that subsequently assumed the seats of power [in France] as a result of a revolutionary political crisis," Heller stepped upon his own message by describing social change in the old regime in *revisionist* fashion. Even though "prior to the Revolution, some among the bourgeoisie . . . had . . . rejected the continued existence of the nobility out of hand," Heller wrote, he went on (contrariwise) to concede that:

> as late as the outbreak of the political crisis of 1788-89 some of the most influential members of the bourgeoisie cannot be said to have had an unequivocally negative view of . . . the nobility. Some of the bourgeoisie were prepared to accept ennoblement for themselves as well as for others based on achievement. One could even suggest that prior to the Revolution, there was a limited integration of the more culturally and economically progressive elements of the nobility with the upper reaches of the bourgeoisie.[24]

Alfred Cobban himself could not have put this more eloquently! Even though Heller hastened to add here that "there were clear limits to such a process," and returned immediately thereafter to the old formulation of a "rapid polarization of opinion" in 1789 and beyond "in which the bourgeoisie became fully conscious of its political interests," he had already betrayed (we suspect) his own indebtedness to revisionist ways of construing social change in late eighteenth-century France.

It was above all the articulation between the *bourgeoisie* as such and "capitalism" as such that seems to have bedeviled Heller. Here he was, characterizing the bourgeois professionals of revisionist social analysis in a very Marxian (i.e., very *capitalist*) manner:

> Many of the so-called professionals were close to those who were . . . involved in business and were . . . dependent on them. Notaries arranged contracts for

merchants. Lawyers represented manufacturers in court proceedings and were silent partners in business. Physicians looked after the families of affluent urban citizens. As for those bourgeois who lived in part or wholly off rent, much of this rent was capitalist rather than feudal . . . such rents were collected from agricultural producers who . . . were themselves producing grain for sale in the market while using wage labor to do so.[25]

And so on. Yet in the same breath Heller could also present eighteenth-century French capitalism in its *productive* aspects as distinctly less modernized than the capitalism on display across the Channel:

> The fundamental difference between the French and British economy was in technology and in the organization of industry. French economic expansion, in general, occurred on the basis of a traditional technology and mode of organization. British growth in manufacturing was more capital-intensive, based on transformative inventions that entailed the factory and the machine as the basis of industry. . . . These innovations were adopted in France but only latterly and not on the same scale.

Ironically, however, in stressing technological and organizational *blockages* "underlying the business and commercial culture of the *ancien régime*" in France, Heller *failed to mention* some recent research that, calling into question the idea of French economic inferiority to England, might have helped—at least to a certain extent—to buttress his arguments about a vibrant, destabilizing capitalism in France.[26]

But, to take up again the main thread of this discussion, there are major studies that contradict the efforts of Heller—and like-minded historians—to cling to simplistic capitalism-centered structuralist readings of the bourgeoisie in *ancien régime* France. We show in the following how a number of scholars have developed more sophisticated approaches to this subject, approaches that *complicate* our view of the French bourgeoisie and, in doing so, open a real interpretative space for the insights of postmodernism and *state-centered* structuralism.

Here, we might well begin with the arguments of sociologist Jack Goldstone's *Revolution and Rebellion in the Early Modern World* (1991). By *any* reading, said Goldstone, the old regime bourgeoisie was as internally divided along economic lines as the French nobility. "The great wholesale merchants of the seaports and the great manufacturers of Paris and Lyon," he wrote, "had fortunes from hundreds of thousands to millions of livres; they had little in common with the doctors, lawyers, small retailers, and minor officials of the provincial towns." And this had implications for upward mobility through the acquisition of offices. "Outbid for advancement by the wealthy bourgeoisie of trade and finance, and with town administrations increasingly in the hands of royal appointees," Goldstone continued, "the *avocats*, notaries, and minor officials of the towns were enraged at the closure of opportunities and the depreciation of their educations and career investments." As this specialist suggested—and as other research has also indicated—pockets of radicalism within this order on the eve of the 1789 revolution may well have originated more from conflicts *within* the bourgeoisie than from doors being slammed in bourgeois faces by an increasingly exclusive *noblesse*.[27]

David Garrioch has similarly complicated our vision of France's prerevolutionary bourgeoisie. His account of the formation of the Paris bourgeoisie began, paradoxically, with a negative assertion: "There was," he announced, "no Parisian bourgeoisie in the eighteenth century. There were merchants and lawyers, teachers, manufacturers, rentiers, *bourgeois de Paris*. But they did not form a united or a citywide class, did not possess the cross-city ties and identity that would make them truly Parisian. The political and social institutions of the city served to fragment rather than to unite the middle classes."[28] Instead, Garrioch saw only the revolution itself as creating a revolutionary bourgeoisie out of political, administrative, social, and cultural tendencies that were, to be sure, nascent but not yet fully developed or fused together in the twilight of the old regime. Undeniably, Garrioch wrote, sociocultural factors loomed large in this process of class formation:

> The ideology of domesticity, with its clearly prescribed gender roles, served to distinguish the middle classes both from the nobility and from the common people. So, too, growing out of the improving material conditions of middle-class life, did a belief that property, virtue, and talent, rather than birth, should be the basis for privilege and advancement. Humanitarianism and a nascent utilitarianism—as well as a confidence in freedom of trade, curiously allied with reliance on state encouragement and assistance—also spread among the Paris middle classes in the final decades of the old regime.[29]

The references here to *ideological* and *cultural* elements in this process of class formation in the Parisian society of the eighteenth century surely mirrored something of what *we* would identify as a moderate postmodernist slant upon old regime social dynamics.

But what was especially noticeable here was Garrioch's ultimate reliance upon the *statist* issue of *political behavior* (with *administrative office* hovering in the background) as decisive in defining the bourgeoisie. "I have taken political behavior as the defining characteristic of the middle classes," said Garrioch with engaging candor. "Political office," he went on to say, "was central to the identity of the middle classes of eighteenth- and nineteenth-century France. For middle-class families, more than for any others, local office was a central facet of social identity and of social power."[30] Hence, for Garrioch, "political behavior," more than any *socioeconomic* attributes, was critical here. But in thus stressing the degree to which officeholding "bestowed not only rank, but also rights, privileges, and power" upon the *bour-*

geoisie in France, Garrioch could not help but broach as well the ever-contentious issue of how the *state* was to be brought back in (if at all) in this analysis. He treated the issue gingerly, saying that while "the state was a key agent in all these changes . . . it was not, of course, a force of nature unconnected with other changes in French society." The state responded, that is, to population growth, to changes in military technology, and to economic development, even as it helped define the "middle class" in France by conferring upon it increasing numbers of local administrative roles.[31]

But if David Garrioch held that there was no *Parisian* bourgeoisie as such in eighteenth-century France, Sarah Maza was willing to venture one step further in a book whose central thesis as stated at the start was, provocatively, that a French bourgeoisie *as such* did not even exist in this period! True, at a later point in her work, Maza apparently relented a bit, concluding that "the bourgeoisie," after all, *did* (in some sense) "certainly exist in Old Regime France."[32] How are we to reconcile these two seemingly irreconcilable assertions? Maza, in this always readable and stimulating essay, was trying to make two cardinal points: (1) Utilizing what she called a method of "cultural constructionism," she suggested that the French bourgeoisie failed the crucial test of "self-awareness" as defined *in language*. "Classes," she maintained, "only exist if they are aware of their own existence, a knowledge which is inseparable from the ability to articulate an identity." The "existence of social groups," she continued on, may be "rooted in the material world," yet it is ultimately "shaped by language and more specifically by narrative."[33] Insofar as (at least according to Maza) the term "bourgeois" in the old regime usually referenced what one *was not* in "group-social" terms rather than what one actually *was*, no *bourgeoisie* as such existed in the France of this era. (2) At the same time, Maza held, a *bourgeoisie* of sorts, when defined as a kind of "shadow nobility," as a "legally distinct, privileged, non-noble upper class" suspended (in Parisian and provincial/urban society) uncomfortably between the *noblesse* and "poorer commoners," undoubtedly *did* have a certain legitimate class existence. Granted, however, that the conception of a *bourgeoisie* as painted in these latter colors was so "problematic," in fact, was "too dangerously democratic for the Old Regime" and yet "too heinously exclusive, indeed aristocratic, for the Revolution," it was destined, alas, for a swift and unceremonious demise after 1789.[34]

Henry Heller's subsequent Marxian grumbling about Sarah Maza's methodology of "cultural constructionism"—we would call it postmodernist "deconstruction"—was, of course, predictable. Yet we, too, cannot help but find it somewhat inconsistent for Maza to see "the existence of social groups" as being, simultaneously, "rooted in the material world" *and* ultimately "shaped by language."[35] Again, the historic term *bourgeois de Paris*, of which Maza made considerable use, may have had a larger *civic* and *political* connotation (as Garrioch and other historians of the Parisian bourgeoisie have intimated) than Maza allowed for. In any case, the larger significance of the work of scholars like Jack Goldstone, David Garrioch, and Sarah Maza is surely that it points us *away from* capitalism-centered structuralism and toward more sophisticated (moderate postmodernist and state-centered structuralist) analyses of the bourgeoisie in *ancien régime* France.

And this is apparently where we are *today* in our search for the elusive French bourgeoisie. In his 2013 anthology of articles on the 1789 revolution, Peter McPhee cited with implicit favor the hoary paradigmatic argument of some historians "that the French Revolution was in large part the work of a bourgeoisie determined to overthrow privilege and [to] be accorded political and social recognition in accord with their economic importance."[36] Yet the two specialists starting off this anthology, namely Peter Campbell and Jean-Pierre Jessenne, hardly appeared to exemplify such an analytic perspective. Campbell, in fact, invoked the classic revisionists—Alfred Cobban and George V. Taylor—when contending as follows: "Overall the 'revolutionary bourgeoisie' has come to look not so much a class as a group of ambitious local notables without a particular class identity but with a fair amount of local or regional administrative and judicial experience." Their ambitions, continued Peter Campbell, "tended toward the noble life-style, and if they were frustrated by the *ancien régime* it was . . . more because their social mobility was jeopardized by greater competition for access to the noble order. Such men were hardly candidates for the label 'capitalists' in Marx's sense."[37] For his part, Jessenne, after presenting "the intermediate class of the middling bourgeoisie" as consisting (in the *ancien régime*) of "merchants, legal men, liberal professions, qualified employees, officials with independent means, and shopkeepers with a house of their own," and as making up "the pivotal class in urban society," asserted rather starkly that, to his way of thinking, "it is a matter of nothing less than starting the debate on the bourgeois revolution from scratch."[38] "Yes," he concluded in this same qualified and *inconclusive* vein, "the Revolution was certainly a social and political crisis, but it can by no means be reduced to being due to a single cause: bourgeoisie or people, peasants or overlords, the acute grain shortage of spring 1789 or the century's long boom. What matters in this revolutionary context . . . is the conjunction of all these contradictions at a particular moment, so as to make ordinary political solutions ineffective and to delegitimize the authorities in power."[39]

Significantly, both Campbell and Jessenne, in voicing their doubts about the traditional scenario identifying a capitalist bourgeoisie as the crucial *social protagonist* in the transition from old regime to revolution in France, seemed motivated to reinvest *politics* in one form or another with a central role in this overall process. Particularly striking in this connection were Peter Campbell's observations about "state failure" in late eighteenth-century France:

Various elements lead to a crisis that is dynamic, transformative by its very nature. . . . This crisis brings forth in response attempts at reform that then invite into politics new groups who find their interests threatened or advanced . . . the crisis snowballs, as ineffectual attempts to resolve it . . . bring in wider groups. . . . Into the vacuum step new . . . groups, alarmed and empowered, having to decide how to replace the discredited regime. . . . So, in this view of revolution as process, what needs to be explained is "state failure."[40]

As Campbell noted, his remarks followed those of other historians concerned with redefining the state in eighteenth-century France.[41] They also presaged—in some ways—the comments (in 2015) of Lauren R. Clay.[42] Clay reacted to the "problem of the conspicuously absent bourgeoisie" in this historiography by focusing upon old regime *commercial capitalists* as "frustrated political actors struggling to find their footing in a rapidly changing political environment." In doing so, she, too, reflected in her own way the overall shift away from capitalism-centered structuralism and toward a state-oriented perspective.

"REVOLUTIONARY BOURGEOISIE" OR "REVOLUTIONARY GENTRY" IN OLD REGIME ENGLAND?

In the English case, our quest for a revolutionary bourgeoisie may have to be reconceived if not altogether abandoned from the start. In 1989, even as Peter McPhee was commemorating the French Revolution in the *American Historical Review* by trying to reemphasize the role of capitalist *bourgeois* in France's *ancien régime*, Alex Callinicos was writing that "the rising gentry . . . was the English bourgeoisie, by and for whom the Great Revolution of 1640 was made."[43] Two years later, Ellen Wood, concurring in this, stated that, in prerevolutionary England, "the aristocracy was as capitalist as the bourgeoisie."[44] That Christopher Hill, the dean of Marxist historians of Stuart England, should have returned repeatedly to a conception of the rising capitalist gentry as the cardinal agent of revolutionary change in England, seems very much in line with this analysis.[45] Given this historiographical legacy, we should first of all revisit the controversy in the late 1980s and 1990s over the "Brenner thesis," which sought to ascertain the *precise nature* of supposedly *capitalist* gentry revolution in Stuart England, and then go on to show how, in English as well as in French revolutionary scholarship, a fundamental shift has been taking place more recently from a capitalism-centered to a state-centered interpretation of social change.

Robert Brenner, erstwhile student of Lawrence Stone at Princeton, saw the key protagonist in the transition from feudalism to capitalism in the era of Charles I as the entrepreneurial gentry rather than the mercantile or industrialist interests. Brenner arrived at this conclusion in a number of studies, culminating (in 1993) in *Merchants and Revolution: Commercial Change, Political Conflict, and London's Overseas Traders, 1550–1653*.[46] To be fair, Brenner did *not* by any means try in his work to gloss over the significance of the constitutional, religious, and international issues that have customarily exercised historians of early Stuart England. He simply insisted upon situating those issues in a larger context of *socioeconomic change*—meaning the transition from feudalism to capitalism that was so central to all Marxist writing on this period in English (and, indeed, in general European) history. For Brenner, then, advocates of the "traditional" (for which, read Marxist-inspired) interpretation of prerevolutionary and revolutionary England "quite properly searched for the roots of . . . seventeenth-century political conflicts in structural problems emerging as a consequence of the long-term transformation of English society in a capitalist direction from the later medieval period."[47]

What was really critical for Brenner, however, was the *specific economic and class nature* of that "long-term transformation of English society in a capitalist direction." By and large, he wrote, the merchant and trading groups, "far from uniformly capitalist or ideologically unified, were divided from, and indeed in crucial ways set against, one another in consequence of their diverse relationships to production, property, and the state." Consequently, the rise of capitalism in England quintessentially "took place within the shell of landlord property and thus, in the long run, not in contradiction with and to the detriment of, but rather to the benefit of, the landed aristocracy." Here, then, we come to the nub of Brenner's argument regarding transformative socioeconomic change in early Stuart England:

> What the transition from feudalism to capitalism on the land thus essentially amounted to was the transformation of the dominant class from one whose members depended economically, in the last analysis, on their juridical powers and their direct exercise of force over . . . a peasantry that possessed its means of subsistence, into a dominant class whose members, having ceded direct access to the means of coercion, depended economically . . . on their absolute ownership of landed property and contractual relations with free, market-oriented commercial tenants (who increasingly hired wageworkers), defended by a state that had come to monopolize force.[48]

The "dominant class" lords in this advantageous situation, able as they now were to take "commercial and competitive" and not solely "customary and fixed" rental payments from their tenants, benefited directly from rising food and land prices as well as from the related (and growing) rivalry among their tenant farmers for those resources so characteristic of this period. Hence, the spectacle of the "greater landed classes" wholeheartedly involved in the growth of agricultural productivity *and* in a concomitant process of "increasing social differentiation" in prerevolutionary England.

Moreover, for Brenner, these beneficiaries of a *specific form* of early modern capitalism—that is, *agricultural* rather than *commercial* or *industrial* capitalism—played a central role in the formation of an English state with which they could coexist in harmony. As Brenner described the situation:

> what the greater landed classes of England now merely required was a state able to protect for them their absolute private property—initially, both from marauding bands of neo-feudal magnates and from peasants seeking to conquer what they believed to be their customary rights to the land; ultimately, from landless squatters. They therefore associated themselves ever more closely during the early modern period with the monarchy in the construction of an increasingly powerful and precociously unified state that succeeded, by the early seventeenth century, in securing . . . a monopoly over the legitimate use of force. This monopoly of force was, from one point of view, extraordinarily effective in guaranteeing landed-class property.[49]

From another point of view, Brenner readily conceded, England's sovereigns (on the bases of economic and political power as described previously) found themselves newly invested with the ability to "pursue their own interests and those of their followers." Admittedly, those interests, which included among other things "the maintenance of the monarchs' self-defined place among the monarchs of Europe," could not be assumed in all situations "to coincide with those of the landed classes." Nonetheless, the bedrock concerns for upholding social deference, day-to-day "law and order," and national unity that were shared equally by servants of the absolutist state *and* by members of the landed classes helped to ensure a prolongation of civil peace in England until well into the fateful seventeenth century.

How, then, did Brenner deal with the transition from old regime to revolution in England—that is, with the issues of the Personal Rule and the civil conflicts of the 1640s? He did so, partly, by allowing (in carefully limited fashion) some other social protagonists into the explanatory picture along with his "landed class" agricultural entrepreneurs. Specifically, he wrote of "colonial aristocratic oppositionists" provoking, in alliance with a "new-merchant leadership of the colonial-interloping trades," a challenge to Charles I's Personal Rule. He spoke of "the consolidation of critical alliances" on what became the royalist and parliamentarian sides in the revolutionary conflicts to come: "on the one hand among the Crown, the merchant political elite and . . . the great majority of overseas company merchants, and on the other hand among key elements in the parliamentary leadership, the new-merchant leadership, [and] a London mass movement . . . of retail shopkeepers, mariners, and artisans."[50] Needless to add, Brenner presented all of this against the backdrop of "the new forms of social-property relations and the new form of state that were the product of the transition to capitalism," and he described clashing élitist attitudes in the crisis-ridden 1630s and

1640s as responding, very specifically, to "differing interests and experiences rooted in differing relationships to capitalist development."[51]

In laying out this complicated and provocative interpretation of socioeconomic and derivative political change in early Stuart England, Robert Brenner complained that scholars had too easily thrown off the "traditional social interpretation" centering upon the roles of "distinct and conflicting feudal and capitalist classes" in seventeenth-century conflicts; they had—so he argued—jumped to the conclusion that the English Revolution had "little or nothing to do with the transition from feudalism to capitalism." The *real* problem, Brenner insisted, was *not* that the traditional long-term analysis and explanation was *in itself* fundamentally flawed, but rather that historians had focused unduly on an assumed "dialectic" between *agricultural* and *urban/bourgeois* varieties of capitalism in early modern England and *not* on the developmental dynamics *within* "landed class" agricultural capitalism *itself*. Along the way, Brenner also became enmeshed in a debate with fellow analysts Patricia Croot and David Parker (among others) over the precise roles to be assigned to *small* and *medium-sized* agricultural producers—as opposed to "larger farmers"—in transforming English landed capitalism in late Tudor and early Stuart times.[52]

But the publication, in 1993, of Brenner's *Merchants and Revolution* also raised larger questions about the "Brenner thesis." A number of experts in the field, however impressed by the amplitude of Brenner's research, his historiographical erudition, and his conceptual originality, nonetheless voiced misgivings about the ideological, even teleological overtones of his work. Robert Ashton, for example, although registering his admiration (in the *English Historical Review*) for this "masterly and provocative synthesis of the factors contributing to the Great Rebellion," spoke in his next breath of "the author's reluctance both to admit that not all of his evidence points unequivocally to his conclusions and to give due weight to other evidence which points in the opposite direction." Much of what Brenner set forth in his study "as proven historical truth," Ashton continued, was "in fact more in the nature of a highly stimulating model, coordinating economic, constitutional, political, and religious developments."[53] Similar reservations came a few years later from R. C. Richardson: "Most of today's social historians," he commented, "are more interested, it seems, in social complexities than in overarching interpretations. . . . They are often more interested in structures rather than dynamics and less concerned with the whole picture."[54] Responding somewhat differently to Brenner's *chef d'oeuvre*, leftist historian David Levine described this (admittedly) "essential reading for specialists" as tarred somewhat with an élitist brush: "Brenner's top-down study of intrigue and factional politics," so Levine wrote, "is a social interpretation with many of the contending social forces left out." *Merchants and Revolution*, that is to say, "focuses on only one particular aspect of the social struggle against absolutism," and as such it is "decidedly *not* an interpretation of state breakdown that is seen in terms of the stresses and fractures induced by social change from the bottom up."[55]

David Levine's critical remarks about Brenner's 1993 study would appear to invite us (at the very least) to shift our attention for the moment from gentry roles in the gestation of social revolution in the early Stuart era to the prospective revolutionary role of the so-called middling sort in English society. It might be perfectly true, opined Jonathan Barry in a 1994 anthology of articles that he co-edited with Christopher Brooks, that, for Marxist scholars, "the leaders of the bourgeoisie" in this period "wanted nothing more than to lose their identity," whereas "the landed elite they sought to join or emulate was already sufficiently equipped with capitalist virtues to bring about political and economic change with no help from the middling sort." Yet Barry had doubts about the adequacy of this kind of gentry-centered interpretation, at least insofar as it applied to the revolutionary 1640s and 1650s in England. "Though a vigorous case has been made for seeing [the English Revolution] as a political and religious crisis within the ruling elite," Barry wrote, "it is harder to ignore the obvious importance of the middling sort both during the [civil] war and in the nonconformist churches it created."[56] Writing in the same anthology, Keith Wrightson and Christopher Brooks expressed similar misgivings about excluding middling-sort (or, we might say, "bourgeois"?) English subjects too hastily from all social explanations of the upheaval of the 1640s and 1650s. Wrightson, it is true, was quick to assure his readers that *he* was "not attempting to enter the debate over the social basis of allegiance in the English Civil War, or to suggest . . . that the English Revolution was above all a revolution of the 'middle sort of people.'" But, at the same time, he *did* accentuate the increasing use of the descriptive term "the middle sort of people" by middle-class English subjects *themselves*, and he regarded *their* frequent use of this term as revealing an "awareness of a continuing process of realignment, a further modification of the principal dividing lines within the English social structure."[57] Meanwhile, Christopher Brooks, in summing up *his* research on the "learned professions" in the 1620s and 1630s, said much the same thing, noting that "social groups between the poor and the elite were sometimes referred to specifically as the middling sort." During these years, he wrote, "a kind of populist politics" emanating from this quarter "was identified as a threat to authority, both monarchical and professional," and it undoubtedly foreshadowed the disasters that were so soon to overwhelm both crown *and* learned professions during the "calamitous years of civil war."[58]

There was, moreover, during the 1990s at least one prominent social historian of *ancien régime* and revolutionary England who was even more forthright about stressing "middling sort" elements than had been scholars such as Jonathan Barry, Keith Wrightson, and Christopher Brooks. Brian

Manning had already plunged into these treacherous interpretative waters in an earlier work,[59] and he returned to the charge in 1996 with a study entitled *Aristocrats, Plebeians and Revolution in England 1640–1660*.[60] This historian took all "conservative" (i.e., revisionist) historiography to task for glossing over "the essential element that made the situation in England different" from that in other countries, that element having been "the presence of a substantial middle rank in the population between the wealthy aristocrats and the impoverished masses." And who, precisely, *were* these "middling" types who (at least in Manning's rendition of events) made the English Revolution such a unique affair?

> The "middle sort of people" were based in the class of independent small producers, but some of these were rising into capitalist employers and others ... declining into wage-earning employees. ... Out of the diversity of the "middle sort" there emerged elements that, without being exactly the same as the growing capitalist or bourgeois tendency, became conscious of the difference between their economic and ideological position and that of others, and found themselves united to defend it against the party which they identified with the aristocracy or ruling class.[61]

Not for Manning, then, simplistic views of early modern English society as polarized neatly between "patrician" and "plebeian" elements. It was necessary, instead, "to put back the 'middle sort' into the English Revolution," even while conceding that the term "middle sort" might not denote precisely what "middle class" signifies for modern historians; additionally, it was crucial "to locate this group both in leadership of broad popular movements and in conflicts of interest with the poor."[62]

And what were the economic/developmental consequences for England of its great mid-century revolution? "Agricultural productivity increased, manufacturing developed and commerce expanded under the impetus of growing home and colonial markets," wrote Manning, in Brenner-style language. Yet always, with Brian Manning, the socioeconomic (and accompanying statist) results of revolution, English style, had to be presented with a certain amount of agency granted to the "middling-sort" types that had been less centrally featured in most elaborations of the "Brenner thesis":

> Urbanisation accelerated and non-landed elements in society grew in importance, "drawn from middling groups, like craftsmen, merchants, artisans, manufacturers and professional people"—"people who gained their living primarily from manufacturing, trade and the provision of professional and other services." There emerged a state adapted to the accumulation of capital and the disciplining of labor, and to commercial and imperial expansion. This rested upon its achievement of legitimacy in the eyes of "middling sorts" as well as aristocrats.[63]

Brian Manning may have studiously avoided use of the term "revolutionary bourgeoisie" in his work, but his assertions at other points that "classes are constantly being shaped and reshaped, a process out of which history itself is made," and that the English Revolution in particular "took place in a society being reshaped by the development of capitalism and the genesis of the modern middle and working classes" might very well have been those, early on, of a (then Marxist-oriented) Christopher Hill.

Yet even before remarking how Hill himself, in some of his last writing on issues of social change and revolutionary origins in early Stuart England, transcended Marxian ways of handling such questions, we should note how some specialists in the 1990s disputed the very notion of a unified bourgeoisie in prerevolutionary England. For instance, Jack Goldstone, whose scholarship, as we saw earlier, depicted a *French* bourgeoisie internally divided along economic lines, made essentially the same point regarding the *English* bourgeoisie. We must discard the idea of a "distinct, emerging bourgeoisie," he wrote, and instead accept a different scenario: "The increase in upward and downward social mobility meant that prerogatives of office and county control were no longer secure; instead, claims to precedence were contested by an increasing number of individuals aspiring to elite status." Such claims were advanced, according to Goldstone, by "court officers, country gentry recruited from the enterprising yeomanry, and domestic and international merchants, who were all divided and in conflict."[64] Moreover, as part of an attempt to correlate *socioeconomic* change with *political* change in the revolutionary era, Goldstone spoke of "a vast body of traders, artisans, apprentices, and workers" (i.e., "middling-sort" individuals) as a "mobilizable body that parliamentary leaders could marshal against the king and his allies in London"; these subjects, in other words, were "a key factor in the origins of the revolution."[65] When leagued with Puritan-leaning elites in the 1640s against the Arminian/royalist cause, they proved formidable indeed.

This kind of analysis, in the English case much as in that of France, allowed for more *complicated* ways of describing social change *and* of relating that change to state/structuralist developments. Thus, for example, English historian Norah Carlin saw nothing inconsistent about stressing, on the one hand, the swelling of the gentry's ranks and, on the other hand, a maturation of middling-sort consciousness and ambitions in early modern times that prefigured some of the dynamics of civil warfare in the 1640s. On the former point, regarding the gentry, Carlin had this to say:

> Most studies of the gentry agree . . . that this group became more independent both socially and politically in the sixteenth and seventeenth centuries. . . . The numbers of landowners who claimed the status of gentlemen trebled between 1540 and 1640, from about 5,000 to 15,000, and there was an especially marked increase in the number of "parish gentry" owning . . . one or two

manors, leading in some areas to a dramatic increase in the proportion of villages which had a resident squire. This suggests a long-term change in the structure and role of the gentry.[66]

Still, by the same token, Carlin, generalizing *on the latter point* from scores of local as well as national monographs, insisted that "the 'middling sort' of seventeenth-century England were prepared to sign political petitions, attend meetings and demonstrations, and ultimately to arm for one side or the other (or even against both) in the English civil war because they had become accustomed to regarding themselves as participants in government rather than [as] the dependents of feudal landlords."[67]

What Goldstone, Carlin, and others like them appeared to be doing *in the larger sense* came down to two things: (1) they were theorizing the English version of a revolutionary bourgeoisie in ways that gave the long-celebrated gentry a leading *but no longer exclusive* role as social protagonists in the drama of England's upheaval; and (2) they were (like Peter Campbell and other specialists in the case of France) suggesting a broader, state-centered structuralist context in which social-élitist activism took on its greatest possible significance. As Norah Carlin herself explained the situation toward the end of her reinterpretative synthesis entitled *The Causes of the English Civil War*:

> If explanations of the English civil war in terms of social change are worth pursuing . . . it is not because they can reduce the complex question of causality to a simple . . . formula of bourgeois revolution, or for their supposedly scientific borrowing from the social sciences, but because they can still attempt to bring together the different strands of explanation; to mediate, in effect, between long-term changes in the economy and short-term political events, and even to aim at that "integrating or totalizing role" towards which social history has frequently aspired, and repair the breach between the history of society and the history of the state.[68]

To "repair the breach between the history of society and the history of the state" may be, as expressed in our *theoretical* terms, to conjoin the elements of a *neostructuralist* approach to this subject.

And, indeed, even some Marxist authorities on the English Revolution have seemed ready to acknowledge this approach—at least in their own fashion. We might even cite Robert Brenner in this connection, however much we still associate him with the "Brenner thesis" provocatively identifying capitalist tensions within the agricultural élite as the *primum mobile* behind the English Revolution. After all, Brenner could concede that "wars certainly did, in many instances, provide the occasion for conflict" in this period, could refer to the pressing "needs of the contemporary state," and could affirm that "the English monarchy's pursuit of war tended to bring to the surface precisely those questions of constitutional and religious principle—concerning parliamentary powers, subjects' liberties, and the character and security of the Protestant settlement—that were most in dispute." The "resolution of these questions," concluded Robert Brenner reasonably enough, "would bear very heavily on what would be the nature of the English state."[69] Granted, Brenner hastened to add here that "one of the best ways to restore principled conflict over the constitution and religion to its proper place at the center of the interpretation of seventeenth-century politics" was "to reassociate constitutional and religious ideas with the sociopolitical and economic contexts from which they arose."[70] How else (he might have put it, in anticipation of Norah Carlin) to "repair the breach between the history of society and the history of the state"? Yet notwithstanding Brenner's predictably Marxian gloss on these issues, his passing invocation of statist/geostrategic concerns must *in itself* quickly draw the attention—and gain the approval—of any neostructuralist scholar in the field today.

Moreover, the most eminent of all English Marxist historians of the seventeenth century seems also to have come, in the twilight of his career, to place these issues in a larger neostructuralist context—that is, to explain revolutionary change in Stuart England in related socioeconomic, religiocultural, and state-centered terms. We noted earlier how, for so many years, Christopher Hill had approached issues of revolutionary causation and process from a strongly (if never altogether simplistically) economic/class point of view.[71] By the time his *Intellectual Origins of the English Revolution Revisited* appeared in 1997, however, Hill was inclined (1) to reconceptualize the revolutionary "protagonist class" *and* (2) to situate England's socioeconomic and religious issues in a framework assuming the interrelatedness of domestic and geostrategic affairs.

On the first point, Hill noted, conventionally enough, that the "two generations before 1640 had seen great changes in English society, a great economic divide in the countryside." The "fortunate few who were conveniently placed to produce for the market and who were sufficiently skilful, industrious, or lucky, and who seized their chance," Hill continued on, "could prosper by taking advantage of rising prices." So far, this was orthodoxy. But, at this point, his characterization of social polarization in early modern England abruptly took on a subtle note of *complication*. "In villages," Hill observed, "new and sharper class divisions were developing—no longer setting gentry against the rest, but gentry, some yeomen, some merchants, some artisans, against the rest. This was so novel that contemporaries had no word to describe the emerging new rich as a social group: the term 'parish elites' is an invention of historians."[72] In other words—as of this writing, in 1997—"some yeomen," "some merchants," and "some artisans" (as well as, possibly, others?) had now joined the oft-celebrated gentry in constituting Christopher Hill's "emerging new rich" or "parish élites" accelerating the pace of revolutionary change in Charles I's England. True, Hill later on (325) reverted to older notions when speaking of "the gentry who took the lead against the crown in the early years of the revolution"; still, the fact remained that, even for this leftist veteran of the post–World War II "storm over the gentry," social-élitist description had now become an unprecedentedly challenging, *complicated* affair.

But the second point, in a sense, had even broader implications, for it exposed Hill's willingness to place long-term causes, along with short-term religious factors, within a state-structuralist nexus of international and domestic developments. On long-term causal analysis, we have this:

> We see here some of the long-term causes of the English Revolution. . . . Opposition to Archbishop Laud linked the desire of the "natural rulers" to be left alone to run their localities with the demand for a . . . commercial imperial policy and fear of royal absolutism. Lurking behind it all was the menace perceived in Catholic victories in the Thirty Years War which led to restoration of confiscated church lands in Germany as well as to religious persecution.[73]

And on the ever-critical short-term *religious* factor in the gestation of revolution in early Stuart England, we have (even more remarkably) this from Hill:

> The Thirty Years War and England's economic and political crisis forced millenarian ideas upon Protestants already predisposed to accept them. Catholics seemed to be winning the war on the continent; English owners of former monastic property could not but be anti-Catholic. In the 1630s it was easy to see an international popish plot, in which Henrietta Maria was a leading figure. The Irish revolt of 1641, for which the Pope sent over his representative to take command, confirmed this view.[74]

Again and again, Hill went out of his way to stress the *intertwined nature* of religious and international questions. As just one example in point: "Theological polarization was a consequence of considerations of foreign-policy issues on which the King's advisers were rightly thought to be unsound. Everything was mixed up."[75]

Everything *was* "mixed up," or tightly interrelated, in the lead-up to (and in the unfolding of) the English Revolution. Yet we hardly need the eleventh-hour ruminations (however illuminating they may be) of a one-time paladin of English Marxism to make us realize how, in English as in French revolutionary historiography, seeking to refine our definition of the bourgeoisie *or its equivalent* may lead us, as good neostructuralists, to insist with renewed confidence upon the worldly context of social-élitist evolution. David Cressy was as aware as any historian of Stuart England of efforts to reinterpret the revolutionary gentry in a more socially inclusive fashion; yet he also pointedly referred to the English Revolution as "a 'world-historical' event," and he went on to sum up what we today would call the neostructuralist thrust in recent writing on the events of the 1640s and 1650s:

> Recent contributions to the debate have emphasized both its ideological and geographical dimensions. . . . The "revolt of the provinces" has expanded into "the wars of the three kingdoms." The revolution, if such it was, is now properly seen to be British as well as English, inexplicable without its Scottish and Irish components. Charles I's problems, like those of Protector Cromwell, are understood in terms of the management of . . . international territories with competing religious and constitutional traditions. Some scholars find even this archipelagian approach too narrow, and emphasize instead the European or even global compass.[76]

Cressey's insight had, significantly, been anticipated years before by Conrad Russell, and it has been powerfully reinforced by the subsequent research of Steve Pincus, Jonathan Scott, Geoffrey Parker, Michael J. Braddick, and a phalanx of other specialists in the field.[77]

That David Cressey would refer to the *ideological* as well as the geographical dimensions of the debate over the English Revolution is also very useful, for it recalls for us the ever-present cultural—in other words, postmodernist—component in any neostructuralist approach to revolution in general and (in this chapter) to the elusive old regime/revolutionary bourgeoisie in particular.

A "REVOLUTIONARY *BURZHUAZIIA*" IN OLD REGIME RUSSIA: ALL BUT NONEXISTENT?

When Marx and Engels declared, in the *Communist Manifesto* of 1848, that "the bourgeoisie, historically, has played a most revolutionary part" in the preparation of major sociopolitical upheavals, they could hardly have anticipated that *Russian* communists in the next century would be deriding their own country's *burzhuaziia* as an abortive class protagonist in the world's first Marxist revolution. But even today, as the following pages show, historians striving to analyze the causes of the 1917 cataclysm in Russia experience extraordinary difficulty in locating a bourgeoisie in late Romanov times. Much like their counterparts in French and English revolutionary studies, they often find themselves investigating other groups in the *ancien régime*—not to mention identifying ideological/cultural elements in a larger, neostructuralist explanation of revolutionary events.

Yet we should perhaps start off here by rejecting social analyses drawing upon extreme versions of either capitalism-centered structuralism (i.e., Marxism) or deconstructionist postmodernism. On the former point, there is no way to deny that some Soviet-inspired scholars have endeavored to stand by the old revolutionary paradigm. Indeed, Thomas C. Owen, contributing to a seminal 1991 anthology of articles on civil society (*obshchestvo*) in late imperial Russia, argued that those specialists, by insistently presenting old regime social dynamics in ideological terms inherited from the past (i.e., *their* past), were obfuscating rather than elucidating Russian social developments that helped pave the way for the 1917 explosion. What Owen referred to here as the "current conceptual muddle" in this field owed much to "Soviet historians, determined to write the history of Russian commerce, manufacturing, and banking in terms of 'finance capital' and 'monopoly.'" Such Leninist ideas, he wrote, "form part of a larger Marxist conception of world history that implicitly assumes the universal applicability of European capitalist and socialist ideas and institutions." If terms such as "modernization" and "economic backwardness" were meant to imply that Russia would someday resemble Great Britain "once the quantitative gaps in steel production and railroad density were closed," Owen went on, they obscured "essential institutional and cultural peculiarities of the Russian experience."[78] On the latter point, Edward Acton complained that "postmodernist" writers, by casting "particular doubt on historical approaches which lay emphasis on objective socio-economic conditions," and by hastening "not only to deconstruct but [also] to reject wholesale the terms and concepts on which social analysis depends," unwittingly *facilitate* reactionary efforts in academia *today* to portray the Russian revolutionary experience as a "conspiracy" advanced through "the propaganda, the language, [and] the discourse infiltrated by socialist intellectuals."[79] Latter-day teleological assumptions encountered at *all* points along the political spectrum, we gather from scholars like Owen and Acton, lie stealthily in wait for researchers who *already* find the terrain of late imperial Russian social history sufficiently treacherous on its own terms.

And in fact, historians seeking *bourgeois* class formation and agency in prerevolutionary Russia have for some years been finding that quest to be frustrating on a number of counts. For one thing, as Gregory Freeze and other specialists have repeatedly stressed, tension between the old juridical estates (*sosloviia*) and associated mentality (*soslovnost'*), on the one hand, and nascent socioeconomic classes, on the other, persisted into the early 1900s, hence delaying the formation of any authentic *burzhuaziia*, among other classes, not to mention inhibiting the state modernization designs of Sergei Witte and of other ministerial dynamos. Freeze, in particular, has remarked that "these *sosloviia* did not inexorably dissolve into classes in the postreform era, as traditionally posited in the estate-class paradigm." Whereas "some new groups, like workers, did tend to develop "class" identities and others, like the professions, endured an undefined . . . status, much of society still tended to think in terms of the prereform *soslovie* system." Freeze saw "the strong hereditary patterns, the persisting legal distinctions, the segregation of groups in administration and law, the deeply-rooted cultural differences among various groups, and the conscious effort of the state to preserve the *soslovie* separation" as factors that "acted to maintain the old social structure even in the face of far-reaching social and economic change."[80]

Thus it is clear that part of the problem with the *sosloviia* stemmed from efforts by opponents of change at St. Petersburg (and in provincial Russia) to retain as many of the customary distinctions in society as they could. The issue, therefore, became *progressively politicized* as the case for social and economic modernization came to be ever more hotly debated between "liberals" and "reactionaries" against the ominous backdrop of Russia's deteriorating geostrategic position. Again, Gregory Freeze:

> The survival of *soslovnost'*, even if in an attenuated form, remained a significant impediment to the political reconstruction of autocracy. . . . Indeed, *soslovnost'*—as a legal principle, as *mentalité*—formed a crucial barrier to the political modernization of the old regime, for it was utterly antithetical to the creation of a modern civil society, which is the *sine qua non* for a democratic order. Hence, *soslovnost'*, if not *sosloviia*, survived to the end of the *ancien régime* and, in some significant respects, even into the Soviet period.[81]

Moreover, as Leopold H. Haimson maintained, the penetration of the Russian countryside by processes of economic, social, and cultural modernization during the *ancien régime* meant that the contradictions between the old corporate, *sosloviia*-dominated society and the newer professional, *class* society that had long characterized urban areas became increasingly characteristic of rural, peasant regions as well. "Such contradictions," in Haimson's words, "contributing there as well to the fragility and potential explosiveness of social relationships and to the growing confusion of social identities," militated all the more dangerously against the efforts of Witte, Stolypin, and other ministerial reformers to modernize the Romanov state and society.[82]

Yet the failure of a Western-style bourgeoisie (*burzhuaziia*) to emerge in old regime Russia was also attributable to factors even more fundamental, perhaps, than the stubborn survival of increasingly obsolescent estates (*sosloviia*), status (*sostoianie*), and rank (*chin*) under the late Romanovs. Abbott Gleason has cited, in this connection, obvious problems such as "the ferocious climate of Great Russia, . . . the extremities of heat and (especially) cold, the poor soil, the irregular rainfall and brief growing season," and "the lack of a useful access to the sea" as making for crudely primitive and exploitative social relations in the tsars' realm. More subtly, however, he has also signaled *mental* or *psychological* impediments to socioeconomic class development—meaning, above all, peasant, gentry, and (perhaps most paradoxically) *intellectual* hostility toward the kind of individual initiative and entrepreneurialism long characteristic of societies in the West:

the culture of the intellectuals, whether of the left or the right, must have been among the most anti-bourgeois in Europe. . . . Both radical and romantic intellectuals hated social rationalism and individualism; it was virtually all they could agree on. So if the *burzhuaziia* was missing in Russia, it was [still] easy to find the [individual] *burzhui*, as well as the kulak and other negative stereotypes of combined greed, cruelty, and calculating rationality.[83]

Further poisoning this witches' brew of physical, psychic, and intellectual impediments to anything resembling Western-style bourgeoisification of pre-revolutionary Russian society were the ethnic/racial demographics and resultant prejudices so prominent in the twilight years of the Empire:

> The communities and groups involved in industrialization tended to keep to themselves; Jewish, Polish, Russian, and German merchants and industrialists had surprisingly little to do with each other . . . stereotypes of Jews and Poles became . . . linked with the bad values of capitalism and thus were often perceived and portrayed as anti-Russian.

"Russian industrialization," concluded Gleason all too persuasively, "was a terrible struggle in cultural as well as social, political, and economic terms."[84]

All of this meant, as Thomas C. Owen has written, that, in the long run—meaning, both before and after the 1905 troubles foreshadowed the much greater explosion-to-come just over a decade later—the Romanov state was caught up with those who *should* have been its "capitalist-industrialist" allies in élitist society in a paradoxical situation fraught with peril for both sides:

> The disarray of the Russian corporate elite appears to have redounded to the benefit of the autocratic state . . . even the most dynamic of tsarist officials, namely Witte and his talented bureaucrats, felt free to administer the economic institutions of the empire by the well-tested methods of bureaucratic tutelage and arbitrariness. To the extent that . . . ministers implanted modern factories by autocratic modes of behavior incompatible with the nature of modern capitalism—through subsidies to favorites, arbitrary restrictions on minority ethnic groups, prohibitions of elective chambers of commerce and industry, preferential credit for the gentry, and the like—the state in fact hindered the development of capitalist industry in Russia.[85]

But by retarding the development of "capitalist industry" in Russia, the tsars' well-intentioned ministers only cut the ground out from beneath any fully autochthonous *burzhuaziia* within imperial borders, thus heightening the country's strategic and economic dependence upon outside Great Powers.

It is intriguing that Owen, anticipating advocates of postmodernism in French and English social history, should in this regard have set so much store by *bourgeois class consciousness*. A social class, he proclaimed, "is more than just an agglomeration of individuals who share roughly the same culture, status, income and economic role within a region or nation." Such individuals cannot be class leaders "unless they share certain beliefs and attitudes, communicate these ideas among themselves, and organize group action in pursuit of common goals, using permanent mechanisms such as membership organizations based on economic or professional function." At a yet higher stage of bourgeois class formation, Owen continued on, "political parties and a whole array of cultural institutions, including schools, newspapers, and publishing houses, buttress the edifice," and the members of the "class" in question effectively announce their feelings of "solidarity" by identifying, even demonizing opposing groups in society. In the end, however, Owen concluded, "bourgeois attitudes" defined in these terms "were nonexistent or weak within the Russian corporate elite prior to 1905; they scarcely influenced the political and economic institutions of the tsarist empire in the decade before World War I."[86]

Sheila Fitzpatrick, placing these issues in an explicitly global context, has stressed how widely expectations about the emergence of a modern, Western-style *burzhuaziia* in Russia were held among patriotic subjects of the Empire at the turn of the century—*and* how closely those expectations were associated in educated minds with the conviction that "the survival of *sosloviia* was an embarrassing anachronism, pointing up the contrast between backward Russia and the progressive West":

> While this [conviction] reflected the popularity of Marxism among Russia's intellectuals, it was by no means only Marxists who thought that a capitalist bourgeoisie and industrial proletariat were necessary attributes of modernity. The belief was widespread; even Russia's conservative statesmen and publicists shared it, though they had a different value judgment of modernity. Even though Russia was still lacking one of the two . . . classes of modern society, the notoriously "missing" bourgeoisie, this did not disturb the general assumption of educated Russians that when . . . classes finally superseded *sosloviia* as the structural underpinning, Russian society would have made the transition from the "artificial" to the "real."[87]

Who at this point could have possibly prophesied that, if and when revolution came to Russia, it would so drastically deconstruct Russian society as to leave (at least temporarily) not even a fully organized urban proletariat, let alone an urban *burzhuaziia* or a rural gentry (*dvorianstvo*), in existence?

Yet long before public affairs took this extreme turn, the fragility or even (some scholars argue) the virtual nonexistence of any bourgeoisie modeled along Western lines was already an entrenched reality. We can retrospectively see this by following the fortunes of some very specific entrepreneurial and professional groups of that era. As James L. West has held, for example, the so-called Riabushinsky circle of progressive Muscovite industrialists "came to personify the effort to create the ideological and organizational basis of a modern entrepreneurial class" in Russia. Yet by spurning the parallel activities of the largely non-Russian capitalists who controlled St. Petersburg's industries, not to mention those of the entrepreneurs in the peripheral regions of this vast country, Pavel P. Riabushinsky and his colleagues only reinforced the centrifugal forces tearing this prospective commercial/industrial *burzhuaziia* apart. "Beneath their liberal rhetoric," West has concluded, "one senses only a weakly developed capacity for cooperation and compromise, skills essential to a well-functioning democratic order."[88] Nancy Frieden discovered similar weaknesses plaguing, specifically, physicians in late nineteenth-century Russia, and Harley Balzer has pictured professional and "intelligentsia" groups generally in similar terms. In such cases, well-intentioned Russian professionals found Western strategies of class formation difficult to emulate, in part because they were caught between an absolute state (*gosudarstvo*) whose intervention in their affairs was essential yet at times stifling and the "people" (*narod*) whose poverty and illiteracy simultaneously saddened and frightened them, but also in part because of inconsistencies in their own class rhetoric and images of themselves.[89] Perhaps, in light of all of this, we should *not* be astonished to find one contributor to the Clowes/Kassow/West anthology, William G. Wagner, concluding bleakly that "the assumption that the existence of a larger middle class in late Imperial Russia would have introduced political democracy and thereby avoided revolution seems problematic." "It would seem," Wagner went so far as to allege, "that a major source of instability in Russia . . . was not the absence but [rather] the presence of a nascent middle class."[90]

At this point, however, the attentive neostructuralist would likely pose the following, eminently reasonable question: if historians of *ancien régime* France could view bourgeois as constituting but one element in a larger élite of *notables* prepared to wield power in revolutionary and postrevolutionary times, and if the gentry were but the "first among equals" in the "emerging new rich" élite of *ancien régime* England, could not a *burzhuaziia* be similarly seen as but one component of a larger "upper crust" of cosmopolitan, educated, and civic-minded advocates of social transformation in *ancien régime* Russia? Samuel D. Kassow has certainly identified fledgling elements of a civil society (*obshchestvo*) inhabiting its Habermasian public sphere in the late decades of tsardom, and has written, optimistically, of such phenomena as "the rise of voluntary societies, the steady if slow development of respect for property rights, the rapid expansion of higher and secondary education, artistic patronage, the growth of professions, the rise of a multilayered press, the emergence of the Duma [that is, after 1906] as a forum for political articulation," and so on, as indicators of such a development.[91] Yet where was the *traditional social "estate" or élite* in all of this? If we are to believe Roberta Manning (and a myriad of other specialists) on this point,

Russia's aristocracy displayed tendencies of social disintegration in the years following on the mid-nineteenth-century Great Reforms, and this process only accelerated as the country approached the political and military crises of the early years of the twentieth century. The landless service nobility crucial to the formulation and implementation of public policy in the ministries, the urban-oriented gentry intelligentsia, and the provincially based landed gentry, all of which had issued from Russia's noble estate, often followed divergent paths during these years, and could never have made common cause with a *burzhuaziia* which, in any case, (as we have already seen) was *itself* hardly a coherent group.[92] Moreover, there is a striking, larger neostructuralist observation to make here: namely, that any "census society" (*tsenzovoe obshchestvo*) of upper- and middle-class Russian *notables* would ineluctably have found itself squeezed perilously between the hammer of the autocratic Romanov state and the anvil of the unenlightened, sometimes anarchic, and forever-exploited masses (workers and peasants) of urban and rural Russia.[93]

All of these centrifugal social tendencies in the Russian old regime were, unsurprisingly, further aggravated in the traumatic circumstances of the Great War, that is, from 1914 on. It is undeniably true that, as Peter Gatrell has noted, "the outbreak of war opened up fresh opportunities for Russian heavy industry. Leading government contractors hurriedly concluded fresh contracts for munitions with the procurement agencies. Other firms in the private sector that had hitherto concentrated on civilian work also joined the headlong rush to manufacture armaments." The metalworking and machine-building firms in Petrograd and the surrounding region especially benefited from all of this.[94] Since, however, the military disasters of late 1914 and 1915 created a munitions crisis, and made the tsarist authorities desperately eager to broaden the manufacturing base and extend their control over the production and distribution of war *matériel* in general, an opening was provided to a novel network of medium-sized and small manufacturers, the so-called War Industries Committees (WICs or *VPKs*), to cooperate in the production of various kinds of military supplies for the war effort.[95] Yet the WICs broached issues that both the ministers and the great industrialists found threatening. In Peter Gatrell's words:

> The WICs protested that neither the state nor big business had sufficient grasp of the scale or type of industrial mobilization that the war necessitated. Complaints were made that the directors of the largest firms in engineering and metallurgy enjoyed too close an association with government officials. The WICs hoped to shatter this cosy relationship. They quickly established themselves in provincial towns and cities, and dedicated themselves not simply to the production of uniforms and munitions for the war effort, but also to the principle of a morally superior form of enterprise that need not disappear with the cessation of hostilities.[96]

In other words, the state's very attempt to enlist all possible entrepreneurial resources in the patriotic campaign against the Central Powers only gave new life to tensions deeply entrenched in the old regime—tensions between the state itself and commercial/industrial society in general, between largely native Muscovite entrepreneurs and predominantly non-Russian capitalists at Petrograd and in the provinces, between large factory owners and medium-sized or small manufacturers, between engineers and metallurgists, on the one hand, and other highly trained professionals, on the other, and so on.

Beyond even this, however, there was the question of how to engage *workers* (i.e., those outside the favored precincts of upper- and middle-class *tsenzovoe obshchestvo*, or census society) in the overall war effort. Merchant-entrepreneurs who had participated in 1913 in founding the liberal "Progressist Party," and who were prominent during the war years in the WICs, agitated not only for their own share of the state's apportionment of contracts for uniforms, munitions, and other war-related *matériel*, but also for an altogether unheard-of partnership between government, capital, and labor in Russia's contribution to the Allied war effort. Peter Gatrell has described this agitation, and the broader challenge it posed to the embattled Romanov regime:

> The issue of labor representation proved particularly explosive in Russia. Aleksandr Guchkov, chairman of the Central War Industry Committee . . . espoused the doctrine of "social peace" and advocated an English-style *rapprochement* between labour and capital. In similar vein, his deputy, Aleksandr Konovalov, maintained that the organized working class "represented the element on which depends ultimate victory over the enemy." According to this perspective, capital should cooperate with labour in modern economic life. The government not surprisingly rejected such a radical view of industrial relations, and found leading industrialists willing to toe the official line.[97]

Indeed, the formation of so-called Workers' Groups" in the WICs proved in the end to be divisive not only in the expected sense of pitting the tsarist regime (and some of its gentry and large industrialist supporters) against Progressists and other liberals in "Privilege Russia" but also in the perhaps somewhat less expected sense of eventually pitting some liberal bourgeois personalities such as Konovalov against others such as Pavel P. Riabushinsky and his closest Muscovite allies. (Konovalov and his old friend Riabushinsky crossed swords over the prioritization to be assigned to "state interests" as opposed to the "autonomous interests" of workers and others in civil society.) Fragmentation *within* the commercial/industrial bourgeoisie, in other words, turned out to be every bit as dangerous in its own way as was the growing isolation of Nicholas and Alexandra's incompetent government within the broader ranks of "respectable" Russian society.[98]

Once 1917 came, and with it the abrupt collapse (in February) of the Romanov regime, the same old forces of fragmentation would continue to hollow out the commercial-industrial *burzhuaziia* from within. Lewis H. Siegelbaum, who has studied the WICs as assiduously as anyone, has demonstrated how, even at *this* specific level *within* Russia's nascent, struggling middle class, those disruptive, centrifugal forces continued to operate—as the larger Russian polity and society were staring affrightedly into the abyss of disaster:

> The *VPK*s advocated national unity in the name of defense, but their own members were more concerned about the defense of their own . . . interests. Technical personnel formed a Union of Engineers with regional branches. Employees of the *VPK*s followed suit. Industrialists, too, felt compelled to exercise the new . . . freedom to organize . . . the Petrograd Society of Factory and Mill Owners hammered out a programme for the protection of their property and later formed the nucleus of an All-Russian Union of Factory and Mill Owner Societies. In Moscow, Riabushinskii chaired the first congress of the All-Russian Union of Trade and Industry on 19 March.[99]

The Central WIC (*TsVPK*) "attempted to accommodate all of these groups, if not their conflicting aims," Siegelbaum has remarked, but when, in May, the third congress of *VPKs* met in Moscow, gloom pervaded the proceedings, as "one speaker after another testified like witnesses in a courtroom to the anarchic situation in industry and transport."[100] The proletariat, in any case, by this time had really no further use for the *VPKs* or for any other institutions sponsored by "census Russia"; they were now receiving their (increasingly radical and *class-oriented*) education from factory committees, trade unions, and soviets. From this time forward, capitalists and workers alike became increasingly caught up in a dialectic of polarized class attitudes and expectations whose final result, in October of that year, would be the Bolshevik seizure of power.[101]

Here, then, we have the "search for the elusive bourgeoisie" in old regime/early revolutionary Russia. And here, too, much as in the cases of old regime France and old regime England, we find that those engaged in the search have ultimately been forced to place their *social* and *cultural* analyses in a larger framework of *state inadequacy* in both domestic and international affairs. In so doing, they have moved in the direction of a fully neostructuralist reading of Russian revolutionary history.

When, for instance, it comes to *domestic* affairs, postmodernist historian Orlando Figes viewed the catastrophic famine of 1891 to 1892 as marking a fundamental turning point, a strategic retreat of state influence in Russia (however autocratic the state might be in theory) before the aroused forces of a civil society (*obshchestvo*) whose most basic needs could no longer be even *anticipated*, let alone sufficiently addressed, by those purportedly speaking and acting in the tsar's name:

> The time was passing when . . . the autocracy had been "the only organized force" in Russia and had been able to dominate a weak and divided society. Now that relationship was being reversed. The institutions of society were becoming more independent and organized, while the tsarist state was steadily becoming weaker and less able to control them. The famine crisis was the crucial turning-point in this process, the moment when Russian society first became politically aware of itself and its powers, of its duties to "the people," and of the potential it had to govern itself.

This was the moment, in a sense, when Russia first became, in Orlando Figes's mind, a "nation."[102]

In this connection, Figes (like so many of his colleagues) also referenced the role played by the *zemstvos*. As we saw in chapter 1, these provincial and district assemblies had been instituted by the government in the post-Crimean era as part of its campaign to establish closer organic ties between St. Petersburg and local élite society. As Leopold Haimson stressed, however, the *zemstvos* also came to serve (significantly, without the authorities' approval) as crucial "institutional foci" for the "emergence . . . of the image of a civil society—an *obshchestvo*—with its principles of order and legitimacy distinct from, and potentially counterposed to, those of the state." As Haimson went on to say:

> By the same token, the crystallization of a sense of the commonweal (*obshchestvennoe delo*), and of an educated elite not only dedicated to serve it but also to infuse it with a sense of dedication to the People, contributed, by the turn of the century, to . . . the conception of a struggle against absolutism, led by a coalition of the liberal and radical groups of a "noncaste," "non-*soslovie*," "nonclass" intelligentsia, to conquer civil rights and political freedom for a "nation" already seen in the making.[103]

Such a development, however, obscured the brutal fact, so soon to be put on display in the unforgiving glare of revolutionary politics, that nebulous notions of a "civil society," and of enlightened service to it, "had failed not only to bridge the divisions between rural and urban-commercial-industrial Russia, and between the upper and lower strata of both, but even to encompass the processes of economic, social, and psychological change actually experienced by various social groups."[104]

But state inadequacy has loomed for Russian social historians in broader *international* terms as well. Samuel D. Kassow, for instance, acknowledged the interrelated dilemmas of domestic and foreign policymaking confronting those who had to govern in late nineteenth- and early twentieth-century Russia: "Faced with an enormous peasant problem, an unstable international situation, a tax base of limited options, [and] an administrative system incapable of governing a vast, disparate, multi-ethnic society," Kassow observed, "many government officials . . . insisted that the state must hold the fist in reserve."[105] When it came to the ultimate crisis precipitated in 1914 by violent events in the Balkans, Imperial Russia had willy-nilly to undergo, Orlando Figes wrote, a "gigantic test of the modern state," a test which *this* particular state, "as the only major European state which had failed to modernize before the war . . . was almost bound to fail."[106] Yet another experienced practitioner of postmodernist history, Sheila Fitzpatrick, tersely endorsed this analysis: "The First World War both exposed and increased the vulnerability of Russia's old regime. The public applauded victories, but would not tolerate defeats. When defeats occurred, the society did not rally behind its government . . . but instead turned sharply against it, denouncing its incompetence and backwardness in tones of contempt."[107] Statements like these make it hard to deny that, in Russian social-revolutionary historiography, much as in French and English scholarship of the same sort, neostructuralist concerns about transcendent questions of state survival have come to loom increasingly large, whether those registering such concerns acknowledge neostructuralism as such or not.

Two major conclusions seem to emerge from this chapter's extended discussion of the scholarly quest for the "elusive *ancien régime* bourgeoisie" in France, England, and Russia.

First, it appears to be all but impossible to derive from the pertinent social-historical literature on these three countries any pat formula regarding their old regime middle classes—and the roles they may have played in their respective sociopolitical upheavals. As we have seen, the French *bourgeoisie*, however differently conceived by different historians, most likely shared the stage in the late eighteenth century with other groups in a *société des notables* that could no longer be accommodated within the outdated chrysalis of the society of "estates" or "orders." In the case of early Stuart England, the gentry seems still to have played a central "initiating" role in the onset of revolution—even if, very likely, it *was* somewhat aided in that process by non-gentry, nonélitist subjects. Finally, with respect to Russia, the relatively incoherent nature, not only of any *burzhuaziia*, but of civil society in general, must strike us (at least with all the clairvoyance of hindsight) as an accompaniment, to be sure, to Romanov autocracy, but also as an ominous harbinger of sociopolitical change likely to be unprecedented in the European revolutionary experience in its violent, "leveling" aspects.

Second, regardless of how, exactly, we are to conceive the middle class and/or other classes in these three specific countries, we can see that our attempt to deal with this general issue *in theoretical terms* has inexorably taken us in a *neostructuralist* direction, as we have defined neostructuralism in this book. We have advanced, that is, from the kind of capitalism-centered structuralism implied in Marxian class analysis toward a state-centered analysis that views social groups against the backdrop of closely interrelated international and domestic developments. At the same time, we have tried wherever possible to draw upon the cultural insights of postmodernism to show how precarious were the bonds unifying the elements of "respectable" society in three European old regimes—and how such weak social bonds presaged in their own way the violent and eventually murderous political infighting of the French, English, and Russian Revolutions.

Chapter Three

To Kill a Monarch

From Proceduralism to Revolutionary Raison d'État

Among the issues looming today in any reassessment of revolutionary change in Europe, none better illustrates neostructuralism's uses of moderate postmodernist and state-centered analysis than does that involving the decisions of Cromwellian Independents, Robespierrist Jacobins, and Leninist Bolsheviks to execute, respectively, Charles I, Louis XVI, and Nicholas II. In recent years, those writing about the English, French, and Russian revolutions have had much to say about this question. English specialist Jason Peacey, for example, describing the trial and execution of Charles I as "an inexplicably understudied subject" that is "seriously under-represented in the literature," has tried to remedy this historiographical oversight by publishing the proceedings of a two-day conference devoted to the 1649 regicide that he had helped to organize at the Institute of Historical Research in London in January 1999.[1] Among Peacey's counterparts in French revolutionary studies, Dan Edelstein has devoted a considerable amount of time in these early years of the new century to "retheorizing" the trial and execution of Louis XVI (December 1792 to January 1793) in comparative-historical terms.[2] Meanwhile, Russian revolutionary specialist Orlando Figes had earlier contended in his 1996 epic, *A People's Tragedy*, that "the murder of the Romanovs assumed such significance in the history of the [Russian] revolution" because "it was a declaration of the Terror. It was a statement that from now on individuals would count for nothing in the civil war."[3] Figes's observations point to a renewed concern in *Russian* scholarship with the violent revolutionary justice meted out to Nicholas II in July 1918. When taken together with the assertions of various English and French historians, they witness more generally to a resurgence of scholarly interest in the phenomenon of European revolutionary regicide.

Chapter 3 aims to reexamine the regicides of 1649, 1793, and 1918, but with a somewhat novel twist. In many treatments of this issue, historians are content to draw a contrast between England and France, on the one hand, as countries in which the rule of law was sufficiently entrenched to *ensure* that monarchs, even when found guilty of treason in *revolutionary* times, could only be dispatched on the basis of legal procedure, and Russia, on the other hand, as a land in which, given the lack of an historic, Western-style rule of law, a decision to have a deposed and "treasonous" monarch *unceremoniously* killed had a certain hard logic. Less well known, however, is the effort mounted unavailingly in the case of France to *theorize* the revolutionary process and to *reify* revolutionary legitimacy to the extent of denying *any* due process (and, thus, *any* possible legitimacy) to Louis XVI. What radical Jacobins failed to do in revolutionary France, Lenin's Bolsheviks would eventually do in revolutionary Russia. In dealing with this issue, chapter 3 utilizes the political-cultural insights of postmodernism and the state-security insights of structuralism to reassess the forces for and against these revolutionary regicides. Moreover, by tracing the progression, in the European revolutionary tradition, from premises of procedural justice to more modern concepts of revolutionary *raison d'état*, chapter 3 ends by underscoring the primacy of *statism* and of state-security calculations in neostructuralist revolutionary analysis.

CHARLES I AND THE "TRADITIONAL LEGAL FORMS AND PROCEDURES"

We may legitimately wonder whether, in the chaotic conditions of civil warfare in the 1640s, a duplicitous monarch such as Charles I could have in any way been shielded from the worst of fates by what John Adamson has referred to as "that peculiarly English preoccupation with the maintenance of traditional legal forms and procedures."[4] Certainly, by the time Oliver Cromwell and the other grandees of the victorious New Model Army had steeled themselves to the need to deal drastically with this "man of blood," the vanquished Charles I had already spent two years engaging in a tortuous game of playing one English (and Scottish) faction off against another.[5] For his many enemies, applying "traditional legal forms and procedures" to the king by now almost automatically meant putting him on trial for his life—whether in the "Rump" of the post-Pride's Purge House of Commons or in some other judicial venue. Yet, in retrospect, we should not be surprised to find significant forces arrayed against as well as in favor of trying (and, conceivably, executing) Charles I. Here, therefore, we draw upon the legalistic and other political-cultural insights of postmodernism *and* the state-security aspects of structuralism to review the factors militating against or in favor of this anointed monarch's execution.

First there were the *legalistic* objections. D. Alan Orr has pointed out that the traditional "law of treason" right up to January 1649 "appeared inimical to regicide." This law, based since 1352 upon Edward III's statute of treasons (*25 Edward III*), defined as "treasonable" such activities as "compassing or imagining the death of the king, queen or eldest male heir to the throne," waging war on "the king in his realm," "counterfeiting the great or privy seal, the king's coin or bringing counterfeit coin into the realm," "killing the chancellor, treasurer or any of the king's justices in the execution of their offices," and so on.[6] As Orr has contended, this statutory conception of "treason" against the king was "neither wholly impersonal nor wholly personal." Under the early modern theory of the "king's two bodies," the monarch's "supra-personal or 'public' authority remained tied to his natural person and the heirs of his body natural." Because (under this theory) the king possessed two "capacities," one being his "natural" body and the other being the immortal "body politic," the king was assured not only of his sovereignty over the emerging bureaucratic state, but also of the transference of his crown to his heirs. In Orr's phrasing: "While the person of the king was mortal and would inevitably perish, the dignity of his office was immortal: upon the death of one monarch the English crown would descend automatically to the heirs of his body without need of formal coronation."[7] As Orr has also noted, English juridical theory in this domain may have drawn sustenance as well from Roman law, with its stress upon monarchical dual "capacities," the *inseparability* of those dual roles, and the special "dignity" and "majesty" of the king's "immortal" capacity as embodying the state's existential continuity.[8]

The extent to which the *constitutional* and *political* application of such juridical theory protected Charles I in his exercise of kingship until very late in the day is reflected, as Orr has acutely observed, in the way the Long Parliament handled the alleged treasons of the king's two most powerful lieutenants, Thomas Wentworth, Earl of Strafford, and Archbishop of Canterbury William Laud:

> The former, as a provincial governor, assumed the mantle of sovereignty in the king's realm of Ireland, in derogation of regal and sovereign authority, and plotted, so to speak, to turn his . . . papists on Rome. The latter erected and maintained an ecclesiastical state within a state—an independent, sovereign sphere of clerical action over and above that emanating from the crown in derogation of the royal supremacy. That both Strafford and Laud acted with the king's complicity and by his leave was conveniently overlooked.

The monarch *himself*, in other words, "could do no wrong—or at least not in early 1641 when articles of impeachment against both these servants of the crown were presented to the Long Parliament."[9] Less than eight years before Charles himself was to be marched to the scaffold, then, treason was still only conceivable as the supreme crime *against* the king, and decidedly *not* as the supreme constitutional crime directly ascribable to the king himself.

Yet, in the end, given the traumata of the "first" civil war and after, this same juridical sense of treasonable behavior *was* to be turned against the king himself. It is suggestive, in this connection, that no one less than the initial parliamentary master strategist John Pym should have all but prophesied such a drastic turn of events as early as 1641 when speaking of the law of attainder brought lethally against Strafford. He alluded to that law, one commentator has written, "as that which unites king and people in a single political body and warned of the dire consequences to the whole political body should the law be subverted or destroyed."[10] Pym himself would not live to see the final fruits of the growing suspicion with which he (and some of his fellows) already regarded the "papistically-inclined" Charles I: as we will see later on, the most radical parliamentarians would in time sever the king's immortal, public capacity from his private, mortal capacity, reduce him to the inferior status of a mere "magistrate," and condemn him to death for having treasonably overstepped the limits of his office in derogation of what was (that is, by 1648/1649) being trumpeted as the *people*'s supreme "sovereignty."[11]

For now, however, we note that social-élitist and constitutional concerns about treating Charles I too harshly, rooted in the political culture of the times, reinforced the legalistic reservations analyzed previously, and in fact they grew as legalistic concerns waned during the war-scarred 1640s. We can see this both on the Presbyterian Right *and* (somewhat more unexpectedly, perhaps) on the Leveller Left. From the Presbyterian viewpoint, there was the tendency, as the conflict between the king and his parliament wore on, to associate war with the threat of social upheaval. Nowhere did this appear more strikingly than in the memoirs of the initially prowar and antiroyalist hotspur Denzil Holles:

> The war, he observed, had undone the ordered harmony of society, had threatened the natural hierarchy. The opening words of his memoirs, written in temporary exile in the winter . . . 1647-8, proclaim Holles's recognition of the connection between war policy and the threat of social revolution, the fulfilment of the "great evil, that servants should ride on horses," a situation in which "the meanest of men, the basest and vilest of the nation, . . . have got the power into their hands; trampled upon the crown; baffled and misused the Parliament; violated the laws; [and] destroyed, or suppressed the nobility and gentry."[12]

Holles's solicitude for "Presbyterian" gentlemen "who had estates which required their looking—after" contrasted sharply with his contempt for the "mercenary Army raised by the Parliament" in which "most of the Colonels and officers [were] mean Tradesmen, Brewers, Taylors, Goldsmiths, Shoemakers and the like; a notable dunghill, if one could rake into it, to find out their several pedigrees."[13] But Holles was scarcely alone in offering such an élitist commentary. "My own endeavors here have been for peace," Sir John Potts had confided to a friend even before hostilities began in 1642; "whensoever necessity shall enforce us to make use of the multitude, I do not promise myself safety."[14] Moreover, numerous Presbyterian divines preaching in London during these increasingly topsy-turvy times rallied, much as did parliamentary Presbyterians, to the safe standard of social hierarchy and deference—as witnessed a sermonizing Edmund Calamy: "We live now in rising times, wherein men raised up from the dunghill doe govern the kingdome almost."[15]

Interestingly—as postmodernists would be quick to stress here—the London Presbyterians' rejection of all escalating talk of regicide in late 1648 was couched in constitutional/ecclesiological as well as in social-élitist terms. Basically, the London divines, looking nostalgically back to the Solemn League and Covenant of 1643 negotiated between John Pym and other leading parliamentarians, on the one hand, and the Scots, on the other, lauded it as the appropriate basis upon which the war against Charles I had (at least initially) been waged:

> as the supreme authority of England rested in the mixed constitution of king, Lords and Commons, the Houses of Parliament were legitimately able to resist a king whose judgement had been perverted by malignant . . . Popish counsel. When this became necessary, as in 1642, parliament had engaged their subjects to fight a defensive . . . war. By commanding subjects in this engagement, parliament had continually declared the legitimate and limited objectives of its aggression against the king. Furthermore, loyal subjects had been obliged to these objectives by a series of oaths and covenants.

Here, the gravamen of the London preachers' complaint against the army—especially in the aftermath of Pride's Purge and in the regicide debate which followed—was that it had "unlawfully" and "sinfully" strayed from the binding principles of the 1643 League and Covenant, hence violating "the ideal of a bounded and reformed monarchy, held in check by a mixed constitution," a monarchy thus "unable to interfere with an autonomous Presbyterian church."[16] Ultimately, however, we can be fairly sure that the idea of the king (in this case, Charles I) as the "keystone in the arch of [social] order" also underlay much of the London preachers' anxiety, and allied them with Presbyterians in the Long Parliament—not to mention with lay Presbyterians from the North negotiating on behalf of Edinburgh.

If, in the end, Presbyterian advocacy of covenant theology, mixed constitutional arrangements favoring an autonomous Presbyterian church, and the traditional social order could do nothing to stop the course of regicide, Leveller agitation on the Left proved equally unavailing. Granted, in his careful reassessment of the Levellers, historian Andrew Sharp portrayed these secular radicals as having, up to Putney (October 1647) and even beyond, "little time for Charles I, for kings, and for kingship." In the eyes of John Lilburne and his confederates, that is, "scripture, reason, and history" argued against the continuation of monarchy in England. "Scripture taught them the basic political and social equality of mankind and their equal access to religious truth. Reason entailed natural equality and freedom. History demonstrated the genesis and continuance of kingship in England in conquest and arbitrary tyranny over 'freeborn Englishmen.'"[17] Yet despite all this, in the months leading up to (and coming after) the regicide, Leveller sentiment on this subject—according to Sharp—shifted remarkably.

This abrupt change in attitudes on the Left toward the possibility (and, soon, the *fait accompli*) of the king's execution seems to have stemmed most basically from the failure of Cromwellian army grandees, on the one hand, and of agitators like Lilburne, Wildman, Overton, and Walwyn, on the other hand, to reach a consensus on constitutional issues at and after Putney—and on the determination of civilian and military Independents to force a regicide through the post-Pride's Purge parliament by what were viewed on the Left as arbitrary, even tyrannical, means. Lilburne had put the whole matter in his inimitable fashion at a conference of army grandees and radicals in September 1648:

> although we should judge the King as arrant a Tyrant as they supposed him, or could imagine him to be; and the parliament as bad as they could make them; yet there being no other balancing power . . . against the Army, but the King and Parliament, it was in our interest to keep one Tyrant to balance another . . . that so we might have something to rest upon, and not suffer the Army . . . and leave no persons nor power to be a counter-balance against them.[18]

In an odd sort of fashion, the invocation here of "balancing" constitutional arrangements by the secular Left recalls for us the similar appeal articulated by London Presbyterians on the moderate Right—all the more so in that, on both sides, it was the victorious and overweening New Model Army that was all too clearly seen as the main threat to such an equilibrium of constitutional forces in England. And, much as in Presbyterian ranks, so in those of secular leftists, the years following upon the regicide of January 30, 1649, would witness bitter disillusionment—a dark mood breeding, at times, armed resistance to the Commonwealth (and Protectorate) that could only prove disastrous.[19]

If elements in seventeenth-century English political culture such as legalism, social élitism, and constitutional scruples seemed to restrain Charles I's multiplying enemies on all sides until fairly late in the day, the structuralist nexus of domestic and foreign politics likewise gave Cromwell and his closest civilian/military associates reasons to pause before embracing the irreversible course of regicide. To begin with, army grandees not overly impressed by the social-élitist anxieties of Presbyterians like Denzil Holles and Edmund Calamy *were* likely to respect the very similar social concerns of what John Adamson has termed "some of the most distinguished members of the 'old nobility'" such as the second Earl of Warwick, current Lord Admiral of the parliament's fleet, the third Earl of Nottingham, descendant of the Lord Admiral who had vanquished the Spanish Armada in 1588, the second Earl of Musgrave, cousin of Lord General Thomas Fairfax, and so on. As Adamson has plausibly argued, such individuals, even in the wake of Pride's Purge, "enjoyed generally cordial relations with the army grandees, and in a world that had not yet fully relinquished its veneration of lineage and rank, they possessed a social eminence and, in the House of Lords, a public platform that gave them a disproportionate influence in politics."[20] Small wonder, then, that, whatever their thoughts about finally settling accounts with the "man of blood," the New Model Army's generals "should have worked hard to mend fences with these aristocratic allies once the Purge had been effected and the immediate threat of a royalist coup had passed."[21]

Moreover, Cromwell and the other army grandees and Independent politicians responsible for guiding English destinies at this juncture had to place likely aristocratic opposition to trying (let alone executing) the king in the larger picture of dialectically interrelated domestic and foreign challenges to their country's security. As Ian Gentles has recently written, those challenges were multifarious as well as urgent, and could easily be construed as arguing powerfully against a regicide:

> So flagrant a defiance of the popular desire for a peaceful settlement would mean that an army would have to be kept perpetually on foot, bringing heavy taxation in its train and inevitable war with Ireland and Scotland. . . . The navy's allegiance was already shaky, and bringing the king to trial could easily tip it into the royalist camp. There was formidable foreign opposition: two of Charles's nephews ruled France and the Netherlands. . . . Within the army itself there were some who argued that having a weak discredited king on the throne would be preferable to executing that king and seeing him replaced with a young heir [i.e., Henry, Duke of Gloucester] over whom they had no power.[22]

Given that (in addition to all these considerations) Cromwell's superior, Lord General Fairfax, adamantly opposed putting the king on trial for his life, we can readily understand the emphatic comment of John Morrill and Philip

Baker, anticipating in this Ian Gentles: "No wonder Cromwell urged caution in moving *to the desired end*."[23] From our theoretical point of view, political culture and the structuralist nexus of domestic and foreign affairs seemed to be working together to ensure such caution.

The fact remains, however, that Morrill and Baker *were* implying here (they are actually more explicit about this at other points) that putting Charles on trial and (possibly) proceeding to execute him *was*, after all, for Oliver, "the desired end." Were they correct in this? We *can* cite a number of factors, both political-cultural and circumstantial, that favored such an outcome. Once again, as in discussing earlier the putative obstacles to a regicide in revolutionary England, we should start with the legalistic and ideological arguments. D. Alan Orr has cited several late sixteenth- and early seventeenth-century treatises, ranging from the Huguenot *Vindiciae Contra Tyrannos* (1579) to Jean Bodin's *The Six Books of a Commonweal* (1606) to Hobbes' *Leviathan* (1651), all of which, Orr has argued, foreshadowed to one extent or another a fundamental transition "from the idea of the ruler 'maintaining his state'—where it simply meant upholding his own position—to the idea that there is a separate legal and constitutional order, that of the State, which the ruler has a duty to maintain."[24] The potential here for the eventual transferal of the allegiance of the *subject* (or, in revolution, *citizen*?) from the *personal* monarch to the *abstract state* as the site of legitimate authority was, patently, enormous—and would in fact bear fruit at Charles I's trial in the form of the *impersonal* statist and protorepublican rhetoric of the king's chief accuser, High Court President John Bradshaw.[25]

Actually, Bradshaw's contractual language, reducing the English king's role from that of God's anointed ruler holding his charge by hereditary right to that of "magistrate" popularly chosen to protect the "people" and preserve the common weal, had both secular and biblical precedents in historic English rhetoric. Patrick Collinson, for instance, has suggested that the prolonged Elizabethan succession crisis had earlier spawned debates in which the monarchy was dampeningly referred to as "a public localised office, like any other form of magistracy," and England was referred to as a "monarchical republic."[26] Patricia Crawford, though she had noted earlier on that the issue of "blood guilt" was useful for royalist and Scottish/Presbyterian as much as for Independent/radical purposes, had agreed that "the discussion of the king's blood guilt undermined his dignity and set him apart from the peace negotiations [in late 1648] as a polluted person." "Recognition of the role of blood guilt," Crawford had concluded, "thus adds a dimension to the conventional accounts of the king's death"—especially when it is invoked to explain the army's frenzied denunciations of Charles I at the famous prayer meeting of April 29, 1648.[27] Sarah Barber, while questioning the tendency of some scholars to see "gentry republican rhetoric" as existing in the counties prior to the regicide, has no less concurred that "the numbers calling for justice against Charles, and the passion of their cry, rose sharply in the summer of 1648," in the London Baptist congregations, to be sure, but above all—as Crawford and others had already argued before Barber—in the victorious Army of the Saints:

> When the second civil war returned the soldiers to action and forced them to fight again a battle which they thought God had given them in 1646, bitterness and emotion pushed them towards the conclusion [that] Charles Stuart was the chief delinquent, responsible for the bloodshed, and the general criticism of kingliness and kings turned into a vicious, regicidal attack, homing in on Charles as an individual. It eventually arrived at the most personalised attack possible. Charles was unlike other men. . . . For Charles, the writing was on the wall.[28]

In a larger sense (as David Scott has recently suggested), secular republicanism and biblical expatiation on blood guilt could conceivably operate *together* to inspire those who, by late 1648, were becoming increasingly insistent on wreaking the ultimate vengeance upon the king.[29]

Still, after all has been duly recorded concerning the ways in which legalistic theorizing, biblical anathemas against "sinful" sovereigns, and élitist and/or popular republican sentiment could operate together to open pathways to the trial and, possibly, execution of Charles I, the essential initiative in this matter lay, in the final analysis, with Cromwell and those of his allies who were *not* (like General Fairfax) inflexibly opposed to such drastic measures. John Morrill and Philip Baker, who have sifted through the pertinent evidence as painstakingly as any scholars, have accepted the main consensus "that Cromwell had never voiced any thought of putting an end to Charles I's rule before October 1647." "We can see no reason to doubt Cromwell's commitment to monarchy in some form before that date," they go on to say, "and no evidence to suggest that he may have had regicide on his mind." Yet the same historians could also conclude, a few pages on, that by November 25, 1648—that is to say, scarcely a year later—Oliver "was resolved to see Charles I put on public trial."[30]

What had happened between these dates? Clearly it was *circumstances*, and not some shift of legalistic or ideological "tectonic plates," that had intervened—the circumstances, that is, associated in geopolitical and domestic/political terms with the king's scheming for and involvement in the "second" civil war of 1648. Hard upon the Putney debates (which had featured, among other things, Cromwell's and Ireton's ever-more-defensive invocation of some form of monarchy) came the devastating news of the king's escape from Hampton Court, his initialing of a treaty with the Scottish opponents of the 1643 Solemn League and Covenant, and—worst of all?—the interception of "treasonous" correspondence between Charles and Henrietta-Maria. The army grandees, it seemed all too obvious, had been rudely deceived by the king, and it was with *that* burning realization in mind that they went forth to defeat one and all in the months ahead. Once it was all over, Oliver, in a letter of November 20, 1648, at Knottingley (near Pontefract), penned bitter words to Robert Jenner and John Ashe in London that augured very ill indeed for the still reigning but now twice-defeated monarch:

> the former quarrel was that Englishmen might rule over one another: this [war] to vassalise us to a foreign Nation. And their fault who have appeared in this Summer's business is certainly double to theirs who were in the first, because it is the repetition of the same offence against all the witnesses that God has borne, by making and abetting a Second War.[31]

No wonder, then, that in seeking to explain Oliver's change of heart toward the king, Morrill and Baker should have pointed to a "coincidence": on the same day that the angry words quoted here were sent on their way to London, the Army's *Remonstrance* was being delivered to the politicians at Westminster. "That theme of the wickedness of the king in seeking foreign arms and giving undertakings to foreigners, starting with the Scots," Morrill and Baker noted, "was at the heart of the indictment of Charles in that *Remonstrance* and it was to appear in the charge against him two months later."[32]

Yet did resolving to put Charles I on trial automatically translate, by late 1648, into an insistence that he be beheaded? C. V. Wedgwood, whose account of the king's trial has been a standard reference on the subject for over fifty years, seemed sure that it did: "Cromwell's conduct during these last days of December," she wrote confidently, "suggests not that he wished to save Charles, but that he wished to bring him to justice with some plausible appearance of legality and Parliamentary consent."[33] More recently, however, scholarly inquiry has yielded some doubts about this. From Morrill and Baker, once again, we have this: "Did Cromwell want to see the king put on trial? Yes. . . . Did he want Charles to cease to be king? *Yes, either by deposition or abdication.* Did he want to see the king dead? *Yes and no—yes in that he deserved it, no in that it might shipwreck the very civil and religious liberties it was intended to safeguard.*"[34] Sean Kelsey's analyses of the *procedure* of the trial, staged at Westminster, have led him to similar conclusions. "The trial preliminaries revealed just how little appetite there was for shedding the blood of England's anointed sovereign," he has written. "Preparations were made for a proceeding from which the King's person, perhaps even some of the authority of his office, if not necessarily his own good name, might emerge unscathed." It was Charles's "almost pathological incapacity to forbear meddling in the quarrels of his enemies," Kelsey reluctantly concluded, that "was to be his undoing."[35]

Yet it may ultimately have been *geopolitics* in the unnerving form of yet *another* civil war envisioned by the unendingly duplicitous Charles I that sealed his fate. True, David Scott resisted this conclusion at one point, holding that "regional concerns or the stresses and strains of British politics" did not necessarily provide "the most compelling motives for regicide. Pride of place in that respect should probably go to Puritan wrath at the king's pride and intransigence in the face of his blood guilt and the evidences of divine providence."[36] Yet, however much this (postmodernist?) assertion might seem to accord with the prior findings of Patrick Collinson, Patricia Crawford, Sarah Barber, and others, Scott conceded at another point that it was likely the prospect of a *third* civil war that moved the Cromwellian statesmen finally in the direction of regicide. In doing so, he agreed with his colleague John Adamson; where the two historians fell out was over the specific question of whether the primary foreign threat in this regard emanated from Scotland or from Ireland.

For Scott, it was the "notion of a reinvigorated regnal union" bringing together England, Ireland, and Scotland, and the king's *apparent* warming to this concept, that did him the most harm. In Scott's version of events, it was the envisaged influence of Edinburgh, more than that of Dublin, that proved in the end to be especially fatal to Charles I's cause:

> Where the Irish were concerned this would probably have entailed some degree of internal political autonomy, with Charles and his prerogative powers providing the only link between England and Ireland. But the Scots, even the Hamiltonians, wanted something more akin to James I's union of crowns. In other words, a larger Scottish presence at the English court; a greater say in the upbringing of Prince Charles; and a stronger voice in royal counsels at Whitehall. The king's willingness to make these concessions, even in defeat, and his refusal to abjure his "foreign" allies raised the spectre of a fourth Scottish invasion.[37]

Perhaps, Scott accordingly mused, it was the regicides' (misplaced) hope that the king's death would dissolve this union and *forever* terminate the "threat of Scottish confederalism" that finally steeled Cromwell and his closest comrades to carry on to the January 30 execution.

Yet John Adamson has couched *his* reading of the situation in a larger (and more persuasive) geopolitical context by keying upon the *Irish* rather than the Scottish connection. "Holding the ring" in *this* version of events was longtime royalist conspirator James Butler, since 1642 the First Marquess of Ormond. Upon returning to Ireland in September 1648 after parleys with the king, Ormond attempted to pull together the multifarious strands of a pro-Stuart alliance that was clearly aimed at encircling and destroying the Independent/parliamentary forces in London and southeastern England. The "junto" of army grandees and their civilian adherents, Adamson has written, "had good reason to be frightened," especially after learning (in December) of successful negotiations bringing together Irish, Dutch (and, possibly, Scottish?) supporters of Charles I:

> Under the terms of the new treaty, rebel-held Ireland was allied defensively with what was probably the world's greatest maritime power. Encouraged by the Stadholder, Prince Willem II of Orange-Nassau, Charles I's forceful and politically ambitious son-in-law, the States-General was already providing a base for royalist naval activity against the parliamentarian regime. It was also expected, in the event of a final treaty being concluded between Kilkenny and the Irish royalists, that the Confederacy would use its own shipping to reinforce the royalist fleet.

Parliament, as a result of all these machinations, was facing "an almost certain alliance of Irish, royalist, and Dutch naval forces, effectively encircling southern England from the Irish sea to the northern approaches to the Channel."[38] There may be much to Adamson's contention that when the news of Ormond's success in finally tying together the many strands of his royalist plot reached London in late January—and when it became clear that Charles would *not* disavow Ormond's negotiations—the king's fate was irredeemably sealed. "For if the king remained adamant that he would not disband the anti-parliamentarian alliance in Ireland," Adamson concluded, "the 'junto' in England were left with no alternative but to dismantle it by force. . . . Take away Charles I and, at a stroke, the lynchpin of the anti-Independent coalition was removed."[39]

Perhaps the safest conclusion to derive from all this rapidly accumulating speculation on the Cromwellian group's motivation going forth in January 1649 is that of Ian Gentles, reached in his 2011 biography of the future Lord Protector:

> Three immediate factors reinforced Cromwell's conviction. . . . First was the constant pressure emanating from the army for vengeance against the king for his treason and blood guilt. . . . Second was Charles's refusal to abandon the Scottish interest after God's judgement upon his cause at Preston. Third was the ever-looming menace of the Marquess of Ormond and his popish Irish army. . . . At this point . . . the critical issue was not the king's guilt for what he had done in the past, but whether or not he would refrain from planning a future war. It was Charles's refusal both to abandon the Scots and to order Ormond to desist from his military preparations that clinched the perception of providential "necessity" in Cromwell's mind.[40]

The comparativist, by the way, may note with amusement the New Model Army's infuriated reaction to a letter from Ormond to Fairfax threatening a violent chastisement of grandees, army rank-and-file, and parliament alike should "one hair of His Majesty's head fall to the ground by their means"; this so clearly will remind him/her of similar dire royalist warnings to be conveyed on Louis XVI's behalf to the Parisian revolutionaries 143 years later in the so-called Brunswick Manifesto![41]

A final indication of the supreme importance of *circumstances* in the undoing of Charles I lies in the very nature of the charges brought against him at his trial. "There can be no doubt," D. Alan Orr has persuasively argued, "that Charles' principal sin was the levying of war. The other allegations of murder, rape and the destruction of property were ancillary to this. Charles was tried largely for bringing war and its attendant destruction on the land."[42] Moreover, any careful reading of the formal accusation presented to the High Court on January 20, 1649, by the clerk, John Cook, takes us inevitably back to the damning *chronology* of the "second" (and presentiments of a "third"?) civil war laid now unequivocally at the king's account by those authorities who at this crucial juncture *really* mattered (i.e., Cromwell and the other Army grandees):

> By which cruel and unnatural wars by him (the said Charles Stuart) levied, continued and renewed as aforesaid, much innocent blood of the free people of this nation hath been spilt, many families have been undone, the public treasury wasted and exhausted, trade obstructed and miserably decayed, vast expense and damage to the nation incurred, and many parts of the land spoiled, some of them even to desolation. And for further prosecution of his said evil designs, he (the said Charles Stuart) doth still continue his commissions to the said Prince [of Wales] and other rebels and revolters, both English and foreigners, and to the Earl of Ormonde and to the Irish rebels and revolters associated with him, from whom further invasions upon this land are threatened upon the procurement and on the behalf of the said Charles Stuart.[43]

And so on. Charles I, redefined now as "chief magistrate" of the redefined "popular state" of England, and tasked in that capacity with England's preservation, had finally—and, we sense, irrevocably—been found fatally wanting. For this deficiency, the Cromwellians and other radicalized Independents could now imagine only the ultimate punishment.

Thus, in a process marked "by that peculiarly English preoccupation with the maintenance of traditional legal forms and procedures," one incorrigible English king was brought to book—in starkly dangerous circumstances. By deploying here the kind of political-cultural analysis associated today with postmodernism *and* the kind of state-security analysis associated with structuralism, we have evaluated (relatively) the forces militating against and in favor of Charles I's execution. And however intriguing we may find Sarah Barber's speculation that "regicidal thinking [at least in England] was reactionary in the sense that it was conservative," and that, consequently, monarchy *as such* might in theory have been preserved at this time with the "right" member of the Stuart family on the throne, we know, in fact, that this is *not* what transpired during the 1649 to 1660 period.[44] Moreover, we are more likely to leave this section of chapter 3 recalling Ian Gentle's recent conclusion that "the critical issue" by 1649 "was not the king's guilt for what he had done in the past, but whether or not he would refrain from planning a future war." In the final analysis, then, it was *circumstances* in their most brutally menacing form, rather than any tendencies in the political culture of those times, that sealed Charles's fate.

LOUIS XVI AND THE CONTENTIOUS COURSE OF REVOLUTIONARY LEGAL PROCEDURE

Can we also speak, in the case of revolutionary France, of a "preoccupation" with maintaining "traditional legal forms and procedures" that was (in consequence) not "peculiarly English" at all? To some extent, the answer seems to have been "yes"; undoubtedly, the clear majority of members of the newly elected National Convention in late 1792 proved in the end to be every bit as determined as their counterparts in mid-seventeenth-century England had been to give their erring and duplicitous monarch a hearing in a trial procedure. In this situation, however, some of the most radicalized and theoretically advanced Jacobins (such as Louis-Antoine Saint-Just and Maximilien Robespierre) attempted to alter the script in unprecedented fashion. Before considering their intervention in the Convention's trial of Louis XVI, however, we need once again to reconsider the political-cultural and circumstantial forces militating against and in favor of subjecting an anointed and formerly "absolute" king to formal judicial procedure in revolutionary times.

First, however, one obvious difference between the English and French situations needs to be underscored: "the English ... brought a reigning king to the bar," Michael Walzer pointed out over forty years ago, "while the French Convention officially summoned *citizen* Louis Capet."[45] In other words, the French, unlike their English predecessors, had *institutionally* done away with monarchy well in advance of deciding, definitively, to put their now *erstwhile* monarch on trial for his life. That, for Louis XVI, this distinction could hardly bode well followed logically enough from events in the first tumultuous years of the Revolution, which had revealed a king opposed to any major deviation from a deeply engrained philosophy of divine-right monarchy, *privilège*, and social inequality.[46] Munro Price, whose personal discovery of private papers of the king's and queen's closest confidants—Count Axel von Fersen, the marquis de Bombelles, and above all the baron de Breteuil—reads like a riveting action novella in itself, has been unequivocal (and, it would seem, unchallengeable) on this cardinal point:

> Many contemporaries, and subsequent historians, have claimed that at various points after 1789 Louis XVI and Marie Antoinette were prepared to compromise with their more moderate opponents, and settle the Revolution on the

basis of an English-style monarchy resting on a bicameral legislature. Breteuil's unpublished letters and memoranda make it absolutely clear that this was never contemplated.... Louis XVI and Marie Antoinette have often been portrayed as weak and vacillating. Far from it; their policy between 1789 and 1792 was entirely consistent, and highly conservative. They were prepared to die for their beliefs, and ultimately did so.[47]

Under such circumstances, Price has concluded, the "royal authority" as still upheld by the royal couple "could only have been restored by civil war or foreign invasion."[48]

We might, therefore, expect to find fewer factors obstructing a decision to try and (conceivably) execute an already dethroned French monarch in late 1792 than we found to be obstructing the earlier decision (in late 1648) to prosecute a still formally reigning (and, of course, still actively defiant) English king; such was indeed the case. Still, there *were* various considerations of a political-cultural and state-security nature invoked to spare Louis XVI a trial and, in the worst instance, the guillotine.

To begin with, Michael Walzer (anticipating in this the analysis later developed by historian Orr in the case of Charles I) discussed the law of treason in his *Regicide and Revolution* (1974). In a gloss equally applicable to England *and* to France, Walzer argued that "under the old regime no laws more perfectly expressed the king's embodiment of the state than did the laws of treason. Although the king could not be conceived to commit any crime, treason was peculiarly alien to him, for it was a crime against his own person."[49] If, Walzer went on to explain, the Long Parliament in the English Revolution had dealt with the Earl of Strafford and Archbishop Laud in a manner that had *not* prevented it, later on, from portraying the *administrative state*, rather than the king, as the ultimate victim of "treason," the French revolutionaries paradoxically may have found their *own* dealings with a "treasonous" Louis XVI more complicated *procedurally* due to their promulgation of a new criminal code and, most notably, of the Constitution of 1791.

This is constitutional territory that a legion of historians—Michael Walzer, Alison Patrick, David Jordan, Ferenc Fehér, Mona Ozouf, and Dan Edelstein, among others—have had to traverse over the years. Patrick's review of the issues is especially lucid. As she noted, the "great stumbling block" in the way of meting out truly revolutionary justice to Louis XVI lay in Articles 2 and 5 of Chapter II of the new Constitution. Article 2 said explicitly that "The person of the king is inviolable and sacred," and Article 5 specified "only three ways in which he could lose his throne: (a) by not taking an oath to the constitution within a designated period, or by retracting it after he had taken it; (b) by leading an armed force against the nation, or by failing to oppose such an undertaking in his name; or (c) by leaving the kingdom and failing to return." The problem for the revolutionaries was that, under these provisions, Louis XVI could be tried as an ordinary citizen *only* for post-abdication (i.e., post August 10, 1792) offenses that (in fact) he could *not* have had the opportunity to commit—and *not* for alleged offenses committed earlier than that, "for which the only penalty prescribed was the loss of the throne."[50] Hence, the strategy of about twenty delegates hoping to save the king was to assert that these constitutional provisions "made the trial of the king for the acts for which he was admittedly responsible a legal and moral impossibility." As Patrick carefully explained the situation:

> His inviolability had been established with the Constitution, and he had lost it only with the throne on 10 August [1792], since when he had self-evidently been unable to do anything which might justify a trial; or alternatively, he could not be tried because there was no law in existence applicable to a man in his position. He could not be tried by existing law because this law did not cover kings; none could be created for the purpose because it would then be retroactive and therefore essentially unjust; and to try him by "the law of nature," as many deputies suggested, would be to put him in a situation where no rules existed, and would result, like the September massacres, in simple murder.[51]

In the end, of course, most *Conventionnels* saw in such tortuous arguments only the tactics of delay, and they reacted accordingly. In fact, every citation of Articles 2 and 5 of Chapter II of the 1791 Constitution could be trumped by citations of Article VI of the prior (and by now sacrosanct) Declaration of the Rights of Man and the Citizen of 1789: "the law must be the same for all." If it *was* the same for all, as Michael Walzer has reasonably enough queried, "how could the king be deposed and nothing more for acts that would have been the death of any other man?"[52]

Interestingly enough, for those *Conventionnels* trying to block the trial and execution of Louis XVI on constitutional grounds, knowing what the Cromwellian Independents had done to Charles I back in 1648 and 1649 came usefully into play. As Patrick put it, these deputies "could assert that the members of the Long Parliament had fatally prejudiced their case by arrogating to themselves an authority which could not rightfully be theirs; thus their "court" had no authority, and they lost the support they should have gained from associating the whole English people with the fate of their king." The result, so these deputies claimed, had been (after the regicide itself) the unprecedented tyranny of Oliver Cromwell—followed (ironically enough) by the Restoration, as personified in Charles II and James II![53] As it turned out, however, Jacobins like Jean-Baptiste Mailhe were quite ready to deflect this line of argumentation by insisting that the English Parliament of 1648 should have in effect "anticipated" the revolutionaries of 1792 by calling for "a Convention representing the sovereign people, which would then have had every right to deal as it wished with Charles I." Such a Convention, embodying the "sovereign people," would have rendered a fully appropriate judgment on Charles I.[54] In this whole debate, as Alison Patrick has so astutely observed, "the greatest play was made with the aftermath of Charles I's execution, which was familiar to all deputies; the Convention was as nervous of a possible Cromwell as the post-1917 Russians were to be of a possible Bonaparte."[55] Palpably, certain protagonists on both sides in this constitutional debate over the dethroned Louis XVI's fate were willing to play the game of "comparative revolutions" insofar as it applied to England and France; yet this in itself appears not to have significantly altered the course of events at this momentous juncture in revolutionary France.

But what about *social-élitist* and/or *popular* opposition to the prosecution of the *ci-devant* king of France? Can we find, in the situation at Paris in late 1792, a *socially based*, eleventh-hour resistance to this drift of events spanning the political spectrum from moderate Right to Left such as that which had (improbably) aligned Presbyterians with Levellers at London in late 1648? The answer appears to be that we *can* find such resistance to a possible French regicide on the moderate Right, but definitely *not* on the Left. Certainly, historians of the Girondists have divined in their vocal (if politically disastrous) delaying tactics on the fate of Louis XVI a dash of social conservatism reminiscent of the élitist stance of Denzil Holles and other Presbyterians in revolutionary England. As David Jordan (among other scholars) observed, this took the form primarily of invective aimed against the plebeian *sans-culotterie* of Paris. "The Girondins," remarked Jordan, "were the first to propose arming one part of the population against the other. They were the first to insist that the antagonisms between the provinces and Paris were irreconcilable, and in fact they encouraged such antagonisms. They were the first to propose seeking support outside the Convention for its actions." As far as the Girondists were concerned, Jordan flatly concluded, "Paris meant social revolution, violence, egalitarianism, the triumph of the vulgar and brutal—in a word, Paris meant the September Massacres."[56] In eventually arguing for an appeal to the nation on the king's fate, however, the leading Girondists were really allowing themselves to be used by those most unappeasable avatars of social conservatism in revolutionary France, the provincial royalists.[57]

But the analogy here fails once we attempt to extend it to the Parisian *sans-culottes*. In light of the scholarship of Albert Soboul and specialists following in his wake, we would find it difficult indeed to detect in the social attitudes of Parisian artisans, shopkeepers, and workers in late 1792 and early 1793 anything at all similar to John Lilburne's belated conversion to the antiregicide cause in revolutionary England.[58] In part, this likely reflected the fact that the trial and regicide in France occurred *earlier in the revolutionary process* than it did in England, and thus could not pose for plebeian types as clear-cut a question of "governmental bureaucratic overreach" as did the trial and execution of Charles I in the England of 1648 and 1649; in part, it probably resulted from the simple fact that it was *civilian politicians*, and *not* army grandees such as Cromwell and others, inclined to resolve issues with military force, who still controlled public affairs in France. Whatever the reasons, we do not encounter in the case of France the same opposition to regicide spanning the political spectrum that we could cite in the case of England. Stating this, nevertheless, in no way palliates the folly of the Girondist politicians in the first year of the Convention: their demonization of the Parisian *sans-culottes* in a time of national wartime emergency, jeopardizing as it did the popular support for the French government, was one of a host of spectacular political miscalculations that lighted them the way to dusty death.[59]

To raise the issue of the national wartime emergency in revolutionary France is, unavoidably, to turn to *geopolitical* factors and to ask if they in any way acted as a deterrent to putting Louis XVI on trial for his life. Undeniably, arguments citing such factors *were* advanced by Girondists and by others in the Convention wishing to save the king from the rigors and possible consequences of such a drastic judicial procedure. Alison Patrick's summary of these arguments should immediately recall for us the debate in revolutionary England over the fate of Charles I. "A number of deputies argued that alive, Louis was a useful hostage and a possible pawn for use in peace negotiations; dead, he could be used by foreign princes to persuade their peoples that the war [i.e., against France] was a just one, and his death would probably provoke England and Spain into open hostility. Louis alive was unpopular and ineffective; dead, he might serve the purposes of all the enemies of the revolutionary regime."[60] Why needlessly augment the ranks of France's enemies? But, once again, those wishing to apply strict justice to the *ci-devant* monarch were ready with their response. Hoisting their opponents with their own petard, they insisted that, far from jeopardizing French security in Europe, executing Louis would, if anything, reinforce it. English and Spanish hostility to Paris, they maintained, depended not at all upon what happened to Louis XVI; it had other, more selfish roots. Trying and executing Louis as a traitor to his own people, by proclaiming to Europe that wearing a crown was no protection against punishment for treason, was the best way to fortify the Republic's position in an always-dangerous Europe—a Europe that was still besotted with "tyranny" and superstition.[61]

We will return later on to the *geostrategic* roots of regicide in revolutionary France. But first, as we continue to reassess factors militating against or in favor of regicide in relative terms, we need to review, in the French case as we did earlier in the English case, political-cultural forces *favoring* such an outcome. Much of what specialists such as Quentin Skinner, Michael Braddick, and D. Alan Orr have written concerning the desacralization of English monarchism and the assertion of impersonal and even (in some measure) protorepublican English statism in the sixteenth and seventeenth centuries applies equally well to developments in France, and has been extended to the "enlightened" eighteenth century by French specialists such as Dale K. Van Kley, Jeffrey W. Merrick, and Roger Chartier.[62] Anticipating all of these latter historians, Michael Walzer contended that, "What happened in the royal household of the last years was simply that the royal embodiment lost its mythic qualities, even before the king himself lost his power to command. . . . [T]he king was still absolute. But he could no longer act out the ideology that made absolutism credible."[63] This was so, Walzer suggested, both because of "transformations in society as a whole" *and* because of "the inability of the court to reflect those transformations, to attract the new men or to shape the changing opinions of the nation."[64] Or, as Enlightenment scholar Robert Darnton has put it succinctly: "The magic had gone out of the Bourbons by the reign of Louis XVI."[65]

Perhaps this was true, at least up to a point. Yet we have to remember—in the French case, as in the English case—that the king in question embarked on the revolutionary experience as a ruler still blessed with mythic, semi-divine qualities in the eyes of many (probably, most?) of his subjects—and with a genuine reservoir of good will to fall back on in both élitist and plebeian ranks of society. Only in the testing times of revolutionary upheaval did Louis squander most of that good will. Clearly, one giant step along this dolorous path was the ill-advised "flight to Varennes" in June 1791. Timothy Tackett has recently written that "the king's flight . . . enormously reinforced the arguments of all those who held to a conspiratorial view of the world," and concluded that retrospective inquiry into the affair divulged, for all to see, "a pattern of boldfaced deceit on the part of Louis himself."[66] Admittedly, the Constituent Assemblymen, loath to confront honestly the existential question mark posed for all of their reformist labors by the royal family's apparent attempt to flee the kingdom, gave Louis XVI a second chance by "reinstating" him as king in September. Yet the enduring damage done to monarchy in France by this incident was suggested in the remarks delivered by Charles de Lameth to his fellow-deputies on June 21: "At present," insisted Lameth, "we are compelled to assume both legislative and executive powers. In periods of crisis, one cannot subject oneself rigorously to the forms of the law, as one would necessarily do in a period of calm. . . . It is better to commit a momentary injustice than to see the loss of the state itself."[67] One traumatic event, it would seem, had done more to confirm the impression of desacralized monarchy and the increasing ascendancy of *abstract statism* in France than could all the philosophizing of the preceding two or three centuries.

But an even more critical step along the road toward desacralization (and, ultimately, regicide) was taken in the short-lived Legislative Assembly of 1791 to 1792 with the antiroyalist rodomontade of the Brissotin deputies—

many of whom, in the Convention of the following year, would be belatedly—and so ironically—striving to save the life of the very king they themselves had so recently been determined to discredit. In late 1791 and early 1792, however, these Girondists-of-the-near-future were out to raise a national demand for war with the traditional enemy Austria, hoping thereby to overthrow the royalist and pacific Feuillant ministers, seize state power for themselves, and so consummate the revolution on their own (rather nebulous) terms. From the very start, this meant that orators such as Jacques-Pierre Brissot himself, Isnard, Vergniaud, Gensonné, Condorcet, Roland, and so on predicated their strategy on their well-founded suspicion that the king's acceptance of the Constitution of 1791 was utterly insincere. But to drive this point home (and this, in the present context, is especially pertinent), they unrelentingly challenged Louis XVI on issues that left him no room for compromise. Thus, the increasingly acidulous exchanges between Brissotin firebrands and sovereign on such questions as the political loyalties of the king's brothers, the comtes de Provence and Artois, the status of all aristocratic émigrés, and the fate of those "refractory" churchmen unable to stomach the Revolution's Civil Constitution of the Clergy.[68] The impact of such rhetoric, unsurprisingly, was further to besmirch the king's already sullied reputation—especially as this rhetoric was accompanied by an increasingly vitriolic campaign, in the assembly and in the popular press, against the king's Austrian Habsburg queen, Marie-Antoinette.[69]

To some extent, then, the abolition of monarchy in France in favor of statist republicanism in September 1792—and the decision, taken soon thereafter in the popularly elected Convention, to put the erstwhile king on trial for his life—were prefigured from a *constitutional/ideological* point of view. But, in revolutionary France as in revolutionary England, it was *state-security* considerations that were most pivotal in determining the course of events. Both John Hardman and Munro Price have identified the French victory over the Prussians at Valmy (September 22, 1792) and the discovery at the Tuileries of the notorious *armoire de fer* holding Louis XVI's correspondence with domestic counterrevolutionaries as developments that sealed the ex-monarch's fate.[70] On December 3, the Convention formally decreed that Louis should be put on trial, primarily on the charge of "conspiring against liberty and . . . against the safety of the state."[71] As Alison Patrick has commented, "if Louis were not in some sense implicated in counterrevolutionary activity, the insurrection of 10 August and the existence of the Convention itself had no justification." Furthermore, as she also noted, "the trial was a useful weapon for the opponents of the Gironde, the Girondins being more influential in the Convention in its early weeks than they were ever to be again."[72] Another way of making this latter point would be to say that, in a supremely ironic turn of events, the selfsame dialectic between international and domestic political forces seized upon previously (and so eagerly) by the formerly prowar Brissotin militants of the Legislative Assembly for their own purposes was starting now to play perilously *against* them, as they belatedly strove to squelch or at the very least mitigate proceedings in the Convention against the now-dethroned Louis XVI.

In fact, as we know today, the eventual decision of the Convention to do with Louis XVI what the purged Rump Parliament had done with Charles I—that is, put him on trial for his life—was (*unlike* the decision in the English case) adopted as a compromise between two more extreme courses of action. On the Right, as we have seen, were the Girondists, unrealistically and disastrously arguing against any procedure at all, or at least against any resort to the scaffold. On the Left, as we shall see in our remarks further on, were those most ideologically inclined Jacobins like Louis-Antoine Saint-Just and Maximilien Robespierre, who inveighed against granting the former king formal judicial procedure precisely because they wanted him dispatched *summarily* as guilty of *kingship as such* rather than of traditionally defined (and procedurally proven) treason. Most of the deputies, however, opted in the end for a course of action much more in line with the English precedent. Michael Walzer, who has analyzed the debates of the *Conventionnels* on this powerfully emblematic question as thoroughly as anyone, has presented the drift of discussion in the Convention in the following terms:

> In the course of the trial, one senses among these centrist delegates who wavered uneasily between the Mountain and the Gironde a growing conviction not only that Louis was ... guilty ... but that he was indeed ... dangerous.... It could not be said that his opposition had ceased merely because he had been captured. He remained the center of all counter-revolutionary activity even in his prison and whatever his personal intentions (and the evidence found in the secret cabinet hardly suggested that his intentions were good). His kingship would be a living reality for many of his subjects so long as he himself was alive; his name was a rallying cry even while he was locked up.[73]

John Bradshaw had argued in much the same starkly practical, state-security vein against Charles I over 140 years before. It may be true, as Patrick has opined, that the *Conventionnels* were sufficiently "well read in the humanitarian literature of their century" to be "reluctant" to pronounce death against Louis, but, given what they knew of his treasonous behavior, and given their ongoing *political* need to remain in the vanguard of the revolutionary drive for "liberty, equality, and fraternity," what alternative course of action could they have possibly embraced?[74]

Yet if the Convention (by a one-vote margin!) eventually *did* render the ultimate verdict against its one-time sovereign, it did not do so before hearing outspoken Jacobin ideologues like Saint-Just and Robespierre anathematize all kings *as kings* and *theorize* the revolutionary process in ways that had *not* been anticipated at the trial of Charles I. In a speech of November 13 that momentarily stunned his listeners in the Convention, Saint-Just held forth in this original and inflammatory manner:

> I say that the king should be judged as an enemy; that we must not so much judge him as combat him; that, as he had no part in the contract which united the French people, the forms of judicial procedure here are not to be sought in positive law, but in the law of nations. . . . The social contract is between citizen and citizen, not between citizen and government. A contract affects only those whom it binds. As a consequence, Louis, who was not bound, cannot be judged in civil law.

"*No man can reign innocently,*" Saint-Just famously went on to proclaim. "The folly is all too evident. Every king is a rebel and a usurper. . . . These are the considerations which a great and republican people ought not to forget when judging a king."[75] Kings, in other words, were beyond the pale of humanity and humanity's contractualism; as such, they should also be excluded from formal judicial procedure.

A few weeks later, Robespierre, in a speech of December 3, took Saint-Just's argument one step farther by portraying the *legitimacy* of *any* trial of the king as amounting, essentially, to a repudiation of the *legitimacy* of the (French) revolutionary process *itself*:

> Louis cannot be judged; he has already been condemned, else the Republic is not cleared of guilt. To propose a trial for Louis XVI of any sort whatever is to step backward toward royal and constitutional despotism. Such a proposal is counter-revolutionary since it would bring the revolution itself before the court. In fact, if Louis could . . . be tried, he might be found innocent. Do I say "found"? He is presumed innocent until the verdict. If Louis is acquitted, where then is the revolution? If Louis is innocent, all defenders of liberty are slanderers. . . . The members of the Federation, the people of Paris, all the patriots of the French empire, are guilty, and this great trial . . . is at last decided in favor of crime and tyranny.[76]

To us today, how anticipatory this all seems to be of Lenin's proclamation, in later Russian revolutionary times, that ex-tsar Nicholas II merited no trial, was outside the pale of humanity, and so must be swiftly dispatched so as not to compromise the *legitimacy* of the revolutionary process *itself*! Here was *theory* taken to an extreme, a postmodernist might say; more significantly, however, here—for the structuralist at least—was *revolutionary raison d'état* taken to an extreme.

And this was not all; for in this jeremiad of December 3, 1792, against *all* royalty Robespierre also began (at a certain distance, to be sure) to presage the subsequent Marxian (and Leninist) conception of the revolutionary "dictatorship of the proletariat":

> Citizens, take care! . . . You . . . confuse the condition of a people in the midst of a revolution with a people whose government is firmly established. . . .
>
> Among a peaceful people free and respected both within and without their country, it would be possible to listen to the counsel of generosity which you are given. But a people which is still struggling for its liberty after so much sacrifice and so many battles; a people among whom the laws are not yet inexorable save for the unfortunate . . . must wish to be avenged.[77]

As a phalanx of historians have pointed out over the years, this Robespierrist differentiation between a people still desperately engaged in revolutionary struggle and a people enjoying the hard-won benefits of peaceful republicanism would be much more fully elaborated in the Incorruptible's celebrated speech "On the Principles of Revolutionary Government," delivered almost exactly a year later (on December 25, 1793) to the Convention.[78]

Obviously, however, the Convention as a whole was not prepared to endorse such *ultra-statist* theorizing on revolutionary issues as was offered by the likes of Saint-Just and Robespierre. True, as Dan Edelstein has recently written, Robespierre in particular "was essentially calling on the state to execute the king on the basis of revolutionary authority," and that "revolutionary authority" *in itself,* once firmly institutionalized, "could be used to establish a normative framework for state action that overrode constitutional and any other legal principles."[79] But that was an issue for future revolutionary theorists and leaders to ponder. Alison Patrick has, in contrast, portrayed a majority reaction in the Convention to such argumentation that, if anything, recalls English procedural-mindedness more than it prefigures the crude *raison d'état* of Bolsheviks like Trotsky and Lenin:

> The proposal that Louis be disposed of by executive decree, without a trial of any sort, was brushed aside . . . by majority opinion. Robespierre's argument that to try the king was to put 10 August on trial was logically unassailable but morally inadmissible; he could not be condemned unheard. The suggestion that this be done was put forward by the brothers Robespierre, but, as far as one can gather from the documents, by very few others. . . . Outside Paris, fewer than a dozen Montagnards took Robespierre's line; these included Robert Lindet, but not, among other well-known members of the Jacobin Club, Couthon, Hentz, J. B. Lacoste, Le Cointre, Merlin of Douai, or Pierre-Louis Prieur.

Indeed, Patrick has hypothesized, the Incorruptible himself may have viewed his address of December 3 more as a "shock tactic," to get the king's trial finally underway, than as a *cri de coeur* articulating a set of nonnegotiable principles on the nature of kingship and the revolutionary process.[80]

In any case, those *Conventionnels* wavering uneasily between Left and Right got their way: the trial of Louis XVI went forward, the former king was judged guilty, a popular appeal of the verdict was rejected, the deputies voted for regicide by the narrowest of margins, and the act was consummated on January 21, 1793. Whether Louis XVI's execution had at least a modicum of "justice" attached to it (procedurally *and politically*) is still debated among historians. Michael Walzer stoutly maintained the affirmative, at least in some measure: "the decision to try the king," he contended, "was also a decision to adopt the formal rules of the judicial process . . . specific charges were brought against the king and evidence was collected to substantiate them; the king and his lawyers were informed of the charges and of the evidence; and Louis was permitted to defend himself in detail and in public against them." This is "hardly a sufficient description of legal fairness," Walzer conceded, "but it is a partial description."[81] Moreover, he insisted, the trial of the ex-king was *not*, as some writers before him had already argued, the beginning of the Jacobin Terror. Perhaps not, but others have rejected such conclusions. Ferenc Fehér, for instance, has stated emphatically that, at least in a *political* sense, the trial and execution of Louis XVI was "a superfluous, rather irrelevant act which solved no problems for the republic," whereas in a *historical* sense "the personal decapitation of an institution can only be crucial for those who intend to crush a tradition by symbolic acts, in other words for those who want to substitute a new mythology for an old one."[82] Yet, new myths, Fehér added, may turn out to be *more* rather than *less* oppressive than the ones they violently replace. Susan Dunn has reasoned along much the same lines, referring to the "traumatic rupture with the past, symbolized by the regicide, and . . . the fratricidal conflict and deep and lasting political divisions that the regicide left in its wake."[83] Perhaps, she continued with more than a touch of irony, the Jacobins, in attempting to desacralize the French monarchy, only "resacralized" it and "revalorized" the dead king "in a different form."[84] The scholarly exchanges on this polarizing subject have endured to the present day and are likely to go on *ad infinitum*.

In reviewing both the English and the French regicides, we have demonstrated that the kinds of political-cultural analysis associated today with postmodernism and statist analysis associated now with structuralism can be utilized to reevaluate the forces that militated against and in favor of these drastic revolutionary actions. In the final analysis, however, we have discovered that, in both cases, structural *state-security* factors were decisive. We will now find that, in the case of Russian regicide, state-security concerns were, if anything, even more decisive: the most audacious theorizing of men like Saint-Just and Robespierre, reformulated during 1917 to 1918 under the unprecedentedly extreme pressure of events by Leon Trotsky and Vladimir I. Lenin, first bore full revolutionary fruit.

NICHOLAS II AND THE INVOCATION OF EXTREME REVOLUTIONARY *RAISON D'ÉTAT*

If, in his massive history of the Russian revolution, veteran Harvard historian Richard Pipes had necessarily to admit that two other European sovereigns prior to Nicholas II had also "lost their lives in consequence of revolutionary upheavals," this was, for him, the extent of any comparison to be drawn between the deaths of Charles I and Louis XVI, on the one hand, and that of Tsar Nicholas, on the other. The "superficial features of events" in these three crises might be familiar, wrote Pipes, but all else was "unique." "Nicholas II was neither charged nor tried. The Soviet Government, which had condemned him to death, . . . never published the relevant documents. . . . The deed, perpetrated in the dead of night, resembled more a gangster type massacre than a formal execution."[85] It would be hard to find much fault with Pipes's indictment of an event that saw the annihilation of an entire family, ex-tsar and all, even though the *immediate role* of V. I. Lenin and his closest cohorts in the July 1918 murders remains (as we will see later on) a matter of scholarly debate. Nonetheless, the comparativist cannot deny the unique aspects of the Russian situation: Nicholas II, forced, unlike his regal counterparts in the earlier upheavals, to abdicate at the very start of the revolutionary process, would play no active role in the ensuing events, whether on the field of battle or in the corridors of counterrevolutionary intrigue. For us, the challenge again is to reevaluate the political-cultural and circumstantial factors militating against or in favor of eventual regicide. In the case of Russia, however, much more than in those of England and France, such analysis appears *almost from the very start* to make a regicidal solution all but certain.

First, however, it might be advisable to explain briefly what actually happened to the ex-tsar and his family during the months intervening between the dramatic abdication at Pskov in early March 1917 and the murder of the Romanovs at Ekaterinburg in the southern Urals region in mid-July 1918.[86] From March 1917 until the middle of August, Nicholas, Alexandra, their children, and the family's old servants lived (not too uncomfortably) under palace arrest at Tsarskoe Selo, close enough to Petrograd to ensure surveillance by the new Provisional Government and the increasingly distrustful proletarian, peasant, and military deputies of the Petrograd Soviet. During this initial period, plans had been mooted to exile the Imperial family to England: this would have allayed the anxieties of Alexander Kerensky and of other government leaders concerning the Romanovs' personal safety, and accorded as well with the desires of Nicholas's royal cousin George V, who had invited him and his family to England as early as March. This design, however, foundered on domestic opposition in both countries: George V withdrew his invitation for fear of alienating—in wartime—the British Labor

Party, and the Petrograd Soviet (after first seeming to fall in with the plan) came to oppose it, favoring instead the imprisonment of the erstwhile tsar in the Peter and Paul Fortress at Petrograd. Eventually, the authorities sent Nicholas and family to Tobolsk, a provincial backwater east of the Urals, where, from August 1917 until the following April, the prisoners lived in a fairly comfortable fashion in the residence of the former Imperial governor. Things, however, took a turn for the worse in the spring and summer of 1918: as a result of a political tug-of-war between two Bolshevik commissars, Vasilii Yakovlev and Fillip Goloshchekin, both of whom were answerable to the new Leninist rulers of Russia, the ex-tsar and his wife were transferred to the nearby Urals industrial town of Ekaterinburg on April 30. (The rest of the family followed there on May 23.) In Ekaterinburg, the Imperial family was confined, in ever more straitened circumstances, in a house commandeered for this purpose from its owner, a retired entrepreneur named Nikolai Ipatiev. It was in this nondescript residence—called, ominously, the House of Special Designation by the Bolsheviks—that the Romanovs were to die, either by order of local militants or, possibly, by order of Lenin himself, in the early hours of the morning of July 17, 1918.

Thus for the bare bones of chronology. We may wonder, as we again turn to postmodernist and structuralist analysis, whether, given a backdrop of unprecedentedly total war, governmental paralysis, and socioeconomic disintegration looming throughout Russia in 1917 and 1918, we could cite *any* factors that might have conceivably shielded the former tsar from the most rigorous application of revolutionary justice. Indeed, even before Russia's involvement in the war of 1914 to 1918 exposed the hollowness of its pretentions to Great Power competitive status for all the world to see, and thus underscored the utter moral and constitutional bankruptcy of tsarism, the balance sheet on the Romanovs in the political culture of the old regime had been, at best, decidedly mixed.

To be sure, the Romanovs (much like the Stuarts and the Bourbons before them) had benefited in prerevolutionary times from the popular attribution to them of magical, religious, and semi-mythic qualities. Indeed, this kind of "monarch-worship," if we can employ such a term, was arguably carried even further in old regime Russia than it had been in old regime England and France. Orlando Figes has described this phenomenon—a phenomenon that the old regime was still trying to cultivate as late as February 1913 when it staged jubilee festivities marking the tercentenary of Romanov rule in Russia:

> In the mind of the ordinary peasant the Tsar was not just a kingly ruler but a god on earth. He thought of him as a father-figure . . . the *Tsar Batiushka* . . . who knew all the peasants personally by name, understood their problems in all their . . . details, and, if it were not for the evil boyars, the noble officials,

who surrounded him, would satisfy their demands in a Golden Manifesto giving them the land. Hence the peasant tradition of sending direct appeals to the Tsar . . . in general the myth of the Good Tsar worked to the benefit of the crown, and as the revolutionary crisis deepened Nicholas's propagandists relied increasingly upon it.[87]

Historically, Figes and others have conceded, this myth of the good, saintly tsar had at times cut *against* traditional deference and hierarchy in Russian society when employed by the peasantry (*muzhiki*) and by their various élitist spokesmen to legitimize rural rebellion; still, on the whole, the near-divinity that long hedged in the tsarist rulers of Russia had been for them a definite plus.

Yet if the late eighteenth and nineteenth centuries witnessed a continuation of this sacralization of monarchy in Russia, and did so in ways that at times highlighted the common interests of Pan-Slavic, Orthodox ecclesiastical, and rural-peasant elements, they also testified to tendencies in the emerging Russian intelligentsia that were much less favorable—and indeed, even violently antipathetic—to the monarchical traditions in this vast Eurasian domain. Helen Rappaport, one of the most recent scholarly inquirers into the events of July 1918 at The House of Special Designation at Ekaterinburg, has pointed this up, and has directly linked it to those events:

> The idea of regicide as an act of national vengeance for crimes against the people was not a new concept in Russia. It had been born among the Russian intelligentsia back in the days of the first great eighteenth-century Russian radical Aleksandr Radishchev, who had lambasted the . . . regime of Catherine the Great and narrowly escaped execution for his outspokenness. The tradition of intellectual protest against tsarism had lived on through the poetry of Pushkin, who was exiled to the Caucasus in 1820 for publishing an "Ode to Liberty," and Lermontov, who more openly alluded to a day of popular reckoning. . . . It reached a high point during the Decembrist Revolt of 1825, when its republican leader Pavel Pestel had advocated the entire wiping-out of the royal dynasty, including its children.[88]

Rappaport suggests that this kind of virulent antimonarchical rhetoric reached a new pitch of violence in the writings of the nineteenth-century nihilist Sergei Nechaev, whose *Catechism of a Revolutionist*, appearing in 1869, became (in her words) "the bible of the Russian revolutionary movement."

Yet Nechaev was only one of a growing number of revolutionary theorists and terrorists—we could mention here Bakunin, Herzen, Belinsky, Dobroliubov, Zaichnevsky, and Chernyshevsky, as well as Sergei Nechaev—whose writings helped motivate extremists to assassinate Tsar Alexander II in March 1881 and, more generally, became part of the Populist and Marxist ideological challenge to Romanov autocracy in Russia. (Marx himself reportedly learned Russian so as to be able to read Chernyshevsky's incendiary novel *What Is To Be Done?*, which appeared in 1862, and V. I. Lenin found in this would-be revolutionist's writings ample raw material for his definition of the modern ruthless revolutionary.[89]) Then, again, in Pyotr Zaichnevsky's 1862 manifesto *Young Russia*, the annihilation of the Romanovs was (at a certain remove) foreshadowed in terms that left even Pavel Pestel's inflammatory prescription of the 1820s somewhat behind:

> Soon, very soon, the day will come when we shall unfurl the great banner of the future, the red flag, and with a mighty cry of "Long Live the Russian Social and Democratic Republic!" we shall move against the Winter Palace to exterminate all its inhabitants. It may be that it will be sufficient to kill only the imperial family, i.e. about 100 people; but it may also happen . . . that the whole imperial party will rise as one man behind the Tsar. . . . If this should happen . . . we shall raise the battle-cry: "To your axes!" and we shall kill the imperial party with no more mercy than they show for us now . . . anyone who is not with us is our enemy, and every method may be used to exterminate our enemies![90]

"Exterminate our enemies!"—such language should have left little doubt in the minds of those Russians potentially aware of it as to what fate likely awaited any tsarist regime seen as irredeemably bankrupt in *moral* as well as financial terms, and as hopelessly discredited in *geopolitical, competitive* terms.

We know now, of course, that such a point of no return came for Nicholas II (and his family) in the unforgiving furies of World War I. Indeed, by early 1917 the situation for them was fast becoming even more untenable than that for Charles I in the latter stages of the English Civil War, or that for Louis XVI in the early stages of the war of 1792. Russia's inability to wage war successfully against the Central Powers (most crucially, against Hohenzollern Germany) meant that Nicholas II had to confront an ever more *consciously revolutionary* opposition—an opposition in and out of government, briefly uniting all ranks of society. This fact is best analyzed and most strikingly perceived in political-cultural terms. In this connection, the association of rumored "dark forces" at court and in general society with Germany and its victorious armies was especially fatal to Nicholas and his family and, thus, to the old regime as a whole. To be sure, as Orlando Figes and Boris Kolonitskii have emphasized, this was a development with roots extending back to the military disasters of 1915. "Such was the mood of despondency following the defeats of 1915," they have written, "that most people naturally assumed there were German spies in the High Command. During that autumn Moscow cabbies claimed that everyone knew the generals were traitors and that, without them, Russian troops would have been in Berlin long ago."[91] Such rumors had persisted throughout 1916, despite the temporary stabilization of forces achieved on the Eastern Front due to the reforms of (now disgraced) War Minister A. A. Polivanov and the battlefield heroics of generals like Alexei Brusilov; with the deepening of the economic crisis behind the lines, and the unending deterioration of morale among the active soldiery, Russia's wartime Germanophobia came to know no bounds.

Specific historical circumstances also facilitated this development, and would have done so even if the tsar, tsarina, and court elements had not also by now been tarred with the brush of sexual scandal long associated with Rasputin.[92] "Many Russian noble families and officers had German names, mostly dating from the eighteenth-century annexation of the Baltic region," Rex Wade has observed; given their natural prominence in military, courtier, and governmental circles in the early twentieth-century tsarist empire, such families and individuals could all too easily—if, in our eyes, questionably—be held responsible for Russia's humiliation at the hands of conspiratorial German (or pro-German) "forces."[93] That, unhappily, the German-born empress herself (like Henrietta-Maria and Marie-Antoinette in the earlier upheavals) was unavoidably branded with the nationality of her adopted country's most natural adversary only made the situation that much worse for the beleaguered authorities.

Further reflecting the government's weakening position was the fact that even those politicians outside the purlieus of power who had every bit as much reason as Nicholas and Alexandra themselves to dread the possibility of revolution in the streets of Petrograd and Moscow were by late 1916 tempted by their frustration with current affairs to fan the flames of Germanophobia, at least indirectly, in that most public of forums, the parliament (Duma), thus further sapping the regime's legitimacy. Thus, Paul Miliukov, principal spokesman of the intensely patriotic Kadet party, bitterly assailed the government in a celebrated speech on November 1, insisting that if the Germans had in fact wanted to foment trouble and disorders in Russia, "they could not do better than to act as the Russian Government has acted." After reviewing the ministers' follies and the "dark rumors of treachery and treason" wildly circulating in the country, Miliukov posed the stunning question: "What is it? Stupidity or treason?" This speech, as Wade has put it, "electrified" opinion from one end of the empire to the other, helped to set a number of *genuine* conspiracies on foot—one of which would soon result in Rasputin's murder—and further cut the ground out from under the tsar and his pathetic coterie of decision-makers.[94] (This was, of course, in addition, reminiscent of the way J. P. Brissot and others had, through their fire-breathing rhetoric in the Legislative Assembly in 1791 and 1792, helped to light the way for the downfall of Louis XVI.)

Perhaps most significant for us, however, in *political-cultural terms*, is how the phenomenon of Germanophobia—in a time of national humiliation administered by German arms—could perform the revolutionary function of temporarily *unifying all social, professional, economic, and ethnic elements in Russian society against the existing régime*, thereby going far toward hurling the isolated Romanov couple from power. As Figes and Kolonitskii have observed, even the Grand Duke Nikolai Mikhailovich, in a letter he wrote to Nicholas II in November 1916, spoke of "the constant intrusion of dark forces into everything" in Russia. As Figes and Kolonitskii go on to argue:

> Fear of the "dark forces" (Black Hundred, Monarchist, Rasputinite and German) united diverse political groups (constitutional monarchists and republicans, liberals and socialists) behind February as a national revolution. During the February Days people in the crowd in Petrograd told foreign correspondents that what they wanted, and were fighting for, was victory over Germany: "Now [that] we have beaten the Germans here, we will beat them in the field."[95]

Hence, the danger of references to the German-born Alexandra as the "German Woman," and of the popular discourse linking the Imperial family, the bungling ministers (including the "German" Prime Minister Boris Stürmer), Rasputin's faction at court, and others with unnamed (but presumably omnipresent) German "spies." Hence, as well, the danger posed for the regime by ordinary soldiers at the front, who—Allan Wildman tells us—were ever more "convinced of the 'German stranglehold,' the treason of government figures, and the German sympathies of the tsarina," and were likely now to ask: "What's the use of fighting if the Germans have already taken over?"[96]

Thus did the Romanovs' unsuccessful involvement in the brutally competitive power politics of early twentieth-century Europe come home to haunt them. For one brief, resplendent moment in early 1917, all those political factions, economic classes, and socioethnic groupings that were fated so soon to struggle viciously among themselves over the succession to state power and the direction of public affairs in modern Russia could at least agree on the absolute necessity of pushing Nicholas II, Alexandra, and their corrupt and incompetent counselors off the stage of history. But what, then, for the toppled tsar? Would he be allowed safe exit from tumultuous wartime Russia, or—at the very least—be granted a formal judicial proceeding harkening back (however imperfectly) to the proceedings accorded in prior upheavals to Charles I and Louis XVI? Or would political-cultural and, above all, geopolitical factors make this impossible, and herald, instead, a more summary and violent justice to be meted out to Russia's erstwhile emperor?

At first, in the immediate aftermath of the abdication drama at Pskov on March 1 and 2, 1917, it appeared that exiling the Imperial family to wartime Britain might be a viable option. As we observed earlier, however, political realities in both George V's realm and the new, revolutionary Russia swiftly eliminated that possibility. The real question to be resolved, after March

1917, was whether Nicholas II, soon confined with his family, first at Tsarskoe Selo and then at other residences in subsequent months, was (like his monarchist counterparts in the earlier upheavals) to be tried formally for treason against his own people, or to be summarily and unceremoniously killed under the aegis of what a subsequent scholar would refer to as a novel "revolutionary authority"?[97]

Initially, our retrospective analysis might indicate elements in the political culture of post-tsarist Russia favoring the former, more traditional method of determining Nicholas II's fate. Indeed, as Mark D. Steinberg and V. M. Khrustalev have suggested in their scrupulously researched study of this general subject, liberals in the newly created Provisional Government might, in the revolution's early days, have wanted to go so far as to spare Nicholas even the rigors of a trial. Unlike the moderate socialist leaders of the more proletarian Petrograd Soviet, constrained to follow their aggrieved constituents in seeing in the revolution "an opportunity to right past inequities and to challenge and punish their oppressors," those élitist leaders ensconced in the new government, such as Paul Miliukov and Alexander Kerensky, placed national reconciliation before class vengeance:

> The liberals in the government held an embracing notion of citizenship that disregarded class and position. They were committed to promoting national unity ... rather than conflict, and ... hesitated to punish former enemies. Their political vocabulary was filled with references to nation, unity, morality, law, duty, and rights. When considering the fate of the former imperial family, these liberals tended to view them as citizens and individuals and thus to be concerned mainly with their personal safety.

When Minister of Justice Alexander Kerensky, who was aware at all times of these clashing views of the February Revolution's meaning, and thus of clashing views about what to do with the ex-tsar, declared before the vengeful Moscow Soviet that he would not be "the Marat of the Russian Revolution," he was exemplifying a tendency, common to the political activists in all camps in these early days of the 1917 maelstrom, to draw analogies with the French revolutionary experience.[98] Yet here, as in the earlier French situation, it was the most radicalized element in the revolutionary political culture that dictated the course of events: that is, an avenging, class-oriented viewpoint on the ex-tsar's fate predominated in Russian politics from start to finish, thus ruling out any show of genuine leniency on the subject.

However, there was, until fairly late in the game, some thought given in revolutionary circles to according the dethroned Nicholas II at least a semblance of English- or French-style judicial procedure. Intriguingly, the suggestion here came most notably from Leon Trotsky, as subsequently documented in his diary. In the words of this longtime socialist revolutionary, who by 1917 and 1918 had wholeheartedly closed ranks with Lenin's Bolsheviks:

> I proposed an open court that would unfold a picture of the entire reign (peasant policy, labor, nationalities, culture, the two wars, etc.). The proceedings of the trial would be broadcast nationwide by radio; in the *volosti*, accounts of the proceedings would be read and commented upon daily. Lenin replied to the effect that this would be very good if it were feasible. But . . . there might not be time enough. . . . No debate took place, since I did not insist on my proposal, being absorbed in different work.[99]

It is possible that this move had been in the works for some time: Orlando Figes, typically, has written that there was in fact "a secret plan, ordered by the Bolshevik Central Committee, to bring the Tsar back to Moscow, where Trotsky was hoping to stage a great show trial for him, in the manner of Louis XVI, with Trotsky himself as chief prosecutor."[100] Again, scholars of this subject ranging from Richard Pipes to Helen Rappaport have cited documents purporting to show that the possibility of staging a public trial of the erstwhile emperor had been mooted in Party circles since the end of 1917. Apparently, on January 29, 1918, the question of the "transfer of Nicholas Romanov to Petrograd in order to be brought to trial" was *officially* discussed, and a resolution to that effect tentatively passed.[101]

Nonetheless, whatever informed speculation can be brought to bear upon this subject, the fact remains that, as the revolution in Russia deepened in the course of 1917 and 1918, *popular* feelings on the question of what to do with Nicholas progressively hardened, thereby placing increasing pressure on the authorities at Petrograd (and, after March 1918, at Moscow) to move beyond any English or French precedents and toward an unceremonious, summary, and violent regicide. This question has been most painstakingly examined and documented, it appears, by Steinberg and Khrustalev. As they have noted, the Romanovs, even while fairly comfortably confined at Tsarskoe Selo in the spring of 1917, were made uneasily aware of the rising chorus of calls in Russian society for vengeance against them:

> From the newspapers, now virtually uncensored, the prisoners learned of the deepening turmoil in the cities. More painfully, they were confronted by a flood of hostile press reports featuring unrestrained stories about the private and public lives of the tsar and tsaritsa. . . . But they did not have to read the papers to witness the angry anti-authoritarianism of many ordinary Russians. Although some of the soldiers who were guarding them were kind and respectful—addressing them as Your Majesties and even working beside them in the garden—others found ways to express their hostility to the old regime.[102]

Yet, as Steinberg and Khrustalev have explained, Nicholas and his family had especially to fear calls for a more draconian settlement of accounts with the *ci-devant* "Imperials" that were increasingly resounding in Soviet and working-class quarters.

> Groups of workers and soldiers, local soviets, and even the entire workers' section of the Petrograd Soviet petitioned the Soviet to imprison the former tsar and his family in the garrison prison at the Kronstadt naval base (Kronstadt sailors were famous for their revolutionary militance) or in the Peter and Paul Fortress (where the tsarist regime had imprisoned many political prisoners) and to put them on trial for their crimes.[103]

Moderate socialists still controlling the Petrograd Soviet might urge "magnanimity" (*velikodushie*) upon their "victorious" revolutionary followers, but by the summer the rising threat of avenging radicalism in Petrograd, Moscow, and the countryside helped persuade the Provisional Government to transfer the Romanovs from Tsarskoe Selo to Tobolsk, a town isolated (as we noted earlier) on the far side of the Ural Mountains.

And, with the collapse of the Provisional Government and accession to power of the Bolsheviks later in the year, things could only go from bad to worse for Nicholas II. The replacement of moderate socialist leaders such as Kerensky, Nikolai Sukhanov, Victor Chernov, and Iraklii Tsereteli by extremist socialists such as Lenin, Trotsky, Stalin, Bukharin, Sverdlov, and Dzerzhinskii meant that, henceforward, there was little ultimately that would be done to shield the ex-tsar and his family from the rage of the urban and rural masses, as focused in soviets and in a bewildering variety of more popular institutions. Such a seismic shift in power at the center "unleashed further rank-and-file radicalism, class revenge and reversal, and utopian visions of breaking with every inheritance and symbol of the past to build a new order," Steinberg and Khrustalev have written in a political-cultural vein of analysis. "The Romanovs fell victim not merely to decisions made by the new regime (the conventional story of their fate) but also to this popular social revolution."[104] And, indeed, this "popular social revolution" now implied a *popular verdict* on the erstwhile emperor (and other Romanovs) that could no longer be satisfied by the classic English- or French-style recurrence to *procedural justice*:

> Nicholas and other Romanovs, as symbols and representatives of the "old world" and the old authorities, were often the targets of . . . verbal assault. And the aggression escalated. Whereas in the early months after the abdication, demands in popular resolutions and appeals tended to be that Nicholas and perhaps Alexandra be imprisoned in a fortress and tried for their crimes, workers and soldiers were now inclined to demand that they be immediately "destroyed" and even to threaten direct action to assure this.[105]

True, Steinberg and Khrustalev have unearthed specific, countervailing cases of kindness and generosity of (often peasant) individuals who may have idealized Nicholas II in the traditional manner almost to the very end; still, we receive the overall impression that such cases were ever more isolated, ever more the exception in a time of growing popular fury directed against the Romanovs.

Hence, when we read that "Lenin and . . . other Bolsheviks began increasingly to use the language of class violence and terror" in the early months of 1918, we can surely discern in this, at least in part, an expedient government response to intensifying proletarian and peasant anger, as well as a predictable articulation of long-held Marxian doctrine.[106] Nonetheless, as even Steinberg and Khrustalev (and most postmodernists stressing political-cultural analysis) would acknowledge, *geopolitical circumstances* may have been the most crucial determinant of the ex-tsar's fate. And here, we, as neostructuralists, can only recall and marvel at the similarly pivotal role played by *geopolitics* (or, perhaps put more exactly, *dialectically interrelated foreign and domestic politics*) in determining the fate of Charles I in 1648 to 1649 and that of Louis XVI in 1792 to 1793.

Is it possible that the murderously complicated international politics of World War I could have somehow played to the *benefit* of Nicholas II and his family? Some writers on the subject (R. K. Massie, Richard Pipes, and Helen Rappaport come most quickly to mind) have, for instance, referenced the ties of cousinhood linking Nicholas II, his German-born wife, Alexandra, and Germany's Kaiser Wilhelm II, and hypothesized that Lenin, in the spring of 1918, just might have delayed retribution against the Imperial family because of his fear of exposing war-ravaged (and German-occupied) Soviet Russia to additional German wrath. Again, historians of this subject have had to deal with the rumors about eleventh-hour negotiations among the warring Great Powers concerning the fate of the Imperial family.[107] Yet to all of this "informed" speculation, Helen Rappaport, for one, returns an emphatic and dampening response:

> In the end, all the various royal initiatives to free the Romanovs were stymied by a flabbiness of will, disunity, internal and international politics, and a conflict of political loyalties and agendas. The official German archives on the Romanov matter are, like the British ones, almost silent about the real role of the Kaiser; the Danish archives have yet to reveal any role their royal family played in the scenario. Whatever these final initiatives might have been, it was a case of too little, too late.

In this fog of war, intrigue, and conflicting geostrategic interests, Rappaport concludes, "the Imperial Family were reduced to the status of helpless pawns in a political game that took no account of their personal fate as human beings but only of the bigger political picture."[108] Harvard historian Richard

Pipes, for his part, had arrived at essentially the same conclusion nearly twenty years before.[109]

We are left, then, with the conviction (in the Russian situation as in the prior cases of England and France) that a revolutionary authority increasingly threatened by exogenous and endogenous circumstances was increasingly likely to apply a drastic solution to the problem of what to do with the "treasonous" monarch. After all, the Bolsheviks' security, already humiliatingly reduced in March 1918 by Germany's imposition upon Soviet Russia of the Carthaginian treaty of Brest-Litovsk, was further imperiled in the late spring and early summer. Even as Hindenburg and Ludendorff prolonged the German occupation of western Russia, British, French, American, and Japanese forces landed in areas ranging from Murmansk and Archangel in the far northwest to the Black Sea region to central Asia to Vladivostok in the Far East. Even more dangerously from Lenin's point of view, stations along the entire Trans-Siberian Railroad, bisecting what was left of the defunct Russian Empire, fell under enemy control. A crucial catalyst here was the seizure of strategic points along the Railroad in midsummer by units of the "Czech Legion," a contingent of former Czech prisoners-of-war destined originally for transference to the Western Front but now essentially immobilized by circumstances in Russia's central provinces. This development abruptly allowed dissident, anti-Bolshevik elements to set up regional governments and armies all over the trans-Urals region—including (fatally for the Imperial family) areas that were disconcertingly close to Ekaterinburg. "By the end of June," Steinberg and Khrustalev have concluded, "the Bolsheviks faced the likelihood that Yekaterinburg would soon fall, putting the tsar in the hands of counterrevolutionaries."[110]

When these last-cited historians go on to comment that "this threatening situation made a trial, at least of the sort that Trotsky envisioned, difficult and unlikely,"[111] they seem to have seized the gist of the matter. Certainly we have, on this pivotal point, the retrospective testimony of Trotsky himself. In a diary entry of April 9, 1935, the now-exiled revolutionist recalled Iakov Sverdlov's explanation for Lenin's purported decision to have the one-time tsar shot in July 1918: "Ilich [i.e., Lenin] thought that we should not leave the Whites a live banner, especially under the present difficult circumstances." Although Pipes cites this entry chiefly to support his contention that Nicholas had been executed, not on the initiative of the Bolshevik militants at Ekaterinburg but rather on Lenin's own initiative at Moscow, his final gloss on the matter—namely, that the execution took place "at a time when the Bolshevik regime felt the ground giving way and feared a restoration of the monarchy"—illustrates in its own way our larger point about the critical role played in the abrupt and bloody demise of the Romanovs by the interacting pressures of total war and looming internal political chaos.[112]

In the final analysis, however, there was more to the story of the sudden decision in July 1918 to have Nicholas—along with his family, as it turned out—executed than the convergence (lethal as it was) of ideological hatreds rooted in the old Russian intelligentsia, political-cultural developments in 1917 and 1918, and the crushing exigencies of total war. Once again, we can begin to deal with issues by citing from the retrospective witness of Trotsky. The decision to kill Nicholas, the ex-war commissar held in 1935, "was not only expedient but necessary. The severity of this punishment showed everyone that we would continue to fight on mercilessly, stopping at nothing. The execution of the Tsar's family was needed . . . to shake up our own ranks, to show that there was no retreating, that ahead lay either total victory or total doom."[113] Building upon Trotsky's reminiscences, and with reference back to the "regicide question" in revolutionary France, Orlando Figes has elaborated upon this question:

> there is no doubt that the murder was also carried out for other reasons. The party leaders were by this stage having second thoughts about the wisdom of a trial. Not that there was any real prospect of finding the ex-Tsar innocent. . . . It was rather the more fundamental problem—one raised by Saint-Just against Louis's trial—that putting the deposed monarch in the dock at all was to presuppose the *possibility* of his innocence. And in that case the moral legitimacy of the revolution would itself be open to question. To put Nicholas on trial would also be to put the Bolsheviks on trial. . . . In the end it was not a question of proving the ex-Tsar's guilt—after all, as Saint-Just had put it, "one cannot reign innocently"—but a question of eliminating him as a rival source of legitimacy. Nicholas had to die so that Soviet power could live.

It was at this critical point, according to Figes, that Lenin and his cohorts "passed from the realm of law into the realm of terror."[114] Although (as *we* well realize) Figes might have done even better to have cited the arguments of Robespierre here as well as those of Saint-Just, his point was essentially correct, and has been driven home in similar fashion by a number of his colleagues in the field.[115]

To revisit the dramatic and symbolically potent issue of revolutionary regicide in the cases of England, France, and Russia is to reaffirm resoundingly the neostructuralist mode of historical analysis. As chapter 3 has demonstrated, explaining the origins of these events draws, in part, upon the kinds of political-cultural insights associated today with moderate postmodernism, but in the end derives even more explanatory power from a state-centered structuralist perspective. Indeed, how could this *not* be the case? After all, we see here a *continuously evolving* reality: namely, the gradual emergence, in the European revolutionary tradition, of a *conscious theorizing* of what (as we noted earlier) Dan Edelstein called "revolutionary authority." In the eyes of a Robespierre, he pointed out, "revolutionary authority" allowed "unlawful actions to be undertaken rightfully; ergo, the state could rightfully execute the king in the name of revolutionary authority." The implication of this was that "revolutionary authority could be used to establish a normative framework for state action that [overrode] constitutional and any other legal principles."[116] Such reasoning, if not deployed in the English revolution, *did* crop up in the rhetoric of advanced Jacobins like Saint-Just and Robespierre in the French revolution, and actually *triumphed as Bolshevik state policy* in the Russian revolution.

Another way of underscoring this point—thus enabling us to trace its progress *in theoretical terms* through the three European upheavals—would be to follow the *linkage between acts of regicide and the implementation of state terror*. In the case of England, this linkage was, in a way, inconceivable insofar as there never *was* any attempt to *theorize* terror in the French or Russian sense. Even for most Londoners exposed in the late 1640s to radical Leveller discourse, Sarah Barber has argued, the "rhetoric of regicide" applied only to "the person-specific evils of one man, the execution of whom would avenge blood-guilt and revive godly magistracy."[117] Small wonder, then, that eventually (if unenthusiastically) England's "natural rulers" threw in their lot with a Stuart Restoration. A similar turn of events would come to pass in postrevolutionary France, where surviving nobles—and chastened *bourgeois* as well—accepted first Napoleonic rule and then a Bourbon Restoration. Yet, in this case, a linkage between regicide and state terror *had* been conceivable, and (if we accept Ferenc Fehér's comments) really *did* take place. After all, radical Jacobins on the Committee of Public Safety such as Saint-Just, Bertrand Barère, and Collot d'Herbois had explicitly *politicized* terror as of September 1793—and this only eight months after Louis XVI went to the scaffold. "The actual form of 'revolutionary justice,' as the rule of the terror," so Fehér therefore argued, "grew organically out of the unhappy compromise whose final result was the 'trial' of the king." Jacobin ideas were "extended to whole social clusters and developed into a fully-fledged system of mass proscriptions," and contributed to a "myth of violence as an inherent necessity of revolutions."[118] Yet at least Louis XVI (*pace* Ferenc Fehér and like-minded historians) was granted the formalities of judicial procedure. In the Russian case, no such considerations were extended to Nicholas II; moreover, the Red Terror that his murder helped to inaugurate was in some respects the harbinger of the even more ghastly Stalinist Terror less than twenty years later. "When a government arrogates to itself the power to kill people, not because of what they had done or even might do, but because their death is 'needed,'" Richard Pipes has said, "we are entering an entirely new moral realm. Here lies the symbolic significance of the events that occurred in Ekaterinburg. . . . The massacre [of the Romanovs] . . . carried mankind for the first time across the threshold of deliberate genocide."[119]

Although we might find Pipes's language a bit extravagant, there can be no doubt that moving from regicide to regicide in these three upheavals has forced us to acknowledge the introduction into the discourse on revolution of an ever more potent principle of revolutionary statism as an *autonomous end-in-itself*. Due to a convergence of ideological, cultural, and, above all, domestic/geopolitical factors, obsolete monarchs were left behind, and were increasingly likely to be replaced in revolutionary times—for better or for worse—by unscrupulous leaders proclaiming—and, in some cases, practicing—a novel and potentially unlimited form of terroristic *raison d'état*.[120] Pointing up this portentous development in the European revolutionary tradition is inevitably, for the neostructuralist historian, a compelling way of advocating for the state-centered core of revolutionary theory. It points, after all, to the full emergence, on the stage of world history, of the *state as historical problem*.

Chapter Four

Circumstances versus Ideas in the Revolutionary "Furies"

If, in chapter 3, neostructuralism's posited reliance upon state security and ideological/cultural analysis helped us reassess the factors working against or in favor of regicide in the English, French, and Russian revolutions, in chapter 4 neostructuralism turns out to be even more transparently useful. It helps us, that is, to approach the origins of revolutionary "terror" through the binary of "circumstances versus ideas." In his comparative analysis of the "Furies" in the French and Russian revolutions, Arno Mayer invoked what we know as state-security structuralism when observing how, for some experts, terror was a weapon "designed to deal with circumstances perceived to endanger the survival of the fledgling . . . revolutionary regime," and was forged "in the heat of refractory domestic and international problems and pressures." By the same token, Mayer conjured up postmodernism when remarking that, for others commenting on the subject, *ideology* was "the essential prerequisite as well as the necessary (if not altogether sufficient) cause and engine of terror." In *this* scenario, "revolutionary leaders" were "moved by ideas and beliefs which instantly [froze] into dogma." A final hypothesis offered by Mayer in this connection would appear to us to be more or less subsumed under a postmodernist rubric, for it spoke of the "mind-set and psychological drives of . . . revolutionary actors who embrace[d] a categorical ideological creed to further their arrogation of power."[1] In the end, Mayer anticipated *our* theorization of this subject by opining that the "underlying issue" here was "that of genetic versus environmental factors in the inception and escalation of revolutionary terror." He might wish for the inclusion of other variables in such analyses (e.g., tensions between city and countryside, or between the secular and the religious, or between innovation and custom), but ultimately he was resigned to the likelihood that most scholars would approach this subject through the explanatory binary of circumstances versus ideas—or, as the French might put it, the *thèse des circonstances* versus the *thèse du complot*.²

Indeed, there *is* a strong case to be made here for Arno Mayer's binary approach—all the more in that it so perfectly lends itself to neostructuralism's uses of ideological/cultural and state-centered structuralist analysis. In extending Mayer's comparative analysis to the English revolution, we contend on these pages that the resort to state-sanctioned terror in revolutionary France, Russia, and England, if incontrovertibly reflecting deep-seated cultural and psychological tendencies inherited from the three countries' old regimes, was above all a response to *circumstances*—that is, to interrelated foreign and domestic challenges to the governments controlled, briefly or for a number of decades, by Jacobins in France, Bolsheviks in Russia, and military/civilian Independents in England. Hence, chapter 4, much like chapter 3, acknowledges the most indispensable insights of both moderate postmodernism and statist structuralism, even if, in the end (again, much like chapter 3), it revalorizes the state-oriented emphasis within neostructuralist revolutionary theory.

THE FOREIGN/DOMESTIC DIALECTIC OF TERROR IN FRANCE

In discussing the causation, statistics, and social incidence of the "Furies" in our three cases of revolution, we might start most logically with France, then move on to Russia, and, finally, cast a glance back at England. France appears to be a natural starting point here, both because the French more or less "invented" the modern discourse of "terror" by *politicizing* and later *theorizing* the word itself and because the Jacobin Terror *as a government-sponsored policy* has been so very painstakingly researched by historians. Because the Leninists in Russia so obviously modeled much of *their* behavior on what their predecessors in France had done before them, and yet at the same time possibly exceeded the Jacobins in the extremes of violence to which they were willing (some would say, forced) to go, the Red Terror of 1918 and beyond should probably be our next port of call. Finally, we need to ascertain to what extent we can discover, in revolutionary England, a pattern of state-sanctioned violence that in hindsight may be viewed as adumbrating—however distantly—the Jacobin Terror in revolutionary France and the Red Terror in revolutionary Russia.

The Jacobin Terror, Richard T. Bienvenu has held, began in earnest only on September 5, 1793, when the National Convention, reacting to deteriorating internal and external circumstances, declared that "punishment and coercion were to be the sole policy of the government towards its enemies." It is probably correct to describe this declaration, as Bienvenu does, as "the psychological turning point in the evolution of the Terror," because, as he notes, it "signaled the Convention's determination to employ ruthlessly instruments of repression that had already been created during the spring and summer."[3] There was, indeed, a most revealing "time lag" between the *creation* of most of those "instruments of repression" and their actual *utilization* on a widespread, institutionalized basis in the besieged republic. As early as March 10, 1793, for example, the Convention had created the Revolutionary Tribunal at Paris to punish crimes against the revolution. Just nine days later came another building block of the future Terror in the form of a statute outlawing "rebels" who, if captured under arms, were to be executed by military commissions in the field within twenty-four hours. Two days later, the Law of March 21 legalized the revolutionary or "surveillance" committees (*comités de surveillance*) that had been springing up at Paris and in the provinces, ordered that more such committees be established, and explicitly authorized them to arrest and detain "suspects." April saw the creation of the soon-to-be-notorious Committee of Public Safety (perhaps modeled, at a distance, on that founded at London in the English revolution), as well as the passage (on April 23) of a decree subjecting "refractory" or non-juring priests to mandatory deportation and, if they returned to France, to death. In May came the *maximum* (price ceiling) on grain. Over the summer, "hoarding commissioners" (*commissaires aux accaparements*) were licensed to hunt down those suspected of illegally stockpiling cereals and other items of *première nécessité*.[4]

Yet, if most of these (and other) measures were in place *before* the *journées* of May 31 to June 2, it required the passage of three more months—*and* the great *sans-culotte* insurrection of September 5 at Paris—to jolt the Jacobins, now securely ensconced in power, into the implementation of Terror on a national scale. "Perhaps it is only fair to conclude," wrote Donald Greer in his renowned statistical study of the Terror, "that the Convention, after having adopted terrorism as an expedient in the spring of 1793, hesitated to make it a permanent policy until conciliation had been tried and failed—until the military disasters of the summer, combined with the menacing agitation of the Parisian *sans-culottes*, left no other alternative."[5] And certainly Greer's classic description of the *temporal* incidence of the Terror—defined as a campaign of officially sanctioned executions—can leave no doubt concerning the existence of a time lag between the installation of the machinery of terror and the actual *unleashing* of that dread machinery on recalcitrant citizens in the infant Republic:

> The curve of executions, beginning in March, 1793, rises to over 200 in April, sinks to less than 100 in May, June, and July, and reaches its nadir in August. In September, October, and November the curve rises steadily, and shoots

upward in December, reaching a peak in January, 1794, with the huge total of 3,517 death sentences, 25% of the number tabulated. Our line falls abruptly in February, continues to decline, though less sharply, in March, rises again in April, sinks in May, and then ascends through June to 1,397 executions in July, the highest point reached since January.[6]

The rising tide of executions in the fall of 1793 and early winter of 1793/1794, Greer concluded, heralded in its own sinister and sanguinary way "the resurgence of the Republic."

Indeed, it seems largely true that this resurgence was France's reaction to a dialectic of external and internal emergencies that achieved its apogee in the late summer and fall of 1793. On the external front, Vienna and London, abetted by other members of what by now was the First Coalition, appeared to be closing in on the revolutionaries. Certainly for Austrian Foreign Minister Franz Maria von Thugut, warring against revolutionary France meant coldly pursuing Habsburg state interests, dealing in the old currency of territorial borders, subject populations, and state revenues. In Baron Thugut's reckoning, the eighteenth century's diplomatic wisdom still seemed to apply: that is, one state's inordinately large acquisition of lands and/or resources required that other major states be commensurately rewarded. Hence, Thugut's attempts, in talks pursued with British envoys, to balance Russian and Prussian gains scored recently at hapless Poland's expense by designating lands (in eastern France, possibly, or, more likely, in Poland) that might go to Austria in the event of victory in the West. And a triumph over Paris seemed to be within Vienna's grasp in 1793. In August, in fact, seasoned Austrian diplomat Florimund Mercy-Argenteau contended that the time had come for a final assault upon France, as the Republic's government, economy, and armies had been so gravely weakened. In hindsight, Karl Roider has argued, August 1793 was the month in which "Austria was closer to defeating revolutionary France than it would ever be again during Thugut's tenure as foreign minister."[7]

If true, this was primarily because Vienna was now concerting its effort against the French with Britain. In August 1793, the key Mediterranean port of Toulon fell to the British; Prime Minister William Pitt's naval forces now were also threatening the French Republic's other coasts. At London, as at Vienna, war was a policy grounded in hard-nosed considerations of national interest. It is important to emphasize that it was the decision at Paris to "revolutionize" the Low Countries, much more than the overthrow of the monarchy or atrocities like the September Massacres of 1792, that had moved Pitt's government from a neutral stance to advocacy of military intervention. The British regarded the Low Countries as the key to their security, not only on the continent but also on the sea routes to India—for did not the Dutch (likely soon to be overrun by the French) have a geostrategic foothold at the Cape of Good Hope and in Ceylon?[8] Moreover, the British (like the Austrians, for that matter) tended to view the French threat in general ideological as well as specifically strategic terms. As one British specialist has somberly observed, the "conflation of the threat posed by the traditional enemy [i.e., France] with a sense that British society and religion were under challenge" was still something to reckon with.[9]

For the leaders of France's Convention, of course, it was precisely this coordinated campaign of Vienna and London that posed the all-absorbing threat, and this threat was all the more urgent, all the more intimidating in that by the late summer and autumn of 1793 it seemed also to be catching up domestic rebellion in its toils. In Normandy and Brittany to the northwest, in the Vendée to the west, and in many regions of the south wracked by "federalism," the Republic felt that it was fending off a counterrevolutionary assault encouraged and in some measure abetted by the First Coalition powers. Clearly, in all these peripheral regions, the fundamental and irreducible tension was that between the war-related demands of an increasingly intrusive, impersonal, and radicalized government, on the one hand, and local values, interests, and sensibilities, on the other. The antigovernment violence in rural Brittany known as *chouannerie*, two experts on the subject have assured us, resulted from traumatic disruptions in the "balance of power" within individual communities caused by intrusive government agents and their local allies. The *chouans* could perceive all too clearly that the revolution would spell an end to the old regime's relative tolerance of self-management in local affairs and naturally tried to turn the "moral unity of the community" against all advocates of integration into national revolutionary politics.[10] In a real sense, this kind of political-sociological (and thus structuralist) interpretation could be extended to the Vendée region immediately south of the Loire, as well as to the Massif Central and to other areas in the Midi. "It hardly needs repeating," one historian has opined, that "the Revolution was ... chiefly a centralizing and modernizing phenomenon centered in the towns; its consequences were most traumatic in the countryside."[11] Another scholar has painted the federalist revolt in southern cities like Bordeaux, Toulouse, Marseilles, and Toulon in similar colors—that is, as "a defense of regional or departmental autonomy" directed against the Parisian authorities.[12]

Yet if the *immediate* question in these restive areas of provincial France was one of rallying to or rejecting the disputed banner of unprecedented governmental interference in people's daily lives, the *transcendent* issue furnishing the cutting edge to the debate (because it directly involved by late 1793 the survival of revolutionary France) was, arguably, the issue of war. "In practical terms," Peter M. Jones has written, "it was the war emergency consequent on the formation of the First Coalition during the spring of 1793 that brought the Terror to every peasant's doorstep." The decree of February 24 calling 300,000 men to the colors was followed by the celebrated *levée en masse* of August; one recruitment drive gave way to another, and government *commissaires* and (in time) *représentants en mission* used the opportunity at hand to "give provincials an elementary lesson in republican politics." This turned out in many cases to be too much for rustic Frenchmen, whose accumulating grievances against Paris exploded when they had to face the prospect of being dragooned into war against other Europeans. "In Burgundy, in the Massif Central, in parts of the South West, in Brittany, and more generally throughout the West," Jones found, "a mood of exasperation prevailed. It was as though the issue of whether or not to fight for the republic had brought to the boil a host of simmering discontents." When the youths of Beaune and Arnay-sur-Arroux, of Dijon and Autun, and of hundreds of other communities protested angrily that those who were profiting most handsomely from the revolution—Jacobin clubbists, state *fonctionnaires*, buyers of *biens nationaux*—should be the very first to march to the frontiers, they were humanizing the diplomatic issues that, in lethal combination with provincial opposition to other policies dictated at Paris, provide the most important explanatory key to the Terror of 1793 and 1794.[13] Most strikingly symptomatic of this dialectic between military and domestic affairs was the civil war that erupted in the Vendée in 1793. However complex the combination of factors that led to this tragic insurrection, Arno Mayer's conclusion that it was, after all, "the implementation of the military draft which unexpectedly triggered the Vendée uprising" seems very much to mirror the findings of Jones, Markoff, and a host of other specialists on the subject.[14]

We would expect, from all of this, to rediscover in Greer's analysis a *geographical* as well as a *temporal* incidence of executions during 1793 and 1794 pointing toward a markedly circumstantial explanation of the Jacobin Terror—and in doing so we would not err. "In the light of numbers of victims" (quoting Greer once again) Paris was "dwarfed by the provinces; and in the provinces the principal swath of the Terror described a crude semicircle, beginning in the upper Rhône Valley, sweeping through southern France, and swinging to a concluding arc in the West." Only about 16 percent of the death sentences were rendered in the capital; 84 percent were carried out in provincial France. Greer's conclusions are inescapable—and, in the terms of our neostructuralist analysis, very significant:

> In summary, it is clear that the Terror barely brushed those départements which manifested little or no opposition to the Republic or had no traffic with the foreign enemy. On endangered frontiers and in the départements of local disturbances, the repression was more severe, and it became harsh on the fringe of the . . . areas in the départements where serious insurrections occurred. In the civil war regions themselves, the Terror wrote its record in blood and reached a peak of severity where the irruption of counter-revolution was most violent.[15]

Another way of putting this: 52 percent of the Terror's executions took place in the thirteen departments of the west, and 19 percent in those of the Rhône Valley in the southeast. Most of the other *provincial* executions occurred in other peripheral regions (the extreme south, menaced by Spain, and the critical northeastern frontier—the Nord, the Pas-de-Calais—threatened by the Austrians). Any consideration of the *social* incidence of the Terror only further buttresses the *thèse des circonstances*, because, in Greer's words: "it is quite clear that the social distribution of the victims varied from region to region, even from département to département, according to the social texture of the counter-revolution." The Republic, in other words, was absolutely "merciless" toward its enemies, *especially its enemies-in-arms*, "whether those enemies were Vendéen peasants, Lyonnais stevedores, or the most exalted aristocrats."[16]

The extent to which Donald Greer's analysis, published back in 1935, has stood the test of time, is really remarkable: indeed, Gilbert Shapiro and John Markoff, though venturing some methodological criticisms of Greer's study in 1975, basically endorsed not only his *statistical treatment* of this subject but also (and more *theoretically*) his major stress on *circumstances* as motivating the Terror of 1793 and 1794. (Ironically enough, Shapiro and Markoff saved their severest strictures, not for Donald Greer, but rather for a statistical commentary on *The Incidence of the Terror* offered by Richard Louie in 1964.[17]) Yet it is equally worthy of note that, long before sociologists Shapiro and Markoff came to grips with this issue, Robert R. Palmer had been induced in his classic study of the Robespierrist Committee of Public Safety to adopt the main outlines of Greer's thesis. "The Terror," Palmer reaffirmed, "was made necessary by circumstances." Moreover, for all of Palmer's prioritization at one point of the *domestic* element in this domestic/international dialectic, he then went on to paint the First Coalition's geopolitical designs upon the French in 1793 in strikingly dire colors:

> The chancelleries . . . looked upon the new France as they did upon Poland, seeing in it a country made helpless by anarchy, in which useful territorial acquisitions might easily be made. Plans circulated among them for the dismemberment of the lands of the late Louis XVI. . . . It was suggested that Austria take Alsace, Lorraine and northern France as far as the river Somme. Sardinia and Spain were invited to occupy parts of the south. The British were to have colonies. All these territories might then either be kept, or used in . . . exchanges among the powers.

Moreover, although Palmer conceded that the Allied offensive against Paris had been "languishing" in the summer of 1793 due to incessant intra-Coalition quarreling, he quite correctly itemized the French reverses on the eve of the September 5 insurrection at Paris: the loss of Valenciennes to the Austrians on July 26, the retreat of the French in the Rhineland, and the crowning fall of Toulon (and, with it, the loss of the Republic's fleet) to the British in August.[18] The larger point here, plainly, is that for Palmer, reassessing the Terror from the vantage point of France's Jacobin rulers led to the same emphasis on interacting external and internal political pressures—that is, on structuralist factors—as had emerged so prominently in Donald Greer's statistical study of 1935.

Significantly, a similar emphasis on *circumstances* as the crucial driving force behind the Jacobin Terror of 1793 and 1794 has emerged in much of the research on the citadels of provincial France, whether of federalist inclination or not. As early as May 1793, for instance, those Bordelais who were still thinking of resisting the dictates of Paris got wind of unnerving rumors of Spanish troops crossing into France and menacing the nearby town of Bayonne. Panic also spread in the department of the Gironde over reports "that 40,000 English troops had disembarked at La Teste on the Bassin d'Arcachon." Small wonder, perhaps, that in the end Bordeaux remained "patriotic."[19] At Marseilles, we learn unambiguously, the Terror "was principally a means of national defense—the immense military effort of a city which was decidedly anti-militaristic." The citizenry there had, in late 1793, to adopt "a more realistic assessment of their interests than they had shown in their involvement in the federalist revolt—interests which hardly would be served by the English at Toulon or the Prussians at Paris."[20] Again, the Committee of Public Safety's draconian treatment of ex-federalists at Lyon during the October 1793 to July 1794 period may have reflected in part Parisian perceptions of Lyonnais "corruption" (and, just possibly, jealousy over a rival city's prosperity?), but the Committee's paramount concern, Bill Edmunds has insisted, "was to deter further revolt at a time of continuing military crisis."[21] At Toulouse, meanwhile, the progress of the revolution through the Terror "followed the progress of French arms in the Pyrenees." The city's *comité de surveillance* had been created in March chiefly "to spur on the recruiting drive"; the guillotine was established there securely only "after the anti-conscription riots of September 1793 had frightened the municipal authorities into repressive action." The eventual relaxation of the Terror at Toulouse—as just about everywhere else—responded directly to the improved military situation in 1794.[22]

It would seem difficult, then, to reject a *primarily* circumstantial interpretation of the Jacobin Terror. Yet Donald Greer himself, almost as if to accommodate in advance later postmodernist notions on the subject, had conceded in his 1935 monograph that the "question of circumstantial motivation" became for historians far more complicated when they had to account for "terror" in the spring and summer of 1794. Specifically, he cited *economic* pressures, and the psychology of overworked, idealistic leaders—"tense, adamant, suspicious," and "apprehensive" as they were—as factors belonging in any satisfactory explanation of the Terror.[23] The sanguinary events of

June 20 to July 27, 1794, at Paris (the so-called Great Terror) in particular elicited from Greer a portrayal of Jacobins like Robespierre as having been "steeped in the psychology of terrorism"; then, again, Greer's contemporary Crane Brinton had already memorably depicted such men as being, in part, religious fanatics bent on imposing a kind of Spartan, civic/moral utopia upon republican France.[24]

Yet even the notorious Great Terror of June to July 1794, which accounted for roughly half of all executions carried out at Paris during the entire period from March 1793 to July 1794, and thus for approximately 8 percent of all officially sanctioned executions throughout the Republic, was, in Greer's eyes, explicable, at least in part, in *circumstantial* terms. As he reminded his readers:

> It is easier to begin than to end repressive regimes, and momentum alone is quite sufficient to account for the continuation of this particular regime during the early summer of 1794. For more than a year the Republic had fought to survive, and this struggle, carried on in the face of what often seemed overwhelming odds, had patterned the psychology of the republicans who governed France. Obliged to fend against multiple attacks, they had unleashed the Terror as a means of defense. They believed that the Republic's survival was the Terror's justification.

It "required," for such men, "the shock of Thermidor to end an anachronism."[25] Again, as Greer noted at another point in his study, fully 36 percent of all death sentences handed down by French law courts during the final two months of the Jacobin Terror were actually "rendered by tribunals or commissions sitting at Laval, Arras, Cambrai, Orange, Nîmes, and Bordeaux"— in other words, in outlying regions of France where, as late as June and July 1794, *circumstantial* considerations (meaning, above all, persisting fears of Coalition military invasion, federalist sabotage, and royalism) still counted for much.[26]

Thus, Donald Greer (and like-minded *érudits*), accentuating a *thèse des circonstances* as applied to the Jacobin Terror, yet all the while foreshadowing (with talk of the terrorist "psychology") insights of a *thèse du complot*. These premonitions of what today we customarily call postmodernism blossomed into a full-blown, novel explanation of the Terror when, in the late 1970s and 1980s, French revisionist François Furet moved on from his long-sustained critique of the Marxist explanatory paradigm to a new engagement with issues of political-cultural analysis. In a landmark book, *Penser la Révolution française*, which appeared in 1978 (and three years later in English translation), Furet offered an interpretation of *ancien régime* and revolution pivoting on the notion of an absolutist political culture common to both periods that insisted on national consensus and that demonized (and, in times of revolutionary crisis, guillotined) those deemed to have deviated from that national consensus. The exclusivist absolutism, prisons, and *lettres de cachet* of late Bourbon times, in other words, gave way (implicitly *had* to give way) to the purges, proscriptions, and executions of the Jacobin Terror.[27] Once the revolution was underway, Furet contended, novel discourses of political legitimacy vied to fill the unprecedented void left in public life by the collapse of the absolute monarchy. From 1789 through the climacteric of the Terror, this increasingly lethal competition of political discourses, all proclaiming fealty to the newly sovereign "people," drove the Revolution relentlessly leftward. For this brief, unforgettable period, ideology was largely independent of—and, indeed, *constitutive of*—sociopolitical reality; only after the overthrow of the Jacobins in Thermidor of Year II (July 1794) would "society" reassume its ordinary role as the *primum mobile* of sociohistorical evolution.

Furet had many an opportunity to elaborate on this view of the Terror during the bicentennial celebrations in 1989. In an article he contributed to his own co-edited *Critical Dictionary of the French Revolution*, for example, Furet argued (among other things) that the actual chronology of events during 1793 made the causal linkage traditionally posited between France's national military emergency and its recourse to Terror largely untenable.[28] Instead, he reiterated, the Jacobin Terror was more *ideological* than *circumstantial*, and he referred back, as he had before, to the political culture and certain social practices (dysfunctions, actually) of the *ancien régime*. The revolution, inheriting as it did the "absolute sovereignty of the king," effectively converted it into *popular* sovereignty. In the end, Furet wrote,

> the Revolution put the people in the place of the king. . . . Wholly obsessed with legitimacy, . . . the Revolution was unwilling to set limits to public authority. It had lived since 1789 on the idea of a new absolute—and indivisible—sovereignty, which excluded pluralism of representation because it assumed the unity of the nation. Since that unity did not exist—and Girondin federalism showed that factions continued to plot in the shadows—the function of the Terror . . . was . . . . to establish it.

Furet conceded a "sociological" dimension to the Terror only in the sense that its violence perpetuated somewhat the "harshness" of the old regime's caste and estate jealousies: in this very limited sense, the Terror "may have stemmed from an egalitarian fanaticism born of an inegalitarian pathology in the old society."[29]

Thus, François Furet, holding forth in the midst of bicentennial celebrations clearly intended by those participating in them to provide a lasting political-cultural exegesis of revolutionary change—and of the Jacobin "Furies" of 1793 and 1794 in particular—in France.[30] However, starting with the bicentennial literature on the subject, and reviewing historiographical developments in subsequent years as well, we find a very mixed verdict at best being rendered upon the Furetist schema.

To begin with, Furet's political-cultural rendition of revolutionary events was swiftly challenged by several historians of international repute.[31] Interestingly enough, this included the redoubtable R. R. Palmer, who seized the occasion of the bicentennial edition of his classic *Twelve Who Ruled* (reassessing the Robespierrist Committee of Public Safety) to express doubts about Furet's postmodernist ideas. If Albert Soboul and other Marxists read historical necessity into the revolution in the form of a "dialectic or class conflict involving a transition from feudalism to capitalism," Palmer wrote, "historical necessity" for Furet amounted to "the persistence of a frame of mind or psychology first expressed by Rousseau, involving concepts of virtue, the general will, the people, and the nation." In either case, this made for a deterministic "take" on the revolution that, Palmer lamented, unfairly shortchanged the "conscious intentions" of the revolutionaries themselves.[32]

Other historians just as readily expressing doubts about Furetist ideas included David Bien and Donald Sutherland (sharing the dais with Furet at the American Historical Association sessions in 1989) and Isser Woloch (in a 1990 review of Furet's and Ozouf's articles in the *Critical Dictionary of the French Revolution*). Bien faulted Furet for highlighting *ideas* at the expense of *circumstances* in his account of the "Furies" in revolutionary France. To begin with, observed Bien reasonably enough, the allegation of some scholars that "liberals and others" had "invented the view that war and counterrevolution caused the Terror" did not in itself mean "that the view is wrong." In any event, he went on to ask, "the large and earlier part of the Terror that involved the so murderously repressive "pacification" in the Vendée, from Lyon to Marseille, and . . . in the North where scores were settled with collaborators—are not these terrible episodes the recognizable byproducts of war? Does one need the political culture of '89 to explain them?" David Bien *did* allow that Furet's argument "for ideas or political culture as cause" was stronger when it came to the Great Terror of June to July 1794; still, he queried as to whether "it was the whole political culture of 1789 that best explains the Terror?" Could not circumstances coming between 1789 and 1793 have favored some elements of that "political culture" at the expense of others?[33] As for Donald Sutherland, *he* essentially agreed with Bien, adding only (from the perspective of someone much given to research in provincial France) that, even in the matter of the Great Terror, state-approved violence had all too often been viewed from an obsessively *Parisian* as opposed to a local viewpoint.[34] Finally, in a similar vein, Isser Woloch took Furet and his colleagues to task for their "blanket denial" that events molded the revolution. "War brought unprecedented mobilization with political ramifications that were indeed linked to the Terror," he argued reasonably enough, and those "ramifications . . . did not abate with the victory at Fleurus or the rout of the 'Catholic and Royalist Army' in the Vendée." The panic may have been over for France's embattled leaders, Woloch conceded, "but the need to prevail [i.e., in French domestic and external affairs] remained."[35]

Although François Furet passed from the scene during the 1990s, the challenge to primarily structuralist readings of the Jacobin Terror that he, Mona Ozouf, and like-minded scholars had raised has remained very much alive in the pertinent historiography. A revealing flashpoint in this connection was the exchange, in 2001, over Arno Mayer's comparison of the "Furies" in revolutionary France with the Red Terror in the revolutionary Russia of 1918 to 1921.[36] Mayer's interpretation, insofar as it concerned the Jacobin Terror, very much privileged dialectically interacting international and domestic pressures on French governance as causing the repressive measures of Robespierre and his colleagues in 1793 and 1794, and as such would hardly have raised the eyebrows of Brinton, Greer, and most of their contemporaries. Still, it stimulated an interesting exchange of views between, on the one hand, Mayer, and, especially, David Bell, on the other. Bell, although certainly critical of the main thrust of what we might term the "Furet/Ozouf" thesis on the Jacobin Terror, also faulted Mayer for eschewing any ideological/cultural analysis of that *bête noire* of circumstantial scholars, the Great Terror of June and July 1794. "This was the Terror," claimed Bell, "that accelerated, rather than slackened, as the military threat diminished, leading members of the Convention to fear for their lives in the summer of 1794." To grasp this phenomenon adequately, he went on, "we cannot refer to the dialectic of revolution and resistance alone, or even to the demands of vengeance. . . . We have to examine the political culture and the political imaginary of revolution."[37] In response, Mayer struck a philosophical note that, we suspect, would resonate with most historians skeptical about postmodernist reconstructions of historical events:

> As a historicist and contextualizer, I do not separate language from the sociopolitical conditions in which it is forged and used. I make this same interactive contextual reading of the . . . unstable emergencies in the "political culture" and "political imagining" during revolutionary convulsions. At the risk of remaining behind the times, I take language, culture, and imagining to have a relative rather than an absolute autonomy, which no doubt makes for arguable but not necessarily "distorted" explanations.

Furthermore, very much in keeping with this perspective (and sounding, in the process, very much like Donald Sutherland in 1989), Mayer found it "analytically more challenging and fruitful" to explore the interactions between Parisian Terror and provincial Terror than to be *exclusively* obsessed (presumably in an ideological/cultural mode of analysis) with Robespierrist "justice" in the capital.[38]

Yet it would oversimplify things unwarrantably to suggest that *all* scholarly commentators on the Furies in revolutionary France would wish to be described categorically as either structuralists *or* deconstructive postmodernists. Patrice Gueniffey, for instance, writing at about the same time as Arno Mayer and his critics, alleged flatly that the Terror was "neither the product of ideology nor a reaction motivated by circumstances. It was ascribable neither to the rights of man, nor to the conspiracies of *émigrés* at Coblentz, nor even to a Jacobin utopia of virtue." The Terror was, rather, a function of the "dynamic of revolutionary politics," which, for Gueniffey, seems to have involved the near-dissolution and subsequent reestablishment of French state power in 1793 and 1794.[39] True, to many of us this would seem to situate Gueniffey (despite himself!) on the side of structuralism, insofar as this has usually involved a state-centered way of looking at issues; yet at least Gueniffey's interpretation can claim to have shed new light on constitutional aspects of the Terror. Gueniffey's compatriot Sophie Wahnich likewise refused to be ensnared altogether in "circumstances vs. ideas/ideologies" altercations over the origins of state-sponsored terror in Jacobin France. She strove to present terror as a reflection of the popular will. The *Conventionnels*, in other words, "had now to fully recognize popular sovereignty, but at the same time prevent the people from having to compromise themselves in unsustainable practices in order to found the Republic." Hence, "putting a brake on the legitimate violence of the people and giving a public and institutionalized form to vengeance" became, for Wahnich, the Jacobin regime's great challenge, especially after the people had, briefly, dishonored themselves during the September Massacres of 1792.[40] Yet, although Wahnich denied that the familiar external circumstances of war and invasion (in particular) could account for the bloodletting of the Great Terror, her cautionary comment that "the people's enemies could always reemerge" (presumably, even in the wake of Fleurus in June 1794) suggests that, for her as well as for Gueniffey, escaping the web of circumstantial explanations remained a difficult enterprise at best.[41]

At least with historians like Patrice Gueniffey and Sophie Wahnich, we can say, the ideological *thèse du complot* as applied to the Jacobin Furies receded somewhat into the background. But a like generalization would scarcely hold for some of the ruminations of Keith M. Baker, Dan Edelstein, and Mary Ashburn Miller, all of whom, in one way or another, have sought to bring ideas, ideologies, and political culture *à la* François Furet back to the center of scholarly discourse on the Terror.

For his part, Baker, in an ingeniously argued article in the *Journal of Modern History*, linked the process of radicalization and the climacteric of terror in France directly to intellectual developments in the ancient—and recent—past. How, he inquired, could the French revolution have been terminated until humanity itself had been utterly transformed? "How could it be assured of the outcome promised by philosophy until all its enemies—ultimately, all those not yet transformed—had been destroyed?" In reacting to such questions, Baker displayed a real originality by describing the "revolutionary dynamic" as an *explosive convergence* of what he termed "classical republicanism" and Enlightenment notions positing limitless progress:

> In effect, the sudden combination of the Enlightenment conception of indefinite progress and the classical-republican notion of (now extended) crisis produced an explosive escalation, a kind of sustained political chain reaction. In these conditions, classical republicanism escaped the constraints of its defensive and oppositional limitations. In the light of infinite promise, it now projected infinite dangers and unending risks. . . . The moment of crisis now evoked a call for extended revolutionary action.

Perhaps most revealingly for our purposes, Baker went on here to insist that historians "who cling to an interpretation of the Terror as an extreme response to extreme circumstances . . . must also recognize that the language in which these circumstances were construed had a powerful life and resonance of its own."[42] How stunningly opposed such an analysis is to Arno Mayer's conception of "language, culture, and imagining" as possessing "a relative rather than an absolute autonomy!" Here is the essence of the debate between discursive postmodernists and state-oriented structuralists reconsidering the question of terror. However ingenious it may be, however, Baker's argument will strike many as glossing over the myriad links between domestic/international politics and terroristic policy in revolutionary France.

Perhaps the most ambitious attempt in recent years to conceive the Jacobin Terror in ideological terms, however, has come from Dan Edelstein. Although Edelstein, in a long monograph of 2009, at first appeared to be proceeding in his analysis from a generally Furetist perspective, he specifically rejected those postmodernists stressing constitutional contract theory, Rousseauist theorizing about the General Will in society, or "classical republicanism" as having fostered revolutionary radicalization and Terror in France. Instead, for Edelstein, "it was under the aegis of natural right . . . that the Montagnards brought 'terror' into the Republic." Thus, he purported to show that many *Conventionnels*, if they had only had their way, would have jettisoned legal procedure for Louis XVI in December 1792 entirely, trying (and, naturally, condemning) him simply on the basis of "natural right" or the (supposedly similar) "right of nations." By the same token, Edelstein wrote, "advanced" Jacobins like Robespierre and (even more) Saint Just would have liked to see revolutionary France discard formal constitutionalism and "popular sovereignty" completely, locating the source of public or statist authority in "nature" rather than in the will of the people. Thus, Dan Edelstein— driving the Furetist interpretation in new directions.[43]

Yet Edelstein's argument, however stimulating, can be disputed on any number of grounds. For one thing, his contention that a "vast majority of deputies" in the Convention deserted "constitutional law for the more nebulous constraints of natural right" in deliberating on the king's fate rested upon a statistical sample of only about 15 percent of the deputies—many of whom, as "prominent" *Conventionnels*, may have been disproportionately pro-Jacobin (and, thus, favoring advanced ideas) from the start.[44] For another thing, his apparently uncritical acceptance of Saint Just's claim that Charles I had been "judged according to the laws of nature" and not by anything "in the laws of England" in January 1649 ignored the consensus among British scholars that, in fact, Charles (like Strafford and Archbishop Laud before him) had been judged, at least partly, on the basis of a 1352 Statute of Treasons dating from the reign of Edward III.[45] Yet again—and perhaps most damagingly—Edelstein appears to have argued against himself in *general terms* by conceding that: "In all likelihood, most deputies did not wish to become Terrorists, and even fewer would have wished to replace positive law altogether with the nebulous constructs of natural right."[46] Concurring with Edelstein that "most deputies did not wish to become Terrorists" (as we assuredly do) would seem fairly obviously to leave us little room for anything other than a primarily *circumstantial* explanation of the Jacobin Terror.

Yet this is not the conclusion that Mary Ashburn Miller reached in her recent study of the Terror, which—if anything—took Edelstein's ideas even farther. The "natural history of revolution," as Miller termed it, "suggests that the Terror was not a result of a radicalization in hopes of realizing the general will, but instead was understood to be, and was portrayed as, the rule of nature." Edelstein, she wrote, was misguided only in that he attributed the radicals' "insertion of the natural world into political life" to "the *weakness* of republicanism in the legal tradition in France," rather than (as Miller did) to the vigor of customary French invocations of "nature" in scientific and literary discourse. For Miller, the Terror seems "to have escalated amid calls for nature to rule."[47] It did not take long, however, for another specialist on the Terror to sound a cautionary note about such an interpretation. "We need to be very specific," wrote Marisa Linton, "about how language and violence were linked" in revolutionary times. "It is not clear," she continued, "why ideas about nature should be more significant than, say, ideas derived from classical antiquity that offered a more specifically political rhetoric of virtue, patriotism, sacrifice, and conspiracy." In concluding that the Jacobins' rule was "founded on the idea of justice—albeit harsh justice—and restoring order," Linton may have gone a long way toward restoring to the Terror a plausible *primary* context of dialectical pressures on governance in revolutionary France.[48]

On one thing *all* scholars of the Jacobin Terror can agree, whether they be of postmodernist or structuralist inclination: namely, that because the old regime's political culture had been marked by a callousness regarding "official" violence, they can discern, in at least some of the Terror's atrocities, a sort of perverse *reenactment* of the worst, most degrading violence that had disfigured the old France. No doubt Richard Cobb had this in mind when, after citing some of the most egregiously inhumane acts committed during the 1790s by both revolutionaries *and* counterrevolutionaries, he alluded to "the violence . . . of the old royal government, of the old royal army, . . . with its barbarous punishments; of the old penal system . . . with its ball and chain and similar refinements; of the old police ordinances and the language of the old administration, which, when addressed to the common people, could express itself only in threats and in the promise of retribution; of the treatment of Protestant children; . . . of the old ruling class, and of their servants," and so on.[49] Moreover, the statist violence that had scarred the *ancien régime* had also had, in its rumor-mongering and panics and general conspiracy-mindedness, a *psychological* dimension as well; this, too, came to haunt the revolutionaries in the searing crucible of foreign invasion and domestic insurrection. "All major revolutions," Timothy Tackett has suggested, "are beset by periods of conspiracy obsession, of intense suspicion and lack of trust, of agonizing uncertainty as to who are one's friends and who are one's enemies, who are the true revolutionaries and who are the wolves in sheep's clothing, hiding behind the mask of revolutionary commitment."[50] And although Tackett is likely justified in seeing this lethal dynamic in 1793 and 1794 as primarily resulting from the *unfolding process of revolution itself* in France—an argument that more or less places him, whether he likes it or not, in the circumstantial school of thought—it was also, just as certainly, a deeply rooted *political-cultural* phenomenon, as even historians skeptical about the fashionable postmodernist turn in French revolutionary historiography must in all fairness acknowledge.

Generally speaking, postmodernist challenges to structuralist interpretations of the Jacobin Terror, however stimulating and however *à la mode*, seem less than fully convincing. Still, at their very best they remind us (alas) how often the prejudices and practices of the Terror resonated with echoes from the "benighted" past. In addition, they remind us that the terrorists, in their *human capacity*, had to be able to find legitimacy and justification for their extreme actions in ideology and culture as well as in the immediate needs of national defense. For these reasons, we see once again the usefulness of neostructuralism, combining as it does the best insights of structuralism and postmodernism.

THE FOREIGN/DOMESTIC DIALECTIC
OF TERROR IN RUSSIA

If anything, it seems that an assiduous reappraisal of state-sanctioned violence in revolutionary Russia leads to even more of an emphasis on circumstances than does a similar exercise in the case of revolutionary France. That is to say, the Bolshevik Terror that got underway in earnest in the summer of 1918 drew much of what Arno Mayer would call its "synchretic driving force" from a menacing dialectic of international and domestic developments—even if, here, too, as in France, revolutionary terror also represented something of a throwback to aspects of the political culture of the *ancien régime*.

There were, to be sure, some genuine differences between the *temporal* profiles of the Jacobin and Red Terrors. Whereas, in the French case, state violence that rapidly intensified in late 1793 ceased fairly quickly at Paris with the overthrow of the Robespierrists in late July 1794 and persisted in most of its provincial bastions only into the early days of August, the analogous phenomenon in Russia waxed and waned in undulations extending over nearly four incarnadined years. One of the more recent of the comparativists examining the Red Terror has summarized its chronology:

> Its first surge came in the fall of 1918, following the attempt on Lenin's life, the British landings at Archangel and Baku, and the seizure of Kazan by Kolchak and the Czech Legion. It receded in November 1918, with the stabilization of the front on the Volga as well as the upheaval in Central Europe and German withdrawal from Ukraine. The Red Terror rose to a second peak in 1919, in face of the difficult struggle with the armies of Kolchak, Deniken, and Iudenich. After their defeat there was another reflux, heralded by the decree of mid-January abrogating capital punishment. But in 1920–21, with the Russo-Polish war, the defiance of Wrangel, and various peasant insurgencies, the first Red Terror again worsened until after the end of the civil war.[51]

Yet, as even this cursory chronology of the Bolshevik Terror offered by Arno Mayer suggests, it rose and fell (much like the earlier, if more compact, Jacobin Terror) primarily (if not exclusively) with the ebb and flow of circumstantial pressures buffeting the revolutionary state.

The applicability of a *thèse des circonstances* is moreover indicated in the Russian case, as in that of France, by the time lag between the *creation* and the actual *utilization*, at least on a widespread basis, of the instruments of terror. True, as early as November 29, 1917, Trotsky, in addressing the executive of the All-Russian Congress of Soviets at Petrograd, warned defiantly that the "naked terror" that he and his Bolshevik comrades were as yet meting out only haphazardly to their "class enemies" would be assuming "more frightful forms, modeled on the terror of the great French revolutionaries." "Not the fortress but the guillotine," intoned Trotsky darkly, "will await our enemies."[52] Still, whatever this determination (expressed so fiercely *and* so soon after the Bolshevik seizure of power) to emulate the heroics of the Jacobin Terror, it took time in Russia, as it had in France, to make of state-sanctioned violence a generalized, *systematic* policy.

This appears most strikingly in connection with the creation and evolution of the Red Terror's chief instrument, the *Cheka*. This "All-Russian Extraordinary Commission to Combat Counterrevolution, Speculation and Administrative Crimes" operated, Alter Litvin has written, "from 7 December 1917 until 6 February 1922."[53] A foundational decree, enacted by the new state executive, the Council of People's Commissars (*Sovnarkom*), assigned this organization the task of fighting against "counterrevolution" and "sabotage" by carrying out preliminary investigations (like the *comités de surveillance* in revolutionary France) and handing "suspects" over to revolutionary courts. Run by a directory consisting for the most part of Bolsheviks (although with the addition, from January 8 until July 6, 1918, of a handful of Leftist Socialist-Revolutionaries [SRs]), and chaired for most of this period by Felix Dzerzhinskii, the Cheka was initially rather small: in December 1917, for example, the central collegium at Petrograd numbered only twenty-three, and when it was transferred (along with the rest of the central government) to Moscow in March 1918, its leadership still numbered only 120. Yet, from February, it seems, and despite Lenin's earlier statements about creating the new Russia without a revival of either the professional army or the *gendarmerie* of the old regime, the Cheka "grew without interruption, both in size and in the range of its activities." The organization began to form armed detachments; by June 1918, these were regrouped into thirty-five battalions of up to forty thousand men, distributed among the central *guberniia* (i.e., administrative units) of European Russia. Of equal significance, the *Cheka* from the start boasted a higher proportion of Bolsheviks (renamed, now, "Communists"), and especially of men loyal to the Party since *before* the October revolution, than any other Commissariat in the new government. And certainly the rhetoric of the new organization was ferocious from the very start. A document circulated as early as February by the *Sovnarkom*, entitled "The Socialist Fatherland is in Danger!" authorized Dzerzhinskii's soon-to-be-dreaded Commissariat to deal with "enemy agents, profiteers, marauders, hooligans, counterrevolutionary agitators and German spies" without going through the courts; a day later, the list was extended to include "saboteurs and other parasites," whom the *Chekists* were enjoined to "shoot on the spot." By the start of the summer, the *Cheka* would be making widespread use of "surveillance, secret agents recruited from among the arrestees and members of 'counterrevolutionary organizations,' interception of domestic and foreign correspondence," and on and on; by July, Dzerzhinskii's legions would have in hand their first detailed instructions as to "who precisely was to be shot."[54]

As all of this suggests, however, the full implementation of a terrorist policy in revolutionary Russia, just as in revolutionary France, waited upon (and responded to) a gradually unfolding crisis much larger than the revolutionaries themselves. The crisis, David S. Foglesong has rightly observed, was

> an international struggle . . . in which not only Russians and Ukrainians but also Latvians, Estonians, Czechs, Germans, Americans and many other nationalities fought and died; a war waged not only behind the lines in Russia but also in the parliaments and streets of foreign countries; a struggle between Reds and Whites not only to mobilize the bodies and sympathies of Russian peasants but also to win the hearts and open the purses of foreign sympathizers.

The *immediate* backdrop to events in Russia in 1917 and 1918 was undeniably the Great War, which had originated in part "in the global rivalry of European powers for territory, markets, natural resources and political dominance."[55] The United States' entry into the war in April 1917 was clearly critical, for in different ways it ratcheted up the pressures on both the Allies and the Central Powers: it stiffened the resolve of England, France, and Italy to hang on grimly until Washington's intervention could decisively affect fortunes on the western front; at the same time, it underlined for Berlin the urgent need to impose peace on Russia (and, eventually, its tardy and hapless ally Rumania) so that substantial German forces could be shifted from the eastern front to the western front in advance of any possible American onslaught. Obviously, the deepening of revolution in Russia (especially in the wake of the abortive "Kerensky offensive" of June 1917 and the Kornilov movement of August 1917) played much more into the hands of Imperial Germany, strategically speaking, than into those of the Western Allies.

The upshot, at least in Russo-German diplomacy, was the Carthaginian treaty of Brest-Litovsk imposed by Berlin on Soviet Russia in March 1918. "By this agreement," John Wheeler-Bennett wrote, "Russia lost 34% of her population, 32% of her agricultural land, 85% of her beet-sugar land, 54% of her industrial undertakings, and 89% of her coal mines." For the Germans, the gains extracted from the October revolution—and from Russia's utter exhaustion—seemed, at this point, decisive:

> At one stroke, Germany had extended her control of Eastern Europe to the Arctic Ocean and the Black Sea, and had acquired the undisputed arbitrament of the fate of 55 million inhabitants of Russia's western fringe—so much for the doctrine of "no annexation" and "self-determination"; while by the agreements with Rumania . . . and with the Ukraine . . . she had gained access to

vast sources of wheat and petroleum. Such was the prospect unfolded before the avid eyes of the Supreme Command; such was the price . . . Lenin paid for the salvation of the . . . Revolution.[56]

Not only had the Germans "successfully broken through the steel ring" of the Allied blockade encircling them and threatening them with starvation; Hindenburg and Ludendorff now had the strategic luxury of deciding how, precisely, to apportion their troops between the eastern front (no longer defended now by the defunct Russian Empire) and the crucial military theater in western Europe.

Yet, precisely for these reasons, the Western Powers tried desperately to intervene in Russia—to intervene, initially, for *geostrategic* reasons, to restore the eastern military front against the Central Powers, but for *ideological*, anti-Bolshevik reasons as well. One specialist, elaborating on the subject, has done well to counsel us to avoid "the false dichotomy between strategic and ideological motives." Although foreign intervention in Russia "*was* in many respects an outgrowth of the Allies' war against the Central Powers," Foglesong has noted, British and French efforts directed against Berlin and Vienna "did not blind them to the rising danger of Bolshevik contagion, and waging the World War did not keep the Allies from pursuing long-term political and economic goals in Eurasia."[57] In any case, British sailors had occupied the far northern port of Murmansk as early as March 1918; in early August, British forces (with American help) seized Archangel, too. London also dispatched troops to central Asia; in addition, British, French, American, and Japanese forces occupied Vladivostok in the Far East and stations along the Trans-Siberian Railroad as far west as the Urals. This latter move was undertaken in part to expedite the evacuation, from Russia, of the so-called Czech Legion, a contingent of former Czech prisoners of war who were to be shifted to the western front to serve as military volunteers in France. Unhappily for Moscow, a sudden Czech mobilization at several points along the Trans-Siberian Railroad in mid-summer represented a virtual military seizure of that vital link between European Russia and the Far Eastern territories of the fledgling Soviet state.

Hence, by August 1918, the Bolsheviks' situation seemed as desperate as that of the Jacobins in another month of August—that of 1793. If Robespierre and his comrades had been caught between the hammer of Britain and the anvil of Austria, Lenin and his associates were caught between the Germans, who still held vast areas of western Russia, and British, French, American, Japanese, and Czech forces mobilized in various peripheral regions of Russia. "Step by step," Richard K. Debo has observed, "the Bolsheviks were forced to retreat from the Urals, the White Sea and Baku. Barely clinging to a foot-hold in the Middle Volga, they were faced with the prospect of losing their last granary as well as the vital link with the Caspian

Sea."[58] Moreover, just as foreign threats had appeared to the revolutionary French to merge dangerously with domestic agitation in the form of *chouannerie*, Vendéen peasant rebellion, and federalism, so foreign threats seemed to the *Sovnarkom* at Moscow to interact with internal agitation—most notably, Left SR insurrectionism and peasant uprisings on the Volga and elsewhere—to weaken further the Bolsheviks' already tenuous hold on power.

The Left SRs had been allowed into *Sovnarkom* and even the *Cheka* in January, but from the very start the working alliance between Bolsheviks and Left SRs like Boris Kamkov and Maria Spiridonova had been uneasy. As the year wore on, the tensions between the two parties—above all, on the questions of Brest-Litovsk and Lenin's ruthless treatment of the peasantry—became explosive. Spiridonova and her allies—for that matter, like extreme leftists within Lenin's own party—denounced Brest-Litovsk as a disgraceful betrayal of the still-expected revolutionary war against international "imperialism," and objected just as bitterly to policies in Russian villages aimed at exacerbating tensions between "rich" and "poor" *muzhiki*. The result, in July to August, was an SR terror campaign culminating in the assassinations of German ambassador Mirbach (July 6, 1918), Marshal von Eichhorn (July 30), Bolshevik Petrograd *Cheka* chief Mikhail Uritsky, and the serious wounding of Lenin himself on August 30. Whether the SRs had either the will or the organization to form an alternative government in Russia was doubtful; in any case, the Bolsheviks, once securely back in control of the situation, retaliated, predictably, with trials and some executions of SRs identified as "enemies of the state." From this point on, the Left SRs, who had already withdrawn earlier in 1918 from the *Sovnarkom*, were forced out of the *Cheka* and most of the soviets. Henceforth, the Bolsheviks ("Communists") would rule Russia alone.[59]

Even as they infuriated partisans on the extreme Left by making peace with Imperial Germany, the Bolsheviks, distinguishing simplistically between rich "kulaks" and "poor peasants" in the villages of Russia, declared a "battle for grain" in the course of which (much like the Jacobins in 1793 to 1794) they sent armed brigades to requisition grain forcibly from rural folk. "Committees of the Rural Poor" (*kombedy*), set up locally by agents loyal to Moscow to help the "food brigades" in their requisitioning activities, only provoked the peasantry to revolt against authorities whose dogmatic Marxist presuppositions seemed ever to blind them to the solidarities and sociological complexities of peasant life in the innumerable rural communities of this vast country.[60]

Significantly, Lenin, gradually shifting Soviet foreign policy from its initial obsession with German occupation to a primary concern with Allied interventionism, marked out the prospective targets of Red Terror by assuming (in what we might call Robespierrist fashion) a wicked collusion between the foreign and domestic enemies of the revolutionary cause. The Western Powers, he warned, were banking "on alliance with the internal enemy of the Soviet government," meaning not only the "capitalists" and the landowners, but also the kulaks. "Ruthless war on the kulaks! Death to them! Hatred and contempt for the parties which defend them—the right SRs, the Mensheviks, and today's left SRs!" Lenin continued on: "The workers must crush the revolts of the kulaks with an iron hand, the kulaks who are forming an alliance with the foreign capitalists against the working people of their own country." An initial wave of *Cheka*-orchestrated Terror had followed the unsuccessful Left SR uprising of early July; in the aftermath of Uritsky's murder and Lenin's near-assassination at the end of August, All-Russian Soviet Executive Chairman Iakov Sverdlov issued a decree calling stridently for "merciless mass terror against all the enemies of the revolution." The Red Terror in its most extreme, *institutionalized* form was now well underway, and it would not cease until late in 1921.[61]

We will probably never be able (in Donald Greer's fashion) to arrive at the number of the Red Terror's victims—archival sources will not allow it—nor can we determine its precise *social* incidence. Nevertheless, we *can* gather, from the available scholarship, that the Bolshevik Terror of 1918 to 1921, as a state-sanctioned campaign of revolutionary repression, *was* quite comparable to the Jacobin Terror in both of these respects. That is to say, for our present purposes, the Terror of 1918 to 1921, like its fearsome predecessor of 1793 and 1794, counted its victims in the tens of thousands, and could be every bit as merciless toward those in the plebeian ranks of society as toward the "high and mighty."

On the first point, one of the lowest estimates (predictably enough) came in 1921 from Soviet authorities, who held that from 1917 into 1920 the *Cheka* had executed somewhat more than 12,700 individuals.[62] Richard Pipes, on the other hand, quoted one scholarly estimate of fifty thousand victims of the Red Terror, and another of up to 140,000. "All one can say with any assurance," averred Pipes, "is that if the victims of Jacobin terror numbered in the thousands, Lenin's terror claimed tens if not hundreds of thousands."[63] Yet we know from Greer's work that France's Terror *also* counted its victims in the tens of thousands, if we add to the roughly seventeen thousand *official* death sentences the many thousands of victims of mass drownings (*noyades*), shootings (*mitraillades*), incarcerations, and so on. There were, also, the facts of the *sheer length* of the Russian Terror, and of Russia's population at the time of its revolution—about six times that of France in the 1790s. It is, perhaps, best to sum up realities as did Arno Mayer: "All these estimates are a mixture of incomplete or flawed data and informed conjectures. Such is likely to continue to be the case even after the surviving Cheka and other archives of the ex-Soviet Union become accessible. For certain, the toll in lives was very heavy, probably corresponding to that in the French Revolution in terms of the proportion of the total population. The contrary would be surprising, given the intensity as well as the extent and duration of the Russian civil war."[64]

On the second point, one grim indication of the inclusiveness of the Red Terror's persecutory outreach came from the all-too-vivid recollections of a former inmate of a *Cheka* jail in Moscow. This individual recalled encountering there "politicians, ex-judges, merchants, traders, officers, prostitutes, children, priests, professors, students, poets, dissident workers and peasants—in short, a cross-section of society."[65] In (Marxist) theory, most of the Red Terror's victims ought to have been the "bourgeois" continually anathematized by Lenin and other leading Bolsheviks as agents of international "imperialist" conspiracy in 1918 and beyond. Yet the most truthful pages of social history give the lie to this sort of propaganda concerning the Red Terror's victims. As Orlando Figes has remarked ironically:

> Of course most of them were not "bourgeois" at all. The round-ups were much too crude for that, sometimes consisting of no more than the random arrest of people on a street blocked off at each end by Cheka guards. People were arrested . . . for being near the scene of a "bourgeois provocation" (e.g., a shooting or a crime); or as the relatives and . . . acquaintances of "bourgeois" suspects. . . . Many people were arrested because someone (and one was enough) had denounced them as [being] "bourgeois counterrevolutionaries." Such denunciations often arose from petty squabbles and vendettas.[66]

Granted, Lenin had written in June 1918: "We must encourage the energy and the popular nature of the terror."[67] The notorious Bolshevik slogan "Loot the Looters!" most likely assured Lenin's party a certain basis of emotional support among the poor, especially in the early days of the Terror: they had, after all, been subject for so long in the old regime to exploitation by those vaunting power, status, and economic affluence in the sunlit pastures of "privilege Russia." Still, as the initial animus against Germans to the west and against Czechs, British, French, Americans, and Japanese to the east, south, and northwest gradually gave way to the intra-Russian furies of the Civil War in 1919 and 1920, the Terror was ever more likely to become an instrument unleashed against *all* members of *all* classes vaguely subsumed under the rubric of "counterrevolutionaries." Hence, as just one example of this, by February 15, 1919, the *Sovnarkom* was ordering Dzerzhinskii's feared cadres "to take hostages from among the peasants, and to shoot them if the snow-clearing is not carried out." The *Cheka*'s subsequent orders from Moscow to "shoot all counterrevolutionaries" and to "let the regional organizations execute [prisoners] on their own account" must have gone a long way toward ensuring that the Red Terror, before it finally ran its course in 1921, had come to affect *all* elements of the population.[68]

Having said all this, there *is* one curious (if limited) respect in which the *social incidence* of the Red Terror actually *did* differ from that of its Jacobin predecessor. Whereas, in the earlier case, terror truly decimated the ranks of those who had struggled to govern revolutionary France prior to 1793 and 1794—that is, Fayettists and Feuillants, Brissotins/Girondists, and even "Dantonist" Jacobins—in the Russian case, terror, whatever its hideous excesses, tended (for whatever reason) to spare those who strove to control events during the topsy-turvy months from February to October 1917. Admittedly, several of the more moderate figures (for instance, Kadets Andrei Shingarev and Fedor Kokoshkin) *did* become early victims of the Furies. The fact remains, nonetheless, that Octobrists such as M. V. Rodzianko and A. I. Guchkov, Kadet and liberal luminaries such as Pavel Miliukov and M. I. Tereshchenko, and, most arrestingly, moderate socialist leaders such as Irakli Tsereteli, Victor Chernov, and Alexander Kerensky emigrated (in some cases, perhaps, were indeed *allowed* to emigrate), and so escaped the firing squads of subsequent Russian history. (Kerensky, in fact, was still very much alive—and alive in New York City, of all places—as late as 1970!) As the flames of Lenin's Terror were subsiding in 1921, the apothegm about social revolutions "devouring their own children" might have appeared to contemporaries of a comparativist tendency to apply more appropriately to France than to Russia. That, in the 1930s, a new outbreak of terror, associated this time with Stalin, would wreak havoc among previously spared (now deemed to be "old") Bolsheviks should not prevent us from noting here this one intriguing exception to a comparison drawn in *general terms* between the two classic revolutionary terrors.

At this point, the structuralist side of our neostructuralist equation might seem to be carrying all before it: that is, the Red Terror, like the Jacobin Terror before it, responded to a dialectic of foreign and domestic pressures on the revolutionary state. Yet postmodernism also has something valuable to say here, pointing as it does to the fact that Lenin's "Furies," like those of Robespierre and his associates, were heavily conditioned by the constitutional, ideological, and cultural legacies of the old regime.

Interestingly enough, flashpoints of scholarly controversy over the gestation of the Furies in French revolutionary historiography found close parallels, in the late 1980s and beyond, in exchanges among experts in Russian history. Indeed, François Furet's accentuation of deep historical continuities linking *ancien régime* with revolutionary terror in the case of France was echoed (consciously or not) by Evan Mawdsley as early as 1987 when he made much of the paradox that the triumph of terrorists and other "extreme radicals" during the civil war in revolutionary Russia had "had much to do with the very strength of the autocracy before 1917." No legal parties had existed in Russia until fewer than ten years before the country had been engulfed in total war. Even more broadly speaking, "the Tsarist state had never tolerated rival forces in the form of political parties or the national minorities, or even in the form of the army or the church. As a result there were no strong forces on hand to take over the country when the autocracy disappeared in February 1917."[69] To a considerable extent, then, the Bolsheviks had been able to "take over . . . because of the state tradition that had been created under the autocracy." The *ideological* counterpoint to this—namely, that Lenin deliberately incorporated into the Red Terror the (often simplistic) class analysis of Marx and other nineteenth-century socialists—cannot help but remind us of how, for François Furet and other French postmodernists, the Jacobins also carried over into *their* Terror something of the exclusionary (and, implicitly, persecutory) social contract theorizing of Rousseau and other Enlightenment *philosophes*.

Indeed, even as François Furet was crossing swords at the 1989 American Historical Association sessions with David Bien and Donald Sutherland over competing conceptions of the Jacobin Terror, a fascinatingly similar difference of opinions was emerging between two Russian revolutionary specialists participating in a "Seminar in Twentieth-Century Russian and Soviet Social History."[70] Sheila Fitzpatrick, very much a paladin of the political-cultural approach to Russian revolutionary history, characteristically cautioned in this forum against "rejecting too much of the old totalitarian orthodoxy" and, specifically, against "forgetting that Bolshevik ideology" had something to do with "the outbreak of civil war" (and, presumably, with the Red Terror that accompanied that civil war). In a more explicitly historiographical vein, Sheila Fitzpatrick then declared that:

> it is surely misleading to suggest that the Bolsheviks were likely under any circumstances to have followed a democratic, pluralist and nonconfrontational path. The old emphasis on ideology (or, to use a newer term, political culture) [is] not entirely misplaced, for the Bolsheviks had always been the tough guys of the Russian SD movement, and in 1917 they were still the intransigents who denounced compromises and coalitions with other parties and called for class war. To labor an obvious point, Bolsheviks were not Mensheviks.[71]

Although Fitzpatrick certainly acknowledged the relevance of geopolitical circumstances to chaos and terror in early Soviet Russia, in her eyes this hardly got the "intransigent" Leninists off the hook: they, too, had contributed (in ideological/cultural terms, that is) to the crisis of those years.

Yet a markedly more structuralist argument emerged here in the commentary of Fitzpatrick's distinguished colleague Moshe Lewin. Even while conceding the significance of (presumably Bolshevik) "ideologies and programs" in the turbulent events of the post-1917 period, Lewin stated unequivocally that the new Soviet system "was not built methodically according to some pre-established blueprint. It was, rather, improvised under the pressure of constant emergencies." After speaking of the virulent partisan hatreds and the "incredible suffering, cruelty, and destruction" tearing at the fabric of Russian society in those years, Lewin raised the structuralist issue of *state-building* that was often downplayed by postmodernists like Fitzpatrick—and saw in it a key to Lenin's triumph in the 1918 to 1921 crisis:

> The Bolsheviks worked feverishly to create a central government as well as important civilian services and local authorities; at the same time they organized a war machine, complete with an armament industry. To sum it all up, they created a state. This achievement testified to a dynamism that the other [extreme Rightist] side lacked. Neither of the main White territories—the Siberian or the southern—managed to produce a credible state administration, despite their claim to superior experience in "statehood" (*gosudarstvennost'*).[72]

That, unhappily, this construction of *gosudarstvennost'* occurred "amidst a disintegrating economy and a decomposing social fabric, at a catastrophic time for the whole country," implied among other things (in Lewin's eyes, at least) an emergency rationale for terror and arbitrary governance that Fitzpatrick's culturally oriented approach could not, perhaps, quite as easily accommodate.[73]

Thus, the *critical tension* between postmodernist and structuralist perspectives on violence in revolutionary Russia—paralleling (in that French bicentennial year) the philosophical disagreements between François Furet and his critics regarding the Robespierrist Terror in France. And, as we have already noted, all of these arguments were dusted off again eleven years later at the New York University conference held to ponder the issues raised in Arno Mayer's comparative study of "the Furies" in these two great sociopolitical upheavals. As we saw earlier, Mayer stoutly defended on this occasion his "old-fashioned" resistance to any explanation of revolutionary terror that was overly reliant on a political-cultural mode of historical analysis. He did this as resolutely in the matter of Bolshevik-style terror as in connection with the Jacobin-style "Furies."[74] It is interesting that, although Sheila Fitzpatrick participated in this forum, she chose *not*, on this occasion, to voice the same "culturalist" ruminations about the Russian Terror of 1918 to 1921 she had expressed earlier at the "Seminar in Russian and Soviet history."[75] Of equal interest is the way Fitzpatrick's colleague William G. Rosenberg, however well known for *his* advocacy of the new cultural approach to Russian revolutionary affairs, chose here to adopt a distinctly structuralist stance. "Although it is obviously true that after the Bolsheviks took power in October 1917 their rule involved an extremely violent political dialectic," he observed, "it is also not too much to say that the revolutionary episode as a whole in Russia was itself an *effect* of violence, foreign and domestic." Again, Rosenberg complained that even striving to focus on the *economic* aspects of crisis in Soviet Russia was "hardly fashionable at a moment when everything 'post' concentrates attention on human agency, ideology, and culturally embedded politics and argues for the end of (social) history, not to mention its lowercase marxist dispositions." Rosenberg's conclusion—that the revolutionary Furies in Russia had been "driven in the first instance by contingent circumstances" and then were "radically accelerated by a politics that could not effectively address" those "contingent circumstances"—would almost certainly have drawn an emphatic endorsement from Moshe Lewin.[76]

However, both before and after William Rosenberg added his voice in this manner to the chorus of structuralists reinterpreting the Furies in revolutionary Russia, a number of scholars—among them, Richard Pipes, Orlando Figes, and Martin Malia—tried to mount a countervailing challenge to the *thèse des circonstances* insofar as it applied to the Red Terror of 1918 to 1921. Yet it must be said that their efforts at times have been *self-contradictory*, and hence less than fully persuasive. Pipes, for example, writing in part against a backdrop of ideological Reaganite/Thatcherite triumphalism in the West, insisted on likening Lenin, as instigator of terror in Russia, to Robespierre at his persecutorial worst: he was, so said Pipes, "quite prepared to resort to [terror] preventively—that is, in the absence of active opposition to his rule. His commitment to it was rooted in a deep-seated belief in the rightness of his cause and in an inability to perceive politics in hues other than pure white and pure black. It was essentially the same outlook that had driven Robespierre. . . . This led [Lenin], like Robespierre, morally to justify the physical elimination of 'bad' citizens."[77] A damning portrayal, no doubt. Yet this selfsame historian conceded, at other points in his vast narrative on the Russian Revolution, that the "early" Red Terror had been "unsystematic" and only came to "assume a more systematic . . . character" in the summer of 1918; that it spared its most prominent SR opponents, such as Chernov, Tsereteli, and Kerensky; and (perhaps most strikingly) that it drew from some of its bitterest critics (such as the incarcerated rightist partisan Victor Purishkevich) the grudging praise that, at least, "Soviet authority [was] firm authority."[78] Perhaps we have, here, a revelatory example of Pipes the empiricist contradicting Pipes the ideologue!

With Orlando Figes, we seem to have an historian who (much like Patrice Gueniffey and Sophie Wahnich in the case of the Jacobin Terror) wanted to slip out of the constraints of the "circumstances vs. ideology" binary by viewing Lenin's Terror as having been (at least in part) *popularly motivated*. "The Terror," maintained Figes, "erupted from below. It was an integral element of the social revolution from the start. The Bolsheviks encouraged but did not create this mass terror. The main institutions of the Terror were all shaped, at least in part, in response to these pressures from below." However tempted the reasonable scholar might be to condemn much that was ugly and violent about the Bolshevik Terror, Figes went on, there could *still* be no doubt "that the Terror struck a deep chord in the Russian civil war mentality, and that it had a strange mass appeal. The slogan 'Death to the Bourgeoisie!' . . . was also the slogan of the street."[79] Perhaps so; yet when Figes hypothesized elsewhere that the Red Terror was "implicit in the regime from the start" and was "bound to follow from Lenin's violent seizure of power and his rejection of democracy," did this *not* once again cast the Terror in *statist* rather than in *popular* terms and indeed beg the question as to whether a genuine "democracy" was *ever* a realistic possibility in the war-ravaged Russia of late 1917 and thereafter?[80] At the very least, Figes's remarks here seemed to give very short shrift to the efforts of liberals and moderate socialists to salvage *their* Russia—a Russia that might have limited the modern state's power—during the eight-month "honeymoon" period from February to October 1917.

Finally, with Martin Malia, we seem to have a political-cultural take on the October Revolution in general, and on the Bolsheviks' terror policies in particular, that was in its own way self-contradictory. At first, Malia seemed to accept the inevitability of a Bolshevik seizure of power (and implementation of ruthless policies) in wartime Russia: "In such a crisis," he wrote, "it is difficult to imagine the cautious Mensheviks or the loosely structured majority SRs organizing the 'defense of the revolution'; so that task would have fallen anyway to the Bolsheviks and fire-breathing left SRs." Yet in the very next instant Malia could go on to excoriate Lenin's cohorts for their "coercive state-building" and argue (on the basis of a partly inaccurate chronology of institutional developments in early Soviet Russia) that "allegations" about the Bolsheviks being "forced into these premature policies by the military emergency" amounted to very little more than an "exculpatory rationalization" of Lenin's initiatives. At the most, "the military emergency led the Bolsheviks to do what they were ideologically programmed to do anyway."[81] Then, writing in a more general fashion, Malia described "Great Revolutions" like that in Russia essentially as "political-constitutional" and "cultural-ideological" rather than as "socioeconomic" in nature. Perhaps, for this historian, regarding the critical motivating force behind such major events as a "special dynamic of crisis politics and ideological intoxication" was a way of attempting to transcend the two sides in the standard explanatory binary of "circumstances vs. ideas." [82] Yet, even if this *was* the case, Malia never fully theorized this in (potentially neostructuralist?) terms.

However this may be, no fair-minded historian at this point could deny *this* central insight of postmodernism: terror, in the Russian as in the French case, carried within itself a savage residue from the *ancien régime*. Indeed, how could this *not* have been so? "Many of the Cheka's most notorious techniques," Figes has noted, "had been borrowed from the tsarist police. The use of provocateurs, stool-pigeons, and methods of torture to extract confessions and denunciations came straight out of the Okhrana's book." Dzerzhinskii, like so many of his minions in the *Cheka*, "had spent half his adult life in tsarist prisons and labour camps." He and the others had truly "learned the system from the inside." Their ghastly practices, in 1918 and beyond, recall for us—and, if possible, even surpass—the infamous *noyades* and *mitraillades* of the Jacobin Terror of 1793 and 1794. Again, insofar as terror in Russia, like terror in France, had a popular as well as official character, it marked the extent to which the old regime, now taking its revenge on the *new* regime, had so thoroughly brutalized and dehumanized its workers and *muzhiki*.[83] Peasant women killing victims with their bare hands at Odessa in 1918, in this sense, can only remind us of peasant women disfiguring and dispatching their captives in the Vendée in 1793.

This having been noted, we no less find in some of the best scholarship a certain critical (if not exclusive) stress on the *circumstances conditioning state-building* in Russia's all-devouring revolutionary crisis. Peter Holquist (for instance) could insist that "Bolshevism as ideology . . . was explicitly antagonistic, envisioning a constant . . . struggle of classes until the achievement of communism." At the same time, he had to concur that "Officials in the Russian state bureaucracy had long held an almost mythic faith in the efficacy of the state," and that, come the statist collapse of 1917 and 1918, *chinovniki* and *literati* from the old regime were thus often predisposed "to side with the tutelary program of the Soviet state, even when they did not sympathize with Bolshevism as an ideology."[84] Holquist's colleague Joshua Sanborn said much the same thing: the Bolsheviks, for sure, "deployed an ideology of violence that was conducive to the further escalation of . . . carnage" *after* 1917; yet they only came to power *in the first place* by riding "the wave of violence that the combination of soldier brutalization and the collapse of authority [had] . . . produced in 1917."[85] Once again, we can see that neostructuralism's reliance on both state-security *and* ideological/cultural analysis furnishes the best key to understanding revolutionary terror.

THE FOREIGN/DOMESTIC DIALECTIC
OF TERROR IN ENGLAND

In casting an analytical glance back at mid-seventeenth-century England, do we in fact perceive there a circumstantially driven but also *cultural* precedent for more modern outbreaks of state terror such as those we have already encountered in France and Russia? The cautious answer would seem to be "yes"—as long as we acknowledge at least one difference between the situation that Cromwell and his confederates faced during 1649 to 1653 and the challenges confronting the Jacobins in 1793 to 1794 and the Bolsheviks in 1918 to 1921. No people before 1649, Ronald Hutton has observed, had ever "formally tried and executed their monarch for crimes against themselves, and there was absolutely no tradition of republican thought in England."

Hence, there could be no *theorizing* about terror in an age unprepared to *politicize* (i.e., in the French/Russian manner) the vocabulary of revolutionary change.[86] Still, if the English, unlike their later French and Russian counterparts, mounted no *theorized*, no bureaucratically coordinated campaign of state violence to preserve their revolutionary gains, they were no less willing to defend themselves against *all* comers, foreign and domestic, and did so with a sporadic ruthlessness that was explicable chiefly in circumstantial but certainly also in ideological/cultural terms.

And defend themselves they assuredly had to do. The much-ballyhooed "insularity" of England notwithstanding, it is arguable that the Commonwealth, in the wake of Charles I's execution in January 1649, had as many solid reasons to fear for its survival as would the French Republic in the late summer and autumn of 1793 and Soviet Russia in the late summer of 1918. The new government, one of its most authoritative historians has written, was "in a position of appalling insecurity":

> Scotland was passively, and most of Ireland actively, hostile. The royalists still had privateer bases in the Scilly Isles, Jersey and the Isle of Man, and a powerful fleet operating out of Irish ports. Not a single foreign state came forward to recognize the Commonwealth, and most were shocked by the unprecedented act of the King's execution. His heir, now styling himself Charles II, was the guest of the Dutch, who maintained one of the world's most formidable navies.

Small wonder, Ronald Hutton has observed, that the Rump Parliament "set frantically about" building up the English navy, commissioning the construction of "77 warships of the latest design and conscripting thousands of seamen (in defiance of *The Agreement of the People*)."[87]

Certainly, Oliver Cromwell entertained few illusions about the challenges facing the regicide Commonwealth in the British Isles—let alone in Europe as a whole. Speaking at the army's General Council on March 23, 1649, before he had accepted the government's offer to lead the impending Irish campaign, Cromwell voiced his fear that everything accomplished so far by God through the agency of the New Model Army might yet be undone by the "strong combination of Scotland and Ireland." The Scots, who had recently declared Prince Charles king, not only of Scotland but also of England, Ireland, and France, were displaying, so Oliver proclaimed, "a very angry, hateful spirit . . . against this Army, as an Army of Sectaries." Yet an even more serious threat to English interests was emanating from Ireland, where thousands of "Papist" troops were allegedly "ready . . . to root out" all local traces of the English, and then—short of a "miracle from heaven"—would descend mercilessly upon the English mainland. In citing Cromwell in this fashion, one of his most recent biographers has aptly summed up a psychology that, for the most pronounced "saints" of the New Model Army, painted the wars of 1649 to 1651 as, in essence, a continuation of the recent "godly" crusade against Charles I:

> Just as it had been God's will that the army should prevail in the English war, so it must be God's will that the army save those English gains from the threats posed by Scotland and, even more pressing, by Ireland. For Cromwell, the same reasoning . . . which had led him to pursue military victory and regicide at home caused him to see the Irish campaign as a just and necessary war. If they shared those beliefs, Cromwell argued, a sense of "love to God and a duty to God" should motivate the soldiers and instill within them a desire to do God's service in Ireland.[88]

If the saints recoiled before the prospect of a violent imposition of Irish Catholicism upon their godly homeland, they probably abhorred with almost equal fervor the Scots' well-advertised intention to foist their notoriously intolerant brand of Presbyterianism upon England.[89]

As Cromwell and the other leaders of the newborn English Republic were well aware, dynastic and other considerations also ensured a strong animus against them on the continent. Indeed, when emissaries of the "Kirk Party" currently ruling at Edinburgh came to terms with "Charles II" in April 1650—terms that augured an eventual assault on the English—they did this on Dutch soil. Close ties between the Stuart and Orange families were then sanctified in the marriage of Charles I's daughter Mary to William of Orange, who reigned as Stadholder William II from 1647 until his death in October 1650. The Dutch, who had provided safe harbor for the English royalist fleet in 1648 and had hosted Charles II's court-in-exile during 1649 and 1650, adamantly refused to recognize the regicide English Republic, and through much of 1650 the Orange faction (backed, it would seem, by public opinion) dreamed of an additional alliance with France to restore the Stuarts by force. Although the Stadholder's sudden death in late 1650 (along with the Dutch States-General's desire to avoid war with London) reduced—for the time being—any chances for an Anglo-Dutch conflict, commercial rivalry between these two countries would soon revive them. At the same time, the longstanding dynastic ties between the Stuarts and the Bourbons ensured the impact of Charles I's execution at Paris. A strongly worded manifesto issued in the youthful Louis XIV's name spoke of "blood-thirsty regicides sending out emissaries 'like locusts' to stir up sedition in every land"; it banned all trade with England and pledged France to finance a military force to help the Stuarts recover their throne. Cardinal Mazarin's government also recommitted itself to maritime hostilities that in fact already existed between Paris and London. At Lisbon and at Madrid as well, the reigning kings denounced the "murder" of Charles I. Only a convincing demonstration of English sea power would elicit, from Spain, Portugal, and eventually France (and from other European states as well), a grudging recognition of the new regime in England.[90]

The leading continental powers never did intervene against the Commonwealth in the early 1650s; this was the decade during which the French and Spanish, already severely strained by their efforts in the recently concluded Thirty Years' War, exhausted themselves altogether by fighting on against each other until 1659. Still, in a manner prefiguring for us what would transpire later on in revolutionary France and revolutionary Russia, events *outside of* England interacted dangerously with developments *within* the newly established republic. For instance, the government's determination to move militarily against the Irish in the wake of Charles I's execution revived Leveller agitation in an army still discontented over its arrears of pay. Over the next few months, Levellers such as Lilburne, Overton, Walwyn, and Prince published reckless, vitriolic attacks on the Commonwealth's military and political leaders, promoted a radical vision of democracy within New Model Army ranks, and were eventually incarcerated on charges of treason. London apprentices and women staged demonstrations outside the House of Commons. "By April 1649," Ian Gentles has written, "the metropolis was in a state of high tension." The funeral of executed army mutineer Robert Lockyer drew a crowd reportedly numbering four thousand; the next month witnessed the suppression of a final military mutiny at Burford in Oxfordshire.[91] Then, again, the New Model's decision to move against the Scots in 1650 breathed new life into the strategic issue of links between the Presbyterians at Edinburgh, who deplored the persisting lack of ecclesiastical discipline and concomitant growth of sectarianism in England, and English Presbyterians. The latter included erstwhile Members of Parliament excluded from the Commons by "Pride's Purge" (in December 1648), powerful financial interests at London, and even Lord General Thomas Fairfax, who "had been drifting towards Presbyterianism since before the regicide," and whose refusal to lead the invasion of Scotland in 1650 elevated Cromwell to supreme command within the army.[92] Finally, the stated resolution of Henrietta-Maria, the Prince of Wales, Prince Rupert, and other royalist exiles flocking together in France and the Low Countries to engineer the overthrow of the English Republic and avenge Charles I's death made for ten years of pro-Stuart conspiracy interweaving, at intervals, all manner of melodramatic events within and beyond English borders.[93]

There appears, then, to be a case for acknowledging, in connection with revolutionary England, circumstances justifying state-sanctioned terror (even if the issue was not yet *theorized*) and presaging the crises that would later beset the Jacobins and Bolsheviks. How, in *institutional* terms, did the English Commonwealth respond to its own existential challenge? It created no Revolutionary Tribunal nor any *comités de surveillance* in the French fashion, let alone anything remotely resembling Felix Dzerzhinskii's murderous

Cheka. It did, however, from time to time establish High Courts of Justice—extraordinary courts whose members, by acting as both jurors and judges in state trials, could forestall any acquittal of dangerous conspirators by juries chosen in the customary way. As Gerald Aylmer has reminded us, a High Court of Justice had been used against Charles I himself. Such an institution was also used against a Scottish royalist, the Duke of Hamilton, and others, in February 1649; against East Anglian plotters in 1650 to 1651; and to try the prominent Presbyterian divine Christopher Love and other conspirators in the summer of 1651. (Exceptionally, a "court martial" was employed against the Earl of Derby and others *after* the 1651 campaign.) In light of these facts, Aylmer concluded that "here the English republicans compare favorably—in humanity and legal correctness at least—with modern revolutionaries."[94]

This may be true—at least as far as the comparativist, painfully steeped in the atrocities of the Jacobin and Bolshevik Terrors, is concerned; yet clearly seventeenth-century contemporaries could not benefit from such a viewpoint. On *three occasions* in particular, the precariously established English Commonwealth lashed out at its adversaries with a savagery that genuinely horrified idealists on both the Left and the Right. First there was the brutal reckoning after the second civil war: in 1649, sacrificial victims were in effect thrown by the Rump parliamentarians to a "godly" army still coveting revenge for the royalist "treason" of 1648. The terror following upon the heels of the civil war and regicide has been graphically described by David Underdown:

> On March 9, after trial by what [diarist] John Evelyn called "the Rebels' new Court of Injustice," Hamilton, Holland, and Capel were beheaded. On April 25 Colonel John Poyer was shot, having lost when he and two others condemned with him by court martial drew lots for the privilege of being executed. In August, Colonel John Morris, who had held out in beleaguered Pontefract for a few hopeless weeks after the King's death, was condemned with his cornet, Michael Blackburne, at York assizes, and also put to death.

"Cromwell's New Slaughter-House," as it was dubbed by some, struck terror into the hearts of royalists throughout England who, especially in the early 1650s, frequently felt dishearteningly abandoned by the factious, intriguing leaders of their cause remaining (safely, of course) abroad.[95]

Then came the sanguinary aftermath of a premature royalist uprising in Norfolk in December 1650. Here, the comparative scholar can point to an admittedly small but still intriguingly anticipatory example of the *inclusive social incidence* of terror in modern revolutionary times. This affair deserves a very close attention to detail—detail worthy of, for instance, an Orlando Figes describing the victims of the much later hecatombs of Russia's Red Terror:

> Most of the prisoners taken in this pathetic affray were men of humble rank and no estates; a few exceptions are worth indentifying. Sir Ralph Skipworth was arrested with his chaplain, and sent to the Tower. . . . Colonel John Saul, Governor of Crowland in the Civil War, was less fortunate: after Parliament had set up a High Court of Justice to deal with the prisoners, . . . he was found guilty and executed at Lynn. A parson named Thomas Cooper, now a schoolmaster, suffered a similar fate at Holt in front of his own school door; a certain Major George Roberts was hanged at Walsingham; and one of the influential Hobart clan went to his death at Dereham. Altogether 24 prisoners were condemned, of whom 20 were executed, and another dozen or so sentenced to varying terms of imprisonment.

The list of condemned men included "a brewer, a woolen draper, a merchant or two—obscure men."[96] As "obscure," we would imagine, as most of the shopkeepers, artisans, laborers, and peasants who were dispatched by guillotine, *noyades*, and *mitraillades* in France in 1793 and 1794, and most of the minor *burzhui*, proletarians, and *muzhiki* executed by Dzerzhinskii's Chekists in the Russia of 1918 to 1921.

Finally—and, possibly, most dangerously—there was the royalist-Presbyterian conspiracy of 1650 and 1651 in an English Commonwealth that would not experience any degree of security until Cromwell had roundly defeated both factions at Worcester (September 3, 1651). From time to time during 1650 and 1651, the Rump arrested leading Presbyterian divines. "The threat from Scotland, and the danger of an alliance between Scottish and English Presbyterianism, overshadowed all parliamentary proceedings between January and September 1650," a leading specialist on the period has explained, and "fears of a royalist coup in England were widespread." All of these anxieties converged even more explosively in the spring and summer of the following year, when (at the time of Cromwell's decisive campaign against the Scots) evidence was uncovered pointing to "a large network of conspiracy, based on the exiled court and the city of London, and involving a number of prominent city Presbyterian ministers." On May 2, three of them—Christopher Love, William Jenkins, and Thomas Case—were arrested, along with five laymen, two of whom were linked to several of the most important Presbyterian Members of Parliament of the pre-Pride's Purge period. In June, Love was sentenced to death by a High Court of Justice; he was beheaded (along with one of the lay figures allegedly implicated in the latest conspiracy) on August 22. Blair Worden has argued (reasonably enough) that "Love would never have died at parliament's hands for his religious views alone. He was executed, at a time of acute political danger, for political misdemeanors." Indeed, on the very day Love went to the block, Charles II's Scottish/royalist army, on its southward advance, was setting up camp at Worcester. However roundly condemned as gratuitously cruel Love's execution may have been on the Right, Worden's conclusion on the affair rings true: "No regime as heavily beset as the Commonwealth government by both internal and external dangers could afford to be lenient towards those whom it found guilty of treason."[97]

But however correct Worden's follow-up observation that Christopher Love's execution "broke the back of clerical opposition to the Rump," Cromwell's victory at Worcester twelve days later brought about much more: it left the longstanding Presbyterian/royalist strategy in ruins, in the process striking down lay as well as Presbyterian enemies of the Republic. True, Charles himself "miraculously" escaped to the continent, but many of his followers were less fortunate. "Lauderdale, Leslie, Massey, and Derby, to name only the most prominent, were all captured, besides many hundreds of lesser rank." And David Underdown pursued this (almost) unrelieved tale of Cavalier woe to its inauspicious end:

> Massey again showed his genius for jail-breaking, but on the day that the King was sailing for France from Shoreham (October 15, 1651) the Earl of Derby was executed at Bolton. Two of his officers, Captain Benbow and Sir Timothy Featherstonehaugh, received similar fates, and shiploads of the nameless rank-and-file made human cargoes for Bermuda and Barbados. Before 1651 was out, the last Royalist standards in the islands came down. . . . As the smoke of Worcester cleared away, it disclosed a wintry scene for the Royalists.[98]

If the Rump's "Act of Oblivion" (February 24, 1652) and Cromwell's widely bruited desire for a policy of conciliation eased matters for some of Charles II's partisans, land confiscations, like the executions and banishments discussed previously, continued to await the Commonwealth's most entrenched, irreconcilable adversaries in England.[99]

Yet the rough justice measured out to English opponents of the Revolution paled, at times, in comparison to that administered to the Irish and Scots—however inclined G. E. Aylmer may have been to praise the Commonwealth's authorities for their (relative) "humanity and legal correctness." The English, after all, considered Ireland (and, increasingly, Scotland) to be their own, and they were clearly prepared, during the climactic 1649 to 1653 phase of their godly revolution, to crush resistance to their sway in those regions, if need be, with a brutality that must foreshadow for us the atrocities committed later on by French revolutionaries in the Vendée or by Russian revolutionaries at, say, Tsaritsyn or Odessa. What transpired in Ireland was, in this respect, particularly revealing. The overall Irish population, it has recently been estimated, actually *shrank* by about three hundred thousand (that is, by 15 to 20 percent) between 1641 and 1652; significantly, the great majority of deaths occurred in the 1649 to 1652 period.[100] Most notorious, of course, was Cromwell's storming of Drogheda (September 10, 1649) and of Wexford (October 11, 1649). The mixed royalist forces opposing the Commonwealth's troops died, quite literally, in their thousands—apparently around three thousand at Drogheda, and another two thousand (on Cromwell's own estimate) at Wexford. In both cases, the massacres of royalists, at least in a strict sense, violated the rules of war prevailing at the time: at Drogheda, they went on long after serious resistance had ceased, and the officers (most of whom had already been taken into what should have been safe custody) were slain in cold blood; at Wexford, the slaughter continued (*without* Cromwell's say-so) while negotiations were still in progress. The ambivalent message sent by Oliver to the Rump in the wake of Drogheda shows that he was aware of the ethical questions raised by such punitive actions, whatever their attendant circumstances.[101] Such questions would also be posed subsequently in Scotland, where General George Monck's storming of Dundee (in late August 1651) reportedly cost the lives of between four hundred and eight hundred townspeople.

If, therefore, we take into account not only the toll exacted by High Courts of Justice, courts martial, and assizes in England, but also the mass killings accompanying military actions in the outlying British territories, viewing them as somewhat analogous to the revolutionary hecatombs in provincial France and Russia, we can plausibly maintain that victims of sporadic terror in revolutionary *Britain* anticipated in their thousands the even more numerous victims in the politically theorized terrors of revolutionary France and Russia. It also seems impossible in this case, as in the two later situations, to deny the crucial motivational role of *circumstances*. As Blair Worden has insisted, the Commonwealth government, "heavily beset" as it was "by both internal and external dangers," had every right to strike back at those (royalists, Presbyterians, etc.) bent on destroying it and avenging the regicide of January 1649. Yet again, it would be a stretch to ignore the role of *unforeseen* circumstances at, for example, Drogheda and Wexford. The garrison of the former community had stubbornly refused a summons to surrender; at Wexford the governor, David Sinnott, had repeatedly made "impossible demands" in likewise resisting calls for surrender that, if acquiesced in from the start, could have staved off massive bloodshed.[102] The question nevertheless remains: were there important ways in which the outbursts of terror in the English Revolution, like the more *theorized* and *systematic* terrors in the later continental upheavals, betrayed certain cultural origins in *ancien régime* practices and patterns of thought?

Unavoidably, in a purely *procedural* sense, the beheadings ordered in revolutionary England by successive High Courts of Justice, if harkening back to no organization remotely resembling the tsarist *Okhrana* in this country's past, should still conjure up for us countless examples of similar punishments (and, for that matter, outright torture) inflicted on "offenders" of one stripe or another in earlier English times. Yet, patently, the problem goes deeper than that. The fact is that, in the English case as in those of France and Russia, no real consensus unites those postmodernist historians seeking meaningful links between cultural/ideological patterns in prerevolutionary times and violent repression in revolutionary times. Indeed, some specialists have come close to denying such hypothetical links altogether. As we noted earlier, for instance, Ronald Hutton claimed that "there was absolutely no tradition of republican thought in England" prior to 1640. Hutton spoke of the Commonwealth frankly as "an event produced by emotion and expediency rather than by theory" and asserted that "in defending itself to the world and to its subjects," the republic found that its "strongest argument . . . lay in its sheer military success."[103] Comparativist Martin Malia went even farther than this, concluding that, at most, the English revolution was "religious and firmly traditionalistic." Because this upheaval (at least, for Malia) was "not consciously experienced as a revolution" and was not "directed toward the creation of a new type of society," but rather was made "in terms of specifically English legal norms and English ecclesiastical issues," it "could not serve as a revolutionary model for the rest of Europe. Unlike the French and Russian Revolutions later, it was not exportable."[104] Yet such a conclusion, beyond denying that *any* revolution in the modern sense (and, thus, any state-sponsored terror) occurred in England, also completely overlooked the very genuine fear struck in many continental leaders' hearts by the heroics of Admiral Robert Blake and other exponents of internationally aggressive English republicanism in the early 1650s.[105]

But even for those historians unwilling to accept such a blanket denial of *any* cultural/ideological roots of revolution in mid-seventeenth-century England, the question of whether to emphasize *religious* or *secular* influences has proven, and still proves, divisive. Certainly David Underdown, in his oft-cited study of anti-Commonwealth conspiracy, unhesitatingly stressed the *religious* motivation of those who (briefly) controlled England after its civil struggles:

> Militant Independency had captured the New Model during the war, and since Pride's Purge the Army was the ultimate arbiter of the nation's destinies. Although the Rump leaders, Vane, Heselrig, and their friends, might strike classical republican attitudes, behind them were the looming figures of Cromwell and Ireton. The Independents, whether inside or outside the Army, were wedded to policies which could be stomached by neither Royalists nor Presbyterians. They rejected the Presbyterian concept of a state church, and advocated a religious toleration limited by the exclusion of Roman Catholics and Anglicans, but which encouraged the existence of the more extreme Protestant sects.

The government, so Underdown stated, was "implacable" in its determination "to suppress the ungodly (the Royalists) in the name of the divine right of the elect."[106]

Yet, however influential Underdown's voice has proven to be in the modern scholarship on this subject, more recent commentators have often tended toward a more *secular* reading of ideological imperatives supposedly driving the revolutionaries (and, thus, by implication, their violent repression of the Royalists) in England. Austin Woolrych, for example, in his *Britain in Revolution*, held that the Rump of the Commons, in preparing the way for the trial of Charles I, laid the ideological foundation for the future Commonwealth by declaring (on January 4, 1649) that "the people are, under God, the original of all just power," and that, accordingly, "the Commons of England, in parliament assembled, being chosen by and representing the people, have the supreme power in this nation." Having fixed upon this point, however, thereby invoking a resonant theme of popular sovereignty destined to run like a Wagnerian *leitmotif* through many a modern revolution, Woolrych admittedly muddied his secular message a bit by describing the High Court's chief prosecutor, John Cook, as "a thorough-paced republican *and* [italics mine] a puritan fanatic."[107] In other words, we still seem here (in Cook's case, at least) to have mixed secular *and* religious motives for the experiment in republican governance in post-Caroline England.

No such complexity of motives figured in Sean Kelsey's analysis of the political culture of the English Commonwealth, a work whose main concerns appear as well in studies by Sarah Barber, David Norbrook, David Zaret, and others.[108] Taking issue spiritedly with the conventional wisdom portraying the Rump as a "feckless, shallow and unconvincing expedient, committed to little more than blindly obstructing the goals of progressive reformers," Kelsey—assuming in good postmodernist fashion the motivational efficacy of ideology—contended that "Englishmen were perfectly adequately equipped to turn the unprecedented circumstance of kinglessness into a set of convictions based upon ideas already long since dominant in early modern English political culture." And Kelsey went on in this vein:

> for at least as long as Englishmen had spoken to one another of the primacy of the common good, and of the priority of service to this "commonwealth," they had in their hands an ideology, based on an abstracted notion of the state-in-society, of at least equal significance to any monarchical or absolute ideal. The codes of honour and prestige which cemented the culture of the early modern gentry republic derived in approximately equal measure from the humanist, neoclassical notion of service to the wider community, on the one hand, and pedigree, on the other.

Kelsey conceded (thereby returning to the issue of *terror*) that this ideologically driven state "erected arbitrary courts that it might execute its enemies judicially," was "more ruthless than any king in its exaction of taxes from the nation," and "deliberately brought hundreds of gentle families to the brink of financial disaster."[109] Nonetheless, he insisted, "republican" notions inherent in Commonwealth beliefs about "the duties of magistracy and virtuous civic responsibility" helped to fill a gaping hole left in the fabric of authority and order by the revolution.[110]

Yet, alas for Kelsey, his fellow-historian Sarah Barber, writing at almost exactly the same time, found in pondering these issues a basic *disunity* rather than any species of *unity*—thereby digging the ground out from under any postmodernist consensus on the *ideological* origins of revolutionary terror. "For a government built on such shaky foundations, the child of a purge, a trial and an execution," so Barber observed dampeningly, "it was both imperative and difficult to establish its ideological and institutional identity. There was little agreement about what constituted a framework for republican government, either among members of the Rump . . . itself or in its wider constituency of supporters." The early days of the Commonwealth saw the Rumpers quarreling about "the status of the Rump parliament itself; the possible need for an executive committee to manage day-to-day affairs; the status of the army; the future of the aristocracy; and a possible oath of loyalty to the new form of government." It was not, so Barber decided, that those advocates of the new regime in England—whether referred to as the "good Party," the "Honest Party," the "godly Party," or the "commonwealthsmen"—failed to know what the Republic's "Good Old Cause" stood for; the problem was, rather, that (as Barber phrased it) "everybody knew; and everybody knew different!"[111] Furthermore, what she called "the practicalities of governing during the 1650s" only exacerbated the tensions already existing among such individuals, and demonstrated the bewildering variety of republican theories to which they adhered.

If postmodernists such as Sean Kelsey and Sarah Barber, writing in the late 1990s, could not even agree about the ideas motivating Commonwealth policy in specifically *English* affairs, it is hardly astonishing that specialists would also differ about the motives lying behind the Republic's policies in the larger *British* sphere. Most controversial in this connection, of course, was Cromwell's whirlwind 1649 campaign in Ireland. Yet most of those remarking upon the dreadful scenes at Drogheda and Wexford seem (1) to have stressed the *multiplicity of factors* lying behind the Irish tragedy, and (2) to have placed the Commonwealth's role in it in a *broader political and geopolitical context*.

With regard to the first point, Woolrych—though regretfully admitting that Cromwell "shared, alas, the prejudice of most of his fellow-countrymen which viewed the Irish as a savage race and inferior people"—argued at the same time that "the real curse of Ireland was not Cromwell but a conjunction of attitudes, largely shared by both English and Scots, which went back to before Cromwell's lifetime: attitudes which assumed Ireland to be a dependent kingdom, looked greedily upon her land as a field wide open for colonization, and equated popery with Idolatry."[112] Certainly Woolrych was right here to underscore England's historic commitment to a major expropriation of Irish land, and to note that the parliamentary "Act for Settling Ireland" of 1652, which set that confiscation in motion, was passed at a time when Oliver himself was "seriously at odds" with the Rump over a number of issues.[113]

With regard to the second point, historians from Christopher Hill to Ian Gentles, while strongly condemning the atrocities in Ireland, have insisted as well upon the *political* and *contextual* element in this tragedy. Hill alluded, "by way of explanation though not justification," to what he termed "the *political* associations of Irish Catholicism," which ensured that, even in the mid-seventeenth century, it remained "a *political* religion in a sense in which Catholicism in England had ceased to be political."[114] Yet Gentles, by placing Cromwell, as a man of his times, in an even more explicitly *international* context, seemed to be suggesting that Catholicism *everywhere* still loomed threateningly in English eyes:

> Cromwell shared the sharp hostility to Roman Catholicism that characterized most English [in] the seventeenth century.... Like most of his compatriots he regarded the pope as either an agent of the Antichrist or as Antichrist himself. English paranoia about the menace of international Catholicism rose dramatically in 1641 when the news flooded in about the atrocities committed by the Catholic Irish against English Protestant settlers. The wildly exaggerated stories, including estimates that over 150,000 Protestants had died, produced in England a state of near-hysteria in which Cromwell was swept up.[115]

In the meantime, Ronald Hutton, writing after Hill but before Ian Gentles, retailed the many atrocities committed in Ireland in the 1640s (some of them by men much less inclined toward religious toleration in *any* situation than Oliver himself) but also accused both the English *and* the Irish of returning to the subject of Drogheda and Wexford for their own political reasons in later periods.[116] Yet, significantly, Hutton, too, like most of his countrymen elaborating on the Irish conundrum, reevaluated the 1649 massacres—as horrendous as they undeniably were—against a backdrop of *international politics.*

In concluding this discussion, we may actually realize how much more useful neostructuralism is than either structuralism by itself or moderate postmodernism by itself in helping us to understand the origins of revolutionary terror in England, France, and Russia. On the one hand, an impressive mass of scholarship seems to confirm our initial suspicion that the relentless dialectic of international and domestic challenges to Cromwellian Independents, Robespierrist Jacobins, and Leninist Bolsheviks, although hardly an isolated variable, was probably even more crucial than were *ancien régime* cultural legacies and revolutionary ideological developments in propelling these protagonists to the ultimate, sanguinary expedients of the block, the guillotine, and the firing squad. Yet, on the other hand, this is emphatically *not* to deny the persistence (in revolutionary times) of old political-cultural tendencies. Moreover, it is also *not* to overlook a "cultural" factor that was ultimately *psychological* as well. After all, the revolutionaries needed to be able—with the Brintonian "Reigns of Terror and Virtue" as with the antecedent regicides—to rationalize and thus *legitimize* their drastic actions. As postmodernism might have it, they had to be able to blend *raisons d'état* and *raisons de révolution* "in a cultural framework in which 'saving' the revolution justified measures that would otherwise be intolerable."[117] Or, as Crane Brinton once phrased it, the terrorists, however engaged at times in unsavory initiatives, needed to *see* their efforts as being "heroic attempts to close once for all the gap between human nature and human aspirations."[118] And so, in the final analysis, neostructuralism, well qualified by virtue of its theoretical assumptions to acknowledge and work out the tensions in the old explanatory binary of "circumstances versus ideas," should thereby be equally well qualified to reevaluate the insights of state-centered and cultural/ideological analysis brought to bear upon the European revolutionaries' most violent and most iconoclastic actions.

Chapter Five

Crises of Revolutionary Legitimacy

Thermidorian Outcomes

The revolutionaries in France, wrote François Furet in postmodernist fashion, became "wholly obsessed" with issues of "legitimacy" in their country's sociopolitical upheaval.[1] The neostructuralist who reappraises revolutionary change in Europe is likely to endorse Furet's insight but, simultaneously, to extend it to the English and Russian revolutions, and, in doing so, show how leaders in all three cases confronted *crises of legitimacy* in the final (Thermidorian) phases of their respective revolutions. To do so means dealing here with a "conundrum within a conundrum." On one level of analysis there is the question, not so much of explaining the origins of the term "Thermidor"—patently, comparativists have appropriated it from the French revolutionary month (July–August 1794) in which the Robespierrists fell from power—or of noting when Thermidor superseded the Terror in England, France, and Russia, as of deciding when, precisely, this final phase of revolution shaded in each case into a subsequent period of history. Granted, the Stuart Restoration (May 1660) and the Bonapartist *coup* of 18–19 Brumaire, Year VIII (November 9–10, 1799) wrote *finis* to the English and French revolutions, respectively. Yet where Russia is concerned, we encounter much more in the way of scholarly disagreement. However, rather than falling in step with those who, like Sheila Fitzpatrick, associate the symptoms of a classic Thermidor with the Russia of the 1930s, we accept here (for the sake of argument) Robert V. Daniel's equation of Thermidor in Russia with the "New Economic Policy" (NEP) period of the 1920s.[2] This would leave us, then, with an English Thermidor largely coinciding with the Protectorate of 1653 to 1659, a French Thermidor coextensive (after October 1795) with the

Directory of 1795 to 1799, and a Russian Thermidor covering the NEP years from 1921 to, say, 1928 or even 1929.

But on a deeper level of analysis, we confront a more troubling question: why, ultimately, did the English and French Thermidorians *forfeit legitimacy*, whereas their later counterparts in Russia (at least for a time) *salvaged* legitimacy? Here, unlike François Furet, we benefit from neostructuralism's marriage of structuralist *state-security* analysis with postmodernist *political-cultural* analysis. In both English and French cases, the "late-revolutionary" or Thermidorian regimes (the Protectorate and the Directory) broke up on the shoals of *delegitimizing* political, cultural, and religious problems—but could do so fairly safely within strategic contexts that were (for one reason or another) less than *existentially threatening*. But in the case of NEP Russia, the challenge to Thermidorian legitimacy was *successfully* addressed because, geopolitically speaking, it simply *had* to be addressed. Here, the challenge took the unprecedented form of a stormy debate in Communist Party leadership circles over strategies of state modernization reflecting both Russian insecurity in global affairs *and* a growing frustration of idealistic expectations in the Party's ranks. Thus, the overall divergence between *failure* in this sense in England and France and *success* in Russia can be best explained in neostructuralist terms that reflect both the state-security concerns of structuralism *and* the political-cultural concerns of postmodernism.

THE CRISIS OF LEGITIMACY IN THE ENGLISH PROTECTORATE

Any reassessment of the English Protectorate's struggle to achieve revolutionary legitimacy will have to commence with the longstanding scholarly debate over issues posed by the fraught relationship between Oliver Cromwell and his parliaments. Yet such a reassessment must also take into account the more recent academic interest in the ill-fated rule of Oliver's son and successor Richard Cromwell—*and* the attendant revival of interest in the tortuous politics that led (in 1659 and 1660) to the Stuart Restoration. Fortunately for the English, their struggles for Thermidorian legitimacy took place on the periphery of a west-central European world that was no longer dominated by the Austro-Spanish Habsburgs, but not yet imperiled by the new ascendancy of Bourbon France.

A preliminary observation might be in order here: namely, that the sudden proliferation of written constitutions in the English revolution (much as in the later French upheaval) was, in itself, something of an indicator of a revolutionary regime that never really managed to establish legitimacy in the citizenry's eyes. The Protectorate was served, first, by the Instrument of Government authored chiefly by John Lambert, and then (after the discredited if generally well-intentioned experiment of the Major-Generals) by the Humble Petition and Advice. Ronald Hutton has noted of the former document that, even if it "suited the Protector and Council too well to be scrapped" in the aftermath of the First Protectorate Parliament's dismissal, it had nonetheless "never received legal endorsement," as the Members of Parliament (MPs) had never finished revising it. If, on the other hand, the latter constitution (adopted in 1657) arguably "did possess a legitimacy, as a decision of Parliament, which the *Instrument* had lacked," this still "did not necessarily mean that it would work." And indeed, at least insofar as this historian is concerned, the Humble Petition and Advice did *not* "work," thereby ensuring that an "atmosphere of the provisional and the unstable still surrounded the regime."[3] This, despite the fact that (as we shall see in the following), Hutton and others have testified to the tentative accomplishments (if not to the enduring success) of Oliver Cromwell's two Protectorate Parliaments.

Oliver himself, of course, continues, as always, to occasion an impassioned debate over the legitimacy (or illegitimacy) of the political regime in late-revolutionary England. There is, to begin with, the question of the *genuine extent* of the Lord Protector's power under the Protectorate. "Oliver Cromwell dominated the political life of England throughout the 1650s," Derek Hirst has gone so far as to aver, "and wielded more raw power than any English ruler before or, perhaps, since."[4] Indeed, by the time of the Second Protectorate Parliament, Hirst has noted, those conservative MPs urging Oliver to take the crown (in 1657) seemed to be wondering whether a "Lord Protector" *as such* could be hedged in by *any* of the "laws and customs" bequeathed to England from its monarchist past.[5] Other specialists, if not prepared to go quite that far in emphasizing the concentration of executive power in Cromwellian hands, *have* conceded that John Lambert's foundational Instrument of Government invested the Lord Protector with a formidable amount of authority from the start. "Under this constitution," wrote G. E. Aylmer, Oliver "enjoyed supreme executive power as head of state," even if in many areas "he had to act with the consent of his Council."[6] He was also expected (under the Instrument) to consult with a unicameral, 460-member legislature representing Scotland and Ireland as well as England and Wales and convening for at least five months every third year. Although these triennial parliaments were "given apparently extensive and supreme legislative rights" along with a supervisory role in important matters of executive governance and administration, their *real* powers, as envisioned under the Instrument, were less than might at first meet the eye. As Peter Gaunt has analyzed the situation:

> the impression of parliamentary omnipotence was illusory, for the legislature was surrounded by potentially severe restrictions, including the prerogative of

> the Protector to veto . . . legislation which in his sole and unquestionable opinion ran counter to the constitution. Several important provisions of the Instrument were specifically deemed inviolable and beyond alteration . . . by future legislation. Indeed, there was no provision for any form of constitutional amendment and Cromwell may have initially considered that the whole document was sacrosanct.[7]

Gaunt has done his best (in revisionist mode) to accentuate the positive in these arrangements and—in particular—to play up the actual cooperation initially attained between the Protector's government and the first Protectorate Parliament in late 1654; nonetheless, he has also conceded that, Oliver's solicitous rodomontade concerning "a free parliament" notwithstanding, the MPs soon found that "there was a distinct limit to Cromwell's brand of freedom."[8]

Successive generations of English revolutionary scholars have found the Lord Protector's uses of power to invite controversy. In a stimulating essay that appeared over forty years ago, for example, Hugh R. Trevor-Roper contended that Cromwell, as an instinctual and hidebound conservative and "back-bencher" unable to transcend the "simple political prejudices of those other backwoods squires whom he had joined in their blind revolt against the Stuart court," had never been able to grasp the subtleties of politics or master issues of patronage and procedure in his dealings with Parliament, as Elizabeth I had so effectively done in prior Tudor times.[9] One of Trevor-Roper's most distinguished students, Roger Howell, Jr., agreed that "the inability to achieve an effective civil settlement" had in fact remained "the essential failure of the Revolution"; still, to affirm this, Howell continued, was merely to acknowledge that the problem had been correctly identified, and not to suggest that Trevor-Roper had provided a valid explanation for it. The "central difficulty with the Trevor-Roper thesis," Howell went on, was that "Elizabethan-style parliamentary management by itself was not the answer to the political problems of the 1650s, nor, for that matter, was it even within the realm of practical possibility."[10] Things had become too polarized in the revolutionary legislatures of the 1650s for the old tactics of compromise and consensus-building to replicate their successes dating from an earlier era.

Yet Howell—like so many other students of the period—remained ambivalent about the Lord Protector. If, on the one hand, Oliver "clearly saw the importance of a civil settlement," was groping toward "the concepts of separation of power and constitutional checks and balances as protective devices against arbitrary government," and was hoping that, somehow, Parliament could function as a vehicle for the expression of "the principle of consent," on the other hand his rule in late-revolutionary England exposed a "darker side" as well:

> It is obvious that his conception of political liberty was substantially moulded in traditional and conservative practices. Anything approaching democracy in a political form was, to his eye, a manifest absurdity. It could not seem otherwise to him in a world where the godly were mixed with the ungodly. He believed firmly too in a 'natural' magistracy and in a system of ranks and orders.... And, if need be, he had few qualms about employing force to curb those who would upset that order.... He could never escape the ambiguity of ruling by military force. Whatever his personal feelings about arbitrary government (and there seem no grounds to doubt his sincerity in this regard), the necessities of preserving order in a divided society, and the desire to bring reform to it, led him in turn to be arbitrary.

The astonishing thing, Howell concluded, was not that Cromwell's contributions to "the story of political liberty" were as limited as they were, but rather "that they were as significant as they were."[11]

As Howell's commentary suggests, scholarly ambivalence toward the Lord Protector often turns upon the charge that he was, in essence, a military dictator in a very modern sense. Ironically, historical writing on this point seems at times to take its cue from politicians of the later revolutions: after all, did not Robespierre's detractors (in Thermidor) frequently liken him to Cromwell, and did not Trotsky's foes accuse him, in the mid-1920s, of having schemed in his earlier stint as War Commissar to become a "Russian Cromwell," militarily subverting the Soviet regime? Happily, today's scholars bring a somewhat more nuanced approach to the subject. Austin Woolrych, for instance, in a seminal article of 1990 and in his magisterial conspectus on the *British* revolution, painted Oliver as, in essence, a traditionalist constable trying to honor his charge to observe the laws, preserve social order, and defend the "people of God."[12] Tellingly, Woolrych stressed the *civilian* character of the Protectorate—at least in certain areas and for certain purposes:

> In Cromwell's England, as under the monarchy, most justice and most local administration lay in the hands of the county magistracy. The only period when their local supremacy was seriously encroached upon by the military was that of the major-generals.... Throughout England and Wales the commission of the peace was an overwhelmingly civilian body ... there were at any one time at least 2,500 JPs in the country, and fewer than 90 among them were serving officers.... There was an even smaller military presence among those other agents of central authority, the commissioners for collecting the monthly assessment.[13]

Yet, all of this notwithstanding, Oliver was still (in Woolrych's rendering, at least) impaled on the horns of two irresolvable dilemmas: (1) his reliance on the army militated against his ability to *civilianize* (and, thus, legitimize) his rule at all levels through a collaboration with regularly elected parliaments;

and (2) his need to accommodate gentry, burgher, and professional interests ran at times against his advocacy of the "people of God," that is, of visible "saints" in the Puritan sense of the term. Actually, for Austin Woolrych, it was the latter, *social/spiritual* contradiction that especially drove the Protector to adopt arbitrary practices of governance.[14]

But others, from Roger Howell to the most recent Cromwellian biographers and commentators on constitutional matters in the Protectorate, have voiced persisting doubts about this thesis. Howell, in refuting Trevor Roper's ideas, pointedly saved for last the question of "the position of the army," and asserted flatly that "the weapon that had won the revolutionary war made the peaceful settlement of it impossible." As long as the army could intrude into the Protectorate's internal politics, Howell wrote, "it both stood in the way of the legitimation of the government via the parliamentary route and heightened the level of the politics of frustration and confrontation within Parliament itself."[15] A similar conclusion, stressing the delegitimizing role of the New Model Army, has latterly emerged in the work of most of the Lord Protector's biographers. Peter Gaunt, for example, however generously he might credit Oliver with "doing God's will" as best he comprehended it and "working for the greater good of the nation and its people," could not, in the final analysis, avoid the reluctant judgment that "the Protector and his entire regime were always an imposition, ultimately surviving only through army backing."[16] Gaunt's most prominent contemporaries in this genre—J. C. Davis and Barry Coward come most immediately to mind—have found themselves constrained to return time and again to the *delegitimizing* significance of this "military factor" throughout the period of the Protectorate.[17]

Even more recently, David L. Smith and Patrick Little, in their careful analysis of parliamentary politics in Protectoral England, have concurred in this commentary on the troubling military element in Cromwellian governance, but they have also gone beyond this to stress the *absolutist tendencies* in that governance. For instance, they have cited Cromwell's "willingness in certain circumstances to bypass Parliament and if necessary even to breach the rule of law," whether in the matter of raising funds in national emergencies or in that of abrogating "the very liberties and privileges for which he had fought in the Civil Wars"; they have found this tendency to be "disconcertingly similar in substance" to Charles I's constitutional behavior. Yet, after all is said and done, they admit, in an effort to *historicize* the Lord Protector, that "such attitudes mark Cromwell as very much a man of his times. He held the view, highly characteristic of early seventeenth-century England, that a mild tyranny was preferable to anarchy."[18] Perhaps so; still, all of this will continue to raise for us the thorny issue of *constitutional legitimacy* in the late-revolutionary England of Oliver Cromwell.

The essential failure of the Protectorate to achieve a requisite degree of legitimacy in the eyes of those in the country who really mattered can best be seen, in *specific terms*, in connection with the fate of Oliver's two parliaments and the intervening episode of the major-generals. Despite truly heroic efforts to rehabilitate the reputation of the First Protectorate Parliament of 1654 and 1655, Gaunt has had to allow after all that government-legislative relations foundered by January 1655 "upon the twin rocks of finance and the army"—issues, moreover, that the MPs correctly saw as inextricably intertwined. To be sure, heated exchanges between the two sides over other issues—aspects of the new constitution, the treatment of religious extremists, the advisability of reviving kingship in one guise or another, and so on— roiled the waters throughout this period.

> But it was when MPs set about reducing the size and cost of the standing forces and rashly attempted to gain future control over the military that the whole edifice collapsed. Parliament called for an army of 30,000 men, all but halving the existing forces, and set a military budget barely adequate to support that number. Moreover, although Cromwell was given joint command of the standing forces for life, members voted that after his death sole control was to pass to parliament, which would then dispose of military command as it 'shall think fit.' Even Cromwell's lifetime joint control was effectively undermined, for the annual military budget was to extend only until December 1659, after which Cromwell, if still alive, would have to apply to parliament for a renewed grant.[19]

The impasse between Whitehall and Westminster over these fiscal/military issues was only aggravated by parliamentary attempts to assert "permanent and sole" control over the local militias as well, and led to the Protector's irritated dismissal of his first Parliament in late January 1655.

The curious episode of the Republic's military rule by the major-generals (1655–1657) took place against the backdrop of Cromwell's continuing failure to legitimize his rule by traditional parliamentary methods. This experiment, Christopher Durston has plausibly argued, "was an attempt to square this particularly vicious political circle by enhancing the security of the regime and furthering godly reform, while at the same time reducing the overall burden of the large military establishment."[20] Historians writing on the major-generals prior to the appearance of Durston's unprecedentedly thorough study disagreed both over the extent to which Cromwell's "swordsmen and decimators" interfered in the ordinary routines of JPs (that is, Justices of the Peace) and other "natural rulers" in the counties *and* over the precise nature of the hostility they undoubtedly encountered in striving to carry out the central government's mandates on their local rounds.[21] Durston, while rejecting the tendency of some scholars to emphasize unduly the disruptive role of the major-generals on the local level, accepts most of his predecessors' explanations for the opposition to these Cromwellian agents that assuredly *did* manifest itself in this period. To some extent, he concedes, the major-generals were disliked because they were "agents of centralization"; even more, they aroused opposition *as soldiers* whose rule, for contemporaries and later English folk, "became a convenient and powerful symbol of the military nature of the unpopular Interregnum state." Yet Durston also cites, as "additional, and probably more potent" reasons for this regime's unpopularity in local eyes, its "lack of constitutional legitimacy and its overtly godly nature." In a manner somewhat reminiscent of Woolrych, Durston especially highlights the reputed "godliness" of the major-generals—and, thus, the *religious/ideological* nature of their mission—as alienating them from the gentry (and, perhaps, others as well) in the shires. "The quintessential feature of the rule of the major-generals," he concludes, "was not that it was army rule, nor that it was London rule, but that it was godly rule, and it was as such that it was decisively rejected by the great majority of the English and Welsh people."[22]

Perhaps. It is, naturally, difficult to establish any hard-and-fast ranking of factors here; maybe the safest thing to do would be to accentuate the mutual interplay, the *interconnectedness* of reasons why this brief experiment did little or nothing to buttress the legitimacy of the Protectorate in the eyes of most English folk in the mid-1650s. Then, again, we need to recall in this connection—as Durston, appropriately, does—the context of extreme *polarization* in which the major-generals struggled from the start to function. On the Left, erstwhile Cromwellian allies like John Bradshaw, Arthur Haselrig, and Edmund Ludlow, convinced that the Lord Protector had irredeemably betrayed the "good old cause" of republicanism, "were by 1655 deeply hostile to the regime and [were] regarded as a major security risk." Fringe groups like the Quakers and Fifth Monarchists added their strident calls for a violent overthrow of all secular authority and for social egalitarianism to the chorus of leftist denunciations of those in power. On the opposite extreme, Cromwell faced what Durston has fairly called "the implacable hostility of the exiled Stuart court and its thousands of supporters within England." For social, economic, political, and ideological reasons, the royalists in the land clung to hopes that "Cromwell's regime might be toppled by an armed uprising, the assassination of its head, or a mutiny by a republican section of the army."[23] Despite Austin Woolrych's sympathetic assertion that the major-generals "do not deserve the kind of anathema that they [have] commonly received" from historians with political axes to grind, he did not challenge the prevailing verdict that they must, in the end, be counted among the Protector's major mistakes.[24] Like the parliament preceding them, and like the one that came immediately *after* them, the "swordsmen and decimators" did not (possibly, in the circumstances, *could* not) solve the regime's most fundamental problem: its failure to *legitimize itself* in the eyes of the country's "natural rulers."

This brings us to what, in hindsight, was likely Oliver's last chance to achieve such acceptance—namely, the Second Protectorate Parliament (1656–1658). Unhappily, with whatever dramatic events it was attended—such as the offer of the crown to Oliver, the adoption of still another "constitution," and so on—retrospective analysis does not really indicate that its two sessions offered the regime any greater chance of securing a durable credibility than had either the First Protectorate Parliament or the subsequent rule of the major-generals. Although Durston has attributed some of Cromwell's difficulties in governing with the 1656 to 1658 Parliament to the inauspicious circumstances under which it was elected in 1656,[25] it is hard to imagine that *any* legislature at this juncture would have looked upon the Protector favorably. Significantly, this parliament (just like its predecessor in 1654) had to be purged before the government could even envision the possibility of managing it successfully; yet, even with this as a *fait accompli* (and most strikingly, perhaps, in its January 25, 1658, session, convened in the wake of Oliver's refusal of the crown) it served notice to the Protector that it was *still* opposing him on the all-important fiscal/military issues. Something of the atmosphere of that session (and of what it recalled, so ironically, from the past!) was conjured up by Ivan Roots:

> the Lord Protector . . . spoke urgently to both Houses, lecturing them on the necessity to resist the temptation to fritter time away on inessentials while the facts of the times, simmering threats at home and abroad, called for drastic and immediate measures. All that stood between them and "another flood of blood and war" was his government and a "poor unpaid army." This strong hint that priority should go to a money grant was ignored. In phraseology reminiscent of that of early parliaments of Charles I, the members claimed that in no circumstances might the grievances of the people be put aside pending a supply vote.[26]

Shades of parliamentary opposition to Charles I—and of the preliminaries to the eleven years' tyranny! That, within days, Oliver had dismissed for good yet another parliament with a bitter tirade against its "obstructionism" was probably foreordained, speaking as it did of intractable political problems upon which many a prospective collaboration between government and parliament had already run aground in England's troubled seventeenth century.

On this occasion, those problems once again involved both a *polarized political culture* and the domestic/international fiscal/military nexus. On the first point: Oliver had recently forfeited whatever lingering chance he might still have had of conciliating his critics on the Right by refusing the crown, whereas, on the Left, thousands of Londoners in early 1658 had signed a petition that, "almost certainly with the connivance of republican MPs, and supported by malcontents in the army, sectaries, and fifth monarchists," was calling militantly for the overthrow of the Protectorate, the restoration of something like the Rump, and complete freedom of conscience.²⁷ On the second point: the Protectorate's way forward, given especially its ambitious and expensive foreign policy, looked increasingly problematic. The "need for money was at the root of all evil," Ivan Roots noted. "[Secretary John] Thurloe saw it as putting the government to the wall in all its enterprises."²⁸ Not only were the county assessments, chief revenue source for the army, already intolerably high in the eyes of most rural gentry, the City of London, too (in yet another throwback to Charles I's reign) would refuse any further financial aid to the authorities. Timothy Venning, for whom Oliver "lacked imagination in this as in other matters and could not see the usefulness of innovation," has accordingly blamed the Lord Protector for not exploring the potential for adopting "money-raising schemes in collaboration with the City that might have offset the impossibility of raising the county assessments to pay for the Army." By the same token, however, Venning has freely admitted that Oliver was "further hampered" by the fact that his government was composed "of a mixture of officers and civilians . . . who conceived of economic matters as not deserving any degree of priority (when they understood such matters at all)."²⁹ In any case, Venning is assuredly correct to argue that, in the last analysis, Cromwell, John Thurloe, and the other leading figures in the government had *above all* to find some way to cater to the needs and sensibilities of the gentry, who were the *natural rulers* in the shires, were fated to dominate any parliament that might be convened, and were crucial to the Protectorate in its efforts to beat back any further royalist conspiracies.

That Oliver and his collaborators ultimately proved unsuccessful in this regard is obvious. But does this mean that, at this point in our analysis, we can remain altogether satisfied with Ivan Root's conclusion, set forth in the mid-1990s, that the Cromwellian system's survival hinged *exclusively* upon "the fast-fraying threads of the life of the present Protector"?³⁰ In the end, it may have come to that: we know now that after Oliver's sudden death in September 1658 the army grandees "made" and then unmade his son and successor Richard Cromwell, and that, in the dizzying period of political instability that followed, anarchy once again threatened and the return of the Stuarts became, first, conceivable, and then all but unavoidable. Yet specialists on the period have—especially in recent years—returned to the interlude between Oliver's demise and the Stuart Restoration of 1660 and in doing so questioned whether the confused course of events from late 1658 to May 1660 was, in fact, all that predetermined. More specifically: *could* Richard Cromwell's brief Protectoral reign have somehow amounted to more than it in fact did; and, if not, did his ouster in April 1659 automatically ensure the triumphant return of the Stuarts to power in England?

Much of the older literature on these two questions assumed that things turned out pretty much the way they had to. Writing in the 1950s, for example, Godfrey Davies cited six primary reasons for the 1660 Restoration: "the constant unpopularity of the army and of godly reform, the divisions of the republican leaders, the waning of ideological fervor among the soldiers, the lack of interest of the reformers in social evils, the corruption of 'Puritanism' by power, and the death of Cromwell who alone had sustained the Interregnum for so long."[31] After summing up Davies's arguments in this fashion, Ronald Hutton (treating the same subject thirty years later) arrived at similarly negative conclusions. He was particularly dismissive of Richard Cromwell's short-lived Lord Protectorship:

> It is a truism to say that he fell because he lost control of the army, and that this was ultimately because he had never been a soldier, but this requires some qualification. He never really 'had' control of the army.... When he believed that he was winning a section of it, he was merely detaching a few officers from their men. In essence, he could only view the army from outside, with no sympathy.... His father had always seen the soldiers as the centre of the whole great movement which had swept him to office, embodying ideals which held good for all. Richard could only see them as rather irritating servants of society.

Yet Hutton's analysis of how things became unglued in the Protectorate actually spared the father no more than it spared the son. "The man who destroyed the Protectorate," stated Hutton, "was Oliver Cromwell, who pushed it into near-bankruptcy, divided its supporters, and elevated as a potential successor a son who had no understanding of the men upon whom he most depended."[32]

Hutton's explanation for the downfall of the Protectorate, then, would actually take us all the way back to Oliver himself, who, by this reading, sowed the seeds of his own regime's destruction! Yet for most subsequent scholars, the transitional crisis of 1658 to 1660 had more complicated causes. Indeed, at least one of them, Ruth E. Mayers, has basically rejected what she sees as the overly *deterministic* historiography on 1658 to 1660. "The collapse of the parliamentary Republic," she has insisted, "was not the predetermined outcome of inveterate hostility or suspicion, but a near adventitious consequence of changing circumstances."[33] Mayers waxes somewhat rhapsodic in describing what, she claims, might have become a permanent regime in *Britain*—had it only been given a decent interval of time: "a unified British republic, religiously tolerant, politically based on the solidarity of the 'well-affected' constituency, incorporating the best of their different ideas, and closely allied with the United Provinces." Granted the time (always that temporal imponderable!) "to re-educate the majority in the principles of popular government," Mayers continues on, "the republicans might have reduced monarchists, demoralized by repeated defeats, to a dissident element no more, and perhaps much less, disruptive than the Roman Catholics, or the

Dutch Orangists." All very well and good; still, as even Mayers in the end must admit, "time was, of course, the commodity that the Commonwealth conspicuously lacked."[34] Disaster finally overtook the Protectorate, she concludes, when the army threw out the restored Rump Parliament in October 1659; yet she insists to the end that it was "contingency" rather than anything more *systemic* that played the largest role in this *dénouement*.

Mayers's contemporaries, however, have not been so sure about this: we sense, in many cases, that they want to push back much as she has against the demons of historical determinism, but cannot—despite themselves, it may be—overlook the basic internal contradictions and *lack of legitimacy* that really *did* bring the Protectorate of the Cromwells down and make King Charles II first conceivable and then unavoidable. Austin Woolrych comes first to mind in this connection. On the one hand, he gamely argued (in 2002)—very much in an "anti-determinist" vein—that it has "often been too easily assumed that only Oliver's strong hand had held the . . . Protectorate together, and that the collapse of both was only a matter of time." Certainly, Woolrych agreed, Oliver's "untimely" death in 1658 created "a precarious situation, but it was an extraordinarily open one. There was always a possibility . . . that things would fall apart, but it was not a foregone conclusion." Moreover, Woolrych complained that the "tendency of old textbooks to race through the twenty months between Cromwell's death and Charles II's return as a period of predictable anarchy with an inevitable outcome committed a serious distortion."[35] Yet this same historian concluded, on later pages, that the passage from Protectoral Republic to Stuart Restoration was, after all, highly likely by 1660. He spoke of "the breadth and depth of the rejoicing that accompanied the Restoration," and of how this event "represented a return to order and stability after a year and more in which the quality of government had deteriorated to the point of threatening the livelihood of ordinary folk, as well as undermining the prosperity of the more well-to-do." In the final analysis, Woolrych concluded, "the Commonwealth perished through its own ineptitude and internal strife before any tide of royalist enthusiasm swept its remnants away."[36]

For David Smith and Patrick Little, explaining those failures ultimately has meant studying them through the prism of government/parliamentary relations. Initially, they contend, Richard Cromwell "displayed considerable skill in handling the difficult and complex circumstances that he inherited from Oliver." As late as March 1659, "events were steadily moving in Richard's direction"—that is, "until the decisive army intervention in April-May proved fatal first to the Parliament and then to the Protectorate itself." Hence, the critical fault line running through government/parliamentary relations under the Protectorate, at least for Smith and Little, was the unresolved army-civilian split—a split implicating *both* Cromwells, as these historians straightforwardly argue:

> The fundamental problem remained the lack of understanding between the army leadership and many ordinary members of Parliament. . . . Whereas under Oliver Cromwell a military Lord Protector excited the suspicion of many within the Parliament, under his son a civilian . . . Lord Protector excited the suspicion of many within the army. Both Cromwells tried in different ways to straddle two essentially incompatible worlds, yet their attempts to do so often tended to destabilize parliamentary proceedings between 1653 and 1659.

This did not automatically signify, Smith and Little conclude cautiously, that the legislators could not function "effectively or productively"; nonetheless, it *did* represent "an inherent source of weakness that had potentially disastrous consequences if the 'single person and Parliament' failed to govern harmoniously together."[37] It would seem, then, that for these two scholars, as for most of their fellow specialists, the drama of 1658 to 1660 had historical roots going well back into the Interregnum.

Even more recently, Blair Worden and H. M. Reece (to go no further) have added their voices to this intensifying discussion of the events of 1658 to 1660. For Worden, this has taken the form of a veritable panegyric about the Parliament as the indispensable guarantor of legitimacy in English governance. What destroyed the Protectorate and ultimately brought back the Stuarts, according to Worden, was the failure of the various contending factions and parties in the Civil War and republican eras to anchor Parliament securely at the heart of the country's constitutional life:

> Something has been lost by [Conrad] Russell's insistence that parliament was "an event" rather than "an institution." It was both. The event mattered because the institution mattered . . . a vision of parliament as the great council of the realm, where ultimate authority, and with it emergency powers, lay: a council, that is, entitled in the last resort not merely to give advice to kings but to make decisions without them. . . . The creation of the Protectorate, which flouted the decisions reached and laws passed by parliament in 1649, was a flagrant violation of a widely accepted principle.[38]

By 1659, Worden has emphasized, "the cry for a 'free parliament,' or a 'full and free' or 'free and full parliament,' set the avalanche of the Restoration in motion." But the Restoration *itself*, Worden has been at pains to add, "was the restoration of parliament before it was the restoration of the monarchy, which was restored through parliament's choice."[39]

Yet it is perhaps Worden's compatriot Henry Reece who has, among recent historians, felt most keenly a lingering need to do battle against the minions of historiographical determinism in the matter of the transition from republic to restored monarchy in mid-seventeenth-century England. After all, he has alleged that "the restoration of the monarchy did not become inevitable with Cromwell's death in September 1658; with the demise of Richard Cromwell in April 1659; with the army's move against the restored Rump in

October 1659; or even with Monck's march into England in January 1660." For Reece, Charles II's accession was guaranteed only, perhaps, when, in February 1660, General Monck gave up irrevocably on the Rump and "arranged for the return of those [parliamentary] members secluded in 1648."[40] Yet, again, like so many of his peers tempted (at times) to kick back against the traces of an excessive determinism, Reece, too, has felt the need to fall back on an analysis pivoting on *something systemically wrong* with the Protectorate, something helping to explain England's reluctant embrace of Charles II. For Reece, not astonishingly, that "something" involved the army—and, inevitably, its always problematic relationship with the MPs at Westminster. Specifically, then, "it was the army's repeated purges and interruptions of successive parliaments that attracted the hostility of civilian politicians, and that eventually left the army leaders in England themselves bereft of any plan for a legislative assembly that they could enlist to legitimize their rule."[41] It was doubtless true as well, Reece conceded, that the army grandees could not adequately control their own junior officers after Oliver's death in late 1658, and that Richard Cromwell and his acolytes "pushed too far and too fast against the army's entrenched political influence" in the circumstances of early 1659. But, for Reece, such contretemps only underline the pivotal role played in the return of the Stuarts by the unresolved—and quite possibly unresolvable—military/civilian split in late Protectoral England.

Significantly, Reece has grasped here one half—the state-security half—of any neostructuralist interpretation of the Thermidorian crisis in English affairs. What could *not* be managed at this time was "military commitments outside England," because "the cost of maintaining forces in Scotland, Ireland, Flanders, and Jamaica was running at nearly twice the amount per month of the cost of the regiments in England, and the huge charge of the navy came on top of that."[42] In concluding that a "major reduction in the scale of these overseas operations would have been essential for the survival of the Protectorate, or indeed any post-1649 regime," Reece was in a sense only reiterating what Timothy Venning's earlier reappraisal of Cromwellian foreign policy had led *him* to conclude. The final resolution of the struggles between the legislative and executive branches of government that delegitimized the Protectorate to the very end, Venning held, would have to involve a "close alliance of personnel between the two which would end with the head of the Executive leading the government via (or from) the Legislature."[43] In our larger *theoretical terms*, this would be the only way to mesh English strategic requirements abroad with political-cultural and constitutional requirements at home. And by 1688 and 1689, for sure, the English would *need*—imperatively—to harmonize these national requirements.

THE CRISIS OF LEGITIMACY IN THE FRENCH DIRECTORY

We do not encounter, in the case of Thermidorian France, any individual as dominant as Oliver Cromwell—Napoleon, after all, only came to power at the end of the period. Still, in reappraising the Directory's political-cultural problems against the backdrop of its increasingly aggressive posture in international affairs, and thus its transcendent neostructural dilemma, we are likely to be impressed by how closely the crisis of legitimacy lurking at the heart of the Directory resembled that which had so insidiously hollowed out the Cromwellian Protectorate nearly a century and a half earlier. Moreover, if the tumultuous circumstances surrounding Richard Cromwell's abortive Protectorate and the ensuing Stuart Restoration have stimulated renewed discussion among English revolutionary historians, the transition from Directory to Bonapartist rule in 1799 has, similarly, provoked a new round of arguments among specialists on late-revolutionary France.

We can begin here with the fact that the constitution drawn up for France by the Thermidorians in 1795, however ingenious in detail, concealed as many pitfalls as had the Instrument of Government and the Humble Petition and Advice in the case of England. Under its terms, power was apportioned between a legislature composed of two chambers, the Council of Five Hundred and the Council of Elders or "Ancients," and a five-man Executive Directory. The Council of Five Hundred (all of whose members had to be at least thirty years old) would propose laws to the upper chamber, whose 250 deputies (aged forty or older) would either sanction or reject those laws. The original Directors were selected by the Elders from a list of ten candidates for each position drawn up by the Five Hundred. One Director was to retire each year, and he would be ineligible for reappointment for five years. Moreover, the Directors were forbidden, without legislative approval, to post troops within sixty kilometers of the assemblies. Thus, the risk of undue pressure being exerted by the executive on the legislature would, it was hoped, be curtailed. Yet the Directors would supervise the daily labors of the ministers and other personnel, and were to be represented in the local departments and cantons (as well as in the tribunals and, at times, in the armies) by *commissaires* overseeing the implementation of laws by elected departmental and cantonal officials, the disposition of justice, and military matters. Finally, all elected officials, from national assemblymen down to local administrators, were to be chosen (yearly) during a ten-day cycle of voting in late March and early April. The electoral system prevailing during 1795 to 1799 recalled those systems instituted at earlier points in the revolution in that it was two-tiered and indirect, permitting a much broader adult (male) franchise at the primary stage than at the secondary stage.[44]

Many years ago, Albert Goodwin contended valiantly that there was "something to be said for the view that the main constitutional difficulties of the Directors were in the course of time solved." He even suggested that the frequent *coups d'états* for which the regime became notorious, "far from being an indication of the essential instability of the government," could be viewed, alternatively, "as a source of strength," as "consonant with the best interests of the country at large."[45] Perhaps; still, critics of the "Constitution of the Year III" have weighed in over time. Martyn Lyons's strictures against its provisions have been fairly typical. He has noted, for example, that a five-man executive might easily fall prey to internal squabbling, and that blind chance might constrain its usefulness, insofar as lots were ostensibly to be drawn annually to decide which Director would retire. More problematic, perhaps, was the rigid separation of powers ordered by the Constitution. The ministers could not sit in the legislature, and the Directors had to communicate with the deputies by official "messages." Additionally, because the Five Hundred managed the purse strings, it could, if dominated by a hostile majority, paralyze the Directors. "The Directory, which had no power of dissolution, and no veto, could only reply by unconstitutional methods." The way was open, in other words, for the coups and executive purges of the legislature and (at times) of local government for which the Directors indeed earned notoriety—and which, for Lyons and many other historians, scarcely betokened governmental stability. There was also the fact that the procedure for amending the Constitution was "almost Byzantine in its complexity."[46] It would be very difficult today to disagree with the inference Lyons has drawn from all of this: namely, that the *politique de bascule* (i.e., seesaw political policy) and the "exceptional laws" of the Directory reflected less than favorably upon the Thermidorians' constitutional handiwork.

Moreover, in this case as in that of Protectoral England, the drawbacks of written constitutions acquired added importance in a political culture characterized by a distrust of pluralistic politics and by deep *social polarization*. Regarding the first point, most scholars now agree that one of the old regime's key legacies to the upheaval in France was its preference for political consensus in society, its mistrust of a contestatory politics of factions/parties. And this tendency hardly expired with the Jacobin Terror. If, in theory, the Directory offered representative governance founded—at least in part—on electoral politics, it never unreservedly accepted the need for a system of freely competing political parties. "It was better to die with honor defending the republic," so Director Louis-Marie La Révellière-Lépeaux revealingly argued, "than to perish or even to live in the muck of parties and . . . factions."[47] Somewhat contradictorily, Bronislaw Baczko has observed, *democracy* in the French revolutionary lexicon "joined together individualism and a true cult of unanimity, representative government and the refusal to allow any interest other than the 'general interest' to be represented, the recognition of the freedom of opinion and the mistrust of divisions in public opinion." "Democracy" in this sense ineluctably "mixed modernity with archaism."[48] The present, in other words, with its untested trust in political pluralism, was now to be awkwardly joined with a past habituated more to the promptings of consensualism.

As for the phenomenon of social polarization, it challenged the Directors and their partisans as implacably as, in Protectoral England, it had dogged Oliver Cromwell and his major-generals. On the Far Right, the authorities could never afford to forget the *émigrés*, nor the ex-nobles sullenly subsisting on their rustic estates—these were individuals who were of one mind in desiring a return to the good old days of *privilège*, social deference, and all the perquisites associated with seigneurialism. The Directors were acutely aware as well of the Declaration of Verona (1795) in which the comte de Provence ("Louis XVIII") promised a complete restoration of the old regime's social structure and prerogatives.[49] By 1796 and 1797, in addition, the Directors would be lashing out against so-called philanthropic institutes engaged in recruiting political candidates and mobilizing voters on the Right. And yet, at the same time, those in governing circles viewed with equal concern the increasingly aggressive campaign on the Left—most markedly in the aftermath of the neo-Jacobin *coup* of Fructidor, Year V (i.e., September 1797)—to broaden the social basis of French politics. As one historian of Jacobin activism in these late days of the Revolution has observed, the politicians and clubbists on the Left did not define their sociopolitical goals with great precision. Still, they *did* share "a minimal preference for a republic where political oligarchy and social pretension would be attacked, and where the 'workingman' had a rightful place in civil and political life." Yet workingmen of all stripes still suffering from a low social status and poor education, still associated in élitist eyes with the recent Jacobin/*sans-culotte* Terror, and involved to some extent now in revitalized Jacobin activism, naturally raised the hackles of the authorities at Paris quite as much as did pro-royalists on the Far Right.[50]

No doubt from the government's point of view, the "solid" Frenchmen to whom it wished to restrict the rights of active citizenship composed what Colin Lucas has called a "political nation": such men "continued to form the *pays légal* of property owners who voted in national elections and provided the personnel of local government."[51] But *was* there in fact a political nation in the center of the political spectrum, a stratum of "natural rulers" (to use the British expression) rooted in socioeconomic interests to whom the Republic's civilian leaders could appeal? Scholarly commentary does very little to validate the Marxian paradigm of a bourgeois Directory anchored securely in the bedrock of entrepreneurial and other middle-class interests. Indeed, Clive Church has gone so far as to state that "the Directory failed precisely because it was not a bourgeois regime. . . . The Directors and their supporters were basically a political group, lacking roots in society, and consequently failing to maintain themselves in power." The regime, he has insisted, had no reason to be surprised if, in the end, businessmen and other notables whose aspirations it had never adequately represented abandoned it, preferring a "leap in the dark" with a charismatic outsider like Napoleon Bonaparte.[52] If, on the other hand, Martyn Lyons has found this approach smacking too much of bureaucratic reductionism, and thus has painted the Directory as reflecting (like all preceding regimes in the revolutionary period) the social biases of middling strata in French society, he has, no less, allowed that "it may indeed be too simple to describe the Directory as a *bourgeois* Republic, since, in the last resort, the *bourgeoisie* abandoned the regime."[53]

The government's legacy appears even more problematic if we take into account *provincial* and *religious* issues. Students of late-revolutionary political culture, for example, have often stressed how unavailing were efforts by the leaders of the so-called First Directory (1795–1797) to persuade prominent local citizens that what transpired at Paris affected them meaningfully (and, of course, favorably). To do so would have required demonstrating to such *provinçiaux* that the government was able to deal fairly with *local* problems, recognized as such in a *local* context. It made little difference what the Directors and assemblymen saw as their diplomatic and domestic objectives if, in the departments and cantons, their *commissaires* and other agents were unable (for instance) to maintain good order on the highways, apply military conscription fairly, defuse subsistence crises, and find ways to mediate arguments for and against governmental intrusion into judicial affairs. Perceived in this light, the regime's problems were daunting, possibly even insoluble, from the start. By 1796, the Directory was finding it hard to convince the "respectable" citizens in the departments that it could solve local problems in a professional and nonpartisan fashion. The Directors subsequently staged the Fructidor *coup* (September 1797) to nullify earlier elections that they (correctly) construed as rejecting their local policies of 1796. Yet, ironically, this only led the so-called Second Directory (of 1797–1799) to adopt illegal political and administrative measures that in turn *further delegitimized* the government in provincial eyes.[54]

Then, there were (in Directorial France, as, earlier, in Protectoral England) *religious* issues. The Republic's ostensibly neutral but actually intolerant and, at times, persecutory stance on such matters only deepened its isolation in the provinces. The Thermidorian/Directorial leaders have earned some scholarly plaudits for trying to instill a new civil religion in the minds and hearts of the citizenry.[55] Yet there is scant evidence to indicate that the new faith, with its transparently political overtones, ever caught on in a major way among the traditionally Catholic masses. What is more, the authorities, even in the relatively tolerant times preceding the leftist Fructidor *coup*, only grudgingly conceded Catholic liberties. Sundays were ordinary working days under the revolutionary calendar, and sacred holidays also fell victim to the new temporal schema. In addition, local officials exercised an intrusive role of surveillance over religious services: preachers were often dismayed to find police spies attending their sermons. Again, priests were subjected to civic tests reminiscent of the Civil Constitution of 1790 and 1791 and were answerable, under penalty of arbitrary deportation, for any violations of the myriad rules against bells and other exterior signs of worship. Yet again, those courageous enough to open Catholic schools could incur official wrath if they failed in any respect to observe the Republican calendar.[56] Predictably, the regime's treatment of Catholic clergy and communicants only hardened in the wake of Fructidor. It imposed a tough loyalty oath on all priests determined still to minister to their flocks and arrogated to itself the power to deport or incarcerate refractory priests by simple administrative fiat.[57]

The Directory's behavior in such matters was explicable (if also self-defeating) on several counts. For one thing, the political culture in which the policymakers of the late 1790s were operating tended to dull their religious sensibilities much as it distorted their political perspective. For, just as the Directors found it hard to accept the idea of organized and freely competing political parties, so they could not in the end resist the temptation to police and even persecute a disestablished Catholic Church supposedly entitled to contend with other faiths for the popular favor. More important, however, was the "force of circumstances." The regime, challenged at home by extremists on both the Right and the Left, and in time besieged on the international front by the Second Coalition, was tempted increasingly to confuse apolitical Catholicism with the royalist-counterrevolutionary cause, and to enlist Jacobin anticlericalism in a patriotic (if sporadic) campaign against recalcitrant priests (and their rumored *émigré* allies) in the provinces. And, just as earlier in the decade, so now, harassing *curés* and *vicaires* only helped to turn the local populace against Paris. "Local documents are full of examples of strife and resistance over the religious issue," Clive Church has commented. "In the quiet department of the Haute Marne this was practically the only cause of public disorder, leading on one occasion to a whole village rioting when two luckless gendarmes tried to arrest a refractory priest." Whereas we may assume that most villages aroused at times from political quiescence in this period were not exercised solely about religious questions, we can agree with Church that the government's draconian treatment of priests and their flocks was "a major cause of the alienation of public opinion during the later stages of the Directory's existence."[58]

Yet if the Directory (like the Protectorate) undercut its own legitimacy on a legion of *domestic* issues reflecting the severely polarized political culture of the times, it likely sealed its own doom most decisively (again, much as had Oliver and Richard Cromwell) on *neostructurally transcendent* issues of finance and geopolitics. Continental warfare and its attendant costs eroded the regime's legitimacy both directly and indirectly: directly, by crippling its finances and alienating its natural constituencies, and indirectly by militarizing internal politics to the point where only the generals and their armies could rescue governance at Paris from the consequences of its own systemic weaknesses.

On the former point: it was the ruinously expensive French foreign policy that prevented the Directory from resolving the protracted financial crisis that had haunted the revolutionaries ever since 1789. Moreover, official efforts to resolve that crisis only cost the government support in what should have been its key constituencies. Thus, for instance, trying to compensate for the widespread failure of French citizens to pay their taxes and for shortfalls in state revenue accruing from the sales of *biens nationaux*—systemic problems greatly aggravated by uncontainable war expenditure—meant (in part) trying to cover ever-widening budget deficits by "allowing" a depreciation of the paper currency (i.e., the old *assignats* and subsequent *mandats territoriaux*). But the decline and eventual demise of this currency must have diminished the Directory in the eyes of its creditors—that is, military and civilian pensioners, salaried employees, and so on—much more than they ingratiated the regime with debtors and speculators fortunate enough to profit from that currency's disastrous depreciation.[59] Even more damaging, probably, from a public relations standpoint, was the notorious "two-thirds bankruptcy" of 1797, which, however necessary it may have seemed to the authorities from a strictly fiscal point of view, effectively wiped out two-thirds of many *rentiers'* most crucial form of income.[60] Then, yet again, there were the shipbuilders, insurance agents, merchants, and refiners in port cities such as Le Havre and Nantes, La Rochelle, Bordeaux, and Marseilles, whose lucrative returns from overseas colonies and trade were in the late 1790s strangled by the British blockade.[61] For every slippery *financier* and war contractor like Gabriel-Julien Ouvrard resourceful enough to batten off the situation by manipulating governmental forced loans, naval outlays, and various war-related expenditures, there must have been a veritable army of bourgeois entrepreneurs financially ruined by the Directory's clash with Britain. As for the masses: Gwynne Lewis has discovered that, in the southern Department of the Gard, the endless war, "although reviving the revolutionary ardor of some, particularly the urban workers, offered little to the rural Catholic population."[62] From the central Department of the Seine-et-Oise came a very similar appraisal of popular attitudes by the state's local *commissaire*: "The French victories appeal to a section of them, but do not touch them greatly, because they are purchased at the cost of their sons' blood, and the peasantry are not sufficiently committed to accept such sacrifices."[63] And no matter what patriotic republican historiography may tell us, nothing was as ideally calculated to spread widespread fear and loathing of Thermidorian war-making among the provincial French as the military conscription that was fully institutionalized in the *loi Jourdan* of 1798.[64]

Insofar as the *indirect* impact of ever-expanding warfare was concerned, it took the form of militarizing both the Right *and* the Left in France, hence further polarizing all political forces in the late Republic. On the Right, the conservative deputies in the assemblies (the so-called Clichyites) were painfully aware of—yet found it increasingly difficult to dissociate themselves from—those implacable royalist foes of the Revolution who tended to discredit even its most moderate critics by taking up arms against France. When the comte de Provence issued his inflammatory and reactionary Declaration of Verona in 1795, when irreconcilable *émigrés* sought to prolong the civil war in the Vendée, assassinate all republicans, or foment military uprisings in the eastern and southern provinces, and when rightist diplomats lobbied the other European powers to form a new coalition against Paris, they were adding to the polarization of politics in Thermidorian France.[65] Yet essentially the same thing was also transpiring on the Left. Most striking in this regard was the sympathetic *entente* that gradually developed between the armies abroad and progressive activists at home.[66] In the unsettled wake of elections in the spring of 1797 reviving the Right, apprehensive patriots found themselves ardently seeking salvation from the victorious republican armies stationed in Italy and Germany. The immediate response to their pleas came in the form of the leftist *coup d'état* of Fructidor (in September 1797). Then, over the ensuing months, Jacobins benefiting from this political purge from one end of the Republic to the other seized every occasion to proclaim solidarity with France's brave *militaires*. Some clubs fraternized noisily with passing detachments of troops. Some even tried to involve army units in local political controversies pitting the "honest" patriots against citizens suspected of sinister designs against the Republic.[67] Most revealing, however, were the attempts of local clubbists to demand that policymakers at Paris mobilize the nation's fiscal resources to award long-promised veterans' bonuses to the intrepid *défenseurs de la patrie*. How better, they apparently calculated, to strengthen the ties between soldiers and reenergized political activists on the Left?[68]

As the Directory struggled to maintain itself amid all of these swirling forces in the late 1790s, it resorted from time to time to its *politique de bascule*, its ploy of purges and counterpurges against irreconcilables on the Right and on the Left. In doing so, it inevitably recalls for us as neostructuralists nothing so much as Oliver Cromwell's Protectorate, with its purges of the First Protectorate Parliament in 1654 and the Second Protectorate Parliament two years later, and its arbitrary, generally detested imposition of major-generals on a rural society as profoundly polarized as French rural society would be 140 years later. Yet we should go on from here to draw the inescapable follow-up analogy between the English and French situations: that between the confused transitional politics of 1658 to 1660 in England and the equally tumultuous transitional politics of 1799 in France.[69] To do this requires, in other words, that we review the most recent historiography on the eventual French resort to Napoleon Bonaparte—much as we have already reassessed the most current scholarly thinking on the developments leading in time to Charles II's accession in England.

One curious difference between these two transitional historiographies is that, whereas in the English case specialists today seem at times torn between a deterministic reading of the passage from Protectorate to Restoration *and* an antideterministic insistence on Richard Cromwell's (or, indeed, the restored Rump's) chances for success, in the analogous case of France historians seem largely to accept the strong likelihood of something like the Bonapartist *coup d'état* of November 1799, disagreeing only on whether they explain this turn of events in structuralist (i.e., state-centered) or in postmodernist (i.e., ideological or political-cultural) terms. Our challenge, as always, is to meld the most valuable insights from both analytical perspectives into a convincing neostructuralist argument.

Certainly, structurally oriented explanations for the Directory's irrevocable loss of legitimacy in 1799 can be cited in much of the recent writing on the subject—however likely that writing may be to acknowledge as well the influences of postmodernism. For instance, Howard G. Brown is very quick to declare (unsurprisingly) that "the state is more than a set of institutions; it is also a mental construct or phenomenon of consciousness that is as historically acquired as the institutions themselves."[70] Having rendered this *hommage* to postmodernism, Brown nevertheless focuses upon the international and domestic roles of (in this case) the French state in endeavoring to explain how and why "the crisis of 1799 . . . brought down the Republic":

> democratic principles had been . . . violated repeatedly since 1789, and there is little reason to think that an upsurge of moral indignation would have sufficed to bring down the regime in 1799. More important was the Directory's failure to achieve its stated aims of victorious peace abroad and the rule of law at home. The regime's accomplishments in these areas were simply too meagre by the summer of 1799 to allow the existing form of government to continue. Thus the débâcle came when a crisis in army management combined with antigovernment elections to precipitate a general paralysis of the state, and thereby made new institutional arrangements almost inevitable.[71]

Brown has returned to this dialectic between the external and domestic roles of the late-revolutionary French state in his subsequent work. "Regardless of its political rhetoric," he has reminded his readers more recently, "most Frenchmen experienced the Republic as a regime that privileged war over social programs, domestic tranquility, and even representative democracy." Military crisis, he has suggested, had originally given birth to the Republic, "and it was military success that largely sustained it." Hence, the inference to be drawn from this was fairly obvious: military reverses (as, in fact, *were* suffered by France in the War of the Second Coalition) were critical in bringing the Directorial republic down.[72]

In all of this, Brown plays up the role (most notably, the *international* role) of the Directory *as a state* in paving the way for its own delegitimization, and, thus, its own destruction. Yet other students of the Directory's terminal crisis in 1799—for instance, James Livesey, Laura Mason, Andrew Jainchill, Bernard Gainot, and Pierre Serna—have, over the past decade or so, attempted to situate this failure of a late-revolutionary state in a larger explanatory context invoking the "agency" (that is, the individual roles) of the Directors and the supposedly novel political culture or cultures generated in France by its revolutionary experience during the 1789 to 1799 period.

James Livesey, for example, in his 2001 study *Making Democracy in the French Revolution*, gave generous play initially to the issue of agency—but in a manner highly unfavorable to the Directors. The "destruction of the republic" in the "crisis of 1799," he felt secure in asserting, "was made possible by the directors themselves ... in a series of coups in Years V and VI, the executive managed to delegitimize the republican state." By undercutting the integrity of the constitutional structures, continued Livesey, "the directors made the republic vulnerable to a crisis like that of 1799."[73] Still, for Livesey, such an explanation of 1799's *dénouement* was, by itself, clearly insufficient. "A line of argument that focuses solely on the personal qualities of the directors as an explanation for the failure of republican political forms in 1799 is highly unsatisfactory," Livesey wrote. "The crisis of 1799 did not come out of thin air. The neo-Jacobin revival in the legislature, which provoked the [Bonapartist] coup of 18 Brumaire, was due to the bad showing of French armies in renewed warfare. The final crisis of the Directory was, in essence, due to foreign policy failures."[74]

This would sound very much like Brown's diagnosis of the Directory's downfall—and, indeed, it recalls classic French republican historiography on the subject. Yet, for Livesey, the Directory's foreign policy failures themselves needed to be understood, ultimately, within a context of *conflicting political cultures*. The Directors, purportedly motivated by what Livesey identifies here as a novel philosophy of "commercial republicanism," were incapable of understanding the very different, "Hobbesian" culture of European geopolitics; hence, they were probably fated to fail in the no-holds-barred world of international affairs. As Livesey deconstructed the situation in the late 1790s:

> [The Directors'] notion of replacing England in a transformed commercial order was a projection of their ideal of the commercial republic, but norms such as utility, happiness, and *industrie*, which had a real social and institu-

tional basis in domestic politics, had none in the sphere of international relations. Relations between states had an irreducibly Hobbesian quality; they were mediated by interest and only marginally by norms. . . . There was no set of concepts through which to articulate the norms of the democratic republic with the facts of international relations.[75]

This, then, was Livesey's undeniably ingenious way of striving to combine the insights of (*his* particular version of) postmodernist analysis with a somewhat more traditionally grounded structuralist emphasis upon state and interstate dynamics—where, that is, the much-mooted question of the Directory's final loss of legitimacy was concerned. What Livesey referred to as the "nexus between formal constitutional politics, democratic political culture, and international affairs" was certainly *not* denied here; it was merely reconceptualized in such a fashion as to allow a *primary stress* upon domestic political-cultural contradictions that were (at least in this account) so instrumental in the final crisis of the Directory.[76]

As suggested earlier, other historians writing recently in a generally postmodernist vein have offered their own thoughts on the loss of Directorial legitimacy in late-revolutionary France. Andrew Jainchill, for instance, has returned to the (apparently irresistible) subject of French foreign policy in the late 1790s, anatomizing it in terms of "classical-republican" and "modern" ideologies. For Jainchill, it was the "interplay" between these two ideologies that helped both to erode the vitality of the Directory *and* to prepare the way for the Bonapartist *coup d'état* of November 1799. Post-Robespierrist debate on foreign policy and the policies actually adopted, according to this historian, "were largely structured by classical-republican anxieties about expansion." Yet "there was also an identifiable modern position that simultaneously pushed the Republic's foreign policy toward more aggressive expansionist programs and helped to lay the conceptual foundation of the Napoleonic Empire." French foreign policy, so wrote Jainchill, has too often been treated separately from domestic politics; in cultural terms, it reflected "the wider post-Terror dialectic between classical-republican and modern political languages."[77] Jainchill's analysis here appears in some respects to resemble that put forth recently by Bernard Gainot, who has written about Directorial attitudes on foreign policy as increasingly torn between incompatible visions of (on the one hand) a hegemonic *grande nation* and (on the other hand) a new France viewed as part of a "federation" of European states.[78] Again, a nexus between late-revolutionary France's foreign and domestic policies seems to be common to the analyses of both of these historians, even if they have differed in their *specific descriptions* of conflicting political visions in the waning days of the Directory.

Bernard Gainot's compatriot Pierre Serna has added to this postmodernist literature on the transition in 1799 from a failing Directory to a new, Bonapartist regime by depicting, as central to this process, the "turncoat" (*la girouette*) who, speaking for an emerging "radical center" in French politics, claimed to represent the "public interest" existing above and beyond any narrowly conceived interests of the state. In Pierre Serna's account (summarized here by James Livesey), the *girouette*, "patterned on the one-time republican allies of Bonaparte, did not maintain the stability of the state by finding the compromise position between social interests." Instead, this transitional individual articulated a brand of "radical moderation," of "ideological centrism between left and right, which insulated the executive from threats to its role generated by different ideas of legitimacy, democratic or constitutional." If this political figure of the *girouette*—and this general phenomenon of "radical centrism"—only emerged fully in the November 1799 coup which ushered in a postrepublican regime in France, it was nonetheless "incubated" in the twilight years of the Directory itself.[79] Here, then, we have yet another attempt to interpret France's fundamental political transition in 1799 in fashionable political-cultural terms.

In the final analysis, however, it may be difficult for historians to resist the kind of approach to the Directory's loss of legitimacy—neostructuralist in all but name—that Brown and others have been grasping at in their work. Even specialists like Isser Woloch who may be tempted initially to analyze the Directory's terminal weaknesses in political-cultural terms will often return, in their efforts to explain the events of 1799, to the drastic impact of the "fiscal-military nexus" on French political fortunes in the late 1790s. To be sure, Woloch has written that the Directorial regime "improbably combined a system of annual elections with a readiness to nullify the results of those elections if they seemed outside the pale." Such political purges, he has observed, may have "provoked appreciative responses at the time from various constituencies, but cumulatively this succession of unconstitutional actions sapped the legitimacy of the republic itself."[80] So, in part, then, the Directory admittedly *was* undone by glaring contradictions in its own political culture—a political culture whose unyielding *secularism*, moreover, alienated in many ways the predominantly Catholic population of the hinterland. Yet ultimately there was the even more fatal obstacle to Directorial success posed by interlocking issues of a *financial* and *geostrategic* nature. As Isser Woloch expressed it: "The treasury was empty and financial stringency inhibited the government at every turn, most visibly in its ability to supply the army. This was especially scandalous since the Directory's diplomacy had provoked the formation of a new anti-French coalition abroad, the outbreak of a war on three fronts, and an early string of victories by its enemies—Britain, Austria, and Russia." A hopelessly compromised attitude toward electoral politics, a persecutorial attitude toward the still-overwhelmingly Catholic masses, and (perhaps most urgently) irresolvable problems of state finance, diplomacy, and war—and all of this (as Woloch has correctly added) "in the absence of an underlying consensus" in society![81] No wonder that the Directory "crashed" and gave way to a charismatic military personality, the convenient "hero of the hour," in the autumn of 1799.[82]

At this point in chapter 5, before moving on to the feverish search for statist legitimacy in early Soviet Russia, we should reiterate that the scholarship on both the Protectorate and the Directory sooner or later invokes the cardinal importance of the fiscal/military nexus—and thereby calls for a fully neostructuralist analysis. We have just seen this point underscored in the French case by Isser Woloch; his remarks on the subject all but anticipated the conclusion arrived at a decade later in the English case by H. M. Reece: "It was the government's military commitments outside England that were sapping its financial viability . . . and that eventually left the army leaders in England themselves bereft of any plan for a legislative assembly that . . . could . . . legitimize their rule."[83] The pages that follow, however, will offer a neostructuralist analysis of revolutionary legitimacy *preserved*—at least for the time being—in historical circumstances that were potentially much more dangerous for the revolutionaries involved.

THE CRISIS OF LEGITIMACY IN NEW ECONOMIC POLICY RUSSIA

To reassess the Bolsheviks' efforts to achieve legitimacy for their rule in NEP Russia is—finally—to confront *fully* the "conundrum within a conundrum" that we identified at the start of this chapter. We have to explain, in other words, how the early Soviet regime—unlike England's Protectorate and France's Directory—managed to weather *its* crisis of legitimacy. As we shall see, *this* particular crisis of revolutionary legitimacy turned on unprecedented imperatives of accelerated, massive, state-sponsored industrialization that harbored enormous implications for Russia's sheer survival in global affairs as well as for the Russian Communist Party's fundamental credibility in the eyes of its domestic acolytes and increasingly impatient critics.

To begin with, the festering disillusionment of V. I. Lenin's successors with the post-Terrorist breathing spell in state economic affairs known as the NEP was reflected, in part, in their obsession with the French revolutionary precedent of Thermidor. To many Communists, Sheila Fitzpatrick has written, "NEP had the smell of Thermidor, the period of degeneration of the great French Revolution." As the debate over strategies of modernization to be pursued heated up, protagonists in that debate accused each other of scheming to impose a Russian version of Thermidorian degeneration on their own revolution—and were not altogether above invoking the "salutary effects of the guillotine" as hedging against such an unthinkable betrayal.[84] Even when consigned, later on, to political oblivion, Leon Trotsky would still be raising

Thermidorian (not to mention Bonapartist) parallels against General Secretary Joseph Stalin, the man who had condemned him to that Carthaginian fate.[85]

But to make this last point is to get ahead of ourselves. Even at the time of its inception in 1921, Lenin's NEP had sowed division in Party ranks, and Lenin himself had always been careful to accentuate the *temporary* nature of this tactical retreat in a country that was never to lose sight of its long-term, historic mission to "build socialism."[86] Paradoxically, the very successes chalked up by NEP by the mid-1920s helped clear the way for a basic reevaluation of how Soviet Russia was to break into the envied precincts of industrialization, urbanization, and modernization most fully defined. On the positive side, Lewis H. Siegelbaum has stated, "the condition of Soviet industry by all accounts took a marked turn for the better in 1924. For the next two years, steady progress was made in the expansion of output, employment, productivity, and profitability. Consumer goods industries continued to lead the way, financing their operations mainly from the quick turnover of sales to an expanding peasant market." Furthermore, during 1924/1925, iron and steel production rose noticeably, "thanks to a more liberal long-term credit policy and the revival of coal production in the Donbass." On the debit side, however, Siegelbaum has noted that the capital goods and extractive industries still could not rival the production quotas achieved before the Great War: if, for instance, cigarette production was at 102 percent of the 1913 total and that of textiles was back to 66 percent, "steel output amounted to only 43.8% and iron ore was no more than 23.8%." Even worse, by 1925 the upward *structural limits* of industrial recovery were already in sight: official estimates pegged existing industrial plants as utilizing up to 85 percent of capacity, and governmental planning agencies such as *Gosplan* and the Supreme Economic Council (*Vesenkha*) were as a result setting up commissions to investigate the fixed capital requirements for a transformation of factories, equipment, and productive processes.[87]

As Siegelbaum and a legion of other historians have explained, this was the point of departure for what scholars still refer to as the "Soviet industrialization debate"—a debate that also caught up in its nets basic questions of Party policy toward the peasantry *and* toward Russian strategic requirements in a world of ever-more-rapidly modernizing Great Powers.[88] Because, as the 1920s wore on (and in part for diplomatic reasons we touch upon subsequently), it became progressively less likely that Soviet Russia could finance its industrialization drive through large-scale foreign commerce and credits, it seemed ever more necessary that the Party look to internal, autochthonous sources for the capital accumulation that was a prerequisite for such industrialization. Given the paucity of *bourgeois* accumulation of capital within Russia, this appeared to point toward a policy of squeezing the peasantry to obtain such funds—even if, conceivably, this might mean a potentially violent confrontation with the *muzhiki* and with other farmers of rural Russia. Although the conclusion drawn in many informed circles in the mid-1920s from a debate between Evgenii Preobrazhensky and Nikolai Bukharin on this subject was that nothing should be done to antagonize the peasantry and thus risk breaking the worker-peasant alliance (the *smychka*) that Lenin, prior to his death in January 1924, had certified as essential in class terms for the NEP, others (including, most critically, General Secretary Stalin) were not so sure.

Stalin by 1925 was making it clear that industrialization (implicitly at any cost) was one of his highest priorities: indeed, on the eighth anniversary of the October Revolution, he likened his Party's recent decision to draw up a Five-Year Plan for accelerated industrialization to Lenin's decision in late 1917 to vault ahead and seize state power. Significantly, too, he was drawing in part on the optimism about the potential for rapid industrial development recently engendered in the Party's caucuses by the impressive advances in productivity—an optimism that found one of its outlets in the increasingly ambitious economic/developmental plans devised by *Gosplan* and *Vesenkha*. When Stalin's erstwhile comrade from Civil War days, Felix Dzerzhinskii, now the head of *Vesenkha*, waxed enthusiastic in 1925 about "these new tasks [of industrialization]" and proclaimed that the Soviets were moving rapidly from the realm of abstract theorizing to formulating the industrialization question "as a definite, concrete objective of all our present economic activity," he was speaking a language soon to find its most famous articulation in the Stalinist doctrine of "Socialism in One Country."[89]

At the same time, we must keep in mind the foreign/domestic dialectic that, as always, was at work in these days of critical decision-making in late-revolutionary Russia. Even as the NEP was, in its productive aspects, coming up against a *domestic* ceiling imposed by worn-out industrial infrastructure and outmoded technology dating from prewar times, the international horizon, to the discomfiture of Foreign Minister Georgi V. Chicherin, his lieutenant Maxim Litvinov, and other Soviet leaders, seemed to be darkening. These were the days of such alarming developments as the British Government's raid on the Soviet trade mission (All Russian Co-operative Society) offices at London, the assassination of a Soviet diplomat in Poland, the break-up of the *Kuomintang*-Chinese Communist Party alliance in China, and (perhaps most worrying) the gradual move of Weimar Germany away from its postwar *Schicksalgemeinschaft* stance implicitly favoring Russia over the Western Powers.[90] Given these shifting external realities, Stalin's decision to "go it alone" in economic/modernizing terms made, for many Russians, a certain geostrategic and, thus, psychological sense. "Leading Bolsheviks" may have "exaggerated and exploited the foreign danger," but, as Arno Mayer has aptly argued, they had been "profoundly marked by the Allied intervention in the civil war," and were "acutely aware of the uncertainty of external relations;

of the anti-Communist *consensus omnium* spanning the outside world; and of Russia's military weakness."[91] That subversive activities staged by the Russian-dominated Comintern in countries from Britain to China helped stoke the fires of anti-Russian sentiment in the world at large does not in itself invalidate those arguments emphasizing the nexus of foreign and domestic factors pushing Soviet Russia down the road toward a relentless tempo of industrialization *and* of collectivization of farms in the countryside. Indeed, the Comintern's own schizoid "aggressive/defensive" psychology in some ways may have *reflected* that nexus of foreign and internal pressures weighing upon Soviet policy formulation.

All of the aforementioned considerations have by no means produced a universal retrospective consensus on the *inevitability* of Soviet abandonment of the NEP in favor of breakneck industrialization and of a forcible collectivization of peasant lands and agricultural equipment in rural Russia. Moshe Lewin, for example, has held that *some* version of NEP might have been retained had the regime only eased the pressures on the *muzhiki* with a combination of imports of grain and industrial commodities, reductions of the glaring inequities between (high) industrial and (low) agricultural prices, and greater utilization of artels, cooperatives, and other alternatives to the "sovietized" collective farming of the 1930s; others have agreed with him.[92] Yet a growing number of historians and economists of note have questioned such revisionism, maintaining either that the NEP constituted in the final analysis an economic blind alley *tout court*, and as such was not capable of yielding the rapid industrialization Russia so urgently needed, or that, as Jon Jacobson has more precisely put it, "by 1926/27 . . . resource allocation and capital investment within the framework of NEP" *could* produce "a level of industrial growth equal to or better than 1909-13 levels, but not an expansion equal to that achieved by the mid-1930s."[93] Jacobson himself, reviewing both the international context *and* the domestic implications of the crash industrialization of the 1930s, has summarized what much of the post–Union of Soviet Socialist Republics historiography has had to say about the contested achievements of the NEP:

> Viewed from a post-Soviet historical perspective, there are good reasons to doubt whether NEP in actuality ever constituted a viable option for agriculture and economic foreign relations. Close examination of these two sectors of the economy indicates that the NEP crisis did not begin in . . . 1927. Rather "a cumulative series of converging crises" plagued NEP from the time it was instituted. The foreign sector of the economy never recovered from the dislocations of the years 1914-1920; and only in 1923/24 and 1926/27 could grain be exported at a level sufficient to fulfill the trade plan for the year.[94]

Still, whatever the actual chronology of NEP's ups and downs may have been, it is undeniable that the grain procurement crisis of 1927 to which

Stalin and his cohorts had to react in one fashion or another served, in the final analysis, as a critical catalyst, "accelerating and sharpening all economic and political processes in the country."[95]

The editors of an anthology on the changes that engulfed rural Russia in 1927 and thereafter—Lynne Viola, V. P. Danilov, N. A. Ivnitskii, and Denis Koslov—have testified to the seriousness of the grain procurement crisis of those years, even as they have regarded it (perhaps inescapably) as serving the *political* as well as the economic purposes of the emerging Stalinist directorate at Moscow. Viola and her colleagues have also been careful to situate this crisis—and the Soviet leaders' perception of it—in a context colored by what we, as neostructuralists, would call the domestic/military/diplomatic nexus of late-revolutionary affairs:

> It was in this context that the regime confronted a crisis in grain procurements in 1927, the first of a series of . . . crises that would continue up to the forced collectivization of Soviet agriculture. State grain procurements first faltered in the spring, reviving in the summer months, and then declining again in the fall. . . . Crop failures in the Ukraine and the Northern Caucasus, which produced two-thirds of the nation's grain, were responsible for the shortfall. The export plan and the internal supply of grain appeared to be in jeopardy. In the face of the war scare, the . . . procurement crisis was viewed as a threat to national security, posing risks to industrialization and defense capacity as well as to internal social stability.[96]

Clearly, according to these specialists, the *muzhiki* and other farmers in the countryside were as capable of divining the potential linkage between domestic and international affairs in this area of public policy as were leaders in Moscow: after all, their diversion of grain and other products from state procurement agents to local purposes (hoarding, fodder for livestock, etc.) responded to the 1927 "war scare" as well as to a "famine" in the availability (or acceptable pricing?) of manufactured goods.[97] But lurking in the background here as well was General Secretary Stalin's all-too-predictable inclination to view the grain procurement crisis through a *political* lens:

> Stalin and his allies continually warned not only of the dangers of war, but of the threat of hunger and urban instability if the grain procurement crisis was not forcefully addressed. . . . It is difficult to say how real the threat to subsistence was. . . . What *is* amply clear is that the regime capitalized on the crisis to push for a final solution to the problems of grain procurement.[98]

For Stalin, rich peasants (*kulaks*), private traders in rural areas, and supposedly lazy local officials were, in 1927 and thereafter, increasingly to be singled out as responsible for the shortages in grain. Looking somewhat ahead, Viola and her associates spelled out what for them would be the manifest *political* implications of all of this: "Collectivization," they concluded, "played a critical role in the development of a police state based on the dictatorial powers of Stalin"; it was "tantamount to the [statist] colonization of the countryside" and "brought with it an unwavering brutality in the subjugation of the peasantry and an end to the peasantry's ability to actively resist the incursions of the state."[99]

Yet this is getting a bit ahead of ourselves; indeed, to some extent it takes us altogether beyond our inquiry into Thermidorian developments in Russia. Suffice it to state at this juncture that we must ultimately situate the debate over the *economics* of the transition from the NEP of the mid-1920s to the Five-Year Plans, heavy industrialization, and collectivization drive of the late 1920s and early 1930s in a larger context of factors that led ultimately to a certain relegitimization of governance in Russia. True, the *economic* historian will, appropriately enough, point out that what Stalin, Trotsky, Preobrazhensky, Bukharin, and the others debating public policy at this time were facing was in some respects merely the latest version of that disjunction between the urban and rural economies, between worker and peasant needs, that had plagued every government in Russia since the late Imperial days of Sergei Witte and Peter Stolypin. Again, the specialist fascinated by the role of personalities in history cannot help but regard Stalin, as he emerged triumphantly from the factional Party in-fighting of the 1920s, as fusing "despotic rule and catch-up modernization" in a manner strikingly reminiscent of Peter the Great and of other modernizing tyrants of the Russian past.[100] For us as neostructuralists, however, the question of a challenge to the legitimacy of this late-revolutionary regime (recalling, in certain respects, the crises of legitimacy in our earlier revolutions) requires above all that we explore the *social* and *cultural* criticisms of the NEP (and, by extension, of the Soviet government itself) that were mounting in the late 1920s.

In his widely read synthesis on the Soviet regime of the 1920s, Lewis H. Siegelbaum has usefully argued that any retrospective explanation of why the Party resorted so abruptly to the extraordinary measures that set the Stalin Revolution in motion at the end of the decade must stress, among other things, "the deep-seated mutual suspicion and antipathy between the party and the peasantry, the commitment of the communists to industrialization which derived from both ideological and national security considerations, the growing consumption needs of an expanding urban population, and the social and political tensions arising out of the NEP system itself."[101] The phrases that really stand out here—at least in *social* terms—are, plainly, "the mutual suspicion and antipathy between the party and the peasantry" and "the growing consumption needs of an expanding urban population." Looming behind these phrases was a *critical alteration in the balance of power between town and countryside in favor of the former*—a demographic/power shift made possible (ironically, perhaps) by the mild but undeniable economic recovery under NEP after 1921. The pronounced "internal migration" of city folk back to the rural peasant villages that had characterized the civil war years (i.e., from 1918 to 1921) was, in other words, *dramatically reversed* in the ensuing period. Ronald G. Suny has recently summarized the initial phase of this seismic shift within Russia:

> As early as 1921-22, with cities recovering from the war and the countryside still reeling from . . . famine, former townspeople and starving peasants streamed into the cities. . . . The number of workers bottomed out in 1922 at about 1.6 million, only 64 percent of what it had been in 1913. Then the number of workers grew steadily. . . . Overpopulation in the countryside, along with the demobilization of the Red Army, constantly fed the cities, and according to the 1926 census the population of the cities had reached their prewar level. But industry could not keep up with the new migrants, and at the end of 1926 over a million workers were unemployed.[102]

This demographic surge, this *repopulation* of urban Russia—with all of its socioeconomic, cultural, and (ultimately) political implications—would only gather steam as the decade wore on. In fact, in the years 1928 to 1932, Sheila Fitzpatrick has found, "urban population in the Soviet Union increased by almost twelve million, and at least ten million persons left peasant agriculture and became wage-earners." Fitzpatrick regards these figures as "enormous," as pointing to "a demographic upheaval unprecedented in Russia's experience and, it has been claimed, in that of any other country over so short a period."[103]

From our perspective, what made this development so significant? It made it all the easier for Russian Communists, urban-based and weaned on simplistic notions about avaricious "kulaks," "middle peasants," and "poor peasants," to continue to think in such primitive "class" terms and to demonize individuals in the first two groups (much as in civil war days) as "class enemies" of poor farmers as well as of workers in the now steadily expanding urban sector. Yet there is a burgeoning corpus of research suggesting that Soviet and Party efforts to "uplift" middle and poor peasants (*seredniaki* and *bedniaki*) and to eliminate their purportedly "backward" ways unavoidably fell short—"unavoidably," that is, due to the chasm separating the fast-paced urban world of bureaucrats (*chinovniki*), Party organizers, and workers from the slower-paced, more traditional world of country farmers. Writing, for instance, back in 1991, Helmut Altrichter argued that "many peasant actions and practices, institutions and customs, had their own internal, compelling logic and functionality . . . the logic and functionality of a precapitalist peasant society, subsistence-oriented and averse to running risks, with the family as the basic unit of production and consumption, and with the village, the *mir*, [as] a world in itself."[104] Teodor Shanin had already reached similar conclusions twenty years earlier in a pioneering work of political sociology. He saw the Russian peasants as increasingly motivated by "defensive conservatism" to defy the pressures brought to bear by Communist ideologues from Moscow; he painted the political leaders at Moscow as "committed to a misleading conception of rural society"; and he depicted their "local representatives" as hopelessly "out of touch with the peasantry in nearly all contexts other than coercive administrative force." Therefore, Shanin concluded, it was probably a foregone conclusion that the Soviet state would achieve next to no legitimacy among those rural Russians who, after all, still constituted at this time the vast majority of the population.[105]

Has scholarship over the past two decades undermined or, generally, lent further weight to this admittedly pessimistic conclusion? For the most part, the latter seems to be the case—especially if we consult the work of historians such as James Heinzen, Lynne Viola, V. P. Danilov, N. A. Ivnitskii, Denis Koslov, Tracy McDonald, and Hugh D. Hudson. Approaching this issue from various angles of research, these inquirers may fairly be said to have strengthened a learned consensus both on the fearsome gap that remained in the late 1920s between the new masters of Russia and their rustic subjects *and* (as a result) on the new regime's imperative need to look for *legitimacy* elsewhere.

James Heinzen has contributed to this growing scholarly consensus from the vantage point of the Commissariat of Agriculture (*Narkomzem*), charged by the Soviet government with the tasks of ensuring the recovery of war-decimated agricultural production, modernizing the peasantry's farming practices, and (in general) trying to "extend the foundation for socialism in the countryside."[106] Heinzen has stressed anew the "great gap fixed" between the opinions on agricultural issues held by Party and *Narkomzem* personnel and those held by most rural *muzhiki*—while simultaneously setting Russia's agricultural/developmental dilemma in an increasingly competitive *international context*. On the former point, we have these observations from Heinzen:

> In the 1920s ... [over] 90% of Communist Party members lived in cities, yet 85% of the population resided in the countryside. The village population was further separated from the regime by an enormous cultural gap, and the Bolsheviks were slow to set down roots and gain legitimacy among the mass of the peasantry. Despite the Party's ambitions, transforming the agricultural sector was not as easy as simply lecturing farmers or distributing new tools. A persistent difference in worldview separated the agricultural specialists, trained mostly in urban schools, from the villagers they were instructing.[107]

Meanwhile, on the latter point, Heinzen reverted to a European, indeed, a global frame of reference popularized for several generations of instructors and students in Russian history by Theodore H. Von Laue[108] and a number of his like-minded colleagues:

> Soviet political leaders and scientists alike felt an urgent need to fix the agricultural "problem." . . . [In] terms of the regime's powerful drive to catch and overtake the West economically, Soviet Russia was in even worse shape than before World War I. The industrial powers of Europe and the United States had moved farther ahead by comparison, having suffered far less in wartime than Russia. Production per capita in the industrialized Western economies was still growing at a more rapid rate than in the USSR; technological change was also leaping ahead more quickly.[109]

In Heinzen's eyes, the tragedy for genuinely idealistic agents in *Narkomzem* (and, by extension, in other Soviet Commissariats as well) was that they were caught, proverbially, between a rock and a hard place in this transitional era—caught, that is, between Communist Party leaders suspicious of "alien non-party government employees" like themselves, on the one hand, and rural peasants every bit as suspicious of Party ideologues and Commissariat *chinovniki*, alike, on the other. This tragic impasse, if we can accept Heinzen's account, "laid the groundwork for the catastrophe of crash collectivization."[110]

In retrospect, the chasm between urban and rural attitudes in this key area of developmental policy was also mirrored in the cautionary language of Party and state figures like Nikolai Bukharin and M. I. Frumkin. As Lynne Viola and her Russian co-editors Danilov, Ivnitskii, and Koslov have repeatedly reminded us, Bukharin sounded the alarm on multiple occasions during the later NEP years about "the possibility of the loss of peasant support" for Party efforts in Russia. Citing Lenin on the dangers posed by a schism between the working class and the peasantry—so that, in effect, the late Bolshevik leader's cherished *smychka* (worker/peasant alliance) might become, perversely, a *razmychka* splitting the two classes apart—Bukharin fearlessly censured the Party leadership's mistaken economic policies, and (in particular) its decision to price agricultural products (meaning, above all, grain) at levels so "artificially" low as to discourage peasant enterprise and, thereby, economic exchanges between rural and urban sectors of Russian society.[111] Yet perhaps an even more remarkable critique emanated, in the course of intra-Party debates in 1928 over agricultural and related issues, from Deputy Commissar of Finance Frumkin. Ironically, Frumkin had been dispatched by order of the Politburo to the Urals region early in the year to oversee grain requisitioning and associated activities; on November 5, 1928, he wrote to the authorities in Moscow condemning the "anti-middle peasant ideology" reportedly being encouraged in Party circles and urging a "go slow" policy when it came to the "socialization" of agriculture. As Viola and her Russian colleagues have noted, Frumkin at this time cried up the need for "ten-twenty years of good relations with the peasantry," during which time (so he hopefully predicted) "socialized" forms of agriculture could steadily develop while the regime worked to modernize small-scale peasant farming.[112] Frumkin's intervention, coming as it did on the very eve of the November Party plenum, earned for him (predictably, perhaps) a much-dreaded arraignment as a "rightist." Yet, however dramatically Frumkin's strictures (like those of Bukharin) may have testified in their own way to the ever-widening divergence between Party and peasant perspectives on economic questions, we may feel no less obligated to ask—especially in the light of Russia's increasingly vulnerable *geostrategic* situation—whether Stalin and his henchmen at Moscow actually *had* "ten-twenty years" to wait upon developments in the countryside.

The subsequent scholarship of Tracy McDonald and Hugh D. Hudson has only reinforced these pessimistic (and well-researched) conclusions regarding the possibility of any lasting *rapprochement* between city and countryside, between Party and Commissariats, on the one hand, and *muzhiki*, on the other. The former historian, working with sources from Riazan province, accentuates the Bolshevik psychology in this gathering tragedy in Thermidorian Russia; the latter scholar, having immersed himself in official political police (i.e., OGPU) archives, provides us with some really stunning *direct* evidence of the peasantry's psychology in this period.[113]

McDonald, it must be said, gives Lenin and his comrades their due. "As early twentieth-century revolutionaries and visionaries," she writes, they were "committed to a complete overthrow of the old order: in their own words, the elimination of its poverty, barbarism, backwardness, slavishness, and exploitation." Whatever the theoretical disagreements among the key Bolshevik figures, "they shared an intense faith in enlightenment and civilization, which could be brought into being through scientific progress and industrial development." This was all noble and good. But, alas, what did the Bolsheviks actually *see* when they looked out upon rural Russia in the mid-1920s?

> When the Bolsheviks turned to face the countryside in 1924 and 1925, they were shaken by what they found. In fact this initial attempt, undertaken in good faith to better understand the countryside, fuelled state insecurities and fears. . . . Peasant culture was considered too backward, too stubborn, too impure, too traditional, far too irreverent for the modern state, and highly inappropriate for the modern citizen. Peasants and especially peasant state representatives had to be trained, professionalized, disciplined, and punished. So that they would behave appropriately, peasants had to be civilized and socialized.[114]

"Civilized" and "socialized"! But was it possible, given the heavy weight of tradition and tribulations, of superstitions and suspicions among the rural folk? McDonald argues that there *was*, in fact, a "window of potential negotiation between peasant and state" between 1924 and 1925, but, as early as 1926, she suggests, that "window" was starting to close. McDonald ends her "story of Bolshevik anxiety," as she calls it, by reflecting, bleakly, that the Leninists were caught in a *double trap*: in theoretical terms, they were "trapped between a . . . commitment to mass participation and their profound distrust of those masses, especially the 'vacillating' peasant population"; in practical terms, they sensed that they simply did *not* have the time requisite for their desired *gradual* transformation of Russian society.[115] Although McDonald does not explicitly conjure up here the "big picture" of Russia's geostrategic vulnerabilities, we can safely assume that those vulnerabilities are, for her, lurking at all times in the background.

But if McDonald tries to enlighten us about Bolshevik "anxieties" stemming from the peasant question in NEP Russia, Hugh D. Hudson, laboring in OGPU archives from the same period, enlightens us about the peasants themselves. Hudson convincingly demonstrates that political police officials in various localities tried, during the winter of 1928, to warn the authorities at Moscow about peasant demoralization caused by the new Soviet state's underpricing of agricultural produce, its overpricing of industrial commodities, its failure to provide sufficient seed loans to the farmers, and so on. (Obviously, the Bukharins and Frumkins in our analysis would have understood—and endorsed—these complaints.) But peasant attitudes surfaced most arrestingly, perhaps, in a letter posted in Kazimirovka village (in Belorussia) by a "middle peasant" (*seredniak*), cited here by Hudson. In this revealing missive, our *seredniak*, dismissing what he viewed as the Bolsheviks' simplistic taxonomy of peasant "classes," tried to lecture his Communist masters at Moscow about the *real* sociology of the Russian peasants with whom *he* was familiar. Though allegedly a supporter of the revolution, he declared stolidly that:

> despite the promises of a new and better life . . . the "untruth" and injustice of tsarism continued. . . . In an impressive display of mastery of Bolshevik discourse, the author argued that rather than being stratified into classes of kulaks, middle peasants, and poor peasants, the peasants . . . actually divided into three "groups:" (1) the hardest working peasants; (2) the middle peasants who worked but were not particularly industrious or intelligent; and (3) the foolish and lazy (and therefore poor) who did not want to work, preferring instead to wait for help from the government.

According to this observer, the Party's bogus stratification of peasant "classes" sapped the initiative of the "hard working, enterprising, and intelligent peasants"; stoked the fires of discontent and enmity among the rural population; and thereby "threatened the economic prosperity of the entire village."[116]

In a sense, then, the final impression we derive from Hudson's research is as dampening as the impressions we have derived from all the other scholarship cited earlier: namely, that *all* governmental agencies, personalities, and social groupings involved in the developmental crisis of rural Russia in the 1920s were foredoomed to frustration in one way or another. For Hudson, specifically, the issue may have been the Soviet regime's failure to heed warnings about economic storm signals from both OGPU agents *and* the rural cultivators they were supposed to be policing; yet the *dramatis personae* could just as easily have been disillusioned *Narkomzem* functionaries, or Party idealists like Nikolai Bukharin, or apprehensive figures in high governmental finance such as M. I. Frumkin. What is indisputable here is Hugh Hudson's *general conclusion*: namely, that the "wholesale collectivization drive announced at the end of 1929 marked the determination of the Stalin regime to resolve forever the 'peasant question.' . . . The peasantry, in the sense of a distinct culture that stood in opposition to the city and its drive to modernize the Soviet Union, would . . . be eliminated."[117]

It really *was*, then, in the *urban* milieu of (especially younger) Party idealists and organizers and workers that the regime had to find and retain its legitimacy if it wished to transcend the developmental constraints of the NEP. Therefore, at least in part, the campaign, underway even in the early 1920s, to "re-proletarianize" the Party (i.e., the "Lenin Levy") by recruiting more than half a million workers into Bolshevik ranks. Such an initiative may have also reflected growing tensions in Party ranks presaging the lethal factional in-fighting of the late NEP period, but surely it helped to restore the Party's proletarian identity—not to mention increasing the weight of the Communist presence in the factories just when "the necessity of raising productivity had become paramount."[118] "Advanced" workers could now play a crucial mediating role between Party and working class: a "re-proletarianized" Party meant, at the same time, a "Bolshevization" of the proletariat. Both Communist Party and Komsomol (Youth) cadres were, in the course of the 1920s, being transformed from within. By the start of the First Five-Year Plan, these cadres had become "mass organizations" boasting largely working-class membership: by 1930, in fact, 56.3 percent of Party members could point to their proletarian origins, and 46.3 percent were officially styled as "workers by current occupation."[119]

Yet the Communist Party's rejuvenation (in the sense of being "re-proletarianized") was hardly an untroubled process in this transitional decade. Lynne Viola has noted, indeed, that Lenin himself had (in 1923) somewhat prematurely exhorted the "working class"—such as it was at that time—to go to the countryside and "lead the peasantry to socialism"; he did not live to see how many hard obstacles *young* workers and Party members would have to surmount before they experienced lasting successes in the modernization campaign and the mature "class-consciousness" of the 1930s. Their challenges, in urban (let alone rural!) Russia, were daunting from the start. As Viola has written:

> In the 1920s factory workers—especially youth, women, and the unskilled—experienced serious economic hardship. Unemployment was endemic in the 1920s and increased dramatically as the decade progressed, largely as a result of rural overpopulation and the consequent influx of peasants to the cities in search of urban employment. Industrialization failed to keep pace with the growing demand for jobs. As the urban population expanded with rural migrants, housing problems became more . . . acute, thereby adding further to the problems of the . . . proletariat. The economic position of the Soviet working class failed to fulfill the rising expectations of material betterment which had come about as a result of the 1917 revolution.[120]

Thus, several results followed here: the same influx of migrants from rural to urban Russia that made it easier for Party leaders to objectify (and, in time, to demonize) "kulaks," allegedly lazy *seredniaki*, and "neobourgeois" Nepmen also deepened worker antipathy toward these same elements in NEP society, and made those workers ever likelier to ascribe their hardships to NEP policies *as a whole*.

It followed easily, then, that Stalin and his acolytes, even as they were isolating and confuting so-called rightists in Communist Party ranks, addressed themselves (in 1929 and ensuing years) to "those workers who identified least with the policies of the NEP period and who had the most to gain from the new, more aggressive policies of the First Five-Year Plan."[121] Hiroaki Kuromiya has given us a fascinating, if rather complicated, group profile of these individuals:

> They were mainly young urban males who had experienced the revolution and civil war in their teens or younger, first entered industrial work shortly after the revolution, and therefore had . . . several years of work experience and some skills by the late 1920s. Predominantly Party and Komsomol members, they were thus in a position to be critical of both the work culture of older workers and the peasant culture of new arrivals from the countryside. They were new forces in the factories who, impatient with the given rate of industrialization, pressed for ever higher tempos; . . . who, intolerant of managerial bureaucratism, pressed for one-man management; who, eager to find "class aliens" in the apparatus, actively sought to be promoted into positions of responsibility.[122]

Such, apparently, were the aspiring young workers upon whose enthusiasm, allied with that of idealistic Party functionaries, the emerging Stalinist leadership would depend over the coming years to *legitimize* Russia's pathbreaking revolution. Lenin's *smychka*, unifying worker and peasant energies, would thus give way to Stalin's *razmychka*, under whose auspices the city, with its factories, Party personnel, and armed worker detachments, would overwhelm the countryside.

There were, finally, myriad *cultural* manifestations of this legitimizing shift from the NEP to the Stalinist revolution from above in the late 1920s and early 1930s. What Fitzpatrick has called a "switch to a class-war concept of cultural revolution" vilifying "bourgeois specialists," technical intelligentsia, so-called Nepmen, and "kulaks" in the countryside, occurred rather abruptly a few months after the Fifteenth Party Congress—and in the wake of Stalin's fateful visit (in January 1928) to Siberia to review one site of the grain procurement crisis. One turning point in this process may well have been the show trial of a large number of mining engineers and technicians from the Shakhty region of the Donbass on charges of sabotage and conspiracy.[123] As a movement aimed at securing legitimacy for the regime on militantly modernistic bases, the "Cultural Revolution," so Fitzpatrick has said, had many aspects: "It was a worker-promotion movement linked to a political campaign to discredit the right opposition within the party. It was an iconoclastic youth movement directed against 'bureaucratic' authority. It was a process whereby militant Communist groups in the professions established local dictatorships and attempted to revolutionize their disciplines. It was, finally, a heyday for revolutionary theorists and 'hairbrained schemers.'"[124] As specialists such as Mark von Hagen, William Chase, and Anne Gorsuch have argued, this transition from one set of economic, cultural, and social policies to another served some very specific interests—for instance, those of junior army personnel increasingly critical of senior officers; of workers bedeviled by chronic housing, health, and workplace problems in Moscow; and of Komsomol youths eager to jettison the constraints and compromises of the "bourgeois" NEP.[125]

Beyond even *these* manifestations of cultural change in late-revolutionary Russia, however, it is arguable that a new kind of *identity politics* was taken in hand by Stalin and his comrades, thus enabling them to legitimize themselves further in the eyes of their (overwhelmingly urban) followers. As we saw in chapter 2, social historians such as Gregory Freeze, Leopold Haimson, Alfred Rieber, and Sheila Fitzpatrick have familiarized us with the notion of a modernizing transition, in old regime and revolutionary Russia, from the *sosloviia* (i.e., ascriptive/hereditary service estates) of tsardom to the (Marxian-prescribed) socioeconomic classes of the Soviet era.[126] As Fitzpatrick in particular has held, the obliteration of the urban and rural social élites of tsarist Russia after 1917, combined with the near disintegration of the working class and city-to-country migration of the civil war and early NEP eras, left Russian society (temporarily) without a satisfactory stabilizing presence of well-defined social classes—and this, at a time when state and society in Russia faced an ever more desperate need for both political and social reconstitution. Fortunately, the economic recovery of the NEP and post-NEP years made it possible for the new Stalinist leadership, having now consigned "kulaks" in the countryside and Nepmen and "bourgeois intellectuals" in the towns to oblivion, to establish itself on the basis of what Fitzpatrick has termed a "Stalinist *soslovnost'*" model of industrialized society.[127] The new proletariat, in an ironic twist of history, unconsciously reaffirmed the "primacy of the state" in Soviet Russia by *allowing itself to be defined in largely traditional terms of service to that state*. Russia's new masters had therefore finally legitimized their rule—that is, by giving rank-and-file Communists, Komsomol activists, and others a way to *redefine* themselves, to anchor their identities securely in a world turned upside-down by the recent storms of world war, revolution, and civil war.[128]

Chapter 5 has provided us with yet another example of how neostructuralism, bringing together as it does the political-cultural insights of moderate postmodernism and the state-centered concerns of structuralism, enables us to analyze a key revolutionary issue. Here, we wanted to know how it was that the *state legitimacy* that ultimately eluded the Protectorate in England and the Directory in France was achieved by V. I. Lenin's successors in Thermidorian Russia. It seems evident now that the English and French were undone by polarized political cultures interacting with less-than-existentially-threatening strategic realities. The Russians, on the other hand, dealt with political-cultural weaknesses in a much more *drastic* fashion so as to be able to address an *existentially* challenging strategic situation. Thus, two points—one involving political culture, the other involving its *strategic context*—are at issue here.

On the first point: both the English and the French Revolutions, for all their sound and fury, left traditional upper- and middle-class élites basically in place, even if altered in some respects. In the case of England, the Protectorate could not in the final analysis overcome the resistance of the natural rulers to its provocative mix of fiscally oppressive militarism and heterodox ecclesiology. In the case of France, the Directors forfeited support in bourgeois quarters as well as rudely alienating the Catholic majority in society. Thus, in both cases, late-revolutionary states were undermined by hopelessly polarized political cultures. No wonder, then, that the natural rulers in England finally threw in their lot with the restored Stuarts, and that the "middle classes" (along with some chastened nobles) in France chanced a "leap in the dark" with the military (and politically ambitious) hero of the hour. In the case of Russia, however, the upheaval of 1917 (and thereafter) radically simplified the social structure by largely obliterating the old urban/rural social élites. The Bolsheviks, admittedly, had their tussles in the 1920s with surviving Intelligentsia, with managerial/technical *spetsialisty*, and with sundry small merchants, shopkeepers, and manufacturers. Still, Russia's new rulers could write upon a relatively "blank" slate in a society of "workers" (frequently betraying peasant origins) and actual peasants, and social realities impelled them (logically enough) to seek, and find, their bases of legitimacy among politicized Soviet citizens in the former group, and then to use them to modernize the cities and towns and overwhelm the countryside. This, for Lenin's successors, was the way to deal *directly* with any danger of a polarized political culture.

On the second point: the implications of state modernization in all of its forms for sheer *survival* in global affairs had an urgency in the Russian case that was surely far greater than in either of the two earlier situations. Here, moving forward from England to France to Russia starkly underscores for us the relevant *state/strategic* realities. The English, in the late 1650s, could "experiment" with revolution in a world no longer menaced by the Austro-Spanish Habsburgs and not yet threatened by Bourbon France. The French, in the late 1790s, faced, in the Second Coalition, an international challenge that their own aggressive foreign policy had been instrumental in creating. But the leaders emerging from the power struggles of the 1920s in Soviet Russia *simply had to take the initiative* on economic/developmental and other issues so as to secure the kind of credibility, of *legitimacy* that had slipped away earlier from the protagonists in England and France. As William Rosenberg has somberly opined, the late-revolutionary Russian state, on the threshold of industrialization, "simply *had* to confront the insularity of the village," as well as revolutionize "attitudes toward work, the quality of production, [and] even productivity itself" in the cities. "The inculcation of more or less uniform values, recognized as legitimate and consequently reinforcing the legitimacy of the regime" was, for the leaders in late-revolutionary Russia, essential in a world of major powers threatening—at the very least—to leave Russia far behind.[129] It was, then, in this sense that the crisis of legitimacy in Thermidorian Russia was genuinely novel in the history of great European revolutions—even though we can see, as neostructuralists *and* with the wisdom of hindsight, that this "novelty" would not necessarily translate into a political legitimacy enduring throughout the twentieth century and beyond, or necessarily grant the long-suffering Russian people a truly permanent emancipation from the autocratic writ of the past.

Conclusion

Neostructuralism and the Postrevolutionary State as Historical Problem

We began this book by identifying five palpably crucial issues in the English, French, and Russian revolutions that can be most rewardingly analyzed through a neostructuralist synthesis of structuralist and postmodernist perspectives. We then proceeded to discuss both structuralism and postmodernism (as they apply to history) in *theoretical* terms, noting in particular that each of these perspectives has tended over the years to split into two principal strains—the former perspective into Marxist/Leninist (or "capitalism-centered") and Weberian/Hintzian (or "state-centered") structuralism, and the latter perspective into moderate (or political-cultural) and radical (or purely discursive) postmodernism. This book has argued throughout that the neostructuralist historian of, specifically, *European* revolutions can usefully employ the first three of these four approaches to revolutionary change; we have found only the radical, purely discursive, or poststructuralist form of postmodernism to be seriously problematic. In this conclusion, we wind up our discussion by doing three things: (1) we delineate one final time the *geographical* and *temporal* parameters of our work; (2) we recapitulate how, in chapters 1 through 5, we have been able to combine the most valuable insights of structuralism and postmodernism; and (3) most originally, perhaps, we explore how the neostructuralist perspective may lead its advocates on to ponder at some length the "postrevolutionary state as historical problem."

On the first point, we once again assert forthrightly that we have *not* claimed—à la Chalmers Johnson, perhaps—to have discovered a set of explanatory keys to *all* sociopolitical upheavals in *all* times and places. We *have* endeavored all along to acquire some understanding of a subset of three classic European revolutions—that is, those that convulsed mid-seventeenth-century England, late eighteenth-century France, and early twentieth-century Russia. As we contended before, so we argue here again that these upheavals, unlike earlier uprisings of a less politically and socially *concentrated* nature and unlike later revolutions in the "developing world," broke out in countries recognized for centuries as sovereign polities untrammeled by any kind of colonial dependency upon more powerful states, and modernized those polities through similarly sequenced phases of *systemic* change. Again, the *international context* of the English, French, and Russian revolutions served notably to stamp them as *unique historical events*. They all played out within (or on the fringes of) a murderously competitive system of semiautonomous states struggling for security, prestige, and (at times) hegemony—a system of international politics rooted in some respects in the localized diplomacy of Renaissance Italy, but then spilling out into the rest of western Eurasia and, eventually, catching up in its toils much of the rest of the world. In acknowledgment of our "decentering" postmodernist friends, we concede again the fact that each of our European upheavals had a significant but ultimately limited *colonial* dimension: for the English and French, that dimension especially involved transatlantic affairs; for the Russians, it might be said to have involved the vast, predominantly Muslim and Turkic regions of central Asia.

On the second point, we start right off by acknowledging once again that our avowed intention to mesh wherever possible the insights of capitalism-centered, state-centered, and "culturalist" analysis has some important scholarly precedents. Without taking the time to reengage here a literature on the subject that we explored in considerable detail in the introduction—the reader can easily enough return to that theoretical discussion at his/her leisure—we *should* at least cite certain remarks of two experts on revolution. In the preface to his invaluable 1997 anthology of articles on this topic, sociologist John Foran observed: "Debates continue about the relative importance of agency versus structure, culture versus political economy, class versus elites and masses, or how race and gender figure in the picture." Here, over twenty years ago, we already had (from Foran) "a call for synthesis, or at least a challenge for [a] more sophisticated integration of diverse analytic elements."[1] In John Foran's case, this was actually a reiteration of his call, issued on the pages of *Sociological Theory* four years earlier, for the creation of a "fourth generation" of revolutionary theory that could accommodate and reconcile the most valuable elements of the various analytic perspectives on revolution.[2] As we observed in the introduction, Jack Goldstone added his voice to the cause eight years later in the *Annual Review of Political Science*.[3] Thus, we obviously do not lay claim to complete originality in attempting—as these and other specialists have attempted in recent decades—to wrestle with the exceedingly complex issues of revolutionary change.

Here, rather, we want simply to recapitulate the ways in which we have tried, on a chapter-by-chapter basis, to interpret through structuralist and postmodernist prisms some carefully defined issues running through (specifically) the English, French, and Russian revolutions.

Thus, chapter 1 argued from a state-centered structuralist perspective that there was an urgent, strategically induced need for state modernization in late *ancien régime* England, France, and Russia; yet simultaneously it borrowed from political-cultural analysis by showing how ideologically "conflicted" the three monarchs were in these situations, and how ideological fault lines in their states helped frustrate the reformist campaigns of their most important ministers. Chapter 2 took up the capitalism-centered concerns of some scholars with questions of bourgeois class identity and politicization in these three old regimes even as it demonstrated (1) how culturalist analysis *complicates* here questions of class identity, and (2) how state-centered analysis increasingly situates these *bourgeoisies* in geostrategic frameworks. Chapter 3, meanwhile, in taking on the grim question of revolutionary regicide, was certainly culturalist or postmodernist in nature by placing all three regicides in political-cultural/psychological contexts, even as it also emphasized (in state/structuralist fashion) the pressing domestic and especially *international* circumstances in which such drastic deeds became not only conceivable but also well-nigh unavoidable. Then, again, chapter 4 tried mediating wherever possible between opposing cultural and circumstantial interpretations of state-sponsored terror ("reigns of terror and virtue") in these three countries, even if (in the end) it found the *thèse des circonstances* to be marginally more persuasive here than the equally ballyhooed *thèse du complot*. Finally, chapter 5 sought—as postmodernists naturally would—to stress the significance of crises of *state legitimacy* in Thermidorian England, France, and Russia; yet in doing so it demonstrated that whether polarized political cultures proved to be fatally delegitimizing in such situations depended, in the final analysis, upon how these *cultural* dynamics played out within the greater contexts of domestic and international politics.

On the third and final point, we need—as advocates of neostructuralism—to *problematize* the postrevolutionary state at some length. How, after all, could we avoid doing so if, as we have frequently stated in this book, the *relentless growth of the state's coercive power in modern times* lies at (or at least fairly near) the heart of (European) revolutionary analysis? To begin with, we should acknowledge here how scholars grappling with questions about revolutionary change in early modern Europe have tried at times to qualify Weberian/Skocpolian conceptions of the administrative state. In the case of England, for instance, specialists ranging from Michael J. Braddick to Jack Goldstone, although surely recognizable to us as "structuralists," have taken up this task. Braddick, for one, has allowed that there *was* a state in the seventeenth century characterized by "a network of offices wielding political power derived from a coordinating center by formal means," and that, therefore, "it makes sense to analyze this network as a whole." Even so, he has also observed, this "early modern state" was only "a partially differentiated and weakly coordinated state." Almost as an afterthought, Braddick added here that state power need not be geographically concentrated in a typically modern sense as long as it is "extensive," endowed, that is, with a degree of coordination between central and local institutions of an administrative nature.[4] For his part, Goldstone has displayed even more caution in ascribing Weberian characteristics to states like that of the late Tudors and early Stuarts: they may have possessed the modern attributes of "centralized national rule-making and rule-enforcing authority," but, he has insisted, they also shared "political space with other actors and authorities" including "semi-autonomous sources of legitimate authority at the regional level or among groups subject to religious law."[5]

At least for structuralists such as Braddick and Goldstone, state formation led, in early modern England, to a bureaucratic entity *somewhat* anticipating the more modern archetype conceived later on by Max Weber and his disciples. In the case of France, however, resisting the tendency to reify the state as an historical "actor" imposing its will more or less independently on society has assumed—especially in recent decades—a more explicitly and defiantly deconstructionist tone. This is perhaps predictable, given the long-standing influence exerted on French historical studies by philosophers such as Michel Foucault and Jacques Derrida and by cultural anthropologists such as Clifford Geertz. One student of the French revolution, Suzanne Desan, has been outspoken on this issue, complaining that, "by and large, as revolutionary historians, we have given relatively little thought to the complexities of the state as an analytic category." Desan accordingly summed up what she regarded as timely revisionism in this area:

> Scholars across a range of disciplines have theorized the state . . . flexibly as a site of structured negotiation over power, resources, and relationships, rather than simply as a coercive entity separate from society. Although it is made up of organizations wielding coercive power and of laws meant to structure power relations and social interactions in a uniform way, the state takes shape only in a set of local practices in which power is repeatedly contested, sometimes reinforced and sometimes redistributed. . . . Finally, recent work conceptualizes the state as both a discursive and institutional entity.[6]

Ironically, Desan's related assurance to her readers (in *French Historical Studies*) that she "is not calling here for "bringing the state back in" as a policy-making entity independent from society" must be seen as alluding fairly obviously to one of Theda Skocpol's co-edited anthologies, thereby suggesting that the shadow of Skocpolian structuralism—whatever its myriad shortcomings—continues to lie across even the elegantly sculpted landscape of French cultural studies.[7] Nor, we suspect, is that shadow likely to be altogether dissipated by Keith Baker's more recent insistence that, most notably in revolutionary politics, "scripts [rather than state initiatives?] generate events."[8]

Whether, as Suzanne Desan has affirmed, the state "takes shape only in a set of local practices" might easily be contested, yet there is no denying that her argument in general would find favor with prominent Russianist postmodernists such as Steve Smith and William Rosenberg. Smith, indeed, has argued that scholars need to extend their "concept of power beyond that of simple coercion" and has specifically deplored the ways in which "historical analysis is handicapped by conceptual dichotomies such as voluntary versus coerced, [and] support versus resistance." Historians of Russia, so Smith has held, must *enlarge* their "understanding of power, to understand it as capacity, as something implicated in all social activity." Such an attitude, naturally enough, extends for this seasoned Russian specialist to applying "some of the techniques of deconstruction" to the political history of the Revolution of 1917: utilizing such techniques, for example, historians "might find it fruitful to dismantle the Bolshevik Party as a unified subject."[9] William Rosenberg, for his part, embraced much the same culturalist approach to statist issues and modern politics in his introductory remarks to a voluminous anthology on Russian revolutionary topics that he co-edited with his colleagues Edward Acton and Vladimir Cherniaev.[10] There can be little doubt, by the same token, that the Sheila Fitzpatricks, Lynn Mallys, Christopher Reads, and Boris Kolonitskiis of Russian revolutionary studies would warmly endorse such culturalist sentiments.

Yet, sooner or later, even culturally oriented specialists, inclined as they may be to deconstruct the state as an analytic category in their research on England, France, or Russia, will find it hard to get away entirely from Weberian ideas on this subject. Some of them, of course, have become habituated to revising, and even in some cases rejecting altogether, Theda Skocpol's derivative argument that the "state properly conceived" is "a set of administrative, policing, and military organizations headed, and more or less well coordinated by, an executive authority."[11] But *are* such scholars equally prepared to dismiss Max Weber's even more classic pronouncement on the subject registered one hundred years ago? Writing for the benefit of his colleagues and acolytes in 1918, that year of prolonged warfare and epochal revolution, this German sociologist insisted that "revolutionary change always results in the development of larger, more pervasive normative institutions to replace the ones the revolutionaries have toppled."[12] It is also worth citing, in this connection, political scientist Noel S. Parker's cautionary (and much more recent) reaction against all theories that purport to consign the bureaucratic state to what we might regard as postmodernist oblivion:

> We should hesitate . . . before jumping to conclusions about the priority of a new "post-national" and discursive arena in place of the collective agent [i.e. the state] embodied in the European revolutionary narrative over more than two centuries. . . . Even a thinker acutely aware of how vulnerable are the nation-state's claims to spatio-temporal identity acknowledges that states are "exceptionally dense political practices" which have not . . . disappeared.[13]

For Parker, then, and for many of us as well, the "nation-state as a place of collective autonomy" must remain, after all is said and done, the formidable construct it has been for centuries. And, after all, was this *not* the case with the rejuvenated postrevolutionary states in England, France, and (most notably) Stalin's Russia? But beyond even this, the most cursory flashback to political events in the Europe of the 1920s and 1930s—as well as any summary of political tendencies throughout the world today—will remind us that the nation-state, however challenged at times locally, has no more been deconstructed away by discursive analysis than it has been submerged in neo-Marxian economic analysis.

When we look back at political developments in interwar Europe, and then compare them to certain tendencies in these early decades of the twenty-first century, we are immediately struck by a common element in the two situations: namely, a merging of structural and political-cultural realities in *authoritarian/populist* states. This is an historical phenomenon that the neostructuralist, concerned as always to mesh structuralist with postmodernist analysis, is well qualified to understand. In the Europe of the 1920s and 1930s, the historic "bureaucratic state" was frequently taken over by unscrupulous politicians (sometimes for explicitly war-making purposes); such protagonists, usually called "fascists," were able to channel into their "cause" popular fears, resentments, and anxieties bred by economic depression, irredentist nationalism, and a presumed Bolshevik threat radiating from the (Russian) East. In the Europe (and in much of the extra-European world) of today, demagogic leaders have again been able frequently to seize state power, again harnessing to their geopolitical and competitive purposes popular fears, resentments, and anxieties. This time, the *popular* element in such authoritarian statism has usually involved insecurity generated by (post-recession) economic globalization and a xenophobia directed against migrants and internal "others" in Europe, the Americas, and Australia/Southeast Asia. Without pursuing this matter any further here, we can perceive, summing things up in neostructuralist fashion, that state/structural and cultural tendencies combined almost a century ago in much of Europe to create postrevolutionary (some would say, counterrevolutionary) states that dangerously challenged the world's democracies, and that something uncomfortably reminiscent of this appears once again to be happening today in Europe—and also in much of the extra-European world.

In a sense, the foregoing discussion of the "postrevolutionary state as historical problem" only takes us back, as neostructuralists, to the classic revolutions of early modern and modern Europe. We may always feel obliged to inquire, in this capacity, as to whether European revolutionary change has actually ameliorated, as claimed, the destinies of Everyman and Everywoman. Perhaps, in the end, it has not done so. Perhaps that is why Max Weber, writing in the apocalyptic year 1918, and obviously disillusioned by the shortcomings of modern revolutionary politics, exhorted his followers to shun the excitement and charisma of revolution and pursue instead careers in reformist politics and bureaucratic service.[14] And perhaps that is why Orlando Figes, reflecting, as we pointed out before, upon the Russian Revolution, admitted that "the state, however big, cannot make people equal or better human beings." Yet Figes also expressed the hope that the state would at least "treat its citizens equally, and strive to ensure that their free activities are directed towards the general good."[15] In developing our analysis of structural and political-cultural forces converging in Europe's great revolutions, we may discover that this is the best that we can realistically hope for in the unfathomable future that awaits us.

Suggestions for Further Reading

It would be impossible to provide here an exhaustive discussion of the scholarship on general revolutionary theory *and* on the more specific questions taken up in each of the chapters of this book. Instead, my intention in this bibliographical chapter is to point interested readers toward some of the classic (but, even more, *most recent*) studies that have informed my arguments. These books and articles would seem to fall naturally under the chapter headings listed in this study's Table of Contents. These are not necessarily hard-and-fast categories: readers unable to locate a specific source under one heading may possibly find it elsewhere. And of course many additional works (especially books and articles published quite recently) appear in the footnoting that accompanies each section of the book.

STRUCTURALISM, POSTMODERNISM, AND—NEOSTRUCTURALISM?

It might be useful for the reader who is confronting issues of structuralism, postmodernism, and neostructuralism in the field of European revolutionary change to begin by consulting some works on English, French, and Russian revolutionary historiography. Reassessments of the literature on the seventeenth-century English Revolution include R. C. Richardson, *The Debate on the English Revolution* (Manchester: Manchester University Press, 1999); Keith Thomas, "When the Lid Came Off England," in *The New York Review of Books*, May 27, 2004; and John Adamson, "Introduction: High Roads and Blind Alleys—The English Civil War and Its Historiography," 1–35, in Adamson, ed., *The English Civil War: Conflict and Contexts, 1640–49* (New York: Palgrave Macmillan, 2009). In the case of revolutionary France, the reader should look at William Doyle, *Origins of the French Revolution*, third edition (New York: Oxford University Press, 1999); and Bailey Stone, *The Anatomy of Revolution Revisited: A Comparative Analysis of England, France, and Russia* (New York: Cambridge University Press, 2014), above all the introduction. Especially valuable reflections on Russian revolutionary studies are offered by (among others) Steve A. Smith, "Writing the History of the Russian Revolution after the Fall of Communism," *Europe-Asia Studies* 46 (1994): 563–78; Ronald G. Suny, "Revisionism and Retreat in the Historiography of 1917: Social History and Its Critics," *Russian Review* 53 (1994): 155–82; and Stephen Kotkin, "1991 and the Russian Revolution: Sources, Conceptual Categories, Analytical Frameworks," *Journal of Modern History* 70 (1998): 384–425.

Classic examples of the revisionist works challenging the long-dominant Marxian interpretative paradigm in French and English revolutionary scholarship from the 1950s on include Alfred Cobban, "The Myth of the French Revolution" (London: University College, 1955), and *The Social Interpretation of the French Revolution* (Cambridge: Cambridge University Press, 1964); George V. Taylor, "Noncapitalist Wealth and the Origins of the French Revolution," *American Historical Review* 72 (1967): 491–92; and Conrad Russell, *Unrevolutionary England, 1603–1642* (London: The Hambledon Press, 1990). For important (if, by Western standards, belated) revisionist ruminations in the case of revolutionary Russia, the reader can do no better than to consult the articles by Steve A. Smith, Ronald G. Suny, and Stephen Kotkin mentioned just earlier. As for the exchanges between postmodernists and structuralists in history *in general*, see (among other studies) Richard J. Evans, *In Defense of History* (New York: W. W. Norton, 1997). On the more specific question of postmodernism versus structuralism in *European revolutionary* analysis, see Noel S. Parker, *Revolutions and History: An Essay in Interpretation* (Cambridge: Polity Press, 1999). More of the literature on this last (and very contentious) question is referenced at subsequent points in this bibliographical chapter.

For as good a general discussion as any of four prestructural approaches to revolution notable in the social-scientific writing of the early and mid-twentieth century, see Michael S. Kimmel, *Revolution: A Sociological Interpretation* (Philadelphia: Temple University Press, 1990), 46–82. Specific examples of "natural history" or "stage-sequence" accounts of revolution are Crane Brinton, *The Anatomy of Revolution* (New York: Prentice-Hall, 1938); Lyford Edwards, *The Natural History of Revolution* (Chicago: University of Chicago Press, 1927); George S. Pettee, *The Process of Revolution* (New York: Harper and Brothers, 1938); and Rex D. Hopper, "The Revolutionary Process," *Social Forces* 28 (1950): 270–79. Probably the best known "structural/functional" theorist of revolution in earlier decades was Chalmers Johnson. See, in particular, *Revolution and the Social System* (Stanford: Hoover Institution Studies, 1964); *Autopsy on People's War* (Berkeley: University of

California Press, 1973); and *Revolutionary Change*, second edition (Stanford: Stanford University Press, 1982). Finally, for examples of theorists stressing individual or "aggregate" social psychological factors in revolutionary situations, the reader should see James C. Davies, *When Men Revolt and Why* (New York: Free Press, 1979); Ted R. Gurr, *Why Men Rebel* (Princeton: Princeton University Press, 1971); and (by the same author) *Rogues, Rebels, and Reformers* (Beverly Hills, CA: SAGE, 1976).

Michael Kimmel provides a competent discussion of the main elements, analytical strengths, and analytical weaknesses of structuralist theory in his *Revolution: A Sociological Interpretation*, esp. 25, 86–87, 145–46. Among the early exponents of what we have termed here capitalism-centered structuralism was Karl Polanyi, *The Great Transformation* (Boston: Beacon Press, 1957). Ellen Kay Trimberger wrote from a similar perspective in *Revolution from Above: Military Bureaucrats and Development in Japan, Turkey, Egypt, and Peru* (New Brunswick: Transaction Books, 1978). But the reader in this connection should above all see the many works of Immanuel Wallerstein. They include (but are hardly limited to) the following: *The Modern World-System: Capitalist Agriculture and the Origins of the European World-Economy in the Sixteenth Century* (New York: Academic Press, 1974); *The Capitalist World-Economy* (New York: Cambridge University Press, 1979); and *The Politics of the World Economy* (New York: Cambridge University Press, 1984). Yet Wallerstein's work has also come in for scholarly criticism. See, in this connection, Robert Brenner, "The Origins of Capitalist Development: A Critique of Neo-Smithian Marxism," *New Left Review* (1977): 25–92; and Theda Skocpol, "Wallerstein's World Capitalist System: A Theoretical and Historical Critique," *American Journal of Sociology* 82 (1977): 1075–90.

As was pointed out in this book's introduction, state-centered structuralism seems to have been much more prominent in the recent theoretical literature on revolution than structuralism based chiefly on *economic* analysis. One of the American sociologists taking the lead here in the 1980s was Randall Collins: see, in particular, his *Sociology Since Midcentury* (New York: Academic Press, 1981); and also *Weberian Sociological Theory* (New York: Cambridge University Press, 1986). But certainly the most influential scholar in this genre since the 1970s has been Collins's fellow sociologist Theda Skocpol. After first setting forth her ideas on revolution in "France, Russia, China: A Structural Analysis of Social Revolutions," *Comparative Studies in Society and History* 18 (1976): 175–210, Skocpol went on to publish her "break-out" monograph: *States and Social Revolutions: A Comparative Analysis of France, Russia, and China* (Cambridge: Cambridge University Press, 1979). Additional structuralist insights on modern revolution from Theda Skocpol (and like-minded specialists) were to come in: Peter B. Evans, Dietrich Rueschemeyer, and Theda Skocpol, eds., *Bringing the State Back In* (New York: Cambridge University Press, 1985); and Theda Skocpol, ed., *Social Revolutions in the Modern World* (Cambridge: Cambridge University Press, 1994).

Still, as this book's introduction also stressed, a healthy number of theorists, even if accepting much of Skocpolian state-oriented structuralism, have in some ways modified and, in actuality, *moved beyond* her ideas on revolutionary causation, process, and consequences. Perhaps the most noteworthy example of this tendency lies in the studies of the late sociologist Charles Tilly. See, for instance, *From Mobilization to Revolution* (London: Addison-Wesley, 1978); "War Making and State Making as Organized Crime," in Evans, Rueschemeyer, and Skocpol, eds., *Bringing the State Back In*, 169–91; and *European Revolutions, 1492–1992* (Oxford: Blackwell, 1993). Almost equally indefatigable in the cause has been Tilly's fellow sociologist Jack A. Goldstone. Goldstone's break-out study was *Revolution and Rebellion in the Early Modern World* (Berkeley: University of California Press, 1991). But see also his "Rethinking Revolutions: Integrating Origins, Processes, and Outcomes," in *Comparative Studies of South Asia, Africa and the Middle East* 29 (2009): 18–32; and, even more recently, *Revolutions: A Very Short Introduction* (Oxford: Oxford University Press, 2014). Other social scientists contributing to this critical literature include Jeff Goodwin, "State-Centered Approaches to Social Revolutions: Strengths and Limitations of a Theoretical Tradition," in John Foran, ed., *Theorizing Revolutions* (London: Routledge, 1997), 11–37; Timothy P. Wickham-Crowley, "Structural Theories of Revolution," in ibid., 38–72; Misagh Parsa, *States, Ideologies, and Social Revolutions: A Comparative Analysis of Iran, Nicaragua, and the Philippines* (Cambridge: Cambridge University Press, 2000); and (once again) Goodwin, *No Other Way Out: States and Revolutionary Movements, 1945–1991* (Cambridge: Cambridge University Press, 2001). I have also had some observations to make regarding the continued usefulness of state-oriented structuralist theories of revolution: see, once again, *The Anatomy of Revolution Revisited*, esp. the introduction.

On the other side of the coin—that is to say, where general revolutionary theory is concerned—are arguments devised by postmodernists or poststructuralists. Among the most articulate adherents of such arguments over the past several decades have been Keith Jenkins, *Rethinking History* (London: Routledge, 1991); Alun Munslow, *Deconstructing History* (London: Routledge, 1997); Frank Ankersmit, *Historical Representation* (Stanford: Stanford University Press, 2001); Beverley Southgate, *Post-modernism in History: Fear or Freedom?* (London: Routledge, 2003); and (by the same author) *What Is History For?* (London: Routledge, 2005). It is only fair to note as well that a number of sociologists have (within limits) credited postmodernism with valuable insights into revolutionary change. See, for examples of this, Eric Selbin, "Revolutions in the Real World: Bringing Agency Back

In," in Foran, ed., *Theorizing Revolutions*, 123–36; Valentine Moghadam, "Gender and Revolutions," in ibid., 137–67; and also John Foran, "Discourses and Social Forces: The Role of Culture and Cultural Studies in Understanding Revolution," in ibid., 203–26. Foran would have more to say on the subject subsequently in *Taking Power: On the Origins of Third World Revolutions* (Cambridge: Cambridge University Press, 2005). Still, the reader intrigued by the postmodernist "turn" in history will also want to consult the social scientists inclined to view this phenomenon somewhat more critically. Anthropologist Ernest Gellner is especially skeptical about it in his *Postmodernism, Reason and Religion* (London: Routledge, 1992). Among those attempting to parse out distinctions between "moderate" and "radical" postmodernism are Pauline Marie Rosenau, *Post-Modernism and the Social Sciences: Insights, Inroads, and Intrusions* (Princeton: Princeton University Press, 1992); and Richard J. Evans, *In Defense of History* (New York: W. W. Norton, 1997). Evans followed up his 1997 monograph with "Postmodernism in History," a contribution to the "Great Debate on History and Postmodernism" staged at the University of Sydney, Australia, in July 2002. Finally, historians in particular may want to mull over the recent pertinent observations offered by Gary Wilder, Judith Surkis, Durba Ghosh, and others in an "AHR Forum: Historiographic 'Turns' in Critical Perspective," *American Historical Review* 117 (2012): 698–813.

In recent years, the postmodernist penchant for linguistics and political culture has been all the rage in French revolutionary studies and has been gradually taken up as well by experts in English and Russian history. Its symbolic starting point (in 1978) was perhaps François Furet's *Penser la Révolution française*—a work soon rendered into English by Elborg Forster as *Interpreting the French Revolution* (Cambridge: Cambridge University Press, 1981). This political-cultural "turn" was reinforced later on by such works as Lynn Hunt's *Politics, Culture, and Class in the French Revolution* (Berkeley: University of California Press, 1984); Emmet Kennedy's *A Cultural History of the French Revolution* (New Haven: Yale University Press, 1989); Keith M. Baker's *Inventing the French Revolution* (Cambridge: Cambridge University Press, 1990); Furet's and Mona Ozouf's anthology *A Critical History of the French Revolution*, trans. Arthur Goldhammer (Cambridge, MA: Harvard University Press, 1989); and Baker's co-edited anthology *The French Revolution and the Creation of Modern Political Culture*, four volumes (Oxford: Pergamon Press, 1987–1994). David Underdown took up the cudgels for postmodernism in English revolutionary studies: see his *Revel, Riot, and Rebellion: Popular Politics and Culture in England, 1603–1660* (Oxford: Clarendon, 1995), and *A Freeborn People: Politics and the Nation in Seventeenth-Century England* (Oxford: Clarendon, 1996). Kevin Sharpe warmly endorsed the cause in such works as *Culture and Politics in Early Stuart England* (Stanford, CA: Stanford University Press, 1993), and *Remapping Early Modern England: The Culture of Seventeenth-Century Politics* (Cambridge: Cambridge University Press, 2000). So have Susan D. Amussen and Mark A. Kishlansky, eds., in *Political Culture and Cultural Politics in Early Modern England* (Manchester: Manchester University Press, 1995); David Zaret, *Origins of Democratic Culture: Printing, Petitions, and the Public Sphere in Early Modern England* (Princeton: Princeton University Press, 2002); and a host of other historians in the field. (In addition, the final section of this bibliographical chapter discusses some of the recent literature on the "transatlantic" aspects of both of the early modern revolutions). In the Russian case, the reader might first of all consult the many works in this genre by Sheila Fitzpatrick, including *The Cultural Front: Power and Culture in Revolutionary Russia* (Ithaca, NY: Cornell University Press, 1992), and then move on to (among innumerable titles) Christopher Read, *Culture and Power in Revolutionary Russia: The Intelligentsia and the Transition from Tsarism to Communism* (New York: St. Martin's Press, 1990); Lynn Mally, *Culture of the Future: The Proletkult Movement in Revolutionary Russia* (Berkeley: University of California Press, 1990); and also Orlando Figes and Boris Kolonitskii, *Interpreting the Russian Revolution: The Language and Symbols of 1917* (New Haven, CT: Yale University Press, 1999).

Finally, postmodernism has recently had to share the limelight—in all three national fields—with structuralist or state-oriented approaches to revolutionary causation and process. I attempted to apply a modified Skocpolian structuralism to the French case in two synthetic studies: see *The Genesis of the French Revolution: A Global-Historical Interpretation* (Cambridge: Cambridge University Press, 1994) and *Reinterpreting the French Revolution: A Global-Historical Perspective* (Cambridge: Cambridge University Press, 2002). Readers will find a similar approach to revolutionary issues in two (similarly titled) books by T. C. W. Blanning: *The Origins of the French Revolutionary Wars* (London: Longman, 1986), and *The French Revolutionary Wars, 1787–1802* (New York: St. Martin's Press, 1996). Jeremy J. Whiteman traced the links between foreign and domestic affairs in early revolutionary France in *Reform, Revolution, and French Global Policy, 1787–1791* (Burlington, VT: University Press of New England, 2003). In the case of England, structuralism (in one form or another) has also found advocates over the past twenty years: see, above all, James S. Wheeler, *The Making of a World Power: War and the Military Revolution in Seventeenth-Century England* (London: Stroud, 1999); Jonathan Scott, *England's Troubles: Seventeenth Century English Instability in European Context* (Cambridge: Cambridge University Press, 2000); and Michael J. Braddick, *State Formation in Early Modern England, c. 1550–1700* (Cambridge: Cambridge University Press, 2000). As for the (somewhat underdeveloped) case of Russia: a classic example of the structuralist approach *avant la lettre* in Russian revolutionary studies has in fact been Theodore H. Von Laue, *Why Lenin? Why Stalin? Why Gorbachev? The Rise and Fall of the Soviet System,* third edition (New York: HarperCollins, 1993). Elements of this rendering of events in Russia have appeared in numerous articles in the anthology co-edited by Edward Acton, Vladimir Cherniaev, and William G. Rosenberg, *Critical Companion to the Russian Revolution 1914–1921* (Bloomington: Indiana University Press, 1997).

MODERNIZERS VERSUS TRADITIONALISTS IN THE EUROPEAN REVOLUTIONS

My intention in this section of the chapter is to familiarize the interested reader with some of the most useful scholarship (both long-standing and of recent vintage) dealing with the latent tensions and eventual full-blown confrontations between modernizing and traditionalist forces and personalities in *ancien régime* and revolutionary England, France, and Russia.

Pursuing this specific issue in the English case might mean first of all consulting some general theoretical works on modernization. Standard references in this area include Samuel P. Huntington, *Political Order in Changing Societies* (New Haven: Yale University Press, 1968); and S. N. Eisenstadt, *Revolution and the Transformation of Societies* (New York: Free Press, 1978). Yet prominent critics of what is loosely called "modernization theory" should also be read in this connection: see, for example, Charles Tilly's classic article "Does Modernization Breed Revolution?" *Comparative Politics* 5 (1973), and Jeff Goodwin, *No Other Way Out: States and Revolutionary Movements, 1945–1991* (Cambridge: Cambridge University Press, 2001). Whether or not Charles I and his leading ministers—most notably Thomas Wentworth, Earl of Strafford, and Archbishop of Canterbury William Laud—can qualify for us as true modernizers has of course provoked extensive scholarly debate over the years. Kevin Sharpe spoke up for the king on this issue in *The Personal Rule of Charles I* (New Haven: Yale University Press, 1991), esp. 407, 455, 557; and so did J. S. Morrill at various points in *The Nature of the English Revolution* (London: Longman, 1993). Yet Charles I is arrayed in much more reactionary garb in most postrevisionist works: see, for example, Ann Hughes, *The Causes of the English Civil War* (New York: St. Martin's Press, 1991); Michael B. Young, *Charles I* (New York: St. Martin's Press, 1997); and Norah Carlin, *The Causes of the English Civil War* (Oxford: Blackwell, 1999). Although we badly need a reexamination of Archbishop Laud's career, fortunately we have many historians remarking upon the modern or not so modern aspects of Strafford's career in J. F. Merritt, ed., *The Political World of Thomas Wentworth, Earl of Strafford, 1621–1641* (Cambridge: Cambridge University Press, 1996). The reader can best reassess the contention between rival (and implicitly *progressive* and *traditionalist*) "conspiracy theories" in late prerevolutionary England by consulting, among other studies, Caroline Hibbard, *Charles I and the Popish Plot* (Chapel Hill: University of North Carolina Press, 1983); and Jonathan Scott, *England's Troubles: Seventeenth-Century English Instability in European Context* (Cambridge: Cambridge University Press, 2000). Finally, following the struggle between modernizing and traditionalist policies (and specifically *military* policies) through the Interregnum years should require the reader to refer to the following studies: David Underdown, *Royalist Conspiracy in England, 1649–1660* (New Haven: Yale University Press, 1960); Bernard Capp, *Cromwell's Navy* (Oxford: Clarendon Press, 1989); Ian Gentles, *The New Model Army in England, Scotland and Ireland 1645–1653* (Oxford: Blackwell, 1991); Ronald Hutton, *The Royalist War Effort, 1642–1646* (London: Routledge, 1999); and Ian Gentles, *The English Revolution and the Wars in the Three Kingdoms, 1638–1652* (London: Pearson, 2007).

There is growing agreement among scholars that readers looking for modernizing values in prerevolutionary France should look to some of Louis XVI's ministers rather than to the king himself. Louis XVI, alas, comes across as a traditionalist and (at critical junctures) downright *reactionary* figure. Witnessing to this unfortunate reality are Pierrette Girault de Coursac, *L'Education d'un roi. Louis XVI* (Paris: Gallimard, 1972); John Hardman, *Louis XVI* (New Haven: Yale University Press, 1993), and *French Politics 1774–1789: From the Accession of Louis XVI to the Fall of the Bastille* (London: Longman, 1995); and Munro Price, *The Fall of the French Monarchy: Louis XVI, Marie-Antoinette, and the Baron de Breteuil* (London: Macmillan, 2002). Among this ill-starred king's reformist ministers, Turgot, Necker, Calonne, Lamoignon de Basville, and Loménie de Brienne stand out. Douglas Dakin still looms (after all these years) as Turgot's most solid biographer: see *Turgot and the Ancien Régime in France* (London: Methuen, 1939). The extensive rehabilitation, in recent years, of Jacques Necker has been led by J. F. Bosher, *French Finances, 1770–1795: From Business to Bureaucracy* (Cambridge: Cambridge University Press, 1970); Jean Egret, *Necker: Ministre de Louis XVI, 1776–1790* (Paris: Champion, 1975); and Robert D. Harris, *Necker: Reform Statesman of the Ancien Régime* (Berkeley: University of California Press, 1979). The major study of Calonne is still that of Robert Lacour-Gayet, *Calonne: Financier, Réformateur, Contre-Révolutionnaire, 1734–1802* (Paris: Hachette, 1963). The notorious sparring between him and his predecessor Necker over the management of royal finances is best handled by Eugene N. White, "Was There a Solution to the Ancien Régime's Financial Dilemma?" *Journal of Economic History* 49 (1989): 545–68. Jean Egret, *The French Prerevolution, 1787–1788*, trans. Wesley D. Camp (Chicago: University of Chicago Press, 1977), deals with

Brienne's and Lamoignon's last-minute efforts at state reform. The *provincial/local* tensions between reformist and reactionary values in the old regime, as reflected in the provincial assemblies of Necker and his successors, have been studied most recently by Peter M. Jones, *Reform and Revolution in France: The Politics of Transition, 1774–1791* (Cambridge: Cambridge University Press, 1995); and Stephen Miller, "Provincial Assemblies, Fiscal Reform, and the Language of Politics in the 1770s and 1780s," *French Historical Studies* 35 (2012): 441–75. The "schizoid political culture" of old regime France is well studied in Dale K. Van Kley, "The Religious Origins of the French Revolution, 1560–1791," in Thomas E. Kaiser and Dale K. Van Kley, eds., *From Deficit to Deluge: The Origins of the French Revolution* (Stanford: Stanford University Press, 2011), chapter 1. Finally, the reader wishing to trace the clash of values through the revolutionary era might start with Jacques Godechot, *La Contre-Révolution: Doctrine et Action* (Paris: Presses Universitaires de France, 1961); D. M. G. Sutherland, *France, 1789–1815: Revolution and Counterrevolution* (New York: Oxford University Press, 1986); and Isser Woloch, *Napoleon and His Collaborators: The Making of a Dictatorship* (New York: Norton, 2001).

In the Russian case, too, modernizing values and policies alienated a stubbornly traditionalist monarch from his visionary ministers. On Nicholas II, the reader should first see Andrew M. Verner, *The Crisis of Russian Autocracy: Nicholas II and the 1905 Revolution* (Princeton: Princeton University Press, 1990); Dominic Lieven, *Nicholas II: Emperor of all the Russias* (London: John Murray, 1993); and M. D. Steinberg and V. M. Khrustalev, *The Fall of the Romanovs: Political Dreams and Personal Struggles in a Time of Revolution* (New Haven: Yale University Press, 1995). In the gallery of modernizing ministers endeavoring to preserve tsarist rule in old regime Russia, the names of Witte, Stolypin, Kokovtsov, and Polivanov seem to stand out. Theodore H. Von Laue focused upon Witte's campaign of state-sponsored industrialization in *Sergei Witte and the Industrialization of Russia* (New York: Columbia University Press, 1963). Alexander Gerschenkron placed Witte's policies in an international developmental context in *Economic Backwardness in Historical Perspective* (Cambridge, MA: Harvard University Press, 1962); more recently, David M. McDonald has reappraised those policies against a *domestic* backdrop in his *United Government and Foreign Policy in Russia, 1900–1914* (Cambridge, MA: Harvard University Press, 1992), esp. chapters 1–3. The most satisfying study of Pyotr Stolypin is by Abraham Ascher, *P. A. Stolypin: The Search for Stability in Late Imperial Russia* (Stanford: Stanford University Press, 2001). For a recent take on his controversial rural reforms, see Judith Pallot, *Land Reform in Russia, 1906–1917: Peasant Responses to Stolypin's Project of Rural Transformation* (New York: Oxford University Press, 1999). We lack studies of V. N. Kokovtsov and A. A. Polivanov, but the interested reader can follow their ill-fated attempts to modernize Imperial Russia's economy and military establishment in McDonald, *United Government and Foreign Policy in Russia*; in Lewis H. Siegelbaum, *The Politics of Industrial Mobilization in Russia, 1914–17: A Study of the War-Industries Committees* (New York: St. Martin's Press, 1983); and in W. Bruce Lincoln, *Passage Through Armaggedon: The Russians in War and Revolution, 1914–1918* (New York: Simon and Schuster, 1986). A solid source on the tensions between progressive and reactionary forces in the *zemstvos* of the old regime is Terence Emmons and Wayne S. Vucinich, eds., *The Zemstvos in Russia: An Experiment in Local Self-Government* (Cambridge: Cambridge University Press, 1982). The often violently clashing Westernizing and Slavophile perspectives in tsarist Russia's intelligentsia are reevaluated carefully in Christopher Read, *Culture and Power: The Intelligentsia and the Transition from Tsarism to Communism* (New York: St. Martin's Press, 1990). Finally, the reader wanting to trace the deepening polarization between radicals and reactionaries in early revolutionary Russia should begin with two articles: William G. Rosenberg and Diane Koenker, "The Limits of Formal Protest: Workers' Activism and Social Polarization in Petrograd and Moscow, March to October, 1917," *American Historical Review* 92 (1987): 296–326; and Paul Flenley, "Industrial Relations and the Economic Crisis of 1917," *Revolutionary Russia* 4 (1991): 184–209.

IN SEARCH OF THE ELUSIVE *ANCIEN RÉGIME* BOURGEOISIE

My purpose in this section of the chapter is to direct the reader to some of the best scholarship by those social historians who are particularly concerned with "locating" and describing "middle-class" (or possibly "genteel") individuals and defining their *political* roles in *ancien régime* and early revolutionary French, English, and Russian society.

In the case of France, whose purportedly bourgeois revolution so fascinated Marx and Engels in the nineteenth century, the reader might start with William Doyle's statistical profile of the old regime's middle classes. See William Doyle, *Origins of the French Revolution* (Oxford: Oxford University Press, 1980), 129–30. Doyle elaborates upon this subject somewhat in *The Oxford History of the French Revolution* (Oxford: Clarendon, 1989). He also shows, in "The Price of Offices in Pre-Revolutionary France," *Historical Journal* 27 (1984), 856–57, that the prices of most venal offices held by bourgeois subjects in the old regime were *rising* rather than (as Alfred Cobban had earlier suggested) *falling*. Historians have also come increasingly to see bourgeois Frenchmen as making up but one element in a larger, multifarious élite of old regime *notables*. See, in this connection, Adeline Daumard and François Furet, *Structures et relations sociales à Paris au milieu du XVIIIe siècle* (Paris: A. Colin, 1961); Georges Lefebvre, "Urban Society in the Orléanais in the Late Eighteenth Century," *Past and Present* 19 (1961), 80, 87; Olwen H. Hufton, *Bayeux in the Late Eighteenth Century* (Oxford: Oxford University Press, 1987); Lynn A. Hunt, *Revolution and Urban Politics in Provincial France: Troyes and Reims, 1786–1790* (Stanford: Stanford University Press, 1978); Robert Darnton, *The Great Cat Massacre and Other Episodes in French Cultural History* (New York: Vintage Books, 1985); and Daniel Roche, *Le siècle des lumières en province: Académies et académiciens provinçiaux, 1680–1789* (Paris: Mouton, 1978). Still, for a few examples of scholars trying to preserve something of the old association between bourgeois *status* and "capitalism" in the old regime, refer to the following: Colin Jones, "Bourgeois Revolution Revivified: 1789 and Social Change," in Colin Lucas, ed., *Rewriting the French Revolution* (Oxford: Clarendon Press, 1991), 69–118; Peter McPhee, *A Social History of France, 1780–1880* (London: Routledge, 1992); Gwynne Lewis, *The Advent of Modern Capitalism in France: The Case of Pierre-François Tubeuf* (Cambridge: Cambridge University Press, 1993); and Henry Heller, *The Bourgeois Revolution in France, 1789–1815* (New York: Berghahn, 2006). Recently, however, specialists endeavoring to "break" this orthodox association between *social status* and economic activities in original ways have proven increasingly assertive. See, for example, David Garrioch, *The Formation of the Parisian Bourgeoisie, 1690–1830* (Cambridge, MA: Harvard University Press, 1996); Sara Maza, *The Myth of the French Bourgeoisie: An Essay on the Social Imaginary, 1750–1850* (Cambridge, MA: Harvard University Press, 2003); and Jack Goldstone, "The Social Origins of the French Revolution Revisited," in Kaiser and Van Kley, eds., *From Deficit to Deluge*, 67–103. Moreover, we now have efforts by some historians to see the state, rather than any "capitalist bourgeoisie," as the crucial protagonist in unleashing revolution in Bourbon France. See, as examples of this tendency, the articles by Peter Campbell and Jean-Pierre Jessenne in Peter McPhee, ed., *A Companion to the French Revolution* (West Sussex, UK: Wiley-Blackwell, 2013).

For many years, Christopher Hill advanced the notion of a rising capitalist gentry as the primary agent of revolutionary change in England. See, for example, *The Century of Revolution, 1603–1714* (London: Nelson, 1961); *Society and Puritanism in Pre-Revolutionary England*, third edition (London: Panther, 1969); *People and Ideas in Seventeenth-Century England* (Brighton: Harvester, 1987); and *Intellectual Origins of the English Revolution* (Oxford: Clarendon Press, 1997). Many historians—too many to list here—had joined Hill in a ballyhooed "storm" over the "rising" (or, perhaps, "declining"?) gentry of early Stuart England in the years following World War II. In the late 1980s and 1990s, Robert Brenner tried to link revolutionary change in seventeenth-century England *specifically with agricultural de-*

velopmental "class" dynamics in writings that culminated in *Merchants and Revolution: Commercial Change, Political Conflict, and London's Overseas Traders, 1550–1653* (Princeton: Princeton University Press, 1993). For the many scholarly contributions to the so-called Brenner debate touched off by this hypothesis, see, in particular, Trevor H. Aston and C. H. E. Philpin, eds., *The Brenner Debate* (Cambridge: Cambridge University Press, 1987); and A. L. Beier, David Cannadine, and James M. Rosenheim, eds., *The First Modern Society: Essays in English History in Honor of Lawrence Stone* (Cambridge: Cambridge University Press, 1989). In addition, R. C. Richardson has left us a timely discussion of the issues raised by Brenner, his supporters, and his critics in *The Debate on the English Revolution*, third edition (Manchester: Manchester University Press, 1998). On the other hand, English revolutionary historiography has never altogether abandoned the notion of *middle-class* "agency" in the coming of the "Puritan" revolution. Earlier efforts to reassess this question included Jack Hexter, "The Myth of the Middle Class in Tudor England," as revised in his *Reappraisals in History* (London: Longman, 1961), 71–116; and C. H. George, "The Making of the English Bourgeoisie 1600–1710," *Science and Society* 35 (1971): 385–414. More recently, other historians have discussed the possible revolutionary role of the "middling sort" in English society: see, for example, the articles anthologized in Jonathan Barry and Christopher Brooks, eds., *The Middling Sort of People: Culture, Society and Politics in England, 1550–1800* (London: Macmillan, 1994); Brian Manning, *The English People and the English Revolution*, second edition (London: Bookmarks, 1991); and (by the same author) *Aristocrats, Plebeians and Revolution in England 1640–1660* (London: Pluto Press, 1996). Yet, in what has been perhaps the most recent "turn" in this contentious literature, a number of post-revisionists have "retheorized" the English version of a "revolutionary bourgeoisie" *and* at the same time related socioeconomic change in early Stuart England to *statist* and *policy-making* developments. See, as examples of this, Carlin, *The Causes of the English Civil War*, esp. 119, 133; Ann Hughes, *The Causes of the English Civil War*, esp. 71; and, most strikingly of all, that leftist veteran of the "storm over the gentry," Christopher Hill, in *Intellectual Origins of the English Revolution Revisited*, esp. 285–86, 297, 300.

Scholarly efforts to locate and study a bourgeoisie in late Romanov times have, of course, been until recently complicated—like so much else in Russian revolutionary historiography—by ideological legacies inherited from Cold War days. The reader will find thoughtful remarks on this issue in: Thomas C. Owen, "Impediments to a Bourgeois Consciousness in Russia, 1880–1905: The Estate Structure, Ethnic Diversity, and Economic Regionalism," in Edith W. Clowes, Samuel D. Kassow, and James L. West, eds., *Between Tsar and People: Educated Society and the Quest for Public Identity in Late Imperial Russia* (Princeton: Princeton University Press, 1991),

75–76; and Edward Acton, "The Revolution and Its Historians: The *Critical Companion* in Context," in Acton, Cherniaev, and Rosenberg, eds., *Critical Companion to the Russian Revolution*, 14–16. Tension, in old regime Russia, between the juridical estates (*sosoloviia*) and nascent socioeconomic classes long delayed bourgeois class formation, and has attracted extensive specialist commentary. See, for example, Gregory L. Freeze, "The Soslovie (Estate) Paradigm and Russian Social History," *American Historical Review* 91 (1986): esp. 35–36; Leopold Haimson, "The Problem of Social Identities in Early Twentieth-Century Russia," *Slavic Review* 47 (1988): 1–20; and Sheila Fitzpatrick, "Ascribing Class: The Construction of Social Identity in Soviet Russia," *Journal of Modern History* 65 (1993): 745–70. Tensions also beclouded the relationship between late Russian autocracy and capitalist elements in *élite* society. See, on this point, Theodore H. Von Laue, "Westernization, Revolution and the Search for a Basis of Authority: Russia in 1917," *Soviet Studies* 19 (1967): 156–80; and Tim McDaniel, *Autocracy, Capitalism, and Revolution in Russia* (Berkeley: University of California Press, 1988). Historians who have followed the fortunes of some *specific* entrepreneurial/professional groups in old regime Russia include A. J. Rieber, *Merchants and Entrepreneurs in Imperial Russia* (Chapel Hill: University of North Carolina Press, 1982); Nancy M. Frieden, *Russian Physicians in an Era of Reform and Revolution, 1856–1905* (Princeton: Princeton University Press, 1981); and James L. West, "The Riabushinsky Circle: *Burzhuaziia* and *Obshchestvennost'* in Late Imperial Russia," in Clowes, Kassow, and West, eds., *Between Tsar and People*, passim. Meanwhile, the *disunity* apparently marking at this time the traditional aristocratic *élite* as well as the bourgeoisie in *ancien régime* Russia is pointed up by Roberta T. Manning, *The Crisis of the Old Order in Russia: Gentry and Government* (Princeton: Princeton University Press, 1982). That all of these centrifugal social tendencies were only exacerbated during the Great War and right into the 1917 Revolution has been very well documented. See, in this connection, Lewis H. Siegelbaum, *The Politics of Industrial Mobilization in Russia, 1914–17: A Study of the War-Industries Committees* (New York: St. Martin's Press, 1983); Peter Gatrell, "Russian Industrialists and Revolution," in Acton, Cherniaev, and Rosenberg, eds., *Critical Companion to the Russian Revolution*, esp. 576–78; and Ziva Galili, "Commercial-Industrial Circles in Revolution: The Failure of 'Industrial Progressivism,'" in Edith R. Frankel, Jonathan Frankel, and Baruch Knei-Paz, eds., *Revolution in Russia: Reassessments of 1917* (Cambridge: Cambridge University Press, 1992). Finally, the reader will want to note how, even for historians embracing political-cultural history, issues relating to bourgeois class formation in prerevolutionary and early revolutionary Russia need increasingly to be viewed against the backdrop of state failure in domestic and, especially, *international* affairs. See, for instance, Orlando Figes, *A People's Tragedy: The Russian Revolution 1891–1924*

(New York: Penguin Books, 1998), 810; and Sheila Fitzpatrick, *The Russian Revolution*, third edition (Oxford: Oxford University Press, 2008), 39.

TO KILL A MONARCH: FROM PROCEDURALISM TO REVOLUTIONARY *RAISON D'ÉTAT*

Because historians of the three great European revolutions have had so much to say (especially in recent years) about the decisions of Cromwellian Independents, Robespierrist Jacobins, and Leninist Bolsheviks to execute, respectively, Charles I, Louis XVI, and Nicholas II, suggestions for further reading on this subject (in both primary *and* secondary sources) would seem to be particularly appropriate.

As one would expect, there are many collections of documents covering the trial of King Charles at Westminster Hall in January 1649. One of the most readily accessible (if rather slender) collections is that co-edited by David Lagomarsino and Charles T. Wood, *The Trial of Charles I: A Documentary History* (Hanover: University Press of New England, 1989). For the political background to these proceedings—including the king's divisive and duplicitous behavior during the latter phases of the English civil wars—refer to the following: David Underdown, *Pride's Purge: Politics in the Puritan Revolution* (Oxford: Clarendon, 1971); and Robert Ashton, *Counter-Revolution: The Second Civil War and Its Origins, 1646–48* (New Haven: Yale University Press, 1994). From the proceedings of a conference held in London in January 1999 come many excellent papers on aspects of the 1649 regicide: they appear in Jason Peacey, ed., *The Regicides and the Execution of Charles I* (Basingstoke and New York: Palgrave, 2001). However, the reader can also delve elsewhere into some of the specific issues taken up at this meeting. Hence, Sarah Barber takes up some of the *ideological* ramifications of the king's trial in "Charles I: Regicide and Republicanism," *History Today* 46 (1996): esp. 30. Again, Daniel P. Klein reviews strictly *legal* issues in "The Trial of Charles I," *Journal of Legal History* 18 (1997): 1–25. On the role of the parliamentary and London Presbyterians in this drama, see Noel H. Mayfield, *Puritans and Regicides. Presbyterian and Independent Differences over the Trial and Execution of Charles (I) Stuart* (London: University Press, 1988); and Ian Gentles, "The Struggle for London in the Second Civil War," *Historical Journal* 26 (1983): esp. 281–91. At the other end of the political spectrum were the Levellers, whose ambivalence at this time about the prospect of executing Charles I is reflected both in Andrew Sharp's article in Jason Peacey's anthology and in Ian Gentles, "The Politics of Fairfax's Army, 1645–9," in John Adamson, ed., *The English Civil War: Conflict and Contexts, 1640–49* (London: Palgrave Mcmillan, 2009), 175–201. On the persistent reluctance of well-connected New Model Army

Grandees like Oliver Cromwell to march the king to his death, refer to John Adamson, *The Noble Revolt: The Overthrow of Charles I* (London: Palgrave Macmillan, 2009); and Ian Gentles, *Oliver Cromwell: God's Warrior and the English Revolution* (New York: Palgrave Macmillan, 2011). On the other hand, the notion of royal "blood guilt" contributing to the determination of Charles's enemies to have him executed is taken up by Christopher Hill, "The Man of Blood," in *The English Bible and the Seventeenth-Century Revolution* (London: Allen Lane, 1993), 324–31, and by Sarah Barber, *Regicide and Republicanism* (Edinburgh: Edinburgh University Press, 1998), esp. 86, 100–01, 111–12. Sean Kelsey's analyses of the actual *theatrics* and *staging* of the trial in January 1649 have led him to stress both Charles's "psychological" inability to compromise with his enemies and *their* determination finally to have done with him: see (in addition to Kelsey's contribution to J. Peacey's anthology) his later article: "The Trial of Charles I," *English Historical Review* 118 (2003): esp. 515–16. Finally, readers interested in European reactions to the regicide of January 1649 should consult C. V. Wedgwood, "European Reaction to the Death of Charles I," in C. H. Carter, ed., *From the Renaissance to the Counter-Reformation: Essays in Honor of Garrett Mattingly* (London: Jonathan Cope, 1966), 401–16; and Richard Bonney, "The European Reaction to the Trial and Execution of Charles I," in J. Peacey, ed., *The Regicides and the Execution of Charles I*, 247–79.

Those desiring access to an original source on the trial and execution of Louis XVI (in December 1792–January 1793) need to consult the *Archives Parlementaires de 1787 à 1860 . . . première série* (Paris: Paul Dupont, 1899), esp. volumes 54–56; they should also consult Albert Soboul, ed., *Le Procès de Louis XVI* (Paris: Collection Archives, 1966), for a useful survey of original documents on the subject. Many of the key speeches by *Conventionnels* at the king's trial have been rendered into English in Michael Walzer, ed., *Regicide and Revolution: Speeches at the Trial of Louis XVI*, trans. Marian Rothstein (Cambridge: Cambridge University Press, 1974). Damning evidence galore of Louis XVI's duplicity in the politics of the early revolution appears in John Hardman, *Louis XVI* (New Haven: Yale University Press, 1993) and in Munro Price, *The Fall of the French Monarchy: Louis XVI, Marie Antoinette and the Baron de Breteuil* (London: Macmillan, 2002). Susan Dunn reviews some cultural aspects of the king's trial in *The Deaths of Louis XVI: Regicide and the French Political Imagination* (Princeton: Princeton University Press, 1994). The constitutional difficulties encountered by those *Conventionnels* wishing to "get at" the king through proper judicial procedures are discussed by Alison Patrick, *The Men of the First French Republic: Political Alignments in the National Convention of 1792* (Baltimore: Johns Hopkins University Press, 1972), 43; and by Ferenc Fehér, *The Frozen Revolution: An Essay on Jacobinism* (Cambridge: Cambridge University Press, 1987), 104–05. Dan Edelstein argues intriguingly (if not altogether convincingly) that trying Louis by the "law of nature" was a real possibility in *The Terror of Natural Right: Republicanism, the Cult of Nature, and the French Revolution* (Chicago: University of Chicago Press, 2009). The dilemmas—and political miscalculations—of the Girondists in the king's trial were covered years ago by M. J. Sydenham, *The Girondins* (London: Athlone Press, 1961), and have been dealt with much more recently by David P. Jordan, *The King's Trial: The French Revolution versus Louis XVI* (Berkeley: University of California Press, 1979), and Gary Kates, *The Cercle Social, the Girondins, and the French Revolution* (Princeton: Princeton University Press, 1985). The reader wishing to learn more about the role of the Parisian *sans-culottes* at this critical point in the revolution should consult (among other studies) Morris Slavin, *The Making of An Insurrection: Parisian Sections and the Gironde* (Cambridge, MA: Harvard University Press, 1986). The most accessible source for the inflammatory speeches (November–December 1792) in which Saint-Just and Robespierre attempted to "theorize" the Revolution and thereby place Louis XVI "beyond the pale" remains Walzer, *Regicide and Revolution*, 21–23, 131–32, 138. For the most updated scholarly analysis of Robespierre's subsequent attempts (in speeches to the Convention of 25 December 1793 and 5 February 1794) to develop and justify his political/constitutional ideas, see Dan Edelstein, "Do We Want a Revolution without Revolution? Reflections on Political Authority," *French Historical Studies* 35 (2012): 269–89. Meanwhile, for a brief and readable account of the king's conduct during his trial (and of how—unlike Charles I—he actually *did* accept legal counsel), see John Hardman, *Louis XVI: The Silent King* (London: Arnold, 2000), chapter 12. Finally, the *international* context of all of this is analyzed in Stone, *Reinterpreting the French Revolution*, esp. 171–72.

Although, of course, Russia's last tsar, Nicholas II, was never granted an English- or French-style trial, the interested reader can glean useful information about his murder in July 1918 from a "carbon copy" of the inquiry of the Commission which, under the direction of Nicholas A. Sokolov, revisited the subject during the 1920s. It is apparently still accessible today in Harvard University's Houghton Library. For general information on the tortuous destiny of the Imperial family during the February 1917 to July 1918 period, see Richard Pipes, *The Russian Revolution* (New York: Alfred A. Knopf, 1990), chapter 17; Orlando Figes, *A People's Tragedy*, esp. 635–42; and Mark D. Steinberg and V. M. Khrustalev, *The Fall of the Romanovs*, passim. Richard Wortman has generated some fascinating work on the myths and symbolism surrounding the historic institution of tsardom in Russia. See, in particular, "Invisible Threads: The Historical Imagery of the Romanov Tercentenary," *Russian History* 16 (1989): 2–4; and his *Scenarios of Power: Myth and Ceremony in Russian Monarchy* (Princeton: Princeton University Press,

1995). On the countervailing forces of terrorism and on would-be revolutionaries in old regime Russia, see these works: Martin Malia, *Alexander Herzen and the Birth of Russian Socialism* (Cambridge, MA: Harvard University Press, 1961); Isaiah Berlin, *Russian Thinkers* (New York: Viking Press, 1978); Abbott Gleason, *Young Russia: The Genesis of Russian Radicalism in the 1860s* (New York: Viking Press, 1980); and Figes, *A People's Tragedy*, esp. 125–38. The impact of rumored "dark forces" (often associated with the Germans) on the Imperial family in wartime Russia is underscored in Orlando Figes and Boris Kolonitskii, *Interpreting the Russian Revolution: The Language and Symbols of 1917* (New Haven: Yale University Press, 1994). As for the damaging impact of Rasputin's scandals on the Romanovs, readers can start here with R. K. Massie, *Nicholas and Alexandra* (New York: Athenaeum, 1967), esp. 152, 299, 346–47, and George Katkov, *Russia, 1917: The February Revolution* (London: Longman, 1967), 157–60, and go on from there! The reluctance of "moderate" revolutionaries in 1917 to deal too harshly with Nicholas II emerges clearly in biographies of the first foreign minister, Paul Miliukov. See Melissa K. Stockdale, *Paul Miliukov and the Quest for a Liberal Russia* (Ithaca: Cornell University Press, 1996). But from the very start, that reluctance was *not* shared by most workers and peasants in 1917 Russia. See, on this question, Michael Melancon, "Soldiers, Peasant-Soldiers, Peasant-Workers and Their Organizations in Petrograd: Ground-Level Revolution in the Early Months of 1917," *Soviet and Post-Soviet Review* 23 (1996): 161–90. Finally, whether or not the actual order for the murder of the ex-tsar emanated from Moscow or from Urals militants at Ekaterinburg has occasioned a minor scholarly controversy in itself. Pipes (in *The Russian Revolution*, 770) assigns blame for this squarely to Lenin; so do both Dominic Lieven in *Nicholas II: Emperor of All the Russias* (London: John Murray, 1993), 242, and Helen Rappaport in *The Last Days of the Romanovs: Tragedy at Ekaterinburg* (New York: St. Martin's Press, 2008), chapter 10. Yet Steinberg and Khrustalev, in *The Fall of the Romanovs*, 293–94, advance the thesis that the initiative in this matter may well have been wrested from the leaders at Moscow by local militants. For obvious reasons, the issue is likely to remain forever unresolved, one way or the other. Incidentally, Leon Trotsky's evolving position on the practicality and, more basically, the *ideological advisability* of even bringing Nicholas to trial can be followed—if retrospectively—in his diary. Refer to the Trotsky Archive, Houghton Library, Harvard University, bMS/Russ 13, T-3731 (various entries).

CIRCUMSTANCES VERSUS IDEAS IN THE REVOLUTIONARY "FURIES"

Most historians writing on the resort to state-sanctioned terror in revolutionary France, Russia, and England approach this subject through the explanatory binary of "circumstances versus ideas." This construct, taken up in Arno Mayer, *The Furies: Violence and Terror in the French and Russian Revolutions* (Princeton: Princeton University Press, 2000), is acknowledged in this study and (for obvious reasons) extended back to England. It is, as such, reflected in this section of our bibliographical chapter.

Richard T. Bienvenu accurately chronicles the creation of the institutions of the Jacobin Terror of 1793 to 1794 in "Terror," in Samuel F. Scott and Barry Rothaus, eds., *Historical Dictionary of the French Revolution, 1789–1799* (Westwood: Greenwood Press, 1985), 942–46. The reader then should see two durable classics on the subject: R. R. Palmer, *Twelve Who Ruled: The Year of the Terror in the French Revolution* (Princeton: Princeton University Press, 1941), and Donald Greer, *The Incidence of the Terror during the French Revolution: A Statistical Interpretation* (Cambridge, MA: Harvard University Press, 1935). For an informed (but hardly devastating) critique of Greer's methodology, see Gilbert Shapiro and John Markoff, "The Incidence of the Terror: Some Lessons for Quantitative History," *Journal of Social History* 9 (1975): 193–218. Major studies of the Jacobin Terror in its *local* settings include Alan Forrest, *Society and Politics in Revolutionary Bordeaux* (New York: Oxford University Press, 1975); Bill Edmunds, *Jacobinism and the Revolt of Lyon, 1789–1793* (Oxford: Clarendon, 1990); William Scott, *Terror and Repression in Revolutionary Marseilles* (London: Macmillan, 1973); Martyn Lyons, *Revolution in Toulouse: An Essay on Provincial Terrorism* (Berne: Peter Lang, 1978); and (for Orange) David Andress, *The Terror: The Merciless War for Freedom in Revolutionary France* (New York: Farrar, Straus and Giroux, 2005). But there is also much solid scholarship on *local opposition* to the Terror. See, for a start, Charles Tilly's classic *The Vendée* (Cambridge, MA: Harvard University Press, 1964), but update this study with Jean-Clément Martin's *La Vendée et la France* (Paris: Seuil, 1987) and *La Vendée et la Révolution* (Paris: Perrin, 2007). Then, again, see D. M. G. Sutherland, *The Chouans: The Social Origins of Popular Counter Revolution in Upper Brittany, 1770–1796* (Oxford: Clarendon Press, 1982). On the "federalist" revolt in general, see Bill Edmunds, "Federalism and Urban Revolt in France in 1793," *Journal of Modern History* 55 (1983): 22–53, and (more recently) Paul Hanson, *The Jacobin Republic Under Fire: The Federalist Revolt in the French Revolution* (University Park: Pennsylvania State University Press, 2003). François Furet presaged postmodernist interpretations of the Jacobin Terror with his remarks in *Interpreting the French Revolution*, passim., and continued his attack in "Terror," in Furet and Ozouf, eds., *A Critical Dictionary of the French Revolution*, 146–50. Other notable cultural renderings of the Terror include Keith M. Baker, "Transformations of Classical Republicanism in Eighteenth-Century France," *Journal of Modern History* 73 (2001): 32–53; Dan Edelstein, *The Terror of Natural Right*, passim.; and Mary Ashburn Miller, *A Natural History of Revolution: Violence and Nature in the French Revolutionary Imagination, 1789–1794* (Ithaca: Cornell University Press, 2011). Similar and yet somewhat different views of the Terror stress its conspiratorial psychology: consult, as examples of this, the articles anthologized in Peter Campbell, Thomas E. Kaiser, and Marisa Linton, eds., *Conspiracy in the French Revolution* (Manchester: Manchester University Press, 2007); and Timothy Tackett's latest book, *The Coming of the Terror in the French Revolution* (Cambridge, MA: Belknap Press of Harvard University Press, 2015). The reader who is curious about international reactions to the Jacobin Terror should consult, among other major works, Karl A. Roider, Jr., *Baron Thugut and Austria's Response to the French Revolution* (Princeton: Princeton University Press, 1987), and Jeremy Black, *British Foreign Policy in an Age of Revolutions, 1783–1793* (New York: Cambridge University Press, 1994). Finally, to ponder once again Arno Mayer's book, consult the "Forum: Comparing Revolutions: On Arno Mayer's *The Furies: Violence and Terror in the French and Russian Revolutions*," *French Historical Studies* 24 (2001): 549–600.

The basic chronology of the Bolshevik or Red Terror is neatly summarized in Mayer, *The Furies*, 311. To study the gradual establishment of the Red Terror is to study the creation and evolution of its primary instrument, the *Cheka*. See, on this subject: George Leggett, *The Cheka: Lenin's Political Police* (Oxford: Oxford University Press, 1981); C. M. Andrew and O. Gordievsky, *KGB: The Inside Story of its Foreign Operations from Lenin to Gorbachev* (London: Hodder and Stoughton, 1990); and Alter L. Litvin, "The Cheka," in Acton, Cherniaev, and Rosenberg, eds., *Critical Companion to the Russian Revolution*, 314–21. Archival sources do not allow us (*à la* Donald Greer) to study the *incidence* of the Red Terror with any precision. Richard Pipes argues that the Terror claimed "tens if not hundreds of thousands" of victims; more cautiously calibrated estimates come from Mayer, *The Furies*, 310, and from Geoffrey Hosking, *The First Socialist Society: A History of the Soviet Union from Within* (Cambridge, MA: Harvard University Press, 1990), 71. The wide *social incidence* of the Terror is graphically illustrated in Figes, *A People's Tragedy*, 642–43, and in Litvin, "The Cheka," in Acton, Cherniaev, and Rosenberg, eds., *Critical Companion to the Russian Revolution*, 317–20. Though Russian revolutionary research does not yet offer the reader the plenitude of local studies devoted to the implementation of—or opposition to—state-sponsored Terror as *does* exist in the case of France, a start can be made with such pioneering works as Teodor Shanin,

The Awkward Class: Political Sociology of Peasantry in a Developing Society, Russia, 1910–1925 (Oxford: Clarendon Press, 1972), esp. 145–62; and O. Figes, *Peasant Russia, Civil War: The Volga Countryside in Revolution, 1917–1921* (Oxford: Oxford University Press, 1989), esp. 66–67, 81–83, 188–89. There is also, in this connection, the role (briefly) played in national Bolshevik politics by the Russian peasantry's advocates, the Left Socialist Revolutionaries. Orlando Figes provides a vivid description of the abortive Left SR uprising of early July 1918 in *A People's Tragedy*, 632–35. But for the latest doubts about the SRs as a *potentially* coherent party in 1918 and after, see Scott B. Smith, *Captives of Revolution: The Socialist Revolutionaries and the Bolshevik Dictatorship 1918–1923* (Pittsburgh: University of Pittsburgh Press, 2011). Furet-style postmodernist interpretations of the Red Terror were widely circulated in a "Seminar in Twentieth-Century Russian and Soviet Social History" in the late 1980s; for the results, consult Diane P. Koenker, William G. Rosenberg, and Ronald G. Suny, eds., *Party, State, and Society in the Russian Civil War: Explorations in Social History* (Bloomington: Indiana University Press, 1989). Since then, however, a structuralist emphasis on the continuity of *war* and *statism* in the Russian Revolution has continued in studies by Peter Holquist, *Making War, Forging Revolution: Russia's Continuum of Crisis 1914–1921* (Cambridge, MA: Harvard University Press, 2002), and Joshua A. Sanborn, *Drafting the Russian Nation: Military Conscription, Total War, and Mass Politics 1905–1925* (De Kalb: Northern Illinois University Press, 2003). Finally, readers interested in the broader setting of the Red Terror should consult Richard K. Debo, *Revolution and Survival: The Foreign Policy of Soviet Russia, 1917–1918* (Toronto: University of Toronto Press, 1979); Evan Mawdsley, *The Russian Civil War* (Boston: Allen and Unwin, 1987); W. Bruce Lincoln, *Red Victory: A History of the Russian Civil War* (New York: Simon and Schuster, 1989); David S. Foglesong, *America's Secret War Against Bolshevism: US Intervention in the Russian Civil War, 1917–1920* (Chapel Hill: University of North Carolina Press, 1995); and on and on!

There was no *theorized, sustained* campaign of Terror in the mid-seventeenth-century English revolution. This is a point that Ronald Hutton underscores correctly in *The British Republic 1649–1660* (New York: St. Martin's Press, 1990), 21–22. Still, the Commonwealth had sporadically to crack down brutally on royalist and other opponents during 1649 to 1653. See, on this issue, these works: Paul Hardacre, *The Royalists during the Puritan Revolution* (The Hague: M. Nijhoff, 1956); David Underdown, *Royalist Conspiracy in England, 1649–1660* (New Haven: Yale University Press, 1960); and (much more recently) Jason McElligott and David L. Smith, eds., *Royalists and Royalism During the Interregnum* (Manchester: Manchester University Press, 2010). The "High Courts of Justice" and other institutions of the episodic state-sanctioned Terror in England are revisited by G. E. Aylmer,

The State's Servants: The Civil Service of the English Republic 1649–1660 (London: Routledge & Kegan Paul, 1973), esp. 31, 35, 355 (n. 16). There is, of course, a copious literature on the sanguinary imposition of Cromwellian "terror" on the Irish in 1649. The connections between persistent Leveller agitation in the New Model Army and the inception of the Irish campaign are explored in Norah Carlin, "The Levellers and the Conquest of Ireland in 1649," *Historical Journal* 30 (1987): 269–88. Cromwell's myriad biographers have been at pains to probe the ethical issues raised by his army's conduct at Drogheda, Wexford, and elsewhere. See, on this controversy, Christopher Hill, *God's Englishman: Oliver Cromwell and the English Revolution* (New York: Harper Torchbooks, 1970); Barry Coward, *Oliver Cromwell* (London: Longman, 1991); Peter Gaunt, *Oliver Cromwell* (New York: New York University Press, 2004); Ian Gentles, *Oliver Cromwell: God's Warrior and the English Revolution* (New York: Palgrave Macmillan, 2011); and so on. The *demographic decline* of the Irish in this period is revisited in Pádraig Lenihan, "War and Population, 1649–52," *Irish Economic and Social History* 24 (1997): 1–21. Inevitably, a Furetist political-cultural analysis has emerged in this field. See, most notably in this connection, Sean Kelsey, *Inventing a Republic: The Political Culture of the English Commonwealth 1649–1659* (Manchester: Manchester University Press, 1997); and Sarah Barber, *Regicide and Republicanism* (Edinburgh: Edinburgh University Press, 1998). Still, those historians stressing the "appalling insecurity" of the newborn Commonwealth in the wake of the regicide would accentuate here the *international* context of all terrorist initiatives. Consult, among other works, Ian Gentles, *The New Model Army in England, Scotland and Ireland 1645–1653* (Oxford: Blackwell, 1991), and *The English Revolution and the Wars in the Three Kingdoms, 1638–1652* (London: Pearson, 2007); Timothy Venning, *Cromwellian Foreign Policy* (New York: St. Martin's Press, 1995); and Bernard Capp, *Cromwell's Navy* (Oxford: Clarendon Press, 1989). Finally, Steve Pincus is able to combine cultural *and* geopolitical analysis in some measure in *Protestantism and Patriotism: Ideologies and the Making of English Foreign Policy, 1650–1668* (Cambridge: Cambridge University Press, 1996).

CRISES OF REVOLUTIONARY LEGITIMACY: THERMIDORIAN OUTCOMES

There is no issue addressed in this book that has given rise to more thoughtful reassessments and, thus, more controversies in recent years than the efforts of the Thermidorian revolutionaries in England, France, and Russia to *legitimize* their new regimes. Consequently, the emphasis here will lie very heavily upon *recent* rather than upon long-standing historical scholarship.

To begin with, Ronald Hutton discusses the phenomenon of proliferating paper constitutions in republican England in *The British Republic 1649–60*, esp. 67, 73–74, 76. The nature and extent of Oliver Cromwell's power in the 1650s are of course taken up in the biographies of Cromwell that have already been referenced, but are also reviewed in the following books: Derek Hirst, "The Lord Protector, 1653–1658," in John Morrill, ed., *Oliver Cromwell and the English Revolution* (London: Longman, 1990), passim; Roger Howell Jr., "Cromwell and His Parliaments: The Trevor-Roper Thesis Revisited," in R. C. Richardson, ed., *Images of Oliver Cromwell* (Manchester: Manchester University Press, 1993), chapter 8; Austin Woolrych, "The Cromwellian Protectorate: A Military Dictatorship?" *History* 75 (1990): 207–31; and also Benjamin Woodford, *Perceptions of a Monarchy Without a King: Reactions to Oliver Cromwell's Power* (Ithaca: McGill-Queen's University Press, 2013). The literature on Oliver's problematic relations with his parliaments ranges from Peter Gaunt, "Law-Making in the First Protectorate Parliament," in Colin Jones, Malyn Newitt, and Stephen Roberts, eds., *Politics and People in Revolutionary England* (Oxford: Oxford University Press, 1986) to David Smith and Patrick Little, *Parliaments and Politics during the Cromwellian Protectorate* (Cambridge: Cambridge University Press, 2007). Superseding all previous works on the Protectorate's major-generals is Christopher Durston, *Cromwell's Major-Generals: Godly Government during the English Revolution* (Manchester: Manchester University Press, 2001). Yet the reader should also refer, on the subject of the army, to Henry Reece, *The Army in Cromwellian England, 1649–1660* (New York: Oxford University Press, 2013). Timothy Venning, *Cromwellian Foreign Policy* (New York: St. Martin's Press, 1995) is probably still the most reliable source on this subject. As for political developments in England *after* Oliver's death, the reader should consult Ronald Hutton, *The Restoration: A Political and Religious History of England and Wales, 1658–1667* (Oxford: Clarendon Press, 1985); Ruth E. Mayers, *1659: The Crisis of the Commonwealth* (Woodbridge: The Boydell Press, 2004); and Blair Worden, *God's Instruments: Political Conduct in the England of Oliver Cromwell* (Oxford: Oxford University Press, 2012). In addition, the reader should consult, in connection with both Oliver Cromwell's Protectorate and that of his ill-omened son Richard, the impressive syntheses of Austin Woolrych, *Britain in Revolution 1625–1660* (Oxford: Oxford University Press, 2002) and of Barry Coward, *The Cromwellian Protectorate* (New York: Palgrave Macmillan, 2002).

The issue of proliferating paper constitutions also came to haunt the Thermidorian politicians in late-revolutionary France. For the actual provisions of the "Constitution of the Year III," consult Denis Woronoff, *The Thermidorean Regime and the Directory, 1794–1799*, trans. Julian Jackson (Cambridge: Cambridge University Press, 1984), 29–42; and Malcolm Crook, *Elections in the French Revolution: An Apprenticeship in Democracy,*

1789–1799 (Cambridge: Cambridge University Press, 1996), 131–57. For a spirited (if questionable) defense of these constitutional arrangements, the reader must—at least in this case—go back to Albert Goodwin, "The French Executive Directory—A Revaluation," *History* 22 (1937): esp. 215–18. Since then, historians have been much more critical of the Constitution of 1795. See, for example, Martyn Lyons, *France Under the Directory* (Cambridge: Cambridge University Press, 1975), 18–20; and (writing in a political-cultural vein) Isser Woloch, *Napoleon and His Collaborators: The Making of a Dictatorship* (New York: Norton, 2001), 5–8. On aspects of the political culture that were antithetical to stable republican governance in Directorial France, see Lynn Hunt, David Lansky, and Paul Hanson, "The Failure of the Liberal Republic in France, 1795–1799: The Road to Brumaire," *Journal of Modern History* 51 (1979): 737–38; and Bronislaw Baczko, *Ending the Terror: The French Revolution After Robespierre*, trans. Michel Petheram (Cambridge: Cambridge University Press, 1994), passim. The Directory's difficulties in dealing with *provincial* issues loom large in Alan Forrest, *The Revolution in Provincial France: Aquitaine, 1789–1799* (New York: Oxford University Press, 1996), and in Howard G. Brown, *Ending the French Revolution: Violence, Justice, and Repression from the Terror to Napoleon* (Charlottesville: University of Virginia Press, 2006). Mona Ozouf discusses religious issues under the Directory in "Revolutionary Calendar" and "Revolutionary Religion" in Furet and Ozouf, eds., *A Critical Dictionary of the French Revolution*, 538–70. On the intersections between the Directory's bellicose foreign policy and domestic political developments, see Howard G. Brown, *War, Revolution, and the Bureaucratic State: Politics and Army Administration in France 1791–1799* (Oxford: Clarendon Press, 1995); and (by the same author) "The New Security State," in Peter McPhee, ed, *A Companion to the French Revolution*, esp. 348–49. For a postmodernist slant on the Directory's hankerings after legitimacy, the interested reader should consult the following works: James Livesey, *Making Democracy in the French Revolution* (Cambridge, MA: Harvard University Press, 2001); Bernard Gainot, *1799, Un Nouveau Jacobinisme?* (Paris: CTHS, 2001); Pierre Serna, *La République des girouettes (1789–1815 et au delà), une anomalie politique: La France de l'extrême centre* (Paris: Champ Vallon, 2005); Andrew Jainchill, *Reimagining Politics After the Terror: The Republican Origins of French Liberalism* (Ithaca: Cornell University Press, 2008); and the many contributions to Pierre Serna, ed., *Républiques soeurs: Le Directoire et la Révolution atlantique* (Rennes: Presses Universitaires de Rennes, 2009). Finally, two excellent works cover the financial, educational, and administrative institutions of the fragile "new regime" in France: Michel Bruguière, *Gestionnaires et profiteurs de la Révolution: L'Administration des finances françaises de Louis XVI à Bonaparte* (Paris: O. Orban, 1986);

and Woloch, *The New Regime: Transformations of the French Civic Order, 1789–1820s* (New York: W. W. Norton, 1994).

The leaders of post-Leninist Russia exposed their concerns about legitimacy by fiercely debating the applicability of the term *Thermidor* to their own situation. See, in this connection, Isaac Deutscher, *Trotsky: The Prophet Unarmed, 1921–29* (London: Oxford University Press, 1970), 312–22; and Michal Reiman, *The Birth of Stalinism*, trans. George Saunders (Bloomington: Indiana University Press, 1987), 22–23. The *economics* of the New Economic Policy (NEP) of the 1920s should be further explored. The reader here, in any case, might want to commence with Sergei V. Iarov, "The Tenth Congress of the Communist Party and the Transition to NEP," in Acton, Cherniaev, and Rosenberg, eds., *A Critical Companion to the Russian Revolution 1914–1921*, 122–27, and then move on to Lewis H. Siegelbaum, *Soviet State and Society between Revolutions, 1918–1929* (Cambridge: Cambridge University Press, 1992), esp. 165–68. Two useful introductory sources on the "industrialization question" in post-Leninist Russia are Alexander Erlich, *The Soviet Industrialization Debate, 1924–1928* (Cambridge, MA: Harvard University Press, 1962), and James R. Millar and Alec Nove, "A Debate on Collectivization: Was Stalin Really Necessary?" *Problems of Communism* 25 (1976): 49–62. The "militarized political culture" that helped to foster anxieties and thus lay the groundwork for crash industrialization in Soviet Russia in the late 1920s is explored by Mark von Hagen, *Soldiers in the Proletarian Dictatorship: The Red Army and the Soviet Socialist State, 1917–1930* (Ithaca: Cornell University Press, 1990). Although Moshe Lewin, Stephen F. Cohen, and other revisionists have argued that the NEP experiment in Russia might have survived if given a reasonable chance, other experts have not been so sure. See on this issue R. W. Davies, *The Industrialization of Soviet Russia: The Soviet Economy in Turmoil, 1929–30* (Cambridge, MA: Harvard University Press, 1989); and Jon Jacobson, *When the Soviet Union Entered World Politics* (Berkeley: University of California Press, 1994). In just the last ten or fifteen years, an entirely new literature has enriched our understanding of the psychology of peasant resistance to Soviet modernization in Russian rural areas. See, for example, James Heinzen, *Inventing a Soviet Countryside: State Power and the Transformation of Rural Russia, 1917–1929* (Pittsburgh: University of Pittsburgh Press, 2004); Lynne Viola, V. P. Danilov, N. A. Ivnitskii, and Denis Koslov, eds., *The War Against the Peasantry, 1927–1930: The Tragedy of the Soviet Countryside*, trans. Steven Shabad (New Haven: Yale University Press, 2005); Tracy McDonald, *Face to the Village: The Riazan Countryside under Soviet Rule, 1921–1930* (Toronto: University of Toronto Press, 2011); and Hugh D. Hudson, *Peasants, Political Police, and the Early Soviet State: Surveillance and Accommodation under the New Economic Policy* (New York: Palgrave Macmillan, 2012). (Yet see also the note of caution sounded on all of this by

Aaron Retish in the *American Historical Review* 118 [2013]: 283–84.) As for the workers' roles in late NEP Russia, see Hiroaki Kuromiya, *Stalin's Industrial Revolution: Politics and Workers, 1928–1932* (Cambridge: Cambridge University Press, 1988); William Chase, *Workers, Society, and the Soviet State: Labor and Life in Moscow, 1918–1929* (Urbana: University of Illinois Press, 1987); Lynne Viola, *The Best Sons of the Fatherland: Workers in the Vanguard of Soviet Collectivization* (New York: Oxford University Press, 1987); and Lewis H. Siegelbaum and Ronald G. Suny, eds., *Making Workers Soviet: Power, Class, and Identity* (Ithaca: Cornell University Press, 1994). Finally, for *cultural* aspects of the quest for legitimacy in Thermidorian Russia, the reader should see the following studies: Lynn Mally, *Culture of the Future: The Proletkult Movement in Revolutionary Russia* (Berkeley: University of California Press, 1990); Sheila Fitzpatrick, *The Cultural Front: Power and Culture in Revolutionary Russia* (Ithaca: Cornell University Press, 1992); and Katerina Clark, *Petersburg, Crucible of Cultural Revolution* (Cambridge, MA: Harvard University Press, 1995); and go on from there.

NEOSTRUCTURALISM AND THE POSTREVOLUTIONARY STATE AS HISTORICAL PROBLEM

There is no need, in this concluding section of our bibliographical chapter, to refer once again to all of the theoretical literature on revolution cited in the first section of the chapter. We limit ourselves here to mentioning some of the works of significance in areas of study whose exploration at any great length would manifestly lie beyond the purview of this book. Those areas are (1) the theorizing of the state, (2) the *geographical contextualization* of (most notably) the English and French revolutions, and (3) the issue of feminist/ gendered roles in the European upheavals. The reader may recall that the introduction briefly discussed the literature on the second of these subjects— namely, the "transatlantic" dimension of the English and French revolutions. The third subject, involving as it does the question of *gender* and of women's roles in the European upheavals, will be fully developed in my next book.

There is no question that social scientists wrestling today with the conceptualization of the state in revolutionary analysis take with abundant caution Theda Skocpol's Weberian pronouncements on the subject. (Refer, again, to Skocpol, *States and Social Revolutions*, 29.) In the case of England, see both Braddick, *State Formation in Early Modern England*, 19–20, and Goldstone, *Revolution and Rebellion in the Early Modern World*, 5n, for evidence of this. For a retheorization of the state that—in the case of France—goes much farther in a "deconstructionist" direction, review again Suzanne Desan, "What's After Political Culture? Recent French Revolutionary Historiography," esp. 194–95. Similar thoughts in the case of Russia are voiced by Steve Smith, "Writing the History of the Russian Revolution after the Fall of Communism," as quoted in Martin A. Miller, ed., *The Russian Revolution: The Essential Readings* (Oxford: Blackwell, 2001), 275–77; and William G. Rosenberg, in Acton, Cherniaev, and Rosenberg, eds., *Critical Companion to the Russian Revolution 1914–1921*, esp. 19–20, 23–24. Yet the reader will also find Weberian (that is to say, structuralist) commentaries on the state in other quarters—as, for instance, in Michael S. Kimmel, *Revolution: A Sociological Interpretation*, 35; and in Noel S. Parker, *Revolutions in History*, 182.

There is also no question that, recently, a number of scholars have pursued the postmodernist project of "decentering" the English and French revolutions by redefining them, at least to some extent, in "Atlanticist" terms. In the former case, see, most notably Carla Pestana, *The English Atlantic in an Age of Revolution, 1640–1661* (Cambridge, MA: Harvard University Press, 2004); and John Donoghue, *Fire Under the Ashes: An Atlantic History of the English Revolution* (Chicago: University of Chicago Press, 2013). Their work draws upon earlier studies, such as Ian K. Steele, *The English Atlantic, 1675–1740: An Exploration of Communication and Community* (New York: Oxford University Press, 1986); Peter Linebaugh and Marcus Rediker, *The Many-Headed Hydra: Sailors, Slaves, Commoners, and the Hidden History of the Revolutionary Atlantic* (Boston: Beacon, 2001); and also David Armitage and Michael J. Braddick, eds., *The British Atlantic World, 1500–1800* (London: Palgrave, 2002). In the latter case, see, above all, Laurent Dubois, "An Atlantic Revolution," *French Historical Studies* 32 (Fall 2009): 655–61; Pierre Serna, "Every Revolution Is a War of Independence," in Suzanne Desan, Lynn Hunt, and William Max Nelson, eds., *The French Revolution in Global Perspective* (Ithaca: Cornell University Press, 2013), 165–82; and David Armitage and Sanjay Subrahmanyam, eds., *The Age of Revolutions in Global Context, 1760–1840* (London: Basingstoke, 2010). Yet the curious reader may also want to consult the somewhat more Eurocentric slant upon all of this in, for example, the works of Jeremy Popkin. They include "Revolution in the Colonies and the French Republican Tradition," in *French Politics, Culture, and Society* 25 (2007): 95–107; and "The French Revolution's Other Island," in David Patrick Geggus and Norman Fiering, eds., *The World of the Haitian Revolution* (Bloomington: Indiana University Press, 2009), 199–222. Gary Wilder draws some incisive contrasts between Dubois's and Popkin's conceptions of the late eighteenth-century "Atlantic" revolutions in the aforementioned "AHR Forum" in the *American Historical Review* 117 (2012): 734–36.

Finally, earlier efforts to *theorize* or historicize feminist/gendered roles in the great European revolutions include Sheila Rowbotham, *Women, Resistance, and Revolution* (London: Allen Lane, 1972); Sian Reynolds, ed.,

Women, State and Revolution: Essays on Power and Gender in Europe Since 1789 (Amherst: University of Massachusetts Press, 1987); Hanna Papanek, "The Ideal Woman and the Ideal Society: Control and Autonomy in the Construction of Identity," in Valentine M. Moghadam, ed., *Identity Politics and Women: Cultural Reassertions and Feminisms in International Perspective* (Boulder: Westview Press, 1994), 42–75; and Valentine M. Moghadam, "Gender and Revolutions," in John Foran, ed., *Theorizing Revolutions* (London: Routledge, 1997), 137–67. In the actual case of revolutionary France, Jennifer N. Heuer has provided thoughts about the literature on the linkages between gendered issues, family dynamics, and the construction of national identity in "Did Everything Change? Rethinking Revolutionary Legacies," in David Andress, ed., *The Oxford Handbook of the French Revolution* (Oxford: Oxford University Press, 2015), 625–41. On the more general question as to whether *gender* actually *remains* a useful category of analysis for the historian of *any* specific country or era, see the reflections of Joan Wallach Scott, *Gender and the Politics of History* (New York: Columbia University Press, 1999), esp. the preface and chapter 10. Obviously there is not enough space here to inventory the most recent works on the roles of women in the English, French, and Russian revolutions, but for some suggestions (updated to 2014) for reading in this area, refer once again to Bailey Stone, *The Anatomy of Revolution Revisited*, esp. 513–14.

Notes

INTRODUCTION

1. For three fairly well-updated reappraisals of revolutionary historiography on England, France, and Russia, consult John Adamson, "Introduction: High Roads and Blind Alleys—The English Civil War and Its Historiography," in John Adamson, ed., *The English Civil War: Conflict and Contexts, 1640–49* (New York: Palgrave Macmillan, 2009), 1–35; Bailey Stone, *The Anatomy of Revolution Revisited: A Comparative Analysis of England, France, and Russia* (New York: Cambridge University Press, 2014), esp. the introduction; and Sheila Fitzpatrick, *The Russian Revolution*, third edition (Oxford: Oxford University Press, 2008), introduction.

2. See, as exemplary of this early revisionism, Alfred Cobban, *The Social Interpretation of the French Revolution* (Cambridge: Cambridge University Press, 1964); George V. Taylor, "Noncapitalist Wealth and the Origins of the French Revolution," *American Historical Review* 72 (1967): 491–92; and Conrad Russell, *Unrevolutionary England, 1603–1642* (London: The Hambledon Press, 1990).

3. For this commentary on these prestructural historical and sociological theories of revolution, see Michael S. Kimmel, *Revolution: A Sociological Interpretation* (Philadelphia: Temple University Press, 1990), 46–82.

4. See, in this connection, Crane Brinton, *The Anatomy of Revolution* (New York: Prentice-Hall, 1938); Lyford P. Edwards, *The Natural History of Revolution* (Chicago: University of Chicago Press, 1927); George S. Pettee, *The Process of Revolution* (New York: Harper and Brothers, 1938); and Rex D. Hopper, "The Revolutionary Process," *Social Forces* 28 (1950): 270–79. A "throwback work" here in later years was Jaroslav Krejci, *Great Revolutions Compared: The Search for a Theory* (New York: St. Martin's Press, 1983).

5. Refer, here, to Chalmers Johnson, *Revolution and the Social System* (Stanford: Hoover Institution Studies, 1964); *Autopsy on People's War* (Berkeley: University of California Press, 1973); and *Revolutionary Change*, second edition (Stanford: Stanford University Press, 1982).

6. Cited in Kimmel, *Revolution: A Sociological Interpretation*, 47. Works exemplifying this genre of revolutionary analysis include Ted R. Gurr, *Why Men Rebel* (Princeton: Princeton University Press, 1971), and *Rogues, Rebels, and Reformers* (Beverly Hills, CA: SAGE, 1976); and James C. Davies, *When Men Revolt and Why* (New York: Free Press, 1979).

7. Citations taken from Kimmel, *Revolution: A Sociological Interpretation*, 25, 86–87, 145–46.

8. Ibid., 151–52.

9. Consult, among his chief works, the following: *The Modern World-System: Capitalist Agriculture and the Origins of the European World-Economy in the Sixteenth Century* (New

York: Academic Press, 1974); *The Capitalist World-Economy* (New York: Cambridge University Press, 1979); and *The Politics of the World Economy* (New York: Cambridge University Press, 1984). Other works that might fall under this rubric range from Karl Polanyi, *The Great Transformation* (Boston: Beacon Press, 1957) to Ellen Kay Trimberger, *Revolution from Above: Military Bureaucrats and Development in Japan, Turkey, Egypt, and Peru* (New Brunswick: Transaction Books, 1978).

10. As cited in Kimmel, *Revolution: A Sociological Interpretation*, 147.

11. As quoted in ibid., 149.

12. Cited in ibid., 151–52.

13. Theda Skocpol, *States and Social Revolutions: A Comparative Analysis of France, Russia, and China* (Cambridge: Cambridge University Press, 1979). Additional structuralist insights on modern revolutions were to come from Skocpol (and others) in Peter B. Evans, Dietrich Rueschemeyer, and Theda Skocpol, eds., *Bringing the State Back In* (New York: Cambridge University Press, 1985); and Theda Skocpol, ed., *Social Revolutions in the Modern World* (Cambridge: Cambridge University Press, 1994). Barrington Moore's *chef-d'oeuvre* was probably *The Social Origins of Dictatorship and Democracy: Lord and Peasant in Early Modern Europe* (Boston: Beacon Press, 1966).

14. Most recently, in the introduction to *The Anatomy of Revolution Revisited*.

15. See, in this connection, Charles Tilly, *European Revolutions, 1492–1992* (Oxford: Blackwell, 1993), 10. Similar insights are developed by Eric Selbin, "Revolutions in the Real World: Bringing Agency Back In," in John Foran, ed., *Theorizing Revolutions* (London: Routledge, 1997), esp. 133.

16. Refer, on this, to Jack Goldstone, "The Social Origins of the French Revolution Revisited," in Thomas Kaiser and Dale K. Van Kley, eds., *From Deficit to Deluge: The Origins of the French Revolution* (Stanford: Stanford University Press, 2011), 67–104. Goldstone has even more recently reviewed the issue of *demographic* origins of modern revolutions *in general* in his brief but provocative study *Revolutions: A Very Short Introduction* (Oxford: Oxford University Press, 2014).

17. Thus Timothy P. Wickham-Crowley, "Structural Theories of Revolution," esp. 43–44, in Foran, ed., *Theorizing Revolutions*. At the same time, even those theorists faulting Skocpol for her alleged neglect of ideological/cultural analysis have agreed with her that *ideas* must always be thoroughly *contextualized* in their times. Misagh Parsa is notably vocal on this point: *States, Ideologies, and Social Revolutions: A Comparative Analysis of Iran, Nicaragua, and the Philippines* (Cambridge: Cambridge University Press, 2000), esp. 7–9, 21.

18. Refer again to Tilly, *European Revolutions, 1492–1992*, 5–6.

19. Martin Malia, *History's Locomotives: Revolutions and the Making of the Modern World*, ed. Terence Emmons (New Haven: Yale University Press, 2006), 5.

20. Dan Edelstein, "Do We Want a Revolution without Revolution? Reflections on Political Authority," *French Historical Studies* 35 (2012): 270.

21. Jack Goldstone, *Revolutions: A Very Short Introduction* (Oxford: Oxford University Press, 2014), esp. 19–20.

22. Stone, *The Anatomy of Revolution*, 489.

23. Thus Ernest Gellner, *Postmodernism, Reason and Religion* (London: Routledge, 1992), 29. In his discipline, so he says, postmodernism "means in effect the abandonment of any serious attempt to give a reasonably precise, documented and testable account of anything." We may find this to be a somewhat simplistic judgment to render upon the entire postmodernist "movement," however.

24. See, for instance, Michel Foucault, *The Archaeology of Knowledge*, trans. A. M. Sheridan Smith (New York: Harper & Row, 1972), and *The History of Sexuality*, trans. Robert Hurley (New York: Vintage, 1980). An accessible account of Jacques Derrida's ideas is Jonathan Culler, *On Deconstruction: Theory and Criticism after Structuralism* (Ithaca: Cornell University Press, 1982).

25. Thus Richard J. Evans, "Postmodernism in History," 1–2. Essay contribution to the "Great Debate on History and Postmodernism" hosted at the University of Sydney, Australia, in July 2002. Evans had already dealt with these issues in a thought-provoking book: *In Defense of History* (New York: W. W. Norton, 1997).

26. Evans, "Postmodernism in History," 1.

27. Beverley Southgate, *Postmodernism in History: Fear or Freedom?* (London: Routledge, 2003), 51. Southgate here was reacting to Evans's 1997 book *In Defense of History* rather than to his later article; yet his response, we suspect, would have been essentially the same in either case.

28. Pauline Marie Rosenau, *Post-Modernism and the Social Sciences: Insights, Inroads, and Intrusions* (Princeton: Princeton University Press, 1992), 3, 14–16, 168–69. Note her use of the terms "post-modernism" and "post-structuralism" to denote the two separate strains in this philosophy. A number of radical feminists (such as Joan Wallach Scott) frequently (if not invariably) follow the same practice.

29. Southgate, *Postmodernism in History*, 58.

30. Ibid., 48–49. Southgate elaborated upon this postmodernist vision of history—and, indeed, of the world of this early twenty-first century—in a subsequent book: *What Is History For?* (London: Routledge, 2005). Other significant works in this genre include Keith Jenkins, *Rethinking History* (London: Routledge, 1991); Alun Munslow, *Deconstructing History* (London: Routledge, 1997); and Frank Ankersmit, *Historical Representation* (Stanford: Stanford University Press, 2001).

31. Southgate, *Postmodernism in History*, 48–49.

32. Keith Michael Baker, "A Script for a French Revolution: The Political Consciousness of the Abbé Mably," in his study *Inventing the French Revolution: Essays on French Political Culture in the Eighteenth Century* (Cambridge: Cambridge University Press, 1990).

33. Cited in Keith M. Baker and Dan Edelstein, eds., *Scripting Revolution: A Historical Approach to the Comparative Study of Revolutions* (Stanford: Stanford University Press, 2015), 3.

34. David A. Bell, as quoted in ibid., 346.

35. Eric Selbin, "Revolutions in the Real World: Bringing Agency Back In," in Foran, ed., *Theorizing Revolutions*, esp. 133. The title here was a pointed rejoinder to Skocpol's earlier title "Bringing the State Back In."

36. Foran, "Discourses and Social Forces: The Role of Culture and Cultural Studies in Understanding Revolutions," in ibid., 219. Foran, by the way, would have much more to say on this subject in a subsequent book: *Taking Power: On the Origins of Third World Revolutions* (Cambridge: Cambridge University Press, 2005).

37. Valentine Moghadam, "Gender and Revolutions," in Foran, ed., *Theorizing Revolutions*, 161–62.

38. Foran, "Discourses and Social Forces," in ibid., 219.

39. Gary Wilder cited in "AHR Forum: Historiographic 'Turns' in Critical Perspective," in *American Historical Review* 117 (2012): 743–44. Admittedly, the same forum also featured comments by several historians of a much more radical persuasion—including at least one who denied the usefulness of the "turn" concept altogether!

40. Rosenau, *Post-Modernism and the Social Sciences*, esp. 155–66 on the issue of postmodernism and Marxism.

41. Noel S. Parker, *Revolutions and History: An Essay in Interpretation* (Cambridge: Polity Press, 1999), 181–83.

42. Thus John Foran, "Theories of Revolution Revisited: Toward a Fourth Generation?" in *Sociological Theory* 11 (1993): 1–20.

43. Thus Jack Goldstone, "Toward a Fourth Generation of Revolutionary Theory," *Annual Review of Political Science* 4 (2001): 139–87. I thank Professor Goldstone for this particular reference culled from his own scholarship.

44. François Furet, *Penser la Révolution française* (Paris: Gallimard, 1978). An interesting "take" on Furet and his work in this period is Michael S. Christofferson, "An Antitotalitarian History of the French Revolution: François Furet's *Penser la Révolution française* in the Intellectual Politics of the Late 1970s," *French Historical Studies* 22 (1999): 557–611.

45. See, in this connection: François Furet and Mona Ozouf, eds., *A Critical Dictionary of the French Revolution*, trans. Arthur Goldhammer (Cambridge, MA: Harvard University Press, 1989); and Keith Baker et al., eds., *The French Revolution and the Creation of Modern Political Culture*, four volumes (Oxford: Pergamon Press, 1887–1894).

46. The two historians collaborated in "Le Problème de l'Atlantique du XVIIIe au XXe siècle," *Relazioni* 5 (1955): 175–239. See also Palmer's classic *The Age of the Democratic Revolution: A Political History of Europe and America, 1760-1800* (Princeton: Princeton University Press, 1959).

47. This recent literature includes David Armitage, *The Declaration of Independence: A Global History* (Cambridge, MA: Harvard University Press, 2007); Wim Klooster, *Revolutions in the Atlantic World: A Comparative History* (New York: New York University Press, 2009); Laurent Dubois, "An Atlantic Revolution," *French Historical Studies* 32 (2009): 655–61; Paul Cheney, *Revolutionary Commerce: Globalization and the French Monarchy* (Cambridge, MA: Harvard University Press, 2010); and Pierre Serna, "Every Revolution is a War of Independence," in Suzanne Desan, Lynn Hunt, and William Max Nelson, eds., *The French Revolution in Global Perspective* (Ithaca: Cornell University Press, 2013), 165–82.

48. Dubois, "An Atlantic Revolution," 655–61. His earlier works (on Haiti) include *A Colony of Citizens: Revolution and Slave Emancipation in the French Caribbean, 1787–1804* (Chapel Hill: University of North Carolina Press, 2004); and *Avengers of the New World: The Story of the Haitian Revolution* (Cambridge, MA: Harvard University Press, 2004).

49. Gary Wilder, "AHR Forum: Historiographic "Turns" in Critical Perspective," esp. 734–36.

50. Refer again to Cheney, *Revolutionary Commerce*, passim.

51. For a discussion of this "Atlantic" tendency in the historiography, see Miranda Spieler, "France and the Atlantic World," in Peter McPhee, *A Companion to the French Revolution* (Oxford: Wiley-Blackwell, 2013), 57–72.

52. Dubois cited here by Gary Wilder in the *American Historical Review* 117 (2012), 734–35.

53. Among Popkin's works: "The French Revolution's Other Island," in David Geggus and Norman Fiering, eds., *The World of the Haitian Revolution* (Bloomington: Indiana University Press, 2009), 199–222; *You Are All Free: The Haitian Revolution and the Abolition of Slavery* (Cambridge: Cambridge University Press, 2010); and "Saint-Domingue, Slavery, and the Origins of the French Revolution," in Kaiser and Van Kley, eds., *From Deficit to Deluge*, esp. 221.

54. Citation again from Wilder's commentary in the *American Historical Review* 117 (2012), 734–35.

55. Thus Peter McPhee, "The French Revolution, Peasants, and Capitalism," *American Historical Review* 94 (1989): 1265–80; *A Companion to the French Revolution*, introduction; and Henry Heller, *The Bourgeois Revolution in France, 1789-1815* (New York: Berghahn, 2006).

56. Consult the following: T. C. W. Blanning, *The French Revolutionary Wars, 1787–1802* (New York: St. Martin's Press, 1996); Bailey Stone, *The Genesis of the French Revolution: A Global-Historical Interpretation* (Cambridge: Cambridge University Press, 1994), and *The Anatomy of Revolution Revisited* (New York: Cambridge University Press, 2014); and Thomas E. Kaiser, "From Fiscal Crisis to Revolution: The Court and French Foreign Policy, 1787–1789," chapter 4 in Kaiser and Van Kley, eds., *From Deficit to Deluge* (2011), and "A Tale of Two Narratives: The French Revolution in International Context, 1787–93," chapter 10 in McPhee, ed., *A Companion to the French Revolution*.

57. David Underdown, *Revel, Riot, and Rebellion: Popular Politics and Culture in England, 1603–1660* (Oxford: Clarendon, 1985). See also a later work very much in the same genre: *A Freeborn People: Politics and the Nation in Seventeenth-Century England* (Oxford: Clarendon, 1996).

58. Kevin Sharpe, *Remapping Early Modern England: The Culture of Seventeenth-Century Politics* (Cambridge: Cambridge University Press, 2000), 3–4.

59. As, for example, in Susan D. Amussen and Mark A. Kishlansky, eds., *Political Culture and Cultural Politics in Early Modern England* (Manchester: Manchester University Press, 1995); and David Zaret, *Origins of Democratic Culture: Printing, Petitions, and the Public Sphere in Early Modern England* (Princeton: Princeton University Press, 2002).

60. Carla Pestana, *The English Atlantic in an Age of Revolution, 1640–1661* (Cambridge, MA: Harvard University Press, 2004). Pestana in turn drew inspiration from earlier works. See, for example, Robert Brenner, *Merchants and Revolution: Commercial Change, Political Con-

flict, and London's Overseas Traders, 1550–1653 (Princeton: Princeton University Press, 1992); and the germane essays in David Armitage and Michael J. Braddick, eds., *The British Atlantic World, 1500–1800* (London: Palgrave, 2002).

61. John Donoghue, *Fire Under the Ashes: An Atlantic History of the English Revolution* (Chicago: University of Chicago Press, 2013). Citation from p. 5. In his introduction, Donoghue singled out for special praise (among recent studies in the field) Peter Linebaugh and Marcus Rediker, *The Many-Headed Hydra: Sailors, Slaves, Commoners, and the Hidden History of the Revolutionary Atlantic* (Boston: Beacon Press, 2001).

62. Donoghue, *Fire Under the Ashes*, 4–5.

63. Pestana's review is found in the *Journal of American History* 101 (2014): 554.

64. Refer to Ian K. Steele's review of *Fire Under the Ashes* in the *American Historical Review* 119 (2014): 1651–52, and to John Coffee's review of the same book in the *English Historical Review* 131 (2016): 914–15.

65. Jonathan Scott, *England's Troubles: Seventeenth-Century English Instability in European Context* (Cambridge: Cambridge University Press, 2000); James S. Wheeler, *The Making of a World Power: War and the Military Revolution in Seventeenth-Century England* (London: Stroud, 1999); David Cressy, *England on Edge: Crisis and Revolution, 1640–42* (Oxford: Oxford University Press, 2006); and—most imaginatively, perhaps—Geoffrey Parker, *The Global Crisis: War, Climate, and Catastrophe in the Seventeenth-Century World* (New Haven: Yale University Press, 2010).

66. Steve A. Smith, "Writing the History of the Russian Revolution After the Fall of Communism," in *Europe-Asia Studies* 46 (1994): 563–78.

67. Thus, see Christopher Read, *Culture and Power in Revolutionary Russia: The Intelligentsia and the Transition from Tsarism to Communism* (New York: St. Martin's Press, 1990); Lynn Mally, *Culture of the Future: The Proletkult Movement in Revolutionary Russia* (Berkeley: University of California Press, 1990); Orlando Figes and Boris Kolonitskii, *Interpreting the Russian Revolution: The Language and Symbols of 1917* (New Haven: Yale University Press, 1999); and Sheila Fitzpatrick, *The Cultural Front: Power and Culture in Revolutionary Russia* (Ithaca: Cornell University Press, 1992). Fitzpatrick has also periodically updated the "cultural turn" in Russian studies: see, for example, *The Russian Revolution*, third edition (Oxford: Oxford University Press, 2008), 185–91.

68. Citations are from Orlando Figes, *A People's Tragedy: The Russian Revolution, 1891–1924* (New York: Penguin Books, 1996), 809–10.

69. Rosenberg cited here in Edward Acton, Vladimir Cherniaev, and William G. Rosenberg, eds., *Critical Companion to the Russian Revolution 1914-1921* (Bloomington: Indiana University Press, 1991), 27.

70. Theodore H. Von Laue, *Why Lenin? Why Stalin? Why Gorbachev? The Rise and Fall of the Soviet System*, third edition (New York: Harper Collins Publishers, 1993).

71. Thus Steven C. A. Pincus, *1688: The First Modern Revolution* (New Haven: Yale University Press, 2009), 33, 36, 45.

1. MODERNIZERS VERSUS TRADITIONALISTS IN THE EUROPEAN REVOLUTIONS

1. Stephen C. A. Pincus, *1688: The First Modern Revolution* (New Haven: Yale University Press, 2009), 476.

2. Ibid., 36–38. On pp. 37–38, Russia's Nicholas II is also closely associated with a wide variety of reforms.

3. His most important work prior to *1688: The First Modern Revolution* was *Protestantism and Patriotism: Ideologies and the Making of English Foreign Policy, 1650–1668* (Cambridge: Cambridge University Press, 1996).

4. For early examples of these (ambivalent) reactions, see Jeremy Black, in *American Historical Review* 115 (2010): 486–88; Scott Hendrix, in *Canadian Journal of History* 45

(2010): 371–73; Melinda Zook, in *Journal of British Studies* 50 (2011): 206–08; and Tony Claydon, in *Journal of Modern History* 83 (2011): 160–62.

5. Pincus, *1688: The First Modern Revolution*, 33.

6. This paraphrases David Cressey, *England on Edge: Crisis and Revolution, 1640–42* (Oxford: Oxford University Press, 2006), 6. Cressey's rehabilitation of the English Revolution of the early 1640s as a truly "world-historical" event comparable in some ways to the later French and Russian Revolutions was anticipated by a number of other studies, including James S. Wheeler, *The Making of a World Power: War and the Military Revolution in Seventeenth-Century England* (London: Stroud, 1999).

7. Consult, for samples of Tocquevillian insight on this subject, *The Old Regime and the French Revolution* (New York: Anchor, 1955), 176–77, 204.

8. See, in this connection, Samuel P. Huntington, *Political Order in Changing Societies* (New Haven: Yale University Press, 1968); and, additionally, S. N. Eisenstadt, *Revolution and the Transformation of Societies* (New York: Free Press, 1978).

9. Charles Tilly, "Does Modernization Breed Revolution?" *Comparative Politics* 5 (1973): esp. 432, 435, 447. Tilly elaborated on issues of state modernization in his later monograph *From Mobilization to Revolution* (Reading, MA: Addison-Wesley, 1978).

10. See, for instance, Michael S. Kimmel, *Revolution: A Sociological Interpretation* (Philadelphia: Temple University Press, 1990), esp. 63–67; and Jeff Goodwin, *No Other Way Out: States and Revolutionary Movements, 1945–1991* (Cambridge: Cambridge University Press, 2001), esp. 17.

11. Peter Lake, "Retrospective: Wentworth's Political World in Revisionist and Post-revisionist Perspective," 252–83. Lake was contributing here to J. F. Merritt, ed., *The Political World of Thomas Wentworth, Earl of Strafford, 1621-1641* (Cambridge: Cambridge University Press, 1996). Citation is from pp. 256–57.

12. Ibid., 257.

13. Pincus, *1688: The First Modern Revolution*, 36.

14. Steve Pincus himself cites the critique of the "modernization" concept offered nearly two decades ago by John D. Kelly: "Alternative Modernities or an Alternative to 'Modernity,'" in *Critically Modern: Alternatives, Alterities, Anthropologies*, ed. Bruce M. Knauft (Bloomington: Indiana University Press, 2002), 262–77.

15. Refer again to Jeremy Black, writing in *The American Historical Review* 115 (2010): 486–88. Other historians speculating very recently about James II's Catholic motivations in the run-up to the "Glorious Revolution" include Edward Vallance, *The Glorious Revolution: 1688: Britain's Fight for Liberty* (New York: Pegasus Books, 2008), passim; and Stephen Taylor, "Afterword: State Formation, Political Stability and the Revolution of 1688," in Tim Harris and Stephen Taylor, eds., *The Final Crisis of the Stuart Monarchy: The Revolutions of 1688–91 in their British, Atlantic and European Contexts* (Woodbridge: The Boydell Press, 2013), esp. 298–99.

16. Scott Sowerby, *Making Toleration: The Repealers and the Glorious Revolution* (Cambridge, MA: Harvard University Press, 2013), 17–18. Sowerby, for his part, argues in his useful study that, for James II, Catholicism was ideally to be "comprehended" within a "transformational politics" of relatively broad religious toleration in England. Reconsidered in this fashion, James II was ahead of his time in *religious* terms rather than in those terms offered by any kind of secular "modernization theory." This subject obviously remains highly controversial.

17. Lionel K. J. Glassey, "In Search of the *Mot Juste*: Characterizations of the Revolution of 1688-9," in Tim Harris and Stephen Taylor, eds., *The Final Crisis of the Stuart Monarchy*, 26–27.

18. Refer to Bailey Stone, *The Anatomy of Revolution Revisited: A Comparative Analysis of England, France, and Russia* (New York: Cambridge University Press, 2014), esp. the introduction.

19. Lawrence Stone, *The Causes of the English Revolution 1559-1642* (London: Routledge and Kegan Paul, 1972), 126–27.

20. As cited in J. R. Tanner, *English Constitutional Conflicts of the Seventeenth Century 1603–1689* (Cambridge: Cambridge University Press, 1971), 72.

21. Ibid., 73.

22. G. E. Aylmer, *A Short History of Seventeenth-Century England: 1603-1689* (New York: Mentor Books, 1963), 87–88.

23. Ibid., 88. Furthermore, as Aylmer reasonably enough notes in this connection, Stuart governance in those agitated years also meant the administrative activities of those in state finances—Weston, and, later, Windebank and Cottington—along with the activities of those in the queen's circle, and of other men as well. Whatever the merits or demerits of their shared philosophy of "Thorough," then, Wentworth and Laud can hardly be said to have monopolized the sources of state power during Charles I's Personal Rule. Ibid.

24. Anthony Milton, "Thomas Wentworth and the political thought of the Personal Rule," 133–56, cited in J. F. Merritt, ed., *The Political World of Thomas Wentworth, Earl of Strafford*. Citation is from p. 149. J. F. Merritt herself discusses Wentworth's long-term career ambitions as he moved from power base to power base (i.e., from Scotland to Ireland to, ultimately, London) in "Power and Communication: Thomas Wentworth and Government at a Distance during the Personal Rule, 1629–1635." Ibid., 109–32.

25. Aylmer, *A Short History of Seventeenth-Century England*, 87–88.

26. Refer to Kevin Sharpe, *The Personal Rule of Charles I* (New Haven: Yale University Press, 1992), esp. 407, 455, 557.

27. Refer, for examples of this, to John S. Morrill, *The Nature of the English Revolution* (London: Longman, 1993), passim.

28. Cited in Ann Hughes, *The Causes of the English Civil War* (New York: St. Martin's Press, 1991), 65.

29. Ibid., 90.

30. Michael B. Young, *Charles I* (New York: St. Martin's Press, 1997), 95.

31. Consult, in this connection, G. E. Aylmer, *The King's Servants: The Civil Service of Charles I, 1625–1642* (New York: Columbia University Press, 1961), esp. 62–63.

32. Young, *Charles I*, 96. Both the origins and the practical impact of the Book of Orders have been extensively reviewed by historians. See, for example, Brian W. Quintrell, "The Making of Charles I's Book of Orders," *English Historical Review* 95 (1980): 553–72; Paul Slack, "Book of Orders: The Making of English Social Policy, 1577–1631," *Transactions of the Royal Historical Society*, Fifth Series (1981): 1–22; and Sharpe, *The Personal Rule of Charles I*, 456–63, 485–87. Anthony Fletcher characterized Charles's Book of Orders as having "highlighted rather than solved . . . the problem of tension between the centre and the localities." Fletcher, *Reform in the Provinces: The Government of Stuart England* (New Haven: Yale University Press, 1986), 59–60.

33. As Cynthia Herrup, for example, has argued. See her article "The Counties and the Country: Some Thoughts on Seventeenth-Century Historiography," in Geoff Eley and William Hunt, eds., *Reviewing the English Revolution: Reflections and Elaborations on the Work of Christopher Hill* (London: Verso, 1988), 289–304.

34. Young, *Charles I*, 97. One exception to this record of generally lackluster achievement, Young has conceded (citing once again Aylmer's research), was reform of the postal system during the 1630s. Ibid., 95.

35. Norah Carlin, *The Causes of the English Civil War* (Oxford: Blackwell, 1999), 100.

36. Ibid., 118.

37. Hirst cited in Jonathan Scott, *England's Troubles: Seventeenth-Century English Instability in European Context* (Cambridge: Cambridge University Press, 2000), 56. One of the very best full-length studies of the subject as it applies to prerevolutionary England is still Caroline Hibbard, *Charles I and the Popish Plot* (Chapel Hill, NC: University of North Carolina Press, 1983).

38. For an especially effective treatment of all of this, see Nicholas Tyacke, *Anti-Calvinists: The Rise of English Arminianism, c. 1590–1640* (Oxford: Clarendon Press, 1987). The issues are further contextualized in Leo F. Solt, *Church and State in Early Modern England 1509-1640* (Oxford: Oxford University Press, 1990).

39. Ann Hughes, *The Causes of the English Civil War*, second edition (Basingstoke: MacMillan, 1998), 81, 89–90.

40. On all of this, see Hibbard, *Charles I and the Popish Plot*, passim; Robin Clifton, "The Popular Fear of Catholics During the English Revolution," *Past and Present* 52 (1971): 23–55;

Peter Lake, "Anti-Popery: The Structure of a Prejudice," in Richard Cust and Ann Hughes, eds., *Conflict in Early Stuart England: Studies in Religion and Politics 1603–1642* (London: Longman, 1989), 72–106; and Jonathan Scott, *England's Troubles*, esp. chapter 1, "Taking Contemporary Belief Seriously." Other, even more recent sources could be cited here as well.

41. There is, of course, a vast and ever-growing literature on the king's last years. The reader might start here with Robert Ashton, *Counter-Revolution: The Second Civil War and Its Origins* (New Haven: Yale University Press, 1994); the essays presented in Jason Peacey, ed., *The Regicides and the Execution of Charles I* (New York: Palgrave Macmillian, 2001); and David Scott, "Rethinking Royalist Politics, 1642–49," in John Adamson, ed., *The English Civil War: Conflict and Contexts, 1640–49* (New York: Palgrave Macmillan, 2009), 36–60. Refer as well to chapter 3 in this book, which places the decision to execute Charles I in a comparative historical context.

42. See, on all of this, Ian Gentles, *The New Model Army in England, Scotland and Ireland 1645–1653* (Oxford: Blackwell, 1991), esp. 38–40 and 118–19; and, by the same author, "The New Model Army Officer Corps in 1647: A Collective Portrait," *Social History* 22 (1997): 127–44. On the royal forces in this period, refer to Ronald Hutton, *The Royalist War Effort, 1642–1646*, second edition (London: Routledge, 1999).

43. In this connection, see the older works of Paul Hardacre, *The Royalists During the Puritan Revolution* (The Hague: M. Nijhoff, 1956), and David Underdown, *Royalist Conspiracy in England, 1649–1660* (New Haven: Yale University Press, 1960), and then go on to Ian Gentles's much more current discussion in *The English Revolution and the Wars in the Three Kingdoms, 1638–1652* (London: Pearson, 2007). Two recent and excellent evaluations of the 1650s in revolutionary England are Austin H. Woolrych, *Britain in Revolution 1625–1660* (Oxford: Oxford University Press, 2002); and Barry Coward, *The Cromwellian Protectorate* (Manchester: Manchester University Press, 2002).

44. Bernard Capp, *Cromwell's Navy* (Oxford: Clarendon Press, 1989), esp. 175–77, 396–401.

45. Refer again to Pincus, *1688: The First Modern Revolution*, 36–37.

46. Pierrette Girault de Coursac, *L'Education d'un roi. Louis XVI* (Paris: Gallimard, 1972), 121.

47. Here the reader should consult John Hardman, *Louis XVI* (New Haven: Yale University Press, 1993); Hardman, *French Politics 1774–1789: From the Accession of Louis XVI to the Fall of the Bastille* (Longman: London, 1995); and Munro Price, *The Fall of the French Monarchy: Louis XVI, Marie-Antoinette, and the Baron de Breteuil* (London: Macmillan, 2002).

48. The best all-around study of Turgot's financial ministry of 1774 to 1776 may still be that of Douglas Dakin, *Turgot and the Ancien Régime in France* (London: Methuen, 1939). On Turgot's constitutional leanings, however, refer also to Gerald J. Cavanaugh, "Turgot: The Rejection of Enlightened Despotism," *French Historical Studies* 6 (1969): 31–58. Turgot's fiscal reforms in office—which, failing French intervention in the American Revolutionary War, might have helped to stave off governmental bankruptcy—are discussed in an updated, "econometric" fashion by Eugene N. White, "Was There a Solution to the Ancien Régime's Financial Dilemma?" *Journal of Economic History* 49 (1989): 545–68.

49. Cited in Hardman, *French Politics 1774–1789*, 50–51. Interestingly enough, Hardman's interpretation of Turgot's behavior may lend credence to Gerald Cavanaugh's argument (in his *French Historical Studies* article referenced in n. 48) that the *Contrôleur-Général des Finances* was moving toward a "rejection" of French-style "Enlightened Despotism."

50. For a thorough discussion of the Paris Parlement's growing opposition to Turgotist reforms during 1775 to 1776, the links between the Parisian magistrates and Hue de Miromesnil, and the impact of all of this on the king, consult Bailey Stone, *The Parlement of Paris, 1774–1789* (Chapel Hill, NC: The University of North Carolina Press, 1981), esp. 93–96.

51. The literature rehabilitating Necker's reputation as a reformist in recent decades has been extensive. See, for examples of this, J. F. Bosher, *French Finances, 1770-1795: From Business to Bureaucracy* (Cambridge: Cambridge University Press, 1970); Jean Egret, *Necker: Ministre de Louis XVI, 1776–1790* (Paris: Champion, 1975); Robert D. Harris, *Necker: Reform Statesman of the Ancien Régime* (Berkeley: University of California Press, 1979); Harris,

Necker and the Revolution of 1789 (Lanham, MD: University Press of America, 1986); and Eugene N. White, "Was There a Solution to the Ancien Régime's Financial Dilemma?"

52. Hardman, *French Politics 1774–1789*, 59–61. Necker actually *did* resign—on May 19—tendering his letter of resignation, not to the king, but rather to Marie Antoinette.

53. The dispute between Necker and the Parisian parlementaires over the issue of the *vingtièmes* in 1778 receives detailed treatment in Stone, *The Parlement of Paris, 1774–1789*, 96–100. See also on this issue the much older but still informative work by Georges Lardé, *Une Enquête sur les vingtièmes au temps de Necker: Histoire des remontrances du Parlement de Paris (1777–78)* (Paris: Letouzey et Ané, 1920).

54. On Calonne, see Robert Lacour-Gayet, *Calonne: Financier, Réformateur, Contre-Révolutionnaire, 1734–1802* (Paris: Hachette, 1963). Because Calonne was a consistent critic of Jacques Necker during the Genevan's first ministry (1776–1781), his own management of royal finances during 1783 to 1787 has been roughly handled by most of those scholars (Bosher, Egret, Harris, etc.) engaged over the past forty years or so in rehabilitating Necker's reputation. For some more balanced (and fairly detailed) comments on this controversy involving the two men, see again Eugene N. White, "Was There a Solution to the Ancien Régime's Financial Dilemma?"

55. These reforms are conveniently summarized in Bailey Stone, *The French Parlements and the Crisis of the Old Regime* (Chapel Hill, NC: The University of North Carolina Press, 1986), 4. For a fuller and more thoroughly contextualized account of these reforms, see Jean Egret, *The French Prerevolution, 1787–1788*, trans. Wesley D. Camp (Chicago: University of Chicago Press, 1977).

56. Hardman, *French Politics 1774–1789*, 84–85.

57. On all of this, see Egret, *The French Prerevolution, 1787–88*, esp. 60–64; Harris, *Necker and the Revolution of 1789*, 233–36; E. N. White, "Was There a Solution to the Ancien Régime's Financial Dilemma?" esp. 565–67; David R. Weir, "Tontines, Public Finance, and Revolution in France and England, 1688–1789," *Journal of Economic History* 49 (1989): 95–124; and, most recently, Gail Bossenga, "Financial Origins of the French Revolution," in Thomas E. Kaiser and Dale K. Van Kley, eds., *From Deficit to Deluge: The Origins of the French Revolution* (Stanford, CA: Stanford University Press, 2011), chapter 1.

58. Hardman, *French Politics 1774–1789*, 91. The king's abandonment of Lamoignon had tragic consequences: the former Keeper of the Seals, forced to resign on September 14, 1788, apparently shot himself on the grounds of his estate at Bâville in May 1789.

59. Georges Lefebvre, *The Coming of the French Revolution*, trans. Robert R. Palmer (Princeton, NJ: Princeton University Press, 1947), 87. I have enlarged on the significance of this session in "23 June 1789: The Most Crucial Day in the French Revolution?" An unpublished paper presented at the University of Houston, Houston, Texas, on February 23, 2002, for "French Historical Studies in Texas."

60. Munro Price, *The Fall of the French Monarchy*, 64. For somewhat differing (but *not*, in the main, radically different) interpretations of what, precisely, Louis XVI was aiming for at the "royal session" of June 23, 1789, refer to Harris, *Necker and the Revolution of 1789*, 506–07, 514–18; and Hardman, *Louis XVI*, 149–53.

61. Price, *The Fall of the French Monarchy*, 66.

62. For further discussion of this point, see Girault de Coursac, *L'Education d'un roi. Louis XVI*, 152, 168, 171–72; and Robert R. Crout, "In Search of a 'Just and Lasting Peace': The Treaty of 1783, Louis XVI, Vergennes, and the Regeneration of the Realm," *International History Review* 5 (1983): 364–98.

63. As cited in Lefebvre, *The Coming of the French Revolution*, 83–84.

64. Price, *The Fall of the French Monarchy*, 69–70. Yet, as John Hardman remarks, even those accommodations of third estate and "popular" demands that Necker had suggested to the king in the days leading up to the June 23 royal session would, in the weeks *after* that session, no longer have been sufficient to appease rapidly radicalizing opinion in non-élitist circles. See, on this point, Hardman, *Louis XVI*, 153.

65. Hardman, *French Politics 1774–1789*, 113.

66. Ibid., 197.

67. Ibid., 245–46. This, despite the likelihood that Charles I's ministers in the 1630s could not have been as "enlightened" in a secularized, French sense (and thus as "conflicted" in their perspectives) as Louis XVI's ministers in the late 1770s and 1780s arguably were. In this latter connection, refer again to Cavanaugh's article, cited in n. 48, on "Turgot: The Rejection of Enlightened Despotism."

68. Refer in this connection to Pierre Renouvin, *Les Assemblées provinciales de 1787: Origines, développements, résultats* (Paris: A. Picard, 1920); and Maurice Bordes, *L'Administration provinciale et municipale en France au XVIIIe siècle* (Paris: S. E. E. S., 1972). There was a long, contentious history of relations between the Parisian parlementaires and the provincial assemblies in their successive iterations under Louis XVI. See, on this point, Stone, *The Parlement of Paris, 1774-1789*, esp. 67–70, 77–79, 113–19, and 164–66.

69. Peter M. Jones, *Reform and Revolution in France: The Politics of Transition, 1774–1791* (Cambridge: Cambridge University Press, 1995), esp. 8–9, 120–21, 123–24, 155–56, 159, 240.

70. Stephen Miller, "Provincial Assemblies, Fiscal Reform, and the Language of Politics in the 1770s and 1780s," *French Historical Studies* 35 (2012): 441–75. The secondary reference is to William H. Sewell, Jr., "Ideologies and Social Revolutions: Reflections on the French Case," *Journal of Modern History* 57 (1985), esp. 66–67.

71. Miller, "Provincial Assemblies, Fiscal Reform, and the Language of Politics," 443.

72. This last phrase is drawn from Renouvin, *Les Assemblées provinciales de 1787*, 79–80.

73. Miller, "Provincial Assemblies, Fiscal Reform, and the Language of Politics," 474. For general discussions of the implications (most notably for Louis XVI's government) of a society still fissured over the issue of *privilège*, consult Bailey Stone, *The Genesis of the French Revolution: A Global-Historical Interpretation* (Cambridge: Cambridge University Press, 1994), esp. 162–94; and Michael Kwass, *Privilege and the Politics of Taxation in Eighteenth-Century France* (Cambridge: Cambridge University Press, 2000).

74. Miller, "Provincial Assemblies, Fiscal Reform, and the Language of Politics," 475. The solidarity posited here between court and provincial nobility in 1789 is also highlighted in Timothy Tackett, *Becoming a Revolutionary: The Deputies of the French National Assembly and the Emergence of a Revolutionary Culture (1789–1790)* (Princeton, NJ: Princeton University Press, 1996), esp. 28–29.

75. Dale K. Van Kley has revisited these ecclesiological and constitutional issues recently in "The Religious Origins of the French Revolution, 1560–1791," in Kaiser and Van Kley, eds., *From Deficit to Deluge*, esp. 120–35. But refer also to his earlier study *The Damiens Affair and the Unraveling of the Ancien Regime, 1750–1771* (Princeton, NJ: Princeton University Press, 1984), from which the quotations in this paragraph are drawn.

76. For an overview of these reforms (especially those legislated in the Constituent Assembly of 1789 to 1791), refer to Stone, *The Anatomy of Revolution Revisited*, esp. 187–99. Earlier analyses of these reforms are also provided in Norman Hampson, *The Constituent Assembly and the Failure of Consensus, 1789–1791* (New York: Blackwell, 1988); Harriet B. Applewhite, *Political Alignment in the French National Assembly, 1789–1791* (Baton Rouge: Louisiana State University Press, 1993); and Michael P. Fitzsimmons, *The Remaking of France: The National Assembly, the Constitution of 1791 and the Reorganization of the French Polity, 1789–1791* (New York: Cambridge University Press, 1994).

77. As quoted by Lefebvre, *The Coming of the French Revolution*, 185.

78. On this memorandum, see Jean Egret, *Necker: Ministre de Louis XVI, 1776–1790* (Paris: Champion, 1975), 372. It is also discussed in considerable detail in Price, *The Fall of the French Monarchy*, 108–09.

79. Timothy Tackett, *When the King Took Flight* (Cambridge, MA: Harvard University Press, 2003), 55. Munro Price fully agrees with all of this, on the basis of his consultation of unpublished correspondence and memoranda of the Baron de Breteuil and others implicated in royalist conspiracies of the early Revolution: "The concessions [Louis XVI and Marie-Antoinette] were prepared to make, to which the declaration of 23 June forms the most credible guide, would not have satisfied even the most moderate of their opponents. Under these circumstances, the royal authority could only have been restored by civil war or foreign inva-

sion." Price, *The Fall of the French Monarchy*, 366. A similar judgment emanates from John Hardman, *Louis XVI*, 153.

80. Price, *The Fall of the French Monarchy*, 367.

81. The best study of republican politics during the Directory remains that of Isser Woloch, *Jacobin Legacy: The Democratic Movement under the Directory* (Princeton, NJ: Princeton University Press, 1970). Woloch has also produced the most comprehensive overview of the postTerrorist reforms in France: see Woloch, *The New Regime: Transformations of the French Civic Order, 1789–1820s* (New York: Norton, 1994). But see also, along these lines: Howard G. Brown, *War, Revolution, and the Bureaucratic State* (New York: Oxford University Press, 1996).

82. On the Declaration of Verona, and other signs of "counterrevolution" both within and outside post-terrorist France, see Jacques Godechot, *La Contre-Révolution: Doctrine et Action* (Paris: Presses Universitaires de France, 1961); and D. M. G. Sutherland, *France, 1789–1815: Revolution and Counterrevolution* (New York: Oxford University Press, 1986).

83. Jacques Godechot, *France and the Atlantic Revolution of the Eighteenth Century, 1770–1799*, trans. Herbert H. Rowen (New York: Free Press, 1965), 246–47. A not altogether dissimilar verdict on the Directory has recently been given by Isser Woloch, in *Napoleon and His Collaborators: The Making of a Dictatorship* (New York: Norton, 2001), 3–5. See also, in this connection, Howard G. Brown, *Ending the French Revolution: Violence, Justice, and Repression from the Terror to Napoleon* (Charlottesville: University of Virginia Press, 2006), who emphasizes the theme of the *progressive militarization* of post-terrorist society in France. The major issue of state legitimacy in post-terrorist France also receives fuller treatment in this book: see chapter 5, "Crises of Revolutionary Legitimacy: Thermidorian Outcomes."

84. Andrew M. Verner, *The Crisis of Russian Autocracy: Nicholas II and the 1905 Revolution* (Princeton, NJ: Princeton University Press, 1990), 61.

85. Ibid., 68, 347.

86. Dominic Lieven, *Nicholas II: Emperor of All the Russias* (London: John Murray, 1993), 42–43. Lieven writes on all of this in "Nicholas II," in Edward Acton, Vladimir Cherniaev, and William G. Rosenberg, eds., *Critical Companion to the Russian Revolution 1914–1921* (Bloomington: Indiana University Press, 1997), 176–81. For similar characterizations of Nicholas II, see R. K. Massie, *Nicholas and Alexandra* (New York: Athenaeum, 1968); and M. D. Steinberg and V. M. Khrustalev, *The Fall of the Romanovs: Political Dreams and Personal Struggles in a Time of Revolution* (New Haven: Yale University Press, 1995).

87. Theodore H. Von Laue, *Why Lenin? Why Stalin? Why Gorbachev? The Rise and Fall of the Soviet System*, third edition (New York: HarperCollins, 1993), 28–29. See also Von Laue's in-depth analysis of this campaign: *Sergei Witte and the Industrialization of Russia* (New York: Columbia University Press, 1963). Some economists, however, have criticized aspects of Witte's policies. See, for example, H. Barkai, "The Macro-Economics of Tsarist Russia in the Industrialization Era: Monetary Developments, the Balance of Payments and the Gold Standard," *Journal of Economic History* 33 (1973): 339–71; and Paul R. Gregory, "Russian Industrialization and Economic Growth: Results and Perspectives of Western Research," *Jahrbücher für Geschichte Osteuropas* 25 (1977): 200–18.

88. This from Dominic Lieven, *Nicholas II*, 75.

89. Verner, *The Crisis of Russian Autocracy*, 56. Lieven, in *Nicholas II*, esp. 75–77, stresses this point as well. David M. McDonald has studied this phenomenon carefully and to great effect in *United Government and Foreign Policy in Russia, 1900–1914* (Cambridge, MA: Harvard University Press, 1992). Specifically, he discusses Witte's intensifying struggles with the other ministers after 1900 in chapters 1 to 3.

90. Lieven, *Nicholas II*, 77. On the tensions between the Finance and Interior Ministries in prerevolutionary Russia see also George L. Yaney, *The Systematization of Russian Government: Social Evolution in the Domestic Administration of Imperial Russia, 1711–1905* (Urbana: University of Illinois Press, 1973), as well as McDonald, *United Government and Foreign Policy in Russia*, esp. the introduction.

91. Von Laue, *Why Lenin? Why Stalin? Why Gorbachev?* 33. Witte's dilemma has been placed in a broader comparative economic/developmental context by Alexander Gerschenkron,

Economic Backwardness in Historical Perspective (Cambridge, MA: Harvard University Press, 1962), esp. 5–30.

92. Von Laue highlights all of this in "Problems of Industrialization," in George Stavrou, ed., *Russia Under the Last Tsar* (Minneapolis: University of Minnesota Press, 1969), 117–53. But also consult once again his major monograph on the subject, *Sergei Witte and the Industrialization of Russia.*

93. Even so, as Verner ironically points out, Nicholas "could ill afford to dispense" with Witte's services in the later matters of trade talks with Germany and peace negotiations with Japan in the wake of the Russo-Japanese War! Verner, *The Crisis of Russian Autocracy*, 58. Witte was even (briefly) prime minister in the aftermath of the 1905 revolution in Russia. Ibid., 319–25. Additional speculation regarding the tsar's motivation in dismissing Witte in August 1903 is provided by McDonald, *United Government and Foreign Policy in Russia*, 63–64.

94. The most satisfying biography of Stolypin is by Abraham Ascher, *P. A. Stolypin: The Search for Stability in Late Imperial Russia* (Stanford, CA: Stanford University Press, 2001). On Stolypin's local reforms, see Neil B. Weissman, *Reform in Tsarist Russia: The State Bureaucracy and Local Government, 1900–1914* (New Brunswick, NJ: Rutgers University Press, 1981). A bit older but still very useful are the essays in Leopold Haimson, ed., *The Politics of Rural Russia, 1905–1914* (Bloomington: Indiana University Press, 1979).

95. Ascher, *P. A. Stolypin*, 162–64. For other "takes" on the Stolypin Reforms, see Teodor Shanin, *The Awkward Class: Political Sociology of Peasantry in a Developing Society: Russia, 1910–1925* (Oxford: Oxford University Press, 1972); D. Atkinson, *The End of the Russian Land Commune, 1905–1920* (Stanford, CA: Stanford University Press, 1983); and Judith Pallot, *Land Reform in Russia, 1906–1917: Peasant Responses to Stolypin's Project of Rural Transformation* (New York: Oxford University Press, 1999).

96. Ascher, *P. A. Stolypin*, esp. 396–99.

97. Ibid., 397–98. On the tsar's resistance to constitutional as well as economic reforms in Russia, see also G. Hosking, *The Russian Constitutional Experiment: Government and Duma, 1907–14* (Cambridge: Cambridge University Press, 1973); Thomas Riha, "Constitutional Developments in Russia," in George Stavrou, ed., *Russia Under the Last Tsar*, 87–116; and Verner, *The Crisis of Russian Autocracy*, passim.

98. For a vivid account of the assassination, see Orlando Figes, *A People's Tragedy: The Russian Revolution, 1891–1924* (New York: Penguin Books, 1996), 229–30. Stolypin died four days later, on September 5.

99. Ascher, *P. A. Stolypin*, 373–74.

100. Ibid., 374–75. Alexandra especially hated Stolypin over concerns he had voiced relating to Rasputin's growing influence at court. See, on this, the personal testimony of Sir Barnard Pares, *The Fall of the Russian Monarchy* (New York: Knopf, 1939), 142–43. Pares's account is substantiated by Lieven, *Nicholas II*, 170, and by Ascher, *P. A. Stolypin*, 355.

101. Ibid., 387–88. Kokovtsov, who was already finance minister, now assumed Stolypin's chairmanship of the Council of Ministers, whereas the Internal Affairs portfolio eventually went to the reactionary N. A. Maklakov. For the prevailing view of Kokovtsov as a fiscally cautious "bureaucrat" who, if lacking Witte's and Stolypin's broad vision and dynamism, still attempted to further the "United Government" reform agenda in Imperial Russia, refer again to Hosking, *The Russian Constitutional Experiment*, 198–99; Weissman, *Reform in Tsarist Russia*, 202–03; and McDonald, *United Government and Foreign Policy in Russia*, 170.

102. The older accounts of the Balkan Wars by Luigi Albertini, Ernst Helmreich, and others have been superseded for the most part by Richard C. Hall, *The Balkan Wars 1912–1913: Prelude to the First World War* (London: Routledge, 2000).

103. See the riveting account of this crisis in L. C. F. Turner, *Origins of the First World War* (New York: Norton, 1970), 43–47. Dominic Lieven has speculated that "hatred of Sukhomlinov" may have led Kokovtsov "to exaggerate the wickedness of the War Minister's plans in November 1912," but even *he* has conceded that "given the existing international tension [it was] dangerous that anyone could even think of ordering any sort of partial mobilization without consulting the Foreign Minister and Chairman of the Council." Lieven, *Russia and the Origins of the First World War* (London: Macmillan, 1983), 62–63. Efforts to rehabilitate War Minister Sukhomlinov as at least something of an old regime military reformer include William

C. Fuller, Jr., *Civil-Military Conflict in Imperial Russia, 1881–1914* (Princeton, NJ: Princeton University Press, 1985), 237–44; and Bruce Menning, "Mukden to Tannenberg: Defeat to Defeat, 1905–1914," in Frederick Kagan and Robin Higham, eds., *The Military History of Tsarist Russia* (New York: Palgrave, 2002). Yet Sukhomlinov's glaring incompetence in the crucial realm of military mobilization planning, notably in 1912 and 1914, has been subsequently underscored by David Alan Rich in his "Russia," in Richard F. Hamilton and Holger H. Herwig, eds., *The Origins of World War I* (Cambridge: Cambridge University Press, 2003).

104. This account of the intriguing against (and eventual disgrace of) Kokovtsov is provided by Verner, *The Crisis of Russian Autocracy*, 347–50. Additional information on these maneuvers at Court appears in McDonald, *United Government and Foreign Policy in Russia*, 190–98. McDonald quite properly points up here the larger issue of the tsar's lack of confidence in (and support for) his "United Government." Kokovtsov's successor I. L. Goremykin was (in the words of one well-placed British diplomat) "an amiable old gentleman, with pleasant manners, of an indolent temperament, and quite past his work." Citation from Turner, *Origins of the First World War*, 59.

105. Verner, *The Crisis of Russian Autocracy*, 347–50.

106. Figes, *A People's Tragedy*, 61. See also in this connection L. C. F. Turner, *Origins of the First World War*, 44, who has the British military attaché to Russia, Colonel Alfred Knox, describing General Polivanov flatly as "the best military organizer in Russia."

107. As quoted in Lieven, *Nicholas II*, 211. That much of this was (tragically) accurate is borne out by subsequent studies of the Imperial Army's performance in World War I. See, in particular, Allan K. Wildman, *The End of the Russian Imperial Army: The Old Army and the Soldiers' Revolt (March–April 1917)* (Princeton, NJ: Princeton University Press, 1980); and David R. Jones, "Imperial Russia's Forces at War," in Allan R. Millett and Williamson Murray, eds., *Military Effectiveness I: The First World War* (Boston: Allen and Unwin, 1988), 249–328.

108. As quoted in Figes, *A People's Tragedy*, 278. Lewis H. Siegelbaum has thoroughly documented Polivanov's efforts to help Guchkov, in his capacity as chair of the Central War Industries Committee (*TsVPK*), to channel war matériel and other supplies to the tsarist government in 1915 and 1916, and to coordinate the patriotic activities of the *VPK*s, of Paul Miliukov and other Progressive Bloc members of the Duma, and of specialists in the War Ministry. See Lewis H. Siegelbaum, *The Politics of Industrial Mobilization in Russia, 1914–17: A Study of the War-Industries Committees* (New York: St. Martin's Press, 1983), esp. 70, 77, 83, 125–26, 133–34, 163.

109. As cited in W. Bruce Lincoln, *Passage Through Armaggedon: The Russians in War and Revolution, 1914–1918* (New York: Simon and Schuster, 1986), 242–43. Lincoln has provided one of the best discussions of the military reforms introduced into the Imperial Army by War Minister Polivanov. Further depressing details about Polivanov's dismissal by the tsar are furnished by George Katkov, *Russia 1917: The February Revolution*, second edition (London: Collins, 1969), 212–17, 258.

110. Ibid., 290. This opinion is also shared by McDonald, *United Government and Foreign Policy in Russia*, 178. The late Allan K. Wildman briefly dissented from this general praise of Polivanov in his 1980 study of the Imperial Army cited earlier, but failed to offer any scholarly substantiation for doing so.

111. Orlando Figes points this out in *A People's Tragedy*, 699n.

112. For some excellent scholarly perspectives on the Great Reforms, refer to the essays in Ben Eklof, John Bushnell, and Larissa Zakharova, eds., *Russia's Great Reforms, 1855–1881* (Bloomington: Indiana University Press, 1994).

113. On the *zemstvos* (and the associated town *dumas* as well), consult the following: Weissman, *Reform in Tsarist Russia*, passim; the essays in Terence Emmons and Wayne S. Vucinich, eds., *The Zemstvos in Russia: An Experiment in Local Self-Government* (Cambridge: Cambridge University Press, 1982); and Charles E. Timberlake, "The Zemstvo and the Development of a Russian Middle Class," in Edith W. Clowes, Samuel D. Kassow, and James L. West, eds., *Between Tsar and People: Educated Society and the Quest for Public Identity in Late Imperial Russia* (Princeton, NJ: Princeton University Press, 1991), 164–79.

114. Weissman, *Reform in Tsarist Russia*, 222.

115. Figes, *A People's Tragedy*, 54. For some of the political ramifications of the struggle, in late prerevolutionary Russia, between the advocates and opponents of the *zemstvos* and of provincial administrative reform in general, see also Robert Edelman, *Gentry Politics on the Eve of the Russian Revolution: The Nationalist Party, 1907–1917* (New Brunswick, NJ: Rutgers University Press, 1980); George Yaney, *The Urge to Mobilize: Agrarian Reform in Russia, 1801–1930* (Urbana: University of Illinois Press, 1982); and Richard G. Robbins, *The Tsar's Viceroys: Russian Provincial Governors in the Last Years of the Empire* (Ithaca, NY: Cornell University Press, 1987).

116. Dorothy Atkinson, "The Zemstvo and the Peasantry," in Emmons and Vucinich, eds., *The Zemstvos in Russia*, 124–25.

117. Terence Emmons, "The Zemstvo in Historical Perspective," in ibid., 423–27. On the apparent bifurcation of the prerevolutionary Russian nobility into landless service nobility and landed gentry (*dvorianstvo*), see especially Roberta T. Manning, *The Crisis of the Old Order in Russia: Gentry and Government* (Princeton, NJ: Princeton University Press, 1982).

118. On the declining fortunes of *zemstvo* reform, and Stolypin's related difficulties in implementing his agrarian policies after 1905, see Roberta T. Manning, "The Zemstvos and Politics, 1864–1914," in Emmons and Vucinich, eds., *The Zemstvos in Russia*, esp. 166–67.

119. Atkinson, "The Zemstvo and the Peasantry," ibid., 124–25.

120. On the late *ancien régime* Russian intelligentsia, consult Christopher Read, *Culture and Power: The Intelligentsia and the Transition from Tsarism to Communism* (New York: St. Martin's Press, 1990); and Jane Burbank, "The Intelligentsia," in Acton, Cherniaev, and Rosenberg, eds., *Critical Companion to the Russian Revolution*, 515–28.

121. See, in this connection: Melissa Stockdale, *Paul Miliukov and the Quest for a Liberal Russia, 1880–1918* (Ithaca: Cornell University Press, 1996); Robert D. Warth, *The Allies and the Russian Revolution: From the Fall of the Monarchy to the Peace of Brest-Litovsk* (Durham, NC: Duke University Press, 1954); and Rex Wade, *The Russian Search for Peace, February–October 1917* (Stanford, CA: Stanford University Press, 1969).

122. See, on this affair, Abraham Ascher, "The Kornilov Affair," *Russian Review* 12 (1953): 235–52; James D. White, "The Kornilov Affair: A Study in Counter Revolution," *Soviet Studies* 20 (1968–69): 187–205; and, most important, George Katkov, *The Kornilov Affair: Kerensky and the Break-Up of the Russian Army* (London: Longman, 1980).

123. Two seminal articles on this deepening social polarization at the capital (and elsewhere) in 1917 are William G. Rosenberg and Diane Koenker, "The Limits of Formal Protest: Workers' Activism and Social Polarization in Petrograd and Moscow, March to October, 1917," *American Historical Review* 92 (1987): 296–326; and Paul Flenley, "Industrial Relations and the Economic Crisis of 1917," *Revolutionary Russia* 4 (1991): 184–209.

124. David S. Foglesong, "Foreign Intervention," in Acton, Cherniaev, and Rosenberg, eds., *Critical Companion to the Russian Revolution*, 112. Foglesong enlarges on much of this in *America's Secret War Against Bolshevism: U.S. Intervention in the Russian Civil War, 1917–1920* (Chapel Hill, NC: University of North Carolina Press, 1995).

125. Evan Mawdsley, "The Civil War: The Military Campaigns," in Acton, Cherniaev, and Rosenberg, eds., *Critical Companion to the Russian Revolution*, 98–101. On the military aspects of the civil war, see also Mawdsley, *The Russian Civil War* (Boston: Allen and Unwin, 1987); and W. Bruce Lincoln, *Red Victory: A History of the Russian Civil War* (New York: Simon and Schuster, 1989).

126. Figes, *A People's Tragedy*, 823–24.

127. See again Pincus, *1688: The First Modern Revolution*, esp. 32–33, 44–45. For instance, Pincus's remark that "revolutions happen only when the old regime commits itself to state modernization" (p. 45) leaves out the fact that, at least in the cases of England, France, and Russia, the whole issue of "state modernization" was *itself* still being contested in the early phases of upheaval—and for a variety of reasons inadequately dealt with in his theoretical discussion.

2. IN SEARCH OF THE ELUSIVE
ANCIEN RÉGIME BOURGEOISIE

1. See the introduction.
2. See Peter McPhee, "The French Revolution, Peasants, and Capitalism," *American Historical Review* 94 (1989): 1265–80; and McPhee, ed., *A Companion to the French Revolution* (West Sussex, UK: Wiley-Blackwell, 2013), esp. the introduction.
3. Thus, Norah Carlin, in *The Causes of the English Civil War* (Oxford: Blackwell Publishers, 1999), 154. Some of Marx's and Engels's thoughts on the origins, process, and results of revolution in mid-seventeenth-century England are found in Karl Marx and Friedrich Engels, *Articles on Britain* (Moscow: Progress Publishers, 1971).
4. For these (and other) statistics, consult William Doyle, *Origins of the French Revolution* (Oxford: Oxford University Press, 1980), 129–30. Doyle enlarges upon this theme somewhat in *The Oxford History of the French Revolution* (Oxford: Clarendon, 1989).
5. As cited in Doyle, "The Price of Offices in Pre-Revolutionary France," *Historical Journal* 27 (1984): 856–57. The same connections between the commerce in offices and demographic developments in *ancien régime* France have been drawn by David Bien, "The *Secrétaires du Roi*: Absolutism, Corps, and Privilege Under the Ancien Régime," in E. Hinrichs et al., eds., *Vom Ancien Régime zur Französischen Révolution* (Göttingen: Vandenhoeck und Reprecht, 1978), esp. 153–68; and by François Furet, *Interpreting the French Revolution*, trans. Elborg Forster (Cambridge: Cambridge University Press, 1981), 106–08. This insight, of course, partially invalidates Alfred Cobban's noted assertion from 1964 that the "revolutionary bourgeoisie" was chiefly a "declining" class of *officiers,* lawyers, and other professional types. Consult in this connection Cobban, *The Social Interpretation of the French Revolution* (Cambridge: Cambridge University Press, 1964), esp. chapter VI.
6. Adeline Daumard and François Furet, *Structures et relations sociales à Paris au milieu du XVIIIe siècle* (Paris: A. Colin, 1961), esp. 80, 87.
7. Georges Lefebvre, "Urban Society in the Orléanais in the Late Eighteenth Century," *Past and Present* 19 (1961): 50–51. Lefebvre's posthumous article was extracted from his much larger monograph, *Etudes Orléanaises: i: Contribution à l'étude des structures sociales à la fin du XVIIIe siècle* (Paris: Commission d'histoire économique et sociale de la Révolution française, 1962).
8. Olwen H. Hufton, *Bayeux in the Late Eighteenth Century* (Oxford: Oxford University Press, 1967), 46, 47–48, 56.
9. Lynn A. Hunt, *Revolution and Urban Politics in Provincial France: Troyes and Reims, 1786–1790* (Stanford: Stanford University Press, 1978), 37–38.
10. Robert Darnton, *The Great Cat Massacre and Other Episodes in French Cultural History* (New York: Vintage Books, 1985), 131, 136.
11. Refer to Daniel Roche, *Le siècle des lumières en province: Académies et académiciens provinçiaux, 1680–1789* (Paris: Mouton, 1978), esp. 255, 393–94. There is also the additional fact that, as Guy Chaussinand-Nogaret demonstrated, many of the *lettres d'anoblissement* bought by wealthy *bourgeois* from the financially straitened French government in the late 1700s proclaimed the authorities' "appreciation" of "meritocratic" values and accomplishments manifested by the Bourbon monarchs' subjects. See, on this issue, Guy Chaussinand-Nogaret, "Aux Origines de la Révolution: Noblesse et Bourgeoisie," *Annales: E. S. C. 30* (1975): 265–77; and, by the same author, *La Noblesse au XVIIIe siècle. De la féodalité aux lumières* (Paris: Hachette, 1976), 268–70.
12. Lefebvre, "Urban Society in the Orléanais in the Late Eighteenth Century," 50–51.
13. Roche, *Le siècle des lumières en province,* 393–94.
14. As quoted by Patrice Higonnet in *Class, Ideology, and the Rights of Nobles during the French Revolution* (Oxford: Clarendon, 1981), 54.
15. Refer, once again, to McPhee, "The French Revolution, Peasants, and Capitalism," 1265–80.
16. Colin Jones, "Bourgeois Revolution Revivified: 1789 and Social Change," in Colin Lucas, ed., *Rewriting the French Revolution* (Oxford: Clarendon Press, 1991), 69–118.

17. Ibid., 109–10. Jones would later elaborate on many of these ideas in "The Great Chain of Buying: Medical Advertisement, the Bourgeois Public Sphere, and the Origins of the French Revolution," *American Historical Review* 101 (1996): 13–40. But see also Daniel Roche, *A History of Everyday Things: The Birth of Consumption in France*, trans. Brian Pearce (Cambridge: Cambridge University Press, 2000); and Jennifer Jones, *Sexing La Mode: Gender, Fashion, and Commercial Culture in Old Régime France* (Oxford: Oxford University Press, 2004), for new discussion of consumption, consumerism, and "capitalism" as socially subversive forces in eighteenth-century France.

18. Jones, "Bourgeois Revolution Revivified," 110–11.

19. Peter McPhee, *A Social History of France, 1780-1880* (London: Routledge, 1992), esp. 14.

20. Ibid., 29. Not surprisingly, McPhee also used this occasion, in 1992, to characterize the French Enlightenment as a "class-based ideology," thereby disagreeing with "those who dispute the correlation of 'enlightened' ideas with a more assertive [and, presumably, more capitalistic/entrepreneurial] bourgeoisie." Ibid., 26–27.

21. Gwynne Lewis, "Introduction" to the second edition of Alfred Cobban, *The Social Interpretation of the French Revolution* (Cambridge: Cambridge University Press, 1999), xxxix. For further documentation on this point, consult Lewis, *The Advent of Modern Capitalism in France: the Case of Pierre-François Tubeuf* (Cambridge: Cambridge University Press, 1993); Thomas Brennan, *Burgundy to Champagne: The Wine Trade in Early Modern France* (Baltimore: Johns Hopkins University Press, 1997); and McPhee, *A Social History of France*, passim.

22. Lewis, "Introduction," xl. Lewis, it should be noted, pointed out as well that leading *cultural* historians of the *ancien régime* were accepting "the crucial importance of increasing wealth as well as the 'incursion of capitalist values'" in their work. See, as examples of this, Daniel Roche, *La France des Lumières* (Paris: Fayard, 1993); and Robert Darnton, *The Forbidden Best-Sellers of Pre-Revolutionary France* (London: Fontana Press, 1997).

23. Henry Heller, *The Bourgeois Revolution in France, 1789–1815* (New York: Berghahn, 2006), 22–23.

24. Ibid., 22–23, 59, 60.

25. Ibid., 55.

26. Ibid., 38–41. See, for example, the following: David Weir, "Tontines, Public Finance, and Revolution in France and England, 1688–1789," *Journal of Economic History* 49 (1989): 95–124; Philip T. Hoffmann, *Growth in a Traditional Society: The French Countryside, 1450–1815* (Princeton: Princeton University Press, 1996); George Grantham, "The French Cliometric Revolution: A Survey of Cliometric Contributions to French Economic History," *European Review of Economic History* 1 (1997): 353–405; and John Nye, "The Importance of Being Late: French Economic History, Cliometrics, and the New Institutional Economics," *French Historical Studies* 23 (2000): 423–37.

27. See Jack A. Goldstone, *Revolution and Rebellion in the Early Modern World* (Berkeley: University of California Press, 1991), esp. 238–39. William Doyle had made the same point in his *Origins of the French Revolution* (Oxford: Oxford University Press, 1980), esp. 135.

28. David Garrioch, *The Formation of the Parisian Bourgeoisie, 1690–1830* (Cambridge, MA: Harvard University Press, 1996).

29. Ibid., 1–2.

30. Ibid., 7. In this connection, Garrioch no doubt had in mind E. P. Thompson's classic study *The Making of the English Working Class* (New York: Vintage Books, 1966).

31. Garrioch, *The Formation of the Parisian Bourgeoisie*, 275–76. On sociological discussions of the "state" in general, refer to Perry Anderson, *Lineages of the Absolutist* State (London: New Left Books, 1974); Peter B. Evans, Dietrich Rueschemeyer, and Theda Skocpol, eds, *Bringing the State Back In* (New York: Cambridge University Press, 1985); and the various "structuralist" essays in John Foran, ed., *Theorizing Revolutions* (London: Routledge, 1997).

32. Sarah Maza, *The Myth of the French Bourgeoisie: An Essay on the Social Imaginary, 1750–1850* (Cambridge, MA: Harvard University Press, 2003), esp. 5, 26.

33. Ibid., 6.

34. Ibid., 22–23, 26.

35. Heller's critique of Maza's "deconstructionist" method may be consulted in Heller, *The Bourgeois Revolution in France*, esp. 17–18.

36. Peter McPhee, ed., *A Companion to the French Revolution*, "Introduction," xvii.

37. Peter Campbell, "Rethinking the Origins of the French Revolution," in ibid., esp. 7–8.

38. Jean-Pierre Jessenne, "The Social and Economic Crisis in France at the End of the *Ancien Régime*," ibid., 29.

39. Ibid., 39–40.

40. Peter Campbell, "Rethinking the Origins of the French Revolution," in ibid., esp. 18–19.

41. See, for example, Jeremy Smith, "Europe's Atlantic Empires: Early Modern State Formation Reconsidered," in *Political Power and Social Theory* 17 (2005): 103–53; and James C. Collins, *The State in Early Modern France*, second edition (Cambridge: Cambridge University Press, 2009). For a more broadly inclusive theoretical discussion of the state in prerevolutionary European situations, the reader is once again directed to Bailey Stone, *The Anatomy of Revolution Revisited*, introduction.

42. Refer to Lauren R. Clay, "The Bourgeoisie, Capitalism, and the Origins of the French Revolution," in David Andress, ed., *The Oxford Handbook of the French Revolution* (Oxford: Oxford University Press, 2015), 20–39.

43. Alex Callinicos, "Bourgeois Revolutions and Historical Materialism," in *International Socialism* 43 (1989): 113–71.

44. Ellen M. Wood, *The Pristine Culture of Capitalism* (London: Verso, 1991), 31.

45. Refer, for example, to these works: *The Century of Revolution, 1603–1714* (London: Nelson, 1961); *Society and Puritanism in Pre-Revolutionary England*, third edition (London: Panther, 1969); *People and Ideas in Seventeenth-Century England* (Brighton: Harvester, 1987); and *Intellectual Origins of the English Revolution Revisited* (Oxford: Clarendon Press, 1997). Needless to add, a postwar generation of scholars—H. R. Trevor-Roper, Lawrence Stone, Jack Hexter, Perez Zagorin, and so on—had also joined Hill in engaging in a "storm" over the "rising" (or, perhaps, "declining"?) gentry in early Stuart England. See Lawrence Stone, *Social Change and Revolution in England, 1540–1640* (London: Longman, 1965) for selections from that celebrated (if rather inconclusive) debate of the 1940s and 1950s.

46. Robert Brenner, *Merchants and Revolution: Commercial Change, Political Conflicts, and London's Overseas Traders, 1550–1653* (Princeton, NJ: Princeton University Press, 1993). Earlier writings leading up to Brenner's *chef-d'oeuvre* included "Agrarian Class Structure and Economic Development in Pre-Industrial Europe" and "The Agrarian Roots of European Capitalism," in Trevor H. Aston and C. H. E. Philpin, eds., *The Brenner Debate* (Cambridge: Cambridge University Press, 1987), 10–63, 213–327, respectively; and "Bourgeois Revolution and Transition to Capitalism," in A. L. Beier, David Cannadine, and James M. Rosenheim, eds., *The First Modern Society: Essays in English History in Honor of Lawrence Stone* (Cambridge: Cambridge University Press, 1989).

47. Brenner, *Merchants and Revolution*, 648–49.

48. Ibid., 650–51.

49. Ibid., 653–54.

50. Ibid., 688.

51. Ibid., 650.

52. Consult, in this connection, Patricia Croot and David Parker, "Agrarian Class Structure and the Development of Capitalism: France and England Compared," in Aston and Philpin, eds., *The Brenner Debate*, esp. 79–81, 83, 85, 87–88. For Brenner's rejoinder to their criticisms, see Brenner, "The Agrarian Roots of European Capitalism," in ibid., esp. 300–02.

53. See Robert Ashton's review of Brenner's *Merchants and Revolution* in *The English Historical Review* 109 (1994): 115–18.

54. R. C. Richardson, *The Debate on the English Revolution*, third edition (Manchester: Manchester University Press, 1998), 148–49.

55. Consult David Levine's lengthy (and largely positive) review of *Merchants and Revolution* in *The American Historical Review* 100 (1995): 156–58.

56. Jonathan Barry, from the "Introduction" to Jonathan Barry and Christopher Brooks, eds., *The Middling Sort of People: Culture, Society and Politics in England, 1550–1800* (London: MacMillan, 1994), 9–10. Earlier efforts to reassess bourgeois contributions to the mid-seven-

teenth-century crisis in Stuart England included Jack Hexter, "The Myth of the Middle Class in Tudor England," revised in his *Reappraisals in History* (London: Longman, 1961): 71–116; and C. H. George, "The Making of the English Bourgeoisie 1600–1710," *Science and Society* 35 (1971): 385–414. Yet see also, in this connection, the general misgivings about sociological renderings of English revolutionary causation expressed by several of the contributors to Adrian Wilson, ed., *Rethinking Social History: English Society 1570–1920 and Its Interpretation* (Manchester: Manchester University Press, 1993).

57. Keith Wrightson, "'Sorts of People' in Tudor and Stuart England," in Barry and Brooks, eds., *The Middling Sort of People*, esp. 45–48.

58. Christopher Brooks, "Professions, Ideology and the Middling Sort in the Late Sixteenth and Early Seventeenth Centuries," in ibid., 136.

59. Consult Brian Manning, *The English People and the English Revolution*, second edition (London: Bookmarks, 1991). Refer, however, in this connection, to Ann Hughes' trenchant criticisms about an earlier edition of Manning's work in *The Causes of the English Civil War* (Basingstoke: MacMillan, 1991), esp. 133–35.

60. Brian Manning, *Aristocrats, Plebeians and Revolution in England 1640–1660* (London: Pluto Press, 1996).

61. Ibid., 4, 71.

62. Ibid., 4.

63. Ibid., 140.

64. Goldstone, *Revolution and Rebellion in Early Modern Europe*, 121.

65. Ibid., 125–26.

66. Norah Carlin, *The Causes of the English Civil War* (Oxford: Blackwell, 1999), 119. This is a point which many sociologically attuned historians of an earlier generation such as Lawrence Stone had also been eager to highlight. See Stone, *Causes of the English Revolution 1529–1642* (London: Routledge, 2002), esp. 72–75.

67. Carlin, *The Causes of the English Civil War*, 133. Ann Hughes (in *The Causes of the English Civil War*, 71) says much the same thing: "There is much evidence that the ranks below the gentry were perfectly capable of independent collective activity to redress practical grievances, attack religious enemies or defend local customs and rights . . . elites' freedom of action was circumscribed by the involvement of a broader political nation which included the . . . 'middling sort'—yeomen, small merchants, prosperous husbandmen and craftsmen—as well as humbler men."

68. Carlin, *The Causes of the English Civil War*, 161–62. For an extended and useful discussion of these issues, consult Adrian Wilson, "Foundations of an Integrated Historiography," in Adrian Wilson, ed., *Rethinking Social History*, 293–335.

69. Refer again to Brenner, *Merchants and Revolution*, 648.

70. Ibid.

71. On this point, refer once again to the monographs by Hill cited in n. 44. For a taste of the *very* young, and *very* Marxist Hill, consult his essay "The English Revolution" in Christopher Hill, ed., *The English Revolution 1640: Three Essays* (London: Lawrence and Wishart, 1940). Robert Brenner (of all people!) outlined the early stages of Hill's intellectual evolution away from the Marxian *parti pris* of his youth in his *Merchants and Revolution*, 638, n. 1. Yet Brenner took the story of Hill's partial "change of heart" only up to the year 1981.

72. Christopher Hill, *Intellectual Origins of the English Revolution Revisited*, 285–86.

73. Ibid., 297.

74. Ibid., 300.

75. Ibid., 297.

76. As cited in David Cressy, *England on Edge: Crisis and Revolution, 1640–1642* (Oxford: Oxford University Press, 2006), 6–7.

77. Consult, for instance, Conrad Russell, *The Fall of the British Monarchies, 1637–1642* (Oxford: Oxford University Press, 1991); Stephen C. A. Pincus, *Protestantism and Patriotism: Ideologies and the Making of English Foreign Policy 1650–1668* (Cambridge: Cambridge University Press, 1996); Jonathan Scott, *England's Troubles: Seventeenth Century English Instability in European Context* (Cambridge: Cambridge University Press, 2000); Geoffrey Parker, *The Global Crisis: War, Climate, and Catastrophe in the Seventeenth-Century World*

(New Haven, CT: Yale University Press, 2010); and Michael J. Braddick, *God's Fury, England's Fire: A New History of the English Civil Wars* (New York: Penguin Books, 2009).

78. Thomas C. Owen, "Impediments to a Bourgeois Consciousness in Russia, 1880–1905: The Estate Structure, Ethnic Diversity, and Economic Regionalism," in Edith W. Clowes, Samuel D. Kassow, and James L. West, eds., *Between Tsar and People: Educated Society and the Quest for Public Identity in Late Imperial Russia* (Princeton, NJ: Princeton University Press, 1991), 75–76.

79. Edward Acton, "The Revolution and Its Historians: The *Critical Companion* in Context," from Edward Acton, Vladimir I. Cherniaev, and William G. Rosenberg, eds., *Critical Companion to the Russian Revolution 1914–1921* (Bloomington: Indiana University Press, 1997), 14–16. Here, Acton had in mind the longtime conservative Russian revolutionary historian Richard Pipes. For similar misgivings about the "postmodernist turn" as applied to Russian revolutionary studies, see, most notably, Robert V. Daniels, "Does the Present Change the Past?" *Journal of Modern History* 70 (1998): esp. 434–35.

80. Gregory L. Freeze, "The Soslovie (Estate) Paradigm and Russian Social History," *American Historical Review* 91 (1986): esp. 35–36.

81. Ibid., 35. On this last point, refer also to the fascinating article by Sheila Fitzpatrick, "Ascribing Class: The Construction of Social Identity in Soviet Russia," *Journal of Modern History* 65 (1993): 745–70. (Reprinted in Martin A. Miller, ed., *The Russian Revolution: The Essential Readings* [Oxford: Blackwell, 2001], 208–34.)

82. Leopold H. Haimson, "The Problem of Social Identities in Early Twentieth-Century Russia," *Slavic Review* 47 (1988): 1–20. See also, in this connection, the remarks by Haimson, William G. Rosenberg, and Alfred. J. Rieber, in "The Problem of Social Identities in Early Twentieth-Century Russia," *Slavic Review* 47 (1989): 1–38; Alfred J. Rieber, "The Sedimentary Society," in Clowes, Kassow, and West, eds., *Between Tsar and People*, 343–66; and Abbott Gleason, "The Terms of Russian Social History," in ibid., 15–27.

83. Ibid., 15–18.

84. Ibid., 17–18. A point that has been convincingly demonstrated as well in the scholarship of modernization theorists such as Theodore H. Von Laue. See Von Laue, *Sergei Witte and the Industrialization of Russia* (New York: Columbia University Press, 1963); "Westernization, Revolution and the Search for a Basis of Authority: Russia in 1917," in *Soviet Studies* 19 (1967): 156–80; and, of course, his classic *Why Lenin? Why Stalin? Why Gorbachev? The Rise and Fall of the Soviet System*, third edition (New York: Harper Collins, 1993). Tim McDaniel, in addition, has theorized the always-problematic relationship between late Russian autocracy and capitalism in interesting ways: see his *Autocracy, Capitalism, and Revolution in Russia* (Berkeley: University of California Press, 1988).

85. Thomas C. Owen, "Impediments to a Bourgeois Consciousness in Russia, 1880–1905: The Estate Structure, Ethnic Diversity, and Economic Regionalism," in Clowes, Kassow, and West, eds., *Between Tsar and People*, esp. 87–88.

86. Ibid., 76–77. Much of this analysis tallies with that offered by (among others) Leopold Haimson: refer again to "The Problem of Social Identities in Early Twentieth-Century Russia," esp. 25–28. Orlando Figes situates the precariousness of any bourgeois class consciousness in late Imperial Russia in a broader social context in his vivid study *A People's Tragedy: The Russian Revolution 1891–1924* (New York: Penguin Books, 1998), esp. 162–64.

87. Sheila Fitzpatrick, "Ascribing Class: The Construction of Social Identity in Soviet Russia," cited here in M. Miller, ed., *The Russian Revolution: The Essential Readings*, 209–11.

88. James L. West, "The Riabushinsky Circle: *Burzhuaziia* and *Obshchestvennost'* in Late Imperial Russia," Clowes, Kassow, and West, eds., *Between Tsar and People*, esp. 55. These themes had already been introduced in A. J. Rieber, *Merchants and Entrepreneurs in Imperial Russia* (Chapel Hill, NC: University of North Carolina Press, 1982); and in Thomas C. Owen, *Capitalism and Politics in Russia* (Cambridge: Cambridge University Press, 1981).

89. Refer to Nancy M. Frieden, *Russian Physicians in an Era of Reform and Revolution, 1856–1905* (Princeton: Princeton University Press, 1981); and Harley Balzer, "The Problem of Professions in Imperial Russia," in Clowes, Kassow, and West, eds., *Between Tsar and People*," 183–98. Teachers, too, dealt with similar predicaments in Imperial Russia. See, for in-

stance, Christine Ruane and Ben Eklof, "Cultural Pioneers and Professionals: The Teacher in Society," in ibid., 199–211.

90. William G. Wagner, "Ideology, Identity, and the Emergence of a Middle Class," in ibid., 161–63.

91. Samuel D. Kassow, "Russia's Unrealised Civil Society," in ibid., 367.

92. On noble estate dynamics in old regime Russia, see Roberta T. Manning, *The Crisis of the Old Order in Russia: Gentry and Government* (Princeton, NJ: Princeton University Press, 1982); Seymour Becker, *Nobility and Privilege in Late Imperial Russia* (DeKalb, IL: Northern Illinois University Press, 1985); and Abraham Ascher, *P. A. Stolypin: The Search for Stability in Late Imperial Russia* (Stanford, CA: Stanford University Press, 2001). The tensions between, specifically, bureaucratic reformers and provincial, landed gentry in the immediate aftermath of the so-called 1905 revolution are teased out by Francis W. Wcislo, "Soslovie or Class? Bureaucratic Reformers and Provincial Nobility in Conflict, 1906–1908," *Russian Review* 47 (1988): 1–24. As for the "gentry intelligentsia," it has long been a commonplace among authorities on this element in *ancien régime* Russia that it was increasingly divided between a "Westernizing" wing, favorable to the cause of modernization, and a "nativist," Slavic-oriented and antimodernizing wing. See, in this connection, the always useful essays in Richard Pipes, ed., *The Russian Intelligentsia* (New York: Columbia University Press, 1969); Christopher Read, *Culture and Power in Revolutionary Russia: The Intelligentsia and the Transition from Tsarism to Communism* (New York: St. Martin's Press, 1990); and Jane Burbank, "The Intelligentsia," in Acton, Cherniaev, and Rosenberg, eds., *Critical Companion to the Russian Revolution 1914–1921*, 515–28.

93. A point made powerfully by, among others, Orlando Figes in *A People's Tragedy*, 163–64, and Samuel D. Kassow, in "Russia's Unrealised Civil Society," 370–71.

94. Peter Gatrell, "Russian Industrialists and Revolution," in Acton, Cherniaev, and Rosenberg, eds., *Critical Companion to the Russian Revolution 1914-1921*, esp. 576–78. For more information on this topic, refer as well to Ruth A. Roosa, "Russian Industrialists during World War I," in G. Guroff and F. V. Carstensen, eds., *Entrepreneurship in Imperial Russia and the Soviet Union* (Princeton: Princeton University Press, 1983), 159–87.

95. On the WICs in wartime Russia, consult especially, Lewis H. Siegelbaum, *The Politics of Industrial Mobilization in Russia, 1914–17: A Study of the War-Industries Committees* (New York: St. Martin's Press, 1983); and Ziva Galili, "Commercial-Industrial Circles in Revolution: The Failure of 'Industrial Progressivism,'" in Edith R. Frankel, Jonathan Frankel, and Baruch Knei-Paz, eds., *Revolution in Russia: Reassessments of 1917* (Cambridge: Cambridge University Press, 1992), 188–216. Gatrell, "Russian Industrialists and Revolution," passim, provides a useful if rather generalized overview of the role played by the WICs in Imperial Russia's war effort against the Central Powers.

96. Ibid., 577–78.

97. Ibid., 581–82. On the developing links between those liberal merchants and industrialists who had helped to found the Progressist Party on the eve of the Great War and the leadership in the WICs during the war years, refer once again to Ziva Galili, "Commercial-Industrial Circles in Revolution: The Failure of 'Industrial Progressivism,'" esp. 190–92. The "Moscow Progressists," Galili remarked, "advocated the building of social coalitions to resist the domination of economic and social life by the autocracy and the landed gentry. Then, during the war, as defeat and mismanagement discredited the forces of the old regime, P. P. Riabushinskii and A. I. Konovalov, the outstanding figures in the faction, openly hailed the 'bourgeoisie' as the force destined to lead Russia's 'vital forces' in the pursuit of political freedom and economic expansion."

98. This last point is also forcefully made by Siegelbaum, *The Politics of Industrialization in Russia, 1914–17*, esp. 209–11. For Siegelbaum, as for Gatrell, Galili, and other specialists on the subject, there was a sort of "double estrangement" steadily intensifying here—between, on the one hand, the tsarist regime and the *VPKs* and, on the other hand, within the industrialist ranks of the *VPKs* (WICs) themselves.

99. Ibid., 201–02.

100. Ibid., 203.

101. The role of the WICs (and of the commercial/industrial "bourgeoisie" in general) in all of this is most carefully elaborated in Galili, "Commercial-Industrial Circles in Revolution: The Failure of 'Industrial Progressivism,'" esp. 190–207. For broader perspectives on the dynamics of class polarization in urban Russia in 1917, however, consult the following: William G. Rosenberg and Diane Koenker, "The Limits of Formal Protest: Workers' Activism and Social Polarization in Petrograd and Moscow, March to October, 1917," *American Historical Review* 92 (1987): 296–326; and, by William G. Rosenberg alone, "The Problem of Market Relations and the State in Revolutionary Russia," *Comparative Studies in Society and History* 36 (1994): 356–86.

102. Orlando Figes, *A People's Tragedy*, 162. For more information on this rural disaster in late nineteenth-century Russia, consult Richard G. Robbins Jr., *Famine in Russia, 1891–1892: The Imperial Government Responds to a Crisis* (New York: Columbia University Press, 1975). See also the general study of George Yaney, *The Urge to Mobilize: Agrarian Reform in Russia 1861–1930* (Urbana: University of Illinois Press, 1982).

103. Haimson, "The Problem of Social Identities in Early Twentieth-Century Russia," 25–26. On the *zemstvos*, refer in particular to the many essays in Terence Emmons and Wayne S. Vucinich, eds., *The Zemstvo in Russia: An Experiment in Local Self-Government* (Cambridge: Cambridge University Press, 1982); and also to Neil B. Weissman, *Reform in Tsarist Russia: The State Bureaucracy and Local Government, 1900–1914* (New Brunswick, NJ: Rutgers University Press, 1981).

104. Leopold Haimson, "The Problem of Social Identities in Early Twentieth-Century Russia," 26. As exemplary of this last tendency, Haimson points to the Muscovite industrialists in the Riabushinsky circle, vacillating between a sense of being *kuptsy*—that is, members of an isolated, discrete interest group in the old society of *sosloviia*—and a sense of belonging to a "big bourgeoisie" (*krupnaia burzhuaziia*) motivated by more modern socioeconomic class interests. Ibid., 28. On the Riabushinsky circle itself, refer once again to James L. West, "The Riabushinsky Circle: *Burzhuaziia* and *Obshchestvennost'* in Late Imperial Russia," in Clowes, Kassow, and West, eds., *Between Tsar and People*, 41–56.

105. Samuel D. Kassow, "Russia's Unrealized Civil Society," ibid., 368.

106. Orlando Figes, *A People's Tragedy*, 810.

107. Sheila Fitzpatrick, *The Russian Revolution*, third edition (Oxford: Oxford University Press, 2008), 39.

3. TO KILL A MONARCH

1. For the results of this initiative, see the many fine papers in Jason Peacey, ed., *The Regicides and the Execution of Charles I* (Basingstoke and New York: Palgrave, 2001).

2. See, in this connection, Dan Edelstein, *The Terror of Natural Right: Republicanism, the Cult of Nature, and the French Revolution* (Chicago: University of Chicago Press, 2009), esp. chapter 3; and "Do We Want a Revolution without Revolution? Reflections on Political Authority," *French Historical Studies* 35 (2012): 269–89.

3. As cited in Orlando Figes, *A People's Tragedy: The Russian Revolution, 1891-1924* (New York: Penguin Books, 1996), 641.

4. See John Adamson, "The Frighted Junto: Perceptions of Ireland, and the Last Attempts at Settlement with Charles I," in Jason Peacey, ed., *The Regicides and the Execution of Charles I*, 39.

5. I have succinctly reviewed Charles I's divisive and duplicitous antics during 1646 to 1648 in *The Anatomy of Revolution Revisited*, 255–57. For somewhat more detailed accounts of all of this, the reader can consult G. E. Aylmer, *A Short History of Seventeenth-Century England: 1603–1689* (New York: Mentor Books, 1963), 130–48; and also Christopher Hill, *The Century of Revolution, 1603–1714* (New York: Norton, 1970), 94–97.

6. D. Alan Orr, "The Juristic Foundation of Regicide," in J. Peacey, ed., *The Regicides and the Execution of Charles I*, 118. Some of the legal issues embedded in this discussion also find elaboration in Michael Walzer, "Regicide and Revolution," *Social Research* 40 (1973):

617–42; and in Daniel P. Klein, "The Trial of Charles I," *Journal of Legal History* 18 (1997): 1–25.

7. Orr, "The Juristic Foundation of Regicide," 118–21. See also, in this connection, the standard work by Ernst L. Kantorowicz, *The King's Two Bodies: A Study in Medieval Political Theology* (Princeton, NJ: Princeton University Press, 1957); and Sarah Barber, "Charles I: Regicide and Republicanism," *History Today 46* (1996), esp. 30.

8. Again, refer to the second half of Kantorowicz, *The King's Two Bodies*, for an in-depth analysis of the Roman law origins of the "dual capacity" view of early modern English kingship.

9. Orr, "The Juristic Foundation of Regicide," 125.

10. Ibid., 119.

11. There are, of course, many edited collections of documents relating to the judicial proceedings at Westminster Hall in January 1649. One of the most readily accessible (if rather slender) collections is that co-edited by David Lagomarsino and Charles T. Wood, *The Trial of Charles I: A Documentary History* (Hanover: University Press of New England, 1989). The documents in this anthology provide the reader with a good sense of the verbatim exchanges during the trial between the king and the Lord President of the High Court of Justice, John Bradshaw. Because Charles never acknowledged the legitimacy of the High Court, there could be, for him, no question of the acceptability of any "counsel for the defense."

12. Citation from David Underdown, *Pride's Purge: Politics in the Puritan Revolution* (Oxford: Clarendon, 1971), 59–60.

13. Cited in Robert Ashton, *Counter-Revolution: The Second Civil War and Its Origins, 1646–48* (New Haven, CT: Yale University Press, 1994), 270–71.

14. Quoted in Underdown, *Pride's Purge*, 59–60.

15. Citation from Ashton, *Counter-Revolution*, 271. On the parliamentary "Presbyterians" themselves, see Noel H. Mayfield, *Puritans and Regicides. Presbyterian-Independent Differences over the Trial and Execution of Charles (I) Stuart* (London: University Press of America, 1988).

16. For all of this, see Elliott Vernon, "The Quarrel of the Covenant: the London Presbyterians and the Regicide," in J. Peacey, ed., *The Regicides and the Execution of Charles I*, esp. 205–08. For more information on the political and ecclesiological stance of the London divines in 1648 and 1649, see Valerie Pearl, "London's Counter-Revolution," in G. E. Aylmer, ed., *The Interregnum: The Quest for Settlement, 1646–1660* (Basingstoke: Palgrave, 1972), 49–50; and Ian Gentles, "The Struggle for London in the Second Civil War," *Historical Journal* 26 (1983), esp. 281, 291. On the "resistance theory," which had helped to fuel Presbyterian defiance of Charles I earlier in the decade, consult (among other scholars) Quentin Skinner, *The Foundations of Modern Political Thought*, two volumes (Cambridge: Cambridge University Press, 1978), II, chapter 7.

17. See Andrew Sharp, "The Levellers and the End of Charles I," in J. Peacey, ed., *The Regicides and the Execution of Charles I*, esp. 185. For Leveller works, see A. L. Morton, ed., *Freedom in Arms: A Selection of Leveller Writings* (New York: International Publishers, 1975); and Andrew Sharp, ed., *The English Levellers* (Cambridge: Cambridge University Press, 1998). For the latest attempt to place the Levellers in a broader "comparative-revolutionary" framework, see Bailey Stone, *The Anatomy of Revolution Revisited*, esp. 293–97, 372–74.

18. Cited in Sharp, "The Levellers and the End of Charles I," 195. On John Lilburne in particular, consult Pauline Gregg, *Freeborn John. A Biography of John Lilburne* (London: George G. Harrap & Co., 1961). The vast literature on the Levellers ranges (in modern times alone!) from Joseph Frank, *The Levellers: A History of the Writings of Three Seventeenth-Century Social Democrats: John Lilburne, Richard Overton, William Walwyn* (Cambridge, MA: Harvard University Press, 1955), to Ian Gentles, "The Politics of Fairfax's Army, 1645–9," in John Adamson, ed., *The English Civil War* (London: Palgrave Macmillan, 2009), 175–201.

19. Leveller disillusionment with the Cromwellian republic of the early 1650s (merging at times with outbursts of royalist sentiment on the Far Right) is reassessed in comparative historical terms in Stone, *The Anatomy of Revolution Revisited*, 372–75.

20. John Adamson, "The Frighted Junto: Perceptions of Ireland, and the Last Attempts at Settlement with Charles I," in J. Peacey, ed., *The Regicides and the Execution of Charles I*, 39–40. Adamson has enlarged upon these issues subsequently in *The Noble Revolt: The Overthrow of Charles I* (London: Palgrave Macmillan, 2007).

21. Adamson, "The Frighted Junto," 38. Obviously, as a member of the East Anglian lesser gentry himself, Cromwell would hardly be advocating a genuinely *social* upheaval in the midst of all of these developments.

22. Ian Gentles, *Oliver Cromwell: God's Warrior and the English Revolution* (New York: Palgrave Macmillan, 2011), 78–79.

23. John Morrill and Philip Baker, "Oliver Cromwell, the Regicide, and the Sons of Zeruiah," in J. Peacey, ed., *The Regicides and the Execution of Charles I*, 30. Morrill and Baker summed up the situation the regicides-to-be faced in terms presaging those of Gentles: "An uncooperative parliament, a divided and volatile army, a resentful, hungry, and hostile populace, all of Scotland and 90 per cent of Ireland in the hands of men implacably opposed to the king's trial and deposition and two of Charles' nephews ruling France and the Netherlands." Ibid.

24. D. Alan Orr, "The Juristic Foundation of Regicide," in ibid., 121. See also, in this connection, two works by Quentin Skinner: *Foundations of Modern Political Thought*, two volumes (Cambridge: Cambridge University Press, 1978), and *Liberty Before Liberalism* (Cambridge: Cambridge University Press, 1998). The case of protobureaucratic statism in early modern England is treated by Michael J. Braddick, *State Formation in Early Modern England, c. 1550–1700* (Cambridge: Cambridge University Press, 2000), and is taken up further in comparative revolutionary theory by Stone, *The Anatomy of Revolution Revisited*, 14–17.

25. As Orr has pointed out in "The Juristic Foundation of Regicide," 130–33.

26. Patrick Collinson, "The Monarchical Republic of Queen Elizabeth I," *Bulletin of the John Rylands Library* LXIX (1987), 406.

27. Patricia Crawford, "Charles Stuart, that Man of Blood," *Journal of British Studies* 16 (1977), esp. 61. Charles himself turned to the concept later on in expressing remorse over his role in Strafford's execution, and wishing to attach "blood guilt" to those parliamentarians who had brought a bill of attainder against him. See also, on the notion of "blood guilt," Christopher Hill, "The Man of Blood," in *The English Bible and the Seventeenth-Century Revolution* (London: Allen Lane, 1993), 324–31.

28. Sarah Barber, *Regicide and Republicanism* (Edinburgh: Edinburgh University Press, 1998), esp. 86, 100–01, 111–12.

29. In Scott's words: "it would be foolish to presuppose too sharp a distinction between . . . civil and religious motives for regicide. Anti-monarchical ideas could in some cases provide a complementary rather than an alternative source of inspiration to that derived from biblical exegesis." David Scott, "Motives for King-Killing," in J. Peacey, ed., *The Regicides and the Execution of Charles I*, 147–48.

30. Citations are from Morrill and Baker, "Oliver Cromwell, the Regicide, and the Sons of Zeruiah," ibid., 15, 31–32.

31. Cromwell's letter cited in Ashton, *Counter-Revolution: The Second Civil War and Its Origins*, 423.

32. Morrill and Baker, "Oliver Cromwell, the Regicide, and the Sons of Zeruiah," 26. The distinction between the "first" and "second" civil wars, accentuated by Cromwell himself at the time, has naturally featured prominently in nearly all subsequent accounts of this critical period. But so has the impact upon Oliver of the intercepted royal correspondence. See, for example, Ashton, *Counter-Revolution: The Second Civil War and Its Origins*, esp. 30–36; and Austin Woolrych, *Soldiers and Statesmen: The General Council of the Army and Its Debates, 1647–48* (Oxford: Clarendon, 1987), esp. 268–76, 305–06.

33. C. V. Wedgwood, *The Trial of Charles I* (London: Collins, 1964), 83. David Underdown a few years later was to register substantial disagreement with this straightforward (if, in relative terms, not-very-nuanced) assessment of the situation in *Pride's Purge*, esp. in chapters 6 and 7.

34. Morrill and Baker, "Oliver Cromwell, the Regicide, and the Sons of Zeruiah," 29.

35. See Sean Kelsey, "The Trial of Charles I," *English Historical Review* 118 (2003), esp. 515–16. Kelsey had already developed a similar argument in "Staging the Trial of Charles I," in J. Peacey, ed., *The Regicides and the Execution of Charles I*, 71–93.

36. Scott, "Motives for King-Killing," in ibid., 153.

37. Scott, ibid., 152–53. For further reflections about Scottish calculations in all of this, see David Stevenson, "The Early Covenanters and the Federal Union of Britain," in R. A. Mason, ed., *Scotland and England 1286–1815* (Edinburgh: John Donald, 1987), esp. 175–76; and John Morrill, "The English, the Scots, and the British," in P. S. Hodge, ed., *Scotland and the Union* (Edinburgh: Edinburgh University Press, 1994), 82.

38. Adamson, "The Frighted Junto," in J. Peacey, ed., *The Regicides and the Execution of Charles I*, 43–44. For additional details on all this, consult Simon Groenveld, "The English Civil War as a Cause of the First Anglo-Dutch War, 1640–1652," *Historical Journal* 30 (1987), 566; and Jonathan Israel, *The Dutch Republic: Its Rise, Greatness, and Fall, 1477–1806* (Oxford: Oxford University Press, 1995), esp. 595–609.

39. Adamson, "The Frighted Junto," 62.

40. Ian Gentles, *Oliver Cromwell: God's Warrior and the English Revolution*, 79–80.

41. Ibid. On the other hand, it was equally the case that any joint intervention in English affairs at the last moment on Charles I's behalf by the French and Spanish (who were still locking horns in grand style on the Continent) was as well-nigh inconceivable as, in the later revolution, would be any intervention on the part of Britain, Prussia, and Austria to save Louis XVI. On the former situation, see Richard Bonney, "The European Reaction to the Trial and Execution of Charles I," in J. Peacey, *The Regicides and the Execution of Charles I*, 247–79, who largely confirms the earlier findings of C. V. Wedgwood, "European Reaction to the Death of Charles I," in C. H. Carter, ed., *From the Renaissance to the Counter-Reformation: Essays in Honor of Garrett Mattingly* (London: Jonathan Cope, 1966), 401–16. On the latter situation, see Bailey Stone, *Reinterpreting the French Revolution: A Global-Historical Perspective* (Cambridge: Cambridge University Press, 2002), 171–72.

42. D. Alan Orr, "The Juristic Foundation of Regicide," 128.

43. Cook's words are cited from Lagomarsino and Wood, eds., *The Trial of Charles I: A Documentary History*, 63.

44. Sarah Barber, *Regicide and Republicanism*, 133–35.

45. Michael Walzer, ed., *Regicide and Revolution: Speeches at the Trial of Louis XVI*, trans. Marian Rothstein (Cambridge: Cambridge University Press, 1974), 13–14. Walzer recapitulated his analysis in "The King's Trial and the Political Culture of the Revolution," in Colin Lucas, ed., *The French Revolution and the Creation of Modern Political Culture*, four volumes (Oxford: Pergamon Press, 1987–1994), volume 2, 184–90. Those readers wishing access to an original source on the trial need to consult the *Archives Parlementaires de 1787 à 1860 . . . première série* (Paris: 1899), esp. 54–56, and should also refer to Albert Soboul, ed., *Le Procès de Louis XVI* (Paris: Collection Archives, 1966), for a useful survey of original documents on the subject.

46. I have summed up much of the evidence to this effect in *Reinterpreting the French Revolution*, esp. 81–86. Much more detail on the subject is convincingly laid out in Munro Price, "The 'Ministry of the Hundred Hours': A Reappraisal," *French History* 4 (1990): 317–39; and in John Hardman, *Louis XVI* (New Haven, CT: Yale University Press, 1993), esp. 145, 149–53.

47. Munro Price, *The Fall of the French Monarchy: Louis XVI, Marie Antoinette and the Baron de Breteuil* (London: Macmillan, 2002), 367.

48. Ibid., 366.

49. Walzer, *Regicide and Revolution*, 42–43. The *Conventionnels* had also to deal (as had the parliamentarians in the English Revolution) with the medieval conception of the "King's two Bodies." For the Jacobins, as earlier for the Independents, trying and executing a king meant dealing with his "immortal" Body Politic as well as with his mortal Body Personal. See, on this, Susan Dunn, *The Deaths of Louis XVI: Regicide and the French Political Imagination* (Princeton, NJ: Princeton University Press, 1994), esp. 16–17.

50. Alison Patrick, *The Men of the First French Republic: Political Alignments in the National Convention of 1792* (Baltimore: Johns Hopkins University Press, 1972), 43. Walzer said much the same thing in his *Regicide and Revolution*, 45–46.

51. Patrick, *The Men of the First French Republic*, 43–44. The constitutional difficulties encountered by those lawyer-deputies desiring to get at the king through proper judicial procedure are also reviewed by Ferenc Fehér, *The Frozen Revolution: An Essay on Jacobinism* (Cambridge: Cambridge University Press, 1987), 104–05. As for trying Louis XVI by the "law of nature," as was the intention of some of the more theoretically inclined deputies, see Dan Edelstein, *The Terror of Natural Right: Republicanism, the Cult of Nature, and the French Revolution* (Chicago: University of Chicago Press, 2009), esp. 146–58.

52. Walzer, *Regicide and Revolution*, 46. Walzer followed up this observation by showing (in chapter 4) how the revolutionaries utilized "contract theory" as an alternative legal foundation upon which to base their prosecution of Louis XVI.

53. Patrick, *The Men of the First French Republic*, 51–52.

54. Ibid., 54.

55. Ibid., 70. Perhaps (in hindsight, which seems always to be so clairvoyant), some of the *Conventionnels* should have been equally mindful of Spartan and ruthless visionaries in their midst such as Louis-Antoine Saint-Just and Maximilien Robespierre!

56. David P. Jordan, *The King's Trial: The French Revolution versus Louis XVI* (Berkeley, CA: University of California Press, 1979), 59–61. Patrick said much the same thing, if a bit less forthrightly: see *The Men of the First French Republic*, esp. 39–82. Older but still useful studies of the Girondists include M. J. Sydenham, *The Girondins* (London: Athlone Press, 1961), and B. Melchior-Bonnet, *Les Girondins* (Paris: 1969).

57. Jordan, *The King's Trial*, 159–60.

58. The standard work here remains Albert Soboul, *The Sans-Culottes: The Popular Movement and Revolutionary Government, 1793-1794*, trans. Rémy Inglis Hall (Princeton, NJ: Princeton University Press, 1980). But refer also to George Rudé, *The Crowd in the French Revolution* (Oxford: Clarendon Press, 1959); and Richard Cobb, "The Revolutionary Mentality in France," *History* 42 (1957): 181–96.

59. The best analysis of the Girondists' political miscalculations in the first year (1792–1793) of the National Convention remains Patrick, *The Men of the First French Republic*, passim. But see also, in this connection, Patrick, "Political Divisions in the French National Convention, 1792-93," *Journal of Modern History* 41 (1969): 421–74; Gary Kates, *The Cercle Social, the Girondins, and the French Revolution* (Princeton, NJ: Princeton University Press, 1985); and Morris Slavin, *The Making of an Insurrection: Parisian Sections and the Gironde* (Cambridge, MA: Harvard University Press, 1986).

60. Patrick, *The Men of the First French Republic*, 71. The reader will recall, here, that precisely the same line of argumentation had been adduced in revolutionary England to save the life of Charles I!

61. Ibid., 73. Jacques-Pierre Brissot, in a speech to the Convention of 12 January, notably elaborated on all the likely reasons for growing British hostility to the French—none of which had much at all to do with Louis XVI's fate. Modern diplomatic historians in the French tradition have tended in general to second Brissot's analysis. See, for example, Jeremy Black, *British Foreign Policy in an Age of Revolutions, 1783–1793* (New York: Cambridge University Press, 1994), esp. 461–63; and T. C. W. Blanning, *The Origins of the French Revolutionary Wars* (London: Longman, 1986), 138.

62. See, for examples of this work, Dale K. Van Kley, *The Damiens Affair and the Unraveling of the Ancien Régime, 1750–1770* (Princeton, NJ: Princeton University Press, 1984); Jeffrey W. Merrick, *The Desacralization of the French Monarchy in the Eighteenth Century* (Baton Rouge: Louisiana State University Press, 1990); and Roger Chartier, *The Cultural Origins of the French Revolution*, trans. Lydia G. Cochrane (Durham, NC: Duke University Press, 1991), esp. chapter 6, "A Desacralized King."

63. Walzer, *Regicide and Revolution*, 32.

64. Ibid.

65. Robert Darnton, *The Literary Underground of the Old Regime* (Cambridge, MA: Harvard University Press, 1982), 205.

66. Timothy Tackett, *When the King Took Flight* (Cambridge, MA: Harvard University Press, 2003), 204–06, 222–23. Similar assessments are provided in John Hardman, *Louis XVI: The Silent King* (London: Arnold, 2000), chapter 10; and in Munro Price, *The Fall of the French Monarchy*, chapter 8.

67. Tackett, *When the King Took Flight*, 124–29.

68. This is especially well covered in Blanning, *Origins of the French Revolution Wars*, 98–99. On the political dilemma posed by all of this for the Feuillant deputies attempting to defend the monarchy—a dilemma that, in many ways, foreshadowed the dilemma of the Brissotins-become-Girondists in the Convention—see Georges Michon, *Essai sur l'histoire du parti feuillant: Adrien Duport* (Paris: Payot, 1924); and Michael L. Kennedy, *The Jacobin Clubs in the French Revolution: The First Years* (Princeton, NJ: Princeton University Press, 1982), passim.

69. In this connection, the reader should consult the many articles of Thomas E. Kaiser. Two especially outstanding examples: "Who's Afraid of Marie-Antoinette? Diplomacy, Austrophobia and the Queen," *French History* 14 (2000): 241–71; and "From the Austrian Committee to the Foreign Plot: Marie-Antoinette, Austrophobia, and the Terror," *French Historical Studies* 26 (2003): 579–617.

70. See, again, Price, *The Fall of the French Monarchy*, esp. 314–18; and Hardman, *Louis XVI: The Silent King*, esp. 158–59. Hardman quite correctly faults historians such as David Jordan and Susan Dunn for stating that the infamous *armoire* actually contained the king's secret correspondence with the Austrians, but, in any case, the impact of the discovery on the *Conventionnels* was essentially the same, for it was all too obvious to them that Louis XVI's *domestic* correspondents *had* been "counterrevolutionaries," and that both king and queen had long been intriguing against the revolution.

71. Price, *The Fall of the French Monarchy*, 318.

72. Patrick, *The Men of the First French Republic*, 40–41.

73. Walzer, *Regicide and Revolution*, 66–67.

74. Patrick, *The Men of the First French Republic*, 72.

75. Saint-Just is cited in Walzer, *Regicide and Revolution*, 21, 23.

76. Robespierre is cited in ibid., 131–32.

77. Robespierre is cited in ibid., 132, 138.

78. Further discussion of this later address does not fall within the purview of our study. See, however, these commentaries on the subject: Robert R. Palmer, *Twelve Who Ruled: The Year of the Terror in the French Revolution* (Princeton, NJ: Princeton University Press, 1941), 264–66; George Rudé, *Robespierre: Portrait of a Revolutionary Democrat* (New York: Viking Press, 1975), 113–15, 198; David P. Jordan, "The Robespierre Problem," 17–34, and Norman Hampson, "Robespierre and the Terror," 155–73, found in Colin Haydon and William Doyle, eds., *Robespierre* (Cambridge: Cambridge University Press, 1999); and also Dan Edelstein, "Do We Want a Revolution without Revolution? Reflections on Political Authority," *French Historical Studies* 35 (2012): 269–89. Robespierre provided further insights into his political/constitutional philosophy in a subsequent address of February 5, 1794, and it, too, has occasioned considerable scholarly commentary, most recently in Dan Edelstein's article in *French Historical Studies*, cited earlier in this footnote.

79. Ibid., 280–84. Edelstein's argument here is more convincing than that adduced in his 2009 study, which saw "natural right" as being "widely accepted" by the *Conventionnels* as providing the "legal grounds for trying Louis XVI." Edelstein's 2009 sample of delegates, although suggestive, still represented only a small proportion of the Convention's membership. Again, Edelstein himself admitted that, even for many of the deputies sampled here, "natural right" was only one of a number of concepts cited as justifying a trial of the ex-monarch. See Edelstein, *The Terror of Natural Right*, 146–58. For a searching appraisal of Edelstein's 2009 monograph, consult Marisa Linton's book review in the *American Historical Review* 116 (2011): 403–06.

80. Patrick, *The Men of the First French Republic*, 49. Patrick also points out (p. 50) that, in his only other major address on this subject, Robespierre seemed quite resigned to a formal judicial procedure. As she notes, this may in part have reflected his realization that some deputies on the Right were (for their own reasons) as opposed to the notion of a trial as were

advanced Jacobin theorists on the Left. The only certain way to frustrate delaying tactics on the Right, in other words, was to press ahead with a formal judicial prosecution of the *ci-devant* king, whatever its theoretical shortcomings in advanced Jacobin eyes.

81. Walzer, *Regicide and Revolution*, 77. It is interesting that Louis XVI, unlike Charles I, did not carry his scorn for the proceedings initiated against him to the point of refusing legal counsel; hence, the courageous efforts of Raymond de Sèze, François-Denis Tronchet, and philosophic luminary Chrétien Guillaume de Lamoignon de Malesherbes to defend the king before the Convention. Yet, in Louis's case as in that of Charles I, accumulated evidence and circumstantial pressures combined to make a guilty verdict a foregone conclusion. John Hardman, in *Louis XVI: The Silent King*, chapter 12, presents a brief, readable account of the king's conduct during his trial.

82. Feher, *The Frozen Revolution: An Essay on Jacobinism*, 99–101.

83. Susan Dunn, *The Deaths of Louis XVI: Regicide and the French Political Imagination* (Princeton, NJ: Princeton University Press, 1994), esp. 165–70.

84. Ibid., 19–20.

85. Richard Pipes, *The Russian Revolution* (New York: Alfred A. Knopf, 1990), 745–46. Inexplicably, Michael Walzer, in *Regicide and Revolution*, 80, gives the date of the Imperial family's demise as "May of 1919," rather than (as we all know) the night of July 16–17, 1918. Pipes drew much of his information from a carbon copy of the inquiry of the Commission which, under the direction of Nicholas A. Sokolov, revisited the subject of the 1918 murders during the 1920s. It may be consulted today in Harvard University's Houghton Library.

86. This discussion draws upon Pipes, *The Russian Revolution*, chapter 17; Orlando Figes, *A People's Tragedy: The Russian Revolution, 1891-1924* (New York: Penguin Books, 1996), esp. 635–42; and Mark D. Steinberg and V. M. Khrustalev, *The Fall of the Romanovs: Political Dreams and Personal Struggles in a Time of Revolution* (New Haven, CT: Yale University Press, 1995), passim.

87. Figes, *A People's Tragedy*, 11–12. For some of the most useful scholarship on the myths and symbolism surrounding the institution of tsardom in Russia, see Richard Wortman, "Invisible Threads: The Historical Imagery of the Romanov Tercentenary," *Russian History* 16 (1989): 2–4; and, by the same author, *Scenarios of Power: Myth and Ceremony in Russian Monarchy* (Princeton, NJ: Princeton University Press, 1995).

88. Helen Rappaport, *The Last Days of the Romanovs: Tragedy at Ekaterinburg* (New York: St. Martin's Press, 2008), 136–37.

89. Orlando Figes, in *A People's Tragedy*, 125–38, provides a good overview of these theorists, terrorists, and would-be revolutionaries. But see also, in this connection, Martin Malia, *Alexander Herzen and the Birth of Russian Socialism* (Cambridge, MA: Harvard University Press, 1961); Richard Pipes, ed., *The Russian Intelligentsia* (New York: Columbia University Press, 1969); Isaiah Berlin, *Russian Thinkers* (New York: Viking Press, 1978); and Abbott Gleason, *Young Russia: The Genesis of Russian Radicalism in the 1860s* (New York: Viking Press, 1980).

90. Cited in Figes, *A People's Tragedy*, 132.

91. Orlando Figes and Boris Kolonitskii, *Interpreting the Russian Revolution: The Language and Symbols of 1917* (New Haven, CT: Yale University Press, 1994). On the mounting difficulties facing the Russian Army by late 1916 and early 1917, see Allan K. Wildman, *The End of the Russian Imperial Army: The Old Army and the Soldiers' Revolt (March–April 1917)* (Princeton, NJ: Princeton University Press, 1980), esp. 105–20; David R. Jones, "Imperial Russia's Forces at War," in Allan R. Millett and Williamson Murray, eds., *Military Effectiveness I: The First World War* (Boston: Allen and Unwin, 1988), 284–85; and John W. Steinberg, *All the Tsar's Men: Russia's General Staff and the Fate of the Empire, 1898–1914* (Baltimore: Johns Hopkins University Press, 2010), passim.

92. On this scandal, and its deleterious impact on the Imperial family, see R. K. Massie, *Nicholas and Alexandra* (New York: Athenaeum, 1967), esp. 152, 299, 346–47; and George Katkov, *Russia, 1917: The February Revolution* (London: Longman, 1967), 157–60.

93. Rex A. Wade, *The Russian Revolution, 1917* (Cambridge: Cambridge University Press, 2000), 22.

94. Ibid. On Miliukov's role in all of this in 1916–1917, refer to Thomas Riha, *A Russian European: Paul Miliukov in Russian Politics* (South Bend, IN: Notre Dame University Press, 1969); and, especially, Melissa K. Stockdale, *Paul Miliukov and the Quest for a Liberal Russia* (Ithaca, NY: Cornell University Press, 1996).

95. Figes and Kolonitskii, *Interpreting the Russian Revolution*, 158–64. Figes enlarges on all this in *A People's Tragedy*, 284–85: "Condemning the court as 'German' was a way of defining and legitimizing . . . revolutionary anger as the patriotic mood of 'the nation,' as if all the country's problems were due to the evil influence of a few highly placed foreigners and could be solved by getting rid of them. The February Revolution of 1917 was identified as a patriotic revolution."

96. Wildman, *The End of the Russian Imperial Army*, 114–15.

97. Refer again in this connection to Edelstein, "Do We Want a Revolution without Revolution? Reflections on Political Authority," esp. 278–89.

98. Refer to Mark D. Steinberg and V. M. Khrustalev, *The Fall of the Romanovs: Political Dreams and Personal Struggles in a Time of Revolution*, 116–17.

99. Richard Pipes cites these words (*The Russian Revolution*, 763) directly from Trotsky's diary. The reader may consult the original entry (from April 9, 1935) in Trotsky Archive, Houghton Library, Harvard University, bMS/Russ 13, T-3731, 110. Orlando Figes also comments upon this reminiscence in *A People's Tragedy*, 636–37. So do Isaac Deutscher in his classic biography of Trotsky, *The Prophet Armed: Trotsky 1879-1921*, second edition (Oxford: Oxford University Press, 1970), 418, and Robert Service, in *Trotsky: A Biography* (Cambridge, MA: Harvard Belknap Press, 2009), 431. Service (and others) have claimed that Trotsky's desire for such a trial was in part thwarted by the rivalry between himself and Lenin's right-hand man Yakov Sverdlov, at that time chair of the executive of the All-Russian Congress of Soviets (*VTsIK*), but this point remains contested. As we will see later on, more basic issues were also at stake in this situation.

100. Figes, *A People's Tragedy*, 636–37.

101. On this specific point, see the following: Pipes, *The Russian Revolution*, 747; and Rappaport, *The Last Days of the Romanovs*, 133–37. Rappaport seems especially skeptical about Lenin's and Sverdlov's intentions on this question, writing as she does of "the smokescreen of a 'trial' for the Tsar."

102. Steinberg and Khrustalev, *The Fall of the Romanovs: Political Dreams and Personal Struggles in a Time of Revolution*, 123.

103. Ibid., 125–26.

104. Ibid., 176–77. For more excellent research on, specifically, the revolutionary political culture in the soviets and other popular bodies during 1917–1918, see John Keep, *The Russian Revolution: A Study in Mass Mobilization* (New York: Norton, 1976), esp. 118–19; Oskar Anweiler, *The Soviets: The Russian Workers, Peasants, and Soldiers' Councils, 1905–1921*, trans. Ruth Hein (New York: Pantheon, 1974); and Michael Melancon, "Soldiers, Peasant-Soldiers, Peasant-Workers and Their Organizations in Petrograd: Ground-Level Revolution in the Early Months of 1917," *Soviet and Post-Soviet Review* 23 (1996): 161–90.

105. Steinberg and Khrustalev, *The Fall of the Romanovs*, 281–83.

106. Ibid, 281.

107. See, for examples of this literature, R. K. Massie, *The Romanovs: The Final Chapter* (New York: Random House, 1995), esp. 12–14; Pipes, *The Russian Revolution*, 780–81; and Rappaport, *The Last Days of the Romanovs*, 156–57.

108. Ibid.

109. Pipes, *The Russian Revolution*, 780–81. Although, interestingly, Pipes interprets the Kaiser's inaction on the Romanov cause in 1918 as stemming, at least in part, from his fear of possible left-wing partisan sabotage of the German war effort. This argument warrants further attention from specialists on wartime Imperial Germany.

110. Steinberg and Khrustalev, *The Fall of the Romanovs*, 288–90. Broader discussions of these issues, and of their implications for Bolshevik survival in Russia, are provided by Richard K. Debo, *Revolution and Survival: The Foreign Policy of Soviet Russia, 1917–1918* (Toronto: University of Toronto Press, 1979); Evan Mawdsley, *The Russian Civil War* (Boston: Allen and Unwin, 1987); and W. Bruce Lincoln, *Red Victory: A History of the Russian Civil War*

(New York: Simon and Schuster, 1989). The best study of the Treaty of Brest-Litovsk is still, after all these years, John Wheeler-Bennett, *The Forgotten Peace: Brest-Litovsk, March 1918* (New York: William Morrow, 1939).

111. Steinberg and Khrustalev, *The Fall of the Romanovs*, 290.

112. Trotsky's entry cited in Pipes, *The Russian Revolution*, 770. Whether or not the actual order for the murder of Nicholas II came from Moscow or from Urals militants at Ekaterinburg has given rise to scholarly controversy in itself. Pipes's version of events is strongly endorsed by Dominic Lieven in *Nicholas II: Emperor of All the Russias* (London: John Murray, 1993), 242, and also (in so many words) by Helen Rappaport in *The Last Days of the Romanovs*, chapter 10, and Orlando Figes (*A People's Tragedy*, 638–39). Yet it is seriously challenged in some of its details by Steinberg and Khrustalev (*The Fall of the Romanovs*, 293–94). In a sense, however, this would seem to be a classic case of a "distinction without much of a difference," at least for most scholars: by July 1918, given all of the converging ideological, political-cultural, and circumstantial factors in place, a swift and non-judicial regicide was most likely all but unavoidable.

113. Cited in Pipes, *The Russian Revolution*, 787.

114. Figes, *A People's Tragedy*, 639–40.

115. Most notably by Pipes, *The Russian Revolution*, 787–88; Edvard Radzinsky, *The Last Tsar: The Life and Death of Nicholas II* (London: Doubleday, 1992), esp. 304–05, 326, 330–31; and Rappaport, *The Last Days of the Romanovs*, 141.

116. Cited in Edelstein, "Do We Want a Revolution without Revolution? Reflections on Political Authority," 282.

117. Sarah Barber, *Regicide and Republicanism*, 133–35.

118. Ferenc Fehér, *The Frozen Revolution: An Essay on Jacobinism*, esp. 108–11. Susan Dunn has reasoned along strikingly similar lines in *The Deaths of Louis XVI*, 165–70. See also, in this connection, Clifford Geertz, "Centers, Kings, and Charisma," in S. Wilentz, ed., *Rites of Power* (Philadelphia: University of Philadelphia Press, 1985), esp. 30; and Hannah Arendt, *On Revolution* (New York: Viking Press, 1963), passim.

119. Pipes, *The Russian Revolution*, 788. The reader will encounter similar language in Radzinsky, *The Last Tsar*, 304–05, 330–31; and in Rappaport, *The Last Days of the Romanovs*, 141. Orlando Figes also links the murders of the Romanovs with the onset of the Red Terror in Russia—if in somewhat more measured tones. For this, consult *A People's Tragedy*, 640–41.

120. In this context, Helen Rappaport writes that "Lenin . . . never thought in terms of individuals, only in terms of the bigger picture—entire classes and groups . . . he was impatient to see all these class enemies wiped out wholesale, destroyed at the root. Not quite genocide but a new kind of necessary, ideological murder, in defence of the greater good of the proletariat. Under his successor, Stalin, it would be perfected on the grand scale." Rappaport, *The Last Days of the Romanovs*, 141. Additionally, as I have pointed out in *The Anatomy of Revolution Revisited*, 13, theorists of comparative revolution such as Martin Malia and Noel Parker have naturally enough focused on the twentieth-century tendency of the revolutionary tradition (with its accompanying "terroristic" and totalitarian aspects) to "migrate" from more technologically and socioeconomically advanced societies to societies less fully developed along those lines—meaning, presumably, from Russia to China and beyond.

4. CIRCUMSTANCES VERSUS IDEAS IN THE REVOLUTIONARY "FURIES"

1. As quoted from Arno Mayer, *The Furies: Violence and Terror in the French and Russian Revolutions* (Princeton: Princeton University Press, 2000), 96–99. Crane Brinton, in his *Anatomy of Revolution* (esp. 198 and 203) had found in all his "reigns of terror and virtue" the "same set of variables . . . all woven together in a complicated pattern of reality" and all of them "in constant interaction one with another, a change in one effecting complex correspond-

ing changes in all the others, and hence in the total situation." I take up Brinton's multi-factoral analysis in somewhat greater detail in *The Anatomy of Revolution Revisited*, 318.

2. Mayer, *The Furies*, 96–99.

3. See Richard T. Bienvenu's article on "Terror" in Samuel F. Scott and Barry Rothaus, eds., *Historical Dictionary of the French Revolution, 1789-1799* (Westwood, CT: Greenwood Press, 1985), 942–46. Bienvenu chronicles the creation—well *before* September 1793—of much of the machinery of what would become the revolutionary government's terrorist campaign of late 1793 and 1794.

4. On all these measures, see also Norman Hampson, *A Social History of the French Revolution* (Toronto: University of Toronto Press, 1963), esp. 168–69. They are also handled masterfully in R. R. Palmer, *Twelve Who Ruled: The Year of the Terror in the French Revolution* (Princeton: Princeton University Press, 1941).

5. Donald Greer, *The Incidence of the Terror during the French Revolution: A Statistical Interpretation* (Cambridge, MA: Harvard University Press, 1935), 114.

6. Ibid., 111–12. For some informed (but hardly devastating) critiques of Greer's work, see Richard Louis, "The Incidence of the Terror: A Critique of a Statistical Interpretation," *French Historical Studies* 3 (1964): 379–89; and Gilbert Shapiro and John Markoff, "The Incidence of the Terror: Some Lessons for Quantitative History," *Journal of Social History* 9 (1975): 193–218.

7. Karl Roider, Jr., *Baron Thugut and Austria's Response to the French Revolution* (Princeton: Princeton University Press, 1987), 131–35. On Austria's vulnerability vis-à-vis Russia and Prussia in this period, consult also Geoffrey Bruun, "The Balance of Power during the Wars, 1793–1814," in *The New Cambridge Modern History, Volume 9: War and Peace in an Age of Upheaval, 1793–1830* (Cambridge: Cambridge University Press, 1965), 250–74; and, more recently, Michael Hochedlinger, *Austria's Wars of Emergence, 1683–1797* (London: Longman, 2003).

8. On these calculations at London, see T. C. W. Blanning, *The Origins of the French Revolutionary Wars* (London: Longman, 1996), 138.

9. Jeremy Black, *British Foreign Policy in an Age of Revolutions, 1783–1793* (New York: Cambridge University Press, 1994), 470.

10. See Tim LeGoff and Don Sutherland, "The Revolution and the Rural Community in Eighteenth-Century Brittany," *Past and Present* 62 (1974): 96–119. Sutherland has enlarged on all of this in *The Chouans: The Social Origins of Popular Counter-Revolution in Upper Brittany, 1770–1796* (Oxford: Clarendon Press, 1982). A recent synthesis is provided by Jean-Clément Martin, "The Vendée, *Chouannerie*, and the State," in Peter McPhee, ed., *A Companion to the French Revolution* (Oxford: Wiley-Blackwell, 2013), 246–59.

11. Harvey Mitchell, "Resistance to the Revolution in Western France," *Past and Present* 63 (1974): 122. But refer again to the studies and syntheses of LeGoff, Sutherland, and Jean-Clément Martin cited in n. 10 for similar analyses of the dynamics of local (and, most notably, rural) opposition to the revolution.

12. Paul Hanson, *The Jacobin Republic Under Fire: The Federalist Revolt in the French Revolution* (University Park, PA: Pennsylvania State University Press, 2003), 244. See also, on this subject, the earlier article of synthesis by Bill Edmonds, "Federalism and Urban Revolt in France in 1793," *Journal of Modern History* 55 (1983): 22–53.

13. P. M. Jones, *The Peasantry in the French Revolution* (Cambridge: Cambridge University, 1988), 207, 223–24. Peasant attitudes toward the government are also studied (in much greater depth) in John Markoff, *The Abolition of Feudalism: Peasants, Lords and Legislators in the French Revolution* (University Park, PA: Pennsylvania State University Press, 1996).

14. Mayer, *The Furies*, 329. This, despite Mayer's earlier suggestion that the "religious element" was also central to this conflict's genesis. Although the classic study of the Vendée remains Charles Tilly, *The Vendée* (Cambridge, MA: Harvard University Press, 1964), readers should also consult the latest work of Jean-Clément Martin: for instance, *La Vendée et la France* (Paris: Seuil, 1987), and *La Vendée et la Révolution: Accepter le mémoire pour écrire l'histoire* (Paris: Perrin, 2007).

15. See Greer, *The Incidence of the Terror*, esp. 38–70, for all of this information.

16. Ibid., esp. 105–10, on the *social* incidence of the Terror.

17. Refer again to Shapiro and Markoff, "The Incidence of the Terror," 193–218. As noted earlier, Louie's article had appeared in *French Historical Studies* 3 (1964): 379–89.

18. See, on all of this, Palmer, *Twelve Who Ruled*, 55–58.

19. The situation at Bordeaux is taken up by Alan Forrest, *Society and Politics in Revolutionary Bordeaux* (New York: Oxford University Press, 1975), 113–14. See also Forrest's more recent studies: *The Revolution in Provincial France: Aquitaine 1789-1799* (Oxford: Oxford University Press, 1996); and *Paris, the Provinces and the French Revolution* (London: Arnold, 2004).

20. For the situation at Marseilles, see William Scott, *Terror and Repression in Revolutionary Marseilles* (London: Macmillan, 1973). On revolutionary (and counterrevolutionary) politics at nearby Toulon, consult M. H. Crook, "Federalism and the French Revolution: the Revolt of Toulon in 1793," *History* 65 (1980): 383–97.

21. Refer here to Bill Edmunds, *Jacobinism and the Revolt of Lyon, 1789-1793* (Oxford: Clarendon Press, 1990), esp. 282–83.

22. For the situation at Toulouse, refer to Martyn Lyons, *Revolution in Toulouse: An Essay on Provincial Terrorism* (Berne: Peter Lang, 1978), esp. 131–33.

23. See again Greer, *The Incidence of the Terror*, esp. 115–28.

24. Ibid., 126–28. For Brinton's earlier description of Jacobins such as Robespierre, Saint Just, Couthon, Billaud Varenne, Collot d'Herbois, etc., as "fanatics of the religion of humanity," refer to *The Jacobins: An Essay in the New History* (New York: Macmillan Co., 1930), esp. 218–22, 231–42.

25. Greer, *The Incidence of the Terror*, 122–23.

26. Ibid., 118–19. On the especially ruthless activities of the "Popular Commission" at Orange, which convicted 432 individuals during the period from June 19 to August 4, consult David Andress, *The Terror: The Merciless War for Freedom in Revolutionary France* (New York: Farrar, Straus and Giraux, 2005), 294–96. Even at Paris, it should be stressed, about half of the guillotine's victims during the last two months of the Terror were *provinçiaux* who had been recently "shipped in" from the war-torn outer regions of France.

27. See François Furet, *Penser la Révolution française* (Paris: Gallimard, 1978). Translated into English by Elborg Forster as *Interpreting the French Revolution* (Cambridge: Cambridge University Press, 1981). An interesting "take" on Furet, his work, and his scholarly contemporaries in this period is provided by Michael Scott Christofferson, "An Antitotalitarian History of the French Revolution: François Furet's *Penser la Révolution française* in the Intellectual Politics of the Late 1970s," *French Historical Studies* 22 (1999): 557–611.

28. See Furet, "Terror," in François Furet and Mona Ozouf, eds., *A Critical Dictionary of the French Revolution*, trans. Arthur Goldhammer (Cambridge, MA: Harvard University Press, 1989), 146–50. He returned to the attack at the 1989 sessions of the American Historical Association. Refer to his contribution in "François Furet's Interpretation of the French Revolution," *French Historical Studies* 16 (1990): 792–802.

29. As one would expect, both Furet and Mona Ozouf tended to view the federalist revolt in several communities in the Midi (like the Terror itself) in primarily *ideological* terms. See their relevant articles in *A Critical Dictionary of the French Revolution*.

30. Prominent among those participants was Keith M. Baker. See Baker et al., eds., *The French Revolution and the Creation of Modern Political Culture*, four volumes (Oxford: Pergamon Press, 1987–1994); and Baker, *Inventing the French Revolution* (Cambridge: Cambridge University Press, 1990).

31. Arno Mayer (in *The Furies*, xiii–xiv) suggested, intriguingly, that the impassioned, often polemical debate over the Jacobin Terror may have "served as a screen" in 1989 for older arguments about certain aspects of France's traumatic twentieth-century experience—as well as reflecting more recent developments such as the decline of the Marxian explanatory paradigm, the advent of *glasnost* and *perestroika* in Gorbachev's Russia and in eastern Europe, and the advent of Thatcherite/Reaganite conservatism in the "Anglo-Saxon" West.

32. See Palmer, *Twelve Who Ruled* (bicentennial edition), 402. The reader here will note the irony of comparing Furet in *any* respect to his detested Marxist nemesis Albert Soboul—not to mention latter-day structuralists such as Theda Skocpol!

33. Refer to David Bien's remarks in "François Furet's Interpretation of the French Revolution," *French Historical Studies* 16 (1990): esp. 779–81.

34. See Sutherland's commentary in ibid., 784–91. In his contribution to this session, Furet said essentially nothing new, reiterating his argument that the *specific chronology of events* in 1793 precluded any circumstantial interpretation of the Terror, and insisting anew (as he already had insisted in his 1978 essay) that the Girondists had originally gone to war in April 1792 for *domestic* rather than geostrategic reasons. Ibid., 792–802.

35. Isser Woloch, "Review Article: On the Latent Illiberalism of the French Revolution," *American Historical Review* 95 (1990): esp. 1467–69. Significantly, Woloch in this book review singled out Palmer's *Twelve Who Ruled* for special praise, writing that the author had "explored the concept of "revolutionary necessity," neither swallowing it whole nor rejecting it categorically."

36. Consult, in this connection, "Forum: Comparing Revolutions: On Arno Mayer's *The Furies: Violence and Terror in the French and Russian Revolutions*," in *French Historical Studies* 24 (2001): 549–600. This forum, staged the preceding December at New York University, gave rise to a number of papers on the two upheavals, several of which were subsequently published either in *French Historical Studies* or in *The Journal of Modern History*.

37. For David Bell's commentary, see "Forum: Comparing Revolutions," esp. 561–63.

38. For Mayer's rejoinder to Bell (and others), refer to ibid., esp. 594, 597. Most intriguing among those commenting on Mayer's work at this forum was Timothy Tackett, whose linking of the French revolutionaries' "obsessive fear of conspiracy" in the early 1790s with an explanatory *thèse des circonstances* seems, in retrospect, to look forward to his latest book, *The Coming of the Terror in the French Revolution* (Cambridge, MA: Belknap Press of Harvard University Press, 2015). See "Forum: Comparing Revolutions," 577, for Tackett's remarks.

39. See Patrice Gueniffey, *La Politique de la Terreur: Essai sur la Violence Révolutionnaire, 1789–1794* (Paris: Fayard, 2000), esp. 1, 14–15, 226–27, 267. My translations here from the French.

40. See Sophie Wahnich, *La Liberté ou la mort: Essai sur la Terreur et le Terrorisme* (Paris: La Fabrique, 2003). Her book has recently been rendered into English as *In Defence of the Terror: Liberty or Death in the French Revolution*, trans. David Fernbach (London: Verso, 2012). Quotations are from the English translation, 63–65.

41. Ibid., 71–72.

42. See Keith M. Baker, "Transformations of Classical Republicanism in Eighteenth-Century France," *Journal of Modern History* 73 (2001): 32–53. Citations are from pp. 46 and 49.

43. See Dan Edelstein, *The Terror of Natural Right: Republicanism, the Cult of Nature, and the French Revolution* (Chicago: University of Chicago Press, 2009), esp. chapter 3. Edelstein has revisited this interpretation and pursued aspects of it in "Do We Want a Revolution without Revolution? Reflections on Political Authority," in *French Historical Studies* 35 (2012): 269–89.

44. For Edelstein's analysis here, see *The Terror of Natural Right*, 149.

45. For this consensus among British scholars regarding the use of the 1352 Statute of Treasons in 1649, see chapter 3 of the current volume, passim.

46. Again, see Edelstein, *The Terror of Natural Right*, 163–64. Moreover, Edelstein (in *Do We Want a Revolution without Revolution?*" esp. 282) seemed much more concerned with Robespierre's invocation of a transcendent "revolutionary authority" that "could be used to establish a normative framework for state action" overriding "constitutional and any other legal principles" than with reaffirming the significance, for the revolutionaries, of "natural law" or the "right of nations." Consult also Marisa Linton's reservations about Edelstein's 2009 study, as expressed in the *American Historical Review* 116 (2011): 403–06.

47. See Mary Ashburn Miller, *A Natural History of Revolution: Violence and Nature in the French Revolutionary Imagination, 1789-1794* (Ithaca: Cornell University Press, 2011), esp. 17–18, 166–67. In fairness to Miller, she *does* place her argument within the established historiographical binary of "circumstances vs. ideas."

48. See Marisa Linton's review of *A Natural History of Revolution* in *American Historical Review* 118 (2013): 600–01.

49. See Richard Cobb, *The Police and The People: French Popular Protest, 1789–1820* (Oxford: Oxford University Press, 1970), 87–90.

50. Timothy Tackett, *The Coming of the Terror in the French Revolution*, 348–49. See also, in this connection, the articles gathered in Peter Campbell, Thomas E. Kaiser, and Marisa Linton, eds., *Conspiracy in the French Revolution* (Manchester: University of Manchester Press, 2007); and Linton, "The Stuff of Nightmares: Plots, Assassinations and Duplicity in the Mental World of the Jacobin Leaders, 1793–1794," in David Andress, ed., *Experiencing the French Revolution* (Oxford: Oxford University Press, 2013), 201–17.

51. Mayer, *The Furies*, 311.

52. As cited in Geoff Swain, *The Origins of the Russian Civil War* (London: Longman, 1995), 257.

53. See Alter L. Litvin, "The Cheka," in Acton, Cherniaev, and Rosenberg, eds., *Critical Companion to the Russian Revolution*, 314–21.

54. Ibid., 314–16. See also, on the *Cheka*, George Leggett, *The Cheka: Lenin's Political Police* (Oxford: Oxford University Press, 1981); and C. M. Andrew and O. Gordievsky, *KGB: The Inside Story of its Foreign Operations from Lenin to Gorbachev* (London: Hodder and Stoughton, 1990).

55. David S. Foglesong, "Foreign Intervention," in Acton, Cherniaev, and Rosenberg, eds., *Critical Companion to the Russian Revolution*, 106–07.

56. John Wheeler-Bennett, *The Forgotten Peace: Brest-Litovsk, March 1918* (New York: William Morrow, 1939), 269–75. See chapter 7 for the military and political details of the treaty. Commercial aspects of Brest-Litovsk were to be fleshed out in later talks. Amazingly, perhaps, this is still the best source on the March 1918 "Peace."

57. Foglesong, "Foreign Intervention," 106–07. See also, on the Allied intervention in Russia, G. A. Brinkley, *The Volunteer Army and Allied Intervention in South Russia, 1917–1921* (Notre Dame, IN: University of Notre Dame Press, 1966); Evan Mawdsley, *The Russian Civil War* (Boston: Allen and Unwin, 1987); M. J. Carley, *Revolution and Intervention: The French Government and the Russian Civil War, 1917–1919* (Montreal: McGill-Queens University Press, 1983); W. Bruce Lincoln, *Red Victory: A History of the Russian Civil War* (New York: Simon and Schuster, 1989); and D. S. Foglesong, *America's Secret War Against Bolshevism: US Intervention in the Russian Civil War, 1917–1920* (Chapel Hill, NC: University of North Carolina Press, 1995).

58. Richard K. Debo, *Revolution and Survival: The Foreign Policy of Soviet Russia, 1917–1918* (Toronto: University of Toronto Press, 1979), 356–57.

59. For a vivid description of the Left SR uprising of early July 1918, consult Orlando Figes, *A People's Tragedy: The Russian Revolution 1891–1924* (New York: Penguin Books, 1998), 632–35. New doubts about the Left SR faction as a cohesive political force in 1918 and thereafter have been recently voiced (and, it must be admitted, very well documented) by Scott B. Smith, *Captives of Revolution: The Socialist Revolutionaries and the Bolshevik Dictatorship 1918–1923* (Pittsburgh, PA: University of Pittsburgh Press, 2011).

60. See, on this issue, Figes, *Peasant Russia, Civil War: The Volga Countryside in Revolution, 1917–1921* (Oxford: Oxford University Press, 1989), esp. 66–67, 81–83, 188–89; and the pioneering work by Teodor Shanin, *The Awkward Class: Political Sociology of Peasantry in a Developing Society, Russia, 1910–1925* (Oxford: Clarendon Press, 1972), esp. 145–62.

61. As cited in Debo, *Revolution and Survival*, 356–58. Richard Pipes claimed that the Red Terror "constituted from the start an essential element of the regime, which now intensified, now abated, but never disappeared, hanging like a permanent dark cloud over Soviet Russia." Pipes, *The Russian Revolution* (New York: Alfred A. Knopf, 1990), 789. Yet Evan Mawdsley, citing from a 1993 volume of statistical data on Red Army losses in this period, suggests a rather more definite end to the Terror in 1921. See Mawdsley, "The Civil War: The Military Campaigns," in Acton, Cherniaev, and Rosenberg, eds., *Critical Companion to the Russian Revolution*, 102–03.

62. A figure cited in Mayer, *The Furies*, 310.

63. Pipes, *The Russian Revolution*, 838.

64. Mayer, *The Furies*, 310. See also, on this question, Geoffrey Hosking, *The First Socialist Society: A History of the Soviet Union from Within* (Cambridge, MA: Harvard University Press, 1990), 71; and also Mawdsley, *The Russian Civil War*, 286.

65. Figes, *A People's Tragedy*, 642.

66. Ibid., 643.

67. In this instance, Lenin is cited in Marc Ferro, *October 1917: A Social History of the Russian Revolution* (London: Longman, 1980), 265.

68. These activities are graphically described in Litvin, "The Cheka," in Acton, Cherniaev, and Rosenberg, eds., *Critical Companion to the Russian Revolution*, 317–20.

69. Mawdsley, *The Russian Civil War*, 284–85.

70. This Seminar, "conceived initially by Moshe Lewin and Alfred Rieber of the University of Pennsylvania," we are informed, "brought together dozens of historians and political scientists to consider broad analytical problems that cut across the imagined dividing line of 1917" in Russian affairs. See Diane P. Koenker, William G. Rosenberg, and Ronald G. Suny, eds., *Party, State, and Society in the Russian Civil War: Explorations in Social History* (Bloomington: Indiana University Press, 1989), ix.

71. For these comments, see Sheila Fitzpatrick, "The Legacy of the Civil War," in ibid., esp. 387–88. Fitzpatrick's imposing corpus of works written in the new cultural mode includes: *The Commissariat of Enlightenment: Soviet Organization of Education and the Arts Under Lunacharsky, October 1917–1921* (Cambridge: Cambridge University Press, 1970); *The Cultural Front: Power and Culture in Revolutionary Russia* (Ithaca, NY: Cornell University Press, 1992); and *Tear off the Masks! Identity and Imposture in Twentieth-Century Russia* (Princeton: Princeton University Press, 2005).

72. Moshe Lewin, "The Civil War: Dynamics and Legacy," in Koenker, Rosenberg, and Suny, eds., *Party, State, and Society in the Russian Civil War*, 399–401.

73. Ibid., 403. Lewin's no-nonsense structuralist approach here carries all the more weight in that, like his fellow-historian Stephen F. Cohen, he has not been at all reticent over the years (in a highly revisionist mode) about excoriating Stalin and his henchmen for the later arbitrariness and evils of forced collectivization of peasant lands, animals, and agricultural equipment in the Soviet countryside.

74. In this connection, see again Mayer's rejoinder to his critics at the December 2000 NYU Forum: "Response," in "Forum: Comparing Revolutions: On Arno Mayer's *The Furies*," in *French Historical Studies* 24 (2001): 589–600.

75. For her comments on Mayer's work at this conference, see Fitzpatrick, "Vengeance and Ressentiment in the Russian Revolution," in ibid., 579–88.

76. For Rosenberg's contributions to this debate, see "Beheading the Revolution: Arno Mayer's 'Furies,'" *The Journal of Modern History* 73 (2001): esp. 911, 917, 930.

77. Cited from Pipes, *The Russian Revolution*, 789–90.

78. For these contradictory remarks by Pipes, see ibid., 816, 821, 556n., respectively. Some of the same contradictions marred Alter Litvin's commentary on the *Cheka* in Acton, Cherniaev, and Rosenberg, eds., *Critical Companion to the Russian Revolution*. "By seizing power in Russia," Litvin wrote at one point, "the Bolshevik leadership had created an extreme situation." But in the next breath, he could admit that the *Cheka*, however "extraordinary" an institution, was "operating in a country in which 'extraordinary measures' were a normal, not an exceptional, phenomenon." See pp. 315–16 and 321 for these observations.

79. Figes, *A People's Tragedy*, 525.

80. Ibid., 630.

81. Martin Malia, *History's Locomotives: Revolutions and the Making of the Modern World*, ed. Terence Emmons (New Haven: Yale University Press, 2006), esp. 270–72. Charles Tilly reviewed Malia's comparative study at length: see his article in *The American Historical Review* 112 (2007): 1120–22.

82. Malia, *History's Locomotives*, 279–80. Obviously, too, Malia's downplaying of *socioeconomics* as a causal factor in the Russian situation would scarcely square with William Rosenberg's analytical contribution to the debate over Arno Mayer's synthesis in 2000 to 2001. Refer again to "Beheading the Revolution," passim.

83. See, in this connection, Figes, *A People's Tragedy*, 645–47; and Richard Cobb, "Quelques aspects de la mentalité révolutionnaire," *Revue d'histoire moderne et contemporaine* 6 (1959): 86–87, 96–104, 116–20.

84. Peter Holquist, *Making War, Forging Revolution: Russia's Continuum of Crisis 1914–1921* (Cambridge, MA: Harvard University Press, 2002), esp. 110–11, 283–87, 384. Interestingly, Holquist invoked Tocquevillian insights frequently throughout his study to underscore the continuity of *statism* running (in Russia as well as in France) from *ancien régime* to revolution.

85. Joshua A. Sanborn, *Drafting the Russian Nation: Military Conscription, Total War, and Mass Politics 1905–1925* (De Kalb: Northern Illinois University Press, 2003), 174.

86. Ronald Hutton, *The British Republic 1649–1660* (New York: St. Martin's Press, 1990), 21–22. For subsequent (and much more extensive) probing of this issue, see Sean Kelsey, *Inventing a Republic: The Political Culture of the English Commonwealth 1649–1659* (Manchester: Manchester University Press, 1997); and Sarah Barber, *Regicide and Republicanism* (Edinburgh: Edinburgh University Press, 1998).

87. Hutton, *The British Republic*, 15. The most imposing study of the personnel, ideology, and campaigns of the Commonwealth's navy is probably still Bernard Capp, *Cromwell's Navy* (Oxford: Clarendon Press, 1989).

88. Peter Gaunt, *Oliver Cromwell* (Oxford: Blackwell, 1996), 112–13. See also, on the Irish/Scottish campaigns, the scholarship of Ian Gentles: especially *The New Model Army in England, Scotland and Ireland 1645–1653* (Oxford: Blackwell, 1991); and *The English Revolution and the Wars in the Three Kingdoms, 1638-1652* (London: Pearson, 2007).

89. The perspective on all of this at Edinburgh is discussed lucidly and in detail by David Stevenson, *Revolution and Counter-Revolution in Scotland, 1644–1651* (London: Royal Historical Society, 1977).

90. All of this is succinctly discussed in Capp, *Cromwell's Navy*, 70–72. Even a Venetian diplomat conceded in 1651 that the Rumpers, if "ignorant mechanics," nonetheless possessed "the finest navy in the world." Ibid., 72. See also, on these matters, Timothy Venning, *Cromwellian Foreign Policy* (New York: St. Martin's Press, 1995); and Stephen Pincus, *Protestantism and Patriotism: Ideologies and the Making of English Foreign Policy, 1650–1668* (Cambridge: Cambridge University Press, 1996).

91. On the connections between the projected Irish campaign and Leveller agitation within the army, consult Norah Carlin, "The Levellers and the Conquest of Ireland in 1649," *Historical Journal* 30 (1987): 269–88. See also Gentles' subsequent commentary: *The English Revolution and the Wars in the Three Kingdoms*, 385–87.

92. Ibid., 418.

93. On this subject, the study by Paul Hardacre, *The Royalists during the Puritan Revolution* (The Hague: M. Nijhoff, 1956) was soon overtaken by David Underdown's still frequently cited *Royalist Conspiracy in England, 1649–1660* (New Haven, CT: Yale University Press, 1960). The much more recent anthology co-edited by Jason McElligott and David L. Smith, *Royalists and Royalism During the Interregnum* (Manchester: Manchester University Press, 2010) may also be consulted, although it is less immediately useful for our purposes.

94. G. E. Aylmer, *The State's Servants: The Civil Service of the English Republic 1649–1660* (London: Routledge & Kegan Paul, 1973), 31, 35, 355 (n. 16) for this assessment of England's High Courts of Justice.

95. Underdown, *Royalist Conspiracy in England*, 12–13, 17.

96. Ibid., 42–45.

97. A. B. Worden, *The Rump Parliament* (Cambridge: Cambridge University Press, 1974), 222–23, 226, 242–48.

98. Underdown, *Royalist Conspiracy in England*, 55. Moreover, Francis Yates, a servant to Derby loyalist Charles Gifford, "was soon to be executed for refusing to betray Charles's movements" in 1651. Ibid., 53. Refer once again to McElligott and Smith, eds., *Royalists and Royalism During the Interregnum*, passim., for further details on some of the pro-Stuart conspirators during this period.

99. Underdown, *Royalist Conspiracy in England*, 57–58.

100. For the actual demographics of this stunning decline, refer to Pádraig Lenihan, "War and Population, 1649–52," *Irish Economic and Social History* 24 (1997): 1–21.

101. See, on Drogheda and Wexford, Gentles, *The English Revolution and the Wars in the Three Kingdoms*, 392–98. Cromwell's numerous biographers have also been at pains to probe the ethical issues raised by his army's conduct in Ireland. Refer, for example, to Christopher Hill, *God's Englishman: Oliver Cromwell and the English Revolution* (New York: Harper Torchbooks, 1970), 116–17, 121–23; Barry Coward, *Oliver Cromwell* (London: Longman, 1991), 72–74; Peter Gaunt, *Oliver Cromwell* (New York: New York University Press, 2004), 84–87; and also Ian Gentles, *Oliver Cromwell: God's Warrior and the English Revolution* (New York: Palgrave Macmillan, 2011), 94–95, 113–14. Other thoughtful comments on this issue appear in Hutton, *The British Republic 1649–1660*, 47–48, and Woolrych, *Britain in Revolution 1625–1660*, 471–80, 577.

102. As emphasized by Gentles, *The English Revolution and the Wars in the Three Kingdoms*, 394, 396–97.

103. Hutton, *The British Republic 1649–1660*, 21–22. "It was also noteworthy," he went on, "that in none of its declarations did the new government attempt to defend itself by promising future reforms to benefit the nation."

104. Malia, *History's Locomotives*, 159–60.

105. On this point, see again Capp, *Cromwell's Navy*, passim.; and Pincus, *Protestantism and Patriotism*, passim.

106. Underdown, *Royalist Conspiracy in England*, 5, 17.

107. Woolrych, *Britain in Revolution 1625–1660*, 431.

108. See, in this connection, Sean Kelsey, *Inventing a Republic: The Political Culture of the English Commonwealth 1649–1659* (Manchester: Manchester University Press, 1997). Other works in this genre include Sarah Barber, *Regicide and Republicanism* (Edinburgh: Edinburgh University Press, 1998); David Norbrook, *Writing the English Republic: Poetry, Rhetoric and Politics, 1627–1660* (Cambridge: Cambridge University Press, 1999); and David Zaret, *Origins of Democratic Culture: Printing, Petitions, and the Public Sphere in Early Modern England* (Princeton, NJ: Princeton University Press, 2002).

109. Kelsey, *Inventing a Republic*, 1, 201.

110. Kelsey here was explicitly challenging the less-than-flattering portrayal of the Rump's capacity (during 1649–1653) for genuine legislative reformism left by Blair Worden in *The Rump Parliament* (Cambridge: Cambridge University Press, 1974).

111. Barber, *Regicide and Republicanism*, 6, 147, 220.

112. Woolrych, *Britain in Revolution 1625–1660*, 469, 479–80.

113. Ibid., 479–80, 577. Woolrych also devoted considerable time to analyzing Cromwell's angry denial of the Irish bishops' charge that he wanted to extirpate the Irish people, and concluded (among other things) that Oliver, however blinkered by pejorative assumptions about the Irish, genuinely would have treated them more humanely over the long run than did the actual post-Cromwellian regimes. Ibid., 474.

114. Hill, *God's Englishman*, 121–22. This, despite Hill's forthright (if, arguably, somewhat hasty?) condemnation of "Cromwell's racial contempt for the Irish, and his commercial-calculating attitude towards the colonization of Ireland."

115. Gentles, *Oliver Cromwell*, 94–95.

116. Hutton, *The British Republic 1649–1660*, 47–48. See also, on this painful subject, the thoughtful commentary of Peter Gaunt, *Oliver Cromwell* (New York: New York University Press, 2004), 85–87.

117. I borrow this phrase more or less verbatim from an always-helpful colleague, sociologist Jack Goldstone.

118. As cited in Brinton, *The Anatomy of Revolution*, 202.

5. CRISES OF REVOLUTIONARY LEGITIMACY

1. Furet is cited here (as before, in chapter 4) from his article entitled "Terror," in his co-edited *A Critical Dictionary of the French Revolution*, 146–50.

2. For these differing opinions, refer to Sheila Fitzpatrick, *The Russian Revolution*, third edition (Oxford: Oxford University Press, 2008), 2–4; and Robert V. Daniels, "Comment: Does the Present Change the Past?" *Journal of Modern History* 70 (1998): 434. On the Communist Party's fierce debates during the 1920s regarding the applicability of the term "Thermidor" to post-Leninist Russia, consult Isaac Deutscher, *Trotsky: The Prophet Unarmed, 1921–29* (London: Oxford University Press, 1970), 312–32; and Michal Reiman, *The Birth of Stalinism*, trans. George Saunders (Bloomington: Indiana University Press, 1987), 22–23. Interestingly, Crane Brinton was still wrestling with this problem in the final (1965) edition of *The Anatomy of Revolution*, as on pp. 227–28 and 233.

3. Ronald Hutton, *The British Republic 1649–60*, second edition (New York: St. Martin's Press, 2000), 67, 73–74, 76. See also, on constitutional and related issues of this period in revolutionary England, the following: Barry Coward, *The Cromwellian Protectorate* (New York: Palgrave Macmillan, 2002); David L. Smith and Patrick Little, *Parliaments and Politics during the Cromwellian Protectorate* (Cambridge: Cambridge University Press, 2007); Patrick Little, ed., *The Cromwellian Protectorate* (Woodbridge: Boydell, 2007); and Patrick Little, *Oliver Cromwell: New Perspectives* (New York: Palgrave Macmillan, 2009). The literature continues to grow!

4. Derek Hirst, "The Lord Protector, 1653–1658," in John S. Morrill, ed., *Oliver Cromwell and the English Revolution* (London: Longman, 1990), 119.

5. Ibid.

6. G. E. Aylmer, *The State's Servants: The Civil Service of the English Republic, 1649–1660* (London: Routledge and Kegan Paul, 1973), 45. For some updated reflections on this relationship, see Blair Worden, "Oliver Cromwell and the Council," in Patrick Little, ed., *The Cromwellian Protectorate*, 82–104.

7. Peter Gaunt, "Law-Making in the First Protectorate Parliament," in Colin Jones, Malyn Newitt, and Stephen Roberts, eds., *Politics and People in Revolutionary England* (Oxford: Oxford University Press, 1986), esp. 165–66.

8. Ibid., 181.

9. See H. R. Trevor-Roper, "Oliver Cromwell and His Parliaments," in Ivan Roots, ed., *Cromwell: A Profile* (New York: Macmillan, 1973), 91–135.

10. For this riposte to Trevor-Roper, see Roger Howell Jr., "Cromwell and His Parliaments: The Trevor-Roper Thesis Revisited," in R. C. Richardson, ed., *Images of Oliver Cromwell* (Manchester: Manchester University Press, 1993), chapter 8.

11. Howell, "Cromwell and English Liberty," in ibid., chapter 10. Citations are from 168–73. On the problematic question of Cromwell's power, as it was perceived by contemporaries, see also Benjamin Woodford, *Perceptions of a Monarchy Without a King: Reactions to Oliver Cromwell's Power* (Ithaca, NY: McGill-Queen's University Press, 2013).

12. Austin Woolrych, "The Cromwellian Protectorate: A Military Dictatorship?" *History* 75 (1990): 207–31; and *Britain in Revolution 1625–1660* (Oxford: Oxford University Press, 2002), esp. 582–83.

13. Ibid. For further discussion about military participation in local government in the England of the 1650s, consult Henry Reece, *The Army in Cromwellian England, 1649–1660* (New York: Oxford University Press, 2013).

14. Woolrych, "The Cromwellian Protectorate: A Military Dictatorship?" esp. 207–13, 215–19. Refer also to this historian's article "Cromwell as a Soldier," chapter 4 in J. S. Morrill, ed., *Oliver Cromwell and the English Revolution* (London: Longman, 1990); and, once again, refer to his subsequent *Britain in Revolution*, passim.

15. Howell, "Cromwell and His Parliaments," 134.

16. Peter Gaunt, *Oliver Cromwell* (Oxford: Blackwell, 1996), 205.

17. See J. C. Davis, *Oliver Cromwell* (London: Arnold, 2001), esp. 200–1; and Barry Coward, *The Cromwellian Protectorate* (Manchester: Manchester University Press, 2002), 162–69.

This despite the fact that both Davis *and* Coward credit Cromwell with the desire to somehow "civilianize" and thereby fully legitimize his regime.

18. Citation from Smith and Little, *Parliaments and Politics During the Cromwellian Protectorate*, 145–46. On the other hand, Patrick Little wrote two years later (i.e., in 2009) that "Cromwell comes across as an honest broker, not a megalomaniac, despite the claims of his enemies. . . . He remained, at heart, the godly hero of the 1640s." At worst, he was, according now to Little, attempting "to balance elements within an unstable regime." Little, *Oliver Cromwell: New Perspectives*, 16–17. Clearly, even the most authoritative scholars remain highly ambivalent about this controversial subject! See also the somewhat earlier thoughts on Cromwellian rule offered by J. S. Morrill, *The Nature of the English Revolution* (London: Harlow, 1993), esp. chapters 1, 15, 18.

19. Gaunt, "Law-Making in the First Protectorate Parliament," 183. The huge and disproportionate importance of *war-related* expenditures in the budgets of the Protectorate has been underlined and, to some extent, quantified by Timothy Venning, *Cromwellian Foreign Policy* (New York: St. Martin's Press, 1995), esp. 246–50. Cromwell's own *naiveté* in technical matters of state finance is stressed by Derek Hirst, "The Lord Protector," 144.

20. Christopher Durston, *Cromwell's Major-Generals: Godly Government during the English Revolution* (Manchester: Manchester University Press, 2001), 4–5.

21. See, notably, on these points, David Underdown, "Settlement in the Counties, 1653–58," in G. E. Aylmer, ed., *The Interregnum: The Quest for Settlement, 1646–60* (New York: Macmillan, 1973), 176; Ivan Roots, "Swordsmen and Decimators," in R. H. Parry, ed., *The English Civil War and After* (London: Macmillan, 1970); and Anthony Fletcher, "Oliver Cromwell and the Localities: The Problem of Consent," in Jones, Newitt, and Roberts, eds., *Politics and People in Revolutionary England*, chapter 10.

22. Durston, *Cromwell's Major-Generals*, 230–32. Durston receives some subsequent support for this chiefly *religious/ideological* interpretation from Smith and Little, *Parliaments and Politics during the Cromwellian Protectorate*, esp. 127, 147. Bernard Capp has more recently contributed to this "cultural interpretation" in *England's Culture Wars: Puritan Reformation and its Enemies in the Interregnum 1649–1660* (Oxford: Oxford University Press, 2012).

23. Durston, *Cromwell's Major-Generals*, 4–5. For reminders on this last point, see David Underdown, *Royalist Conspiracy in England, 1649–1660* (New Haven, CT: Yale University Press, 1960); and Jason McElligott and David L. Smith, eds., *Royalists and Royalism during the Interregnum* (Manchester: Manchester University Press, 2010).

24. Woolrych, *Britain in Revolution*, 629–30.

25. Specifically, Durston has faulted the major-generals for pressuring Oliver to hold parliamentary elections at this time, underestimating as they allegedly did the "hostile climate of public opinion" that was bound (in 1656) to lead to political results unfavorable to the Protectoral regime. Durston, *Cromwell's Major-Generals*, 201–2.

26. Ivan Roots, *The Great Rebellion: 1642–1660*, revised edition (Gloucestershire: Allan Sutton, 1995), 223–30. Roots had devoted earlier thoughts to this subject in "Lawmaking in the Second Protectorate Parliament," in H. Hearder and H. R. Loyn, eds., *Studies in British Government and Administration* (Cardiff: University of Wales Press, 1974).

27. Roots, *The Great Rebellion*, 223–30.

28. Ibid.

29. Venning, *Cromwellian Foreign Policy*, 241–42. For Cromwell's candid admission of his own lack of expertise in state/fiscal matters, refer once again to Hirst, "The Lord Protector," 144.

30. Roots, *The Great Rebellion*, 230–31.

31. This summation of Davies' enumeration of Protectoral weaknesses in 1658 and 1659 is furnished by Ronald Hutton, *The Restoration: A Political and Religious History of England and Wales, 1658–1667* (Oxford: Clarendon Press, 1985), 119–23. But refer also to the original source: Godfrey Davies, *The Restoration of Charles II 1658–1660* (San Marino, CA: Huntingdon Library, 1955).

32. Hutton, *The Restoration*, 41.

33. Ruth E. Mayers, *1659: The Crisis of the Commonwealth* (Woodbridge: The Boydell Press, 2004), 229.

34. Ibid., 273–74.
35. Woolrych, *Britain in Revolution 1625–1660*, 702.
36. Ibid., 779. For Woolrych's fair-minded but, in the end, rather dampening evaluation of Richard Cromwell's leadership abilities, refer to ibid., 708–13. Interestingly, Woolrych also cites on these pages William Prynne's remark (in May 1659) attributing Richard's downfall to "the confederated triumvirate of republicans, sectaries, and soldiers." Ibid., 712–13. Clearly, Richard had to deal with disunity in both State Council and Army at the same time during his abortive rule, and unsurprisingly he found this in the end to be an impossible task. Barry Coward also stresses this point in *The Cromwellian Protectorate*, 111–12: "what actually happened illustrates that power during the last days of the Protectorate was wielded not by the grandees but by the Commonwealthsmen and their junior army officer allies meeting at St. James's."
37. Smith and Little, *Parliaments and Politics during the Cromwellian Protectorate*, 168–70.
38. Blair Worden, *God's Instruments: Political Conduct in the England of Oliver Cromwell* (Oxford: Oxford University Press, 2012), 239–40.
39. Ibid., 257–59. For a fuller discussion of this vision of the parliament as the institution most critical to the legitimacy of governance in England, consult also James S. Hart Jr., "Rhetoric and Reality: Images of Parliament as Great Council," in Michael J. Braddick and David L. Smith, eds., *The Experience of Revolution in Stuart Britain and Ireland* (Cambridge: Cambridge University Press, 2011), 74–95.
40. Reece, *The Army in Cromwellian England, 1649–1660*, 173.
41. Ibid., 234.
42. Ibid.
43. Venning, *Cromwellian Foreign Policy*, 250.
44. On these arrangements, see Denis Woronoff, *The Thermidorean Regime and the Directory, 1794–1799*, trans. Julian Jackson (Cambridge: Cambridge University Press, 1984), 29–42; and Malcolm Crook, *Elections in the French Revolution: An Apprenticeship in Democracy, 1789–1799* (Cambridge: Cambridge University Press, 1996), 131–57. The role of a reemergent, post-Terror Abbé Sieyès in helping to draw up this "Constitution of the Year III" is discussed in Bronislaw Baczko, *Ending the Terror: The French Revolution After Robespierre*, trans. Michel Petheram (Cambridge: Cambridge University Press, 1994), 225–30, 248–58.
45. For this valiant (if debatable) argument, see Albert Goodwin, "The French Executive Directory—A Revaluation," *History* 22 (1937): esp. 215–18.
46. For this detailed critique of the Constitution of 1795, see Martyn Lyons, *France Under the Directory* (Cambridge: Cambridge University Press, 1975), esp. 18–20. Isser Woloch has updated this constitutional critique by placing it within a political-cultural context: see *Napoleon and His Collaborators: The Making of a Dictatorship* (New York: W. W. Norton, 2001), esp. 5–8.
47. Cited by Lynn Hunt, David Lansky, and Paul Hanson, "The Failure of the Liberal Republic in France, 1795-1799: The Road to Brumaire," *Journal of Modern History* 51 (1979): 737–38. This point, again, is heartily endorsed by Woloch, *Napoleon and His Collaborators*, 5–8.
48. Baczko, *Ending the Terror*, 109–10.
49. On the social views of those on the Far Right, see Jacques Godechot, *La Contre-Révolution: Doctrine et Action* (Paris: Presses Universitaires de France, 1961); and, again, D. M. G. Sutherland, *France, 1789–1815: Revolution and Counterrevolution* (New York: Oxford University Press, 1986).
50. A foundational work on the Jacobin revival in the late 1790s is Isser Woloch, *Jacobin Legacy: The Democratic Movement Under the Directory* (Princeton, NJ: Princeton University Press, 1970), esp. 92–93, 95–96, 112. But see also, more recently, Bernard Gainot, *1799, Un Nouveau Jacobinisme?* (Paris: CTHS, 2001); and the relevant essays in Howard G. Brown and Judith Miller, eds., *Taking Liberties: Problems of a New Order from the French Revolution to Napoleon* (New York: Manchester University Press, 2002).
51. Colin Lucas, "The First Directory and the Rule of Law," *French Historical Studies* 10 (1977): 258.

52. Clive Church, "In Search of the Directory," in J. F. Bosher, ed., *French Government and Society, 1500–1850: Essays in Memory of Alfred Cobban* (London: Athlone Press, 1973), esp. 274–76, 279–80, 288–89.

53. Lyons, *France Under the Directory*, 236–37. For useful updates to this 1970s exchange between Church and Lyons on the nature of the Directory, refer to the following: Catherine Kawa, *Les Ronds-de-cuir en Révolution: Les Employés du ministre de l'intérieure sous la première République* (Paris: CTHS, 1996); and Ralph Kingston, "The Bricks and Mortar of Revolutionary Administration," *French History* 20 (2006): 405–23.

54. For this provincial perspective: Richard Cobb, *Paris and Its Provinces, 1792–1802* (New York: Oxford University Press, 1975); Lucas, "The First Directory and the Rule of Law," 231–60; Hunt et al., "The Failure of the Liberal Republic in France," 736–38; Alan Forrest, *The Revolution in Provincial France: Aquitaine, 1789–1799* (New York: Oxford University Press, 1996); and Howard G. Brown, *Ending the French Revolution: Violence, Justice, and Repression from the Terror to Napoleon* (Charlottesville: University of Virginia Press, 2006).

55. See, for example, Mona Ozouf, *Festivals and the French Revolution*, trans. Alan Sheridan (Cambridge, MA: Harvard University Press, 1988); and Ozouf's articles on the "Revolutionary Calendar" and "Revolutionary Religion" in François Furet and Mona Ozouf, eds., *A Critical Dictionary of the French Revolution*, trans. Arthur Goldhammer (Cambridge, MA: Harvard University Press, 1989), 538–70.

56. John McManners has discussed all of this in *The French Revolution and the Church* (Westport, CT: Greenwood Press, 1982), 120–21. The Thermidorian Convention had officially disestablished the Catholic Church in statutes of September 1794 and February 1795. On this, consult William Doyle, *Oxford History of the French Revolution*, second edition (Oxford: Oxford University Press, 2002), 287–88.

57. McManners, *The French Revolution and the Church*, 121–27.

58. Church, "In Search of the Directory," 286–87. For similar examples of alienation in the southern department of the Gard, see Gwynne Lewis, *The Second Vendée: The Continuity of Counter-Revolution in the Department of the Gard, 1789–1815* (Oxford: Clarendon Press, 1978), 134–35.

59. On the *assignats*: Seymour Harris, *The Assignats* (Cambridge, MA: Harvard University Press, 1930); Goodwin, "The French Executive Directory," 322–23; and also Elise S. Brezis and François Crouzet, "The Role of Assignats During the French Revolution: An Evil or a Rescuer?" in *Journal of European Economic History* 24 (1995).

60. On the partial bankruptcy of September 1797, the standard (if by now dated) analysis is still that of Goodwin, "The French Executive Directory," esp. 201–18. But see also the much more recent work of Michel Bruguière, *Gestionnaires et profiteurs de la Révolution: L'Administration des finances françaises de Louis XVI à Bonaparte* (Paris: O. Orban, 1986), for a contextual discussion of this bankruptcy.

61. On this point, see François Crouzet, "Wars, Blockade, and Economic Change in Europe, 1792-1815," *Journal of Economic History* 24 (1964): 567–88.

62. Lewis, *The Second Vendée*, 134–35.

63. An official report cited in Church, "In Search of the Directory," 286. Moreover, as Isser Woloch has pointed out, the war militated directly against the government's goal of generating more taxable revenue via economic development, not only by cutting French entrepreneurs out of international trade, but also by drafting young men away from (consequently) "neglected arts, agriculture, and commerce" at home. Isser Woloch, *The New Regime: Transformations of the French Civic Order, 1789–1820s* (New York: W. W. Norton, 1994), 388.

64. Ample evidence to this effect is cited in the works of Alan Forrest. See, in particular, *Conscripts and Deserters: The Army and French Society during the Revolution and Empire* (New York: Oxford University Press, 1989); and *The Soldiers of the French Revolution* (Durham, NC: Duke University Press, 1990). The Jourdan Decree of 1798 is most thoroughly discussed by Isser Woloch, *The New Regime*, esp. 389–91.

65. See, on these points, Harvey Mitchell, *The Underground War Against Revolutionary France* (Oxford: Clarendon Press, 1965); and, much more recently, the following articles in Peter McPhee, ed., *A Companion to the French Revolution* (Oxford: Wiley-Blackwell, 2013): D. M. G. Sutherland, "Urban Crowds, Riot, Utopia, and Massacres," 231–45; Jean-Clément

Martin, "The Vendée, Chouannerie, and the State," 246–60; and Stephen Clay, "The White Terror: Factions, Reactions, and the Politics of Vengeance," 359–78.

66. See Woloch, *Jacobin Legacy*, 70–76, for this discussion of a military/civilian understanding and eventual political collaboration on the Left.

67. Ibid., 134–35.

68. Ibid., 165–69, for Woloch's thorough discussion of the veterans' bonus as a political issue in late Directorial France.

69. Obviously, too, postmodernists dealing with *intellectual* history are bound to be fascinated by the parallels that they can draw between the final, dramatic efflorescence of revolutionary idealism in both late-revolutionary situations—involving, that is, the short-lived revival of the "Good Old Cause" under the restored Rump Parliament in England in 1659 and the neo-Jacobin revival due to the crisis of the War of the Second Coalition in France in 1799.

70. Howard G. Brown, *War, Revolution, and the Bureaucratic State: Politics and Army Administration in France 1791–1799* (Oxford: Clarendon Press, 1995), 265.

71. Ibid., 235–36.

72. Consult Brown, "The New Security State," in McPhee, ed., *A Companion to the French Revolution*, 348–49. Brown's analysis of the Directory's crisis of legitimacy was even more explicit in his *Ending the French Revolution: Violence, Justice, and Repression from the Terror to Napoleon*, passim.

73. James Livesey, *Making Democracy in the French Revolution* (Cambridge, MA: Harvard University Press, 2001), 237–38.

74. Ibid., 238–39.

75. Ibid., 243. Livesey, we should point out, has much more recently elaborated upon his political/cultural rendering of the French Directory's downfall in "The Political Culture of the Directory," in Peter McPhee, ed., *A Companion to the French Revolution*, 328–42.

76. Interestingly, Livesey was cited for (in a sense) not being *sufficiently postmodernist* by Laura Mason. In a review of his 2001 book appearing in the *American Historical Review*, Mason faulted Livesey for isolating the essence of "commercial republicanism" from "the factionalized political world in which its practices were formulated." She then went even farther by criticizing Livesey for turning to a discussion of foreign policy *at all* in his account of the Directory's 1799 collapse; thus, she refused to endorse his argument regarding a "nexus" between international and domestic (French) affairs. See Laura Mason's review in *American Historical Review* 107 (2002): 1302–03. Of course, diplomatic historians might contend that both Livesey *and* Mason have failed to grasp the larger historical continuity (extending from the old regime through the entire revolutionary era and beyond) of a French outreach (on land *and sea*) toward something approaching supremacy in international affairs.

77. Andrew Jainchill, *Reimagining Politics After the Terror: The Republican Origins of French Liberalism* (Ithaca: Cornell University Press, 2008), 24.

78. Refer in this connection to Bernard Gainot, *1799, Un Nouveau Jacobinisme?* (Paris: CTHS, 2001); and "Vers une alternative à la Grande Nation: Le Projet d'une confédération des Etats-nations en 1799," in Pierre Serna, ed., *Républiques soeurs: Le Directoire et la Révolution atlantique* (Rennes: Presses Universitaires de Rennes, 2009), 75–86.

79. Pierre Serna developed this postmodernist interpretation of the transition from Directorial to Bonapartist rule in his study *La République des girouettes (1789-1815 et au delà), une anomalie politique: La France de l'extrême centre* (Paris: Champ Vallon, 2005). I have cited here from Livesey's commentary on Serna's ideas in his *Making Democracy in the French Revolution*, esp. 330.

80. Woloch, *Napoleon and His Collaborators*, 5–6. Refer also to Woloch's earlier analysis of these issues in his *Jacobin Legacy*, passim.

81. Woloch, *Napoleon and His Collaborators*, 5–6.

82. It is also relevant to point out, in this connection, that early on in the French Revolution, observers as utterly dissimilar in ideological terms as Edmund Burke in England and Maximilien Robespierre in France had predicted the possibility of a military finale to this upheaval.

83. Refer once more to H. M. Reece, *The Army in Cromwellian England*, 234.

84. A point made by Sheila Fitzpatrick, *The Russian Revolution*, third edition (Oxford: Oxford University Press, 2008), 119. On the Russian Bolshevik (i.e., Communist) Party's

frequent invocation of Thermidorian parallels during the 1920s, refer again to Deutscher, *Trotsky: The Prophet Unarmed*, 312–32, and Reiman, *The Birth of Stalinism*, 22–23.

85. See, for example, Leon Trotsky, *The Revolution Betrayed: What Is the Soviet Union and Where Is It Going?* trans. Max Eastman (Garden City, NY: Doubleday, Doran and Co., 1937), 5–8, 19–20, 45–47, 54–56, 275–79.

86. On the *economics* of the NEP, see the following: M. Dobb, *Soviet Economic Development After 1917* (London: Routledge and Kegan Paul, 1951); Esther Kingston-Mann, *Lenin and the Problem of Marxist Peasant Revolution* (Oxford: Oxford University Press, 1983); and Sergei V. Iarov, "The Tenth Congress of the Communist Party and the Transition to NEP," in Edward Acton, Vladimir Cherniaev, and William Rosenberg, eds., *A Critical Companion to the Russian Revolution 1914–1921* (Bloomington: Indiana University Press, 1997), esp. 122–27.

87. For all of these statistics, see Lewis H. Siegelbaum, *Soviet State and Society between Revolutions, 1918–1929* (Cambridge: Cambridge University Press, 1992), 165–68.

88. Two excellent sources on this subject are Alexander Erlich, *The Soviet Industrialization Debate, 1924–1928* (Cambridge, MA: Harvard University Press, 1962), and James Millar and Alec Nove, "A Debate on Collectivization: Was Stalin Really Necessary?" in *Problems of Communism* 25 (1976): 49–62.

89. Dzerzhinskii cited in Fitzpatrick, *The Russian Revolution*, 114. See also Siegelbaum, *Soviet State and Society*, esp. 179–80, for further discussion of the activities, at this time, of *Gosplan* and *Vesenkha*. Dzerzhinskii actually died prematurely before the year was out.

90. Sources on these developments include John P. Sontag, "The Soviet War Scare of 1926–27," *Russian Review* 34 (1975): 66–77; Kurt Rosenbaum, *Community of Fate: German-Soviet Diplomatic Relations, 1922–1928* (Syracuse, NY: Syracuse University Press, 1965), esp. 247; and Timothy E. O'Connor, *Diplomacy and Revolution: G. V. Chicherin and Soviet Foreign Affairs, 1918-1930* (Ames: Iowa State University Press, 1988), 154–56.

91. Arno J. Mayer, *The Furies: Violence and Terror in the French and Russian Revolutions* (Princeton, NJ: Princeton University Press, 2000), 623. Mark von Hagen has noted a militarized political culture in Soviet Russia in the late 1920s that helped to heighten *domestic* anxieties in this period: see his *Soldiers in the Proletarian Dictatorship: The Red Army and the Soviet Socialist State, 1917–1930* (Ithaca, NY: Cornell University Press, 1990).

92. See, for example, these works by Lewin: *Russian Peasants and Soviet Power: A Study of Collectivization*, trans. Irene Nove (London: Allen and Unwin, 1968); *Political Undercurrents in Soviet Economic Debates* (Princeton, NJ: Princeton University Press, 1974); and *The Making of the Soviet System: Essays in the Social History of Interwar Russia*, trans. Catherine Porter (New York: Pantheon Books, 1985). For a similar viewpoint, see Stephen F. Cohen, *Bukharin and the Bolshevik Revolution: A Political Biography, 1888–1938*, revised edition (New York: Alfred A. Knopf, 1980); and *Rethinking the Soviet Experience: Politics and History since 1917* (New York: Oxford University Press, 1985).

93. Jon Jacobson, *When the Soviet Union Entered World Politics* (Berkeley: University of California Press, 1994), 241–42. One of the best scholarly attempts to establish a compromise position on these immensely controversial issues is R. W. Davies, *The Industrialization of Soviet Russia: The Soviet Economy in Turmoil, 1929–30* (Cambridge, MA: Harvard University Press, 1989).

94. Jacobson, *When the Soviet Union Entered World Politics*, 259–60.

95. Siegelbaum, *Soviet State and Society*, 190.

96. Lynne Viola, V. P. Danilov, N. A. Ivnitskii, and Denis Koslov, eds., *The War Against the Peasantry, 1927–1930: The Tragedy of the Soviet Countryside*, trans. Steven Shabad (New Haven, CT: Yale University Press, 2005), 17–19.

97. The peasants' reaction to the possibility of war in 1927 has been stressed recently by Hugh D. Hudson, in his *Peasants, Political Police, and the Early Soviet State: Surveillance and Accommodation under the New Economic Policy* (New York: Palgrave Macmillan, 2012), esp. 124–25.

98. Viola et al., eds., *The War Against the Peasantry, 1927–1930*, 18–19. In this connection, consult also these historians' discussion of Stalin's crucial trip to Siberia in January 1928. Ibid., 58–60.

99. Ibid., 325–26. For similarly bleak depictions of the implications of collectivization for the *muzhiki* of rural Russia, see Sheila Fitzpatrick, *Stalin's Peasants: Resistance and Survival in the Russian Village after Collectivization* (New York: Oxford University Press, 1994); and Lynne Viola, *Peasant Rebels under Stalin: Collectivization and the Culture of Peasant Resistance* (Oxford: Oxford University Press, 1996).

100. A point made recently by Arno Mayer, *The Furies*, 616–18. But see also, on this point, Robert C. Tucker, *Stalin in Power: The Revolution from Above, 1928-1941* (New York: W. W. Norton, 1990), esp. 50–65, 114–18.

101. Siegelbaum, *Soviet State and Society*, 188.

102. Ronald Grigor Suny, *The Soviet Experiment: Russia, the USSR, and the Successor States*, second edition (New York: Oxford University Press, 2011), 190–91.

103. Fitzpatrick, *The Russian Revolution*, 141. In-depth documentation for these assertions is marshaled in Sheila Fitzpatrick, "The Great Departure: Rural-Urban Migration in the Soviet Union, 1929–1933," in William R. Rosenberg and Lewis H. Siegelbaum, eds., *Social Dimensions of Soviet Industrialization* (Bloomington: Indiana University Press, 1993), esp. 21–22.

104. Helmut Altrichter, "Insoluble Conflicts: Village Life between Revolution and Collectivization," in Sheila Fitzpatrick, Alexander Rabinowitch, and Richard Stites, eds., *Russia in the Era of NEP: Explorations in Soviet Society and Culture* (Bloomington: University Of Indiana Press, 1991), 192–209.

105. Teodor Shanin, *The Awkward Class: Political Sociology of Peasantry in a Developing Society: Russia 1910–1925* (New York: Oxford University Press, 1972), 198–99. For similar takes on the mutually antagonistic relationship between Communists and peasants in the late twentieth-century literature, see Lewin, *Russian Peasants and Soviet Power*, esp. 415, 417–18, 419–20; and Siegelbaum, *Soviet State and Society*, 143–44.

106. James Heinzen, *Inventing a Soviet Countryside: State Power and the Transformation of Rural Russia, 1917–1929* (Pittsburgh: University of Pittsburgh Press, 2004), esp. 3–4.

107. Ibid., 4.

108. Refer in this connection to (among other classic works) Theodore H. Von Laue, *Why Lenin? Why Stalin? Why Gorbachev? The Rise and Fall of the Soviet System*, third edition (New York: HarperCollins, 1993).

109. Heinzen, *Inventing a Soviet Countryside*, 4.

110. Ibid., 9–10. Intriguingly, Heinzen also complains here—in a comment on historiography—that "until recently" scholars in his field have not only "neglected the importance of the Commissariat of Agriculture in their discussions of the 1920s," but, more generally, have "downplayed the importance of the state altogether." He commends fellow specialists such as David Shearer, Peter Holquist, and Don K. Rowney for helping to refocus attention on "the critical role of the early Soviet state." Ibid.

111. Not to mention discouraging *foreign* exchanges as well. See Viola, et al., eds., *The War Against the Peasantry, 1927–1930*, esp. 64–65. This is, of course, a point that Stephen F. Cohen had also been at pains to make in revisionist studies such as *Bukharin and the Bolshevik Revolution* and *Rethinking the Soviet Experience*.

112. Viola et al., eds., *The War Against the Peasantry, 1927–1930*, 66.

113. Tracy McDonald, *Face to the Village: The Riazan Countryside under Soviet Rule, 1921–1930* (Toronto: University of Toronto Press, 2011); and Hugh D. Hudson, *Peasants, Political Police, and the Early Soviet State: Surveillance and Accommodation under the New Economic Policy* (New York: Palgrave MacMillan, 2012).

114. McDonald, *Face to the Village*, 10, 299.

115. Ibid., 300–04. James Heinzen had made essentially the same points about the "anxiety-inducing" dilemmas faced by Lenin's immediate successors. Refer again to Heinzen, *Inventing a Soviet Countryside*, esp. 3–4.

116. Hudson, *Peasants, Political Police, and the Early Soviet State*, 91–92.

117. Ibid., 113. Admittedly, more nuanced statements regarding the inevitability of a "face-off" between state authorities and the Russian peasantry under NEP have come from some scholarly quarters. See, for example, the cautionary remarks of Aaron B. Retish, *American Historical Review* 118 (2013): 283–84. See also his subtle handling of issues in *Russia's Peasants in Revolution and Civil War: Citizenship, Identity, and the Creation of the Soviet

State, 1914–1922 (Cambridge: Cambridge University Press, 2008). Still, the pessimistic consensus in the literature on this subject, if not necessarily watertight, remains formidable.

118. Siegelbaum, *Soviet State and Society*, 180–83. See also, on these issues, Sheila Fitzpatrick, "The Bolsheviks' Dilemma: Class, Culture, and Politics in Early Soviet Years," *Slavic Review* 47 (1988): 599–613; John Hatch, "The 'Lenin Levy' and the Social Origins of Stalinism: Workers and the Communist Party in Moscow, 1921–1928," *Slavic Review* 48 (1989): 558–77; and several of the essays in Lewis H. Siegelbaum and Ronald Grigor Suny, eds., *Making Workers Soviet: Power, Class, and Identity* (Ithaca: Cornell University Press, 1994).

119. These statistics on the evolution of Communist Party membership are culled from T. H. Rigby, *Communist Party Membership in the USSR, 1917–1967* (Princeton, NJ: Princeton University Press, 1968), esp. 116.

120. Lynne Viola, *The Best Sons of the Fatherland: Workers in the Vanguard of Soviet Collectivization* (New York: Oxford University Press, 1987), 23–26. On housing and other shortages experienced by workers in Moscow under NEP, see William Chase, *Workers, Society, and the Soviet State: Labor and Life in Moscow, 1918–1929* (Urbana: University of Illinois Press, 1987). On the roles of *women* and *youth* in all of this, consult Anne G. Gorsuch, *Youth in Revolutionary Russia. Enthusiasts, Bohemians, Delinquents* (Bloomington: Indiana University Press, 2000).

121. Viola, *The Best Sons of the Fatherland*, 72.

122. Hiroaki Kuromiya, *Stalin's Industrial Revolution: Politics and Workers, 1928–1932* (Cambridge: Cambridge University Press, 1988), 113–15. Much of this was anticipated in Kuromiya's earlier article: "The Crisis of Proletarian Identity in the Soviet Factory, 1928–1929," *Slavic Review* 44 (1985): 280–97. As he noted, these "core workers" were also likely recruits for the latest technical training in the Soviet regime's new engineering schools.

123. On this so-called Shakhty trial and the subsequent trial of alleged "Industrial Party" *saboteurs*, consult Kendall E. Bailes, *Technology and Science Under Lenin and Stalin* (Princeton, NJ: Princeton University Press, 1978).

124. Sheila Fitzpatrick, *The Cultural Front: Power and Culture in Revolutionary Russia* (Ithaca, NY: Cornell University Press, 1992), 118. See also, on the Soviet culture of the NEP era, Katerina Clark, *Petersburg, Crucible of Cultural Revolution* (Cambridge, MA: Harvard University Press, 1995); and Lynn Mally, *Culture of the Future: The Proletkult Movement in Revolutionary Russia* (Berkeley: University of California Press, 1990).

125. Consult again the works by von Hagen, Chase, and Gorsuch referenced in notes 91 and 120.

126. Consult, for instance, Gregory Freeze, "The Soslovie (Estate) Paradigm and Russian Social History," *American Historical Review* 91 (1986): 11–36; Leopold Haimson, "The Problem of Social Identities in Early Twentieth-Century Russia," *Slavic Review* 47 (1988): 1–20; and Sheila Fitzpatrick, "Ascribing Class: The Construction of Social Identity in Soviet Russia," *Journal of Modern History* 65 (1993): 745–70. Other sources in this literature are cited in the notes to chapter 2.

127. Fitzpatrick, "Ascribing Class," 233–34.

128. See also, on this issue, Fitzpatrick, "The Problem of Class Identity in NEP Society," in Fitzpatrick, Rabinowitch, and Stites, eds., *Russia in the Era of NEP*, 12–33. Of course, this "bottom-up" or postmodernist approach to cultural questions in early Soviet Russia has not lacked its challengers. Their criticisms of scholars like Fitzpatrick are reviewed by Siegelbaum, *Soviet State and Society*, esp. 219–23. William Chase offers a compromise on this matter: the Stalinist "revolution from above," he suggests, "interacted ... along unforeseen lines" with a societal "revolution from below." *Workers, Society, and the Soviet State*, 299–300.

129. William Rosenberg, "Conclusion," in Fitzpatrick, Rabinowitch, and Stites, eds., *Russia in the Era of NEP*, 316, 319–20.

CONCLUSION

1. As cited in the Introduction (p. 7) to John Foran, ed., *Theorizing Revolutions* (London: Routledge, 1997).
2. Refer again to Foran, "Theories of Revolution Revisited: Toward a Fourth Generation?" *Sociological Theory* 11 (1993): 1–20.
3. See again Jack A. Goldstone, "Toward a Fourth Generation of Revolutionary Theory," *Annual Review of Political Science* 4 (2001): 139–87. Goldstone has since had further thoughts about this issue in subsequent commentaries. See, for example: "Rethinking Revolutions: Integrating Origins, Processes, and Outcomes," in *Comparative Studies of South Asia, Africa and the Middle East* 29 (2009): 18–32; and *Revolutions: A Very Short Introduction* (Oxford: Oxford University Press, 2014).
4. For this discussion of the Tudor-Stuart state, see Michael J. Braddick, *State Formation in Early Modern England, c. 1550-1700* (Cambridge: Cambridge University Press, 2000), 14, 19–20.
5. See again Goldstone, *Revolution and Rebellion in the Early Modern World*, p. 5n.
6. As cited from Suzanne Desan, "What's After Political Culture? Recent French Revolutionary Historiography," *French Historical Studies* 23 (2000): 194–95.
7. The reference, of course, is to Evans, Rueschemeyer, and Skocpol, eds., *Bringing the State Back In*.
8. Consult again Baker and Edelstein, eds., *Scripting Revolution*, 3.
9. Steve Smith, "Writing the History of the Russian Revolution after the Fall of Communism," as quoted in Martin A. Miller, ed., *The Russian Revolution: The Essential Readings* (Oxford: Blackwell, 2001), 275–77.
10. See his prefatory words in Edward Acton, Vladimir Cherniaev, and William G. Rosenberg, eds., *Critical Companion to the Russian Revolution 1914-1921* (Bloomington: Indiana University Press, 1997), esp. 19–20, 23–24. Yet we should also recall in this connection Rosenberg's impatient observation several years later (at the NYU seminar devoted to Arno Mayer's *The Furies*) that, these days, "everything 'post' concentrates attention on human agency, ideology, and culturally embedded politics and argues for the end of (social) history, not to mention its lower-case marxist dispositions." Rosenberg was cited to this effect in chapter 4 of the present book.
11. As cited in Skocpol, *States and Social Revolutions*, 29.
12. See, for this citation, Kimmel, *Revolution: A Sociological Interpretation*, 35. Kimmel was paraphrasing here (quite accurately) from Weber's famous treatise entitled "Politics as a Vocation," which appeared in 1918.
13. Refer once again, in this connection, to Parker, *Revolutions in History*, 182.
14. Refer once again to Kimmel's discussion of Weber's 1918 treatise in *Revolution: A Sociological Interpretation*, 35–36.
15. Figes, *A People's Tragedy*, 823–24.

Index

absolutism, 160; *of ancien régime*, 17; of Louis XVI, 15; reforming, 21; Walzer on, 93
abstract statism, 93
Act of Oblivion, 147
Acton, Edward, 63, 201
Adamson, John, 81, 85
affirmative postmodernism, xvi
aggregate social psychology, x
agriculture: capitalism and, 55, 56; collectivization of, 184–185; socialization of, 188
Alexander II (Tsar), 101
Alexander III (Tsar), 34, 35–36
Alexandra (Empress), 30, 103, 104, 244n100
alienation, class, 35
Altrichter, Helmut, 186
American Historical Association, 137
American Historical Review, 53
Amussen, Susan, xxi
The Anatomy of Revolution (Brinton), x
The Anatomy of Revolution Revisited (Stone, B.), xiv, xix, 5
ancien régime, xxiv, 7, 11, 21, 24, 63, 68; absolutism of, 17; bourgeoisie in, 42–53; capitalism and, 48; Furet on, 121; middle classes of, 73
Anglican Church, 10
Annual Review of Political Science (journal), xix

anti-Catholicism, 10; Charles I and, 11
antiroyalists, 78, 93–94
aristocracy, 10; traditional, 10
Aristocrats, Plebeians and Revolution in England, 57
Armitage, David, xx
Ascher, Abraham, 29; on Stolypin, 29–30
Ashe, John, 84
Ashton, Robert, 56
Atkinson, Dorothy, 35
Austria-Hungary, 31
authoritarianism: modernization and, 34; state, 202
Aylmer, G. E., 7, 8, 145, 147, 157; on Charles I, 7

Baczko, Bronislaw, 170–171
Baker, Keith M., 83, 125; on Enlightenment, 125–126; on Jacobin Terror, 126; on texts, xvii
Baker, Philip, 81–82, 83, 84
balance of power, 117
bankruptcy, two-thirds, 174
Barber, Sarah, 82–83, 85, 150; on Charles I, 87; on regicide, 111
Barère, Bertrand, 111
barin, 35
Barry, Jonathan, 57; on gentry, 57
Bell, David, xviii, 124
Bien, David, 137; on Furet, 123
biens nationaux, 174

Bienvenu, Richard T., 114–115
Black, Jeremy, 4
Blake, Robert, 149
Blake, William, 13
Blanning, T. C. W., xxi
blood guilt, 82
Bodin, Jean, 82
Bolsheviks, ix, xxiii, 37, 71, 109, 130, 132–133; crisis of legitimacy of, 180–195; Holquist on, 141; Litvin on, 266n78; Mayer on, 182; McDonald on, 189–190; opposition to, 109; peasants and, 190; power accessed by, 107; in Red Terror, 135; Sanborn on, 141; slogans of, 135
Bolshevization, 191
Bonapartist *coups*, 178
Book of Orders, 8
Bordes, Maurice, 21
Bourbon Restoration, 111
bourgeoisie, xxiv, 199; in *ancien régime*, 42–53; Campbell on, 52–53; capitalism and, 48; class consciousness of, 66; class formation and, 64–65, 66; in English Revolution, 59; in French Revolution, 42–53; Garrioch on, 50–51; Jessenne on, 52–53; Maza on, 51; McPhee on, 46, 52; revolutionary, 45–46, 53–63; self-awareness of, 51; as social protagonist, 52
The Bourgeois Revolution in France (Heller), 48
Braddick, Michael, 92, 199–200
Bradshaw, John, 82, 95, 162
Brenner, Robert, 53, 60; Levine on, 56–57; on Personal Rule, 55–56; on Stuart England, 54
Brenner Thesis, xxii, 53, 56, 60–61
Brest-Litovsk, 109, 131
Brinton, Crane, x, 152
Brissot, Jacques-Pierre, 94
Britain in Revolution (Woolrych), 150
Brooks, Christopher, 57
Brown, Howard G., 179; on French Revolution, 176–177; on postmodernism, 176
Brumaire coup, 155
Brunswick Manifesto, 86
Brusilov, Alexei, 32

Bukharin, Nikolai, 182, 185, 191; on NEP, 188
Burke, Edmund, 273n82
burzhuaziia, 63–71. *See also* bourgeoisie
Butler, 85, 86

Calamy, Edmund, 79, 81
Callinicos, Alex, 53
Calonne, Charles-Alexandre de, 19, 241n54; dismissal of, 17–18; Hardman on, 17; Louis XVI and, 16–17, 17; reforms of, 17
Campbell, Peter: on bourgeoisie, 52–53; on state failure, 52–53
Capet, Louis, 88
capitalism: agricultural, 55, 56; *ancien régime* and, 48; bourgeoisie and, 48; early forms of, 55; English Revolution influenced by, 56; feudalism and transition to, 53–54, 56; French Revolution and, 49; industrialization and, xi; rise of, 54; in Russia, 66; urban, 56
capitalism-centered structuralism, xi, xxiii; extreme versions of, 63; Marxism and, 45; McPhee on, 45; state-centered structuralism and, 41, 49, 53, 198
Capp, Bernard, 13
Carlin, Norah, 7, 59, 60; on Charles I, 9–10
Case, Thomas, 146
Catechism of a Revolutionist (Nechaev), 101
Catholicism, 152, 165–166, 172–173, 238n16; anti-Catholicism, 10, 11
Catholic modernity, Pincus on, 4
The Causes of the English Civil War (Carlin), 60
census society, 69, 71
Charles I (King), xxii, xxiv, 1, 3, 28, 108, 256n41; anti-Catholicism and, 11; Aylmer on, 7; Barber on, 87; Carlin on, 9–10; crusade against, 142–143; denunciations of, 82–83; escape of, 147; execution of, 1, 13, 84, 87, 90–91, 92, 143–144; governance style of, 9; Hughes on, 8; ministers of, 242n67; Orr on, 87; parliamentary opposition to, 163; Personal Rule of, 6, 7, 21, 55; Pincus on, 14; on popery, 11–12;

Index

Sharpe on, 7–8; social philosophy of, 9; as traditionalist, 8, 14; traditional legal forms and, 76–88; trial of, 84, 87, 127, 150; Young on, 8–9, 9
Charles II (King), 90, 143, 146, 147, 166, 168
Chartier, Roger, 93
Chase, William, 193
Chaussinand-Nogaret, Guy, 247n11
Cheka, 130–131, 133, 135, 145; Figes on, 140
Cheney, Paul, xx
Chernov, Victor, 107, 136, 139
Chernyshevsky, Nikolay, 101
Chicherin, Georgi V., 182
chinovnik, 35
chouannerie, 117
Church, Clive, 173
citizenship, 171
Civil Constitution of the Clergy, 94
class consciousness: of bourgeoisie, 66; modernization and, 191; of peasants, 186
class formation, xxvi, 46, 68; bourgeoisie and, 64–65, 66; Garrioch on, 50; Gleason on, 65–66; language and, 51; Owen on, 66
classical republicanism, 126, 178
Clay, Lauren R., 53
Cobb, Richard, 128
Cobban, Alfred, ix, 45, 46, 52, 247n5; Lewis on, 47–48
Coffee, John, xxii
Cohen, Stephen F., 266n73
Cold War, ix
collectivization, 188, 191; of agriculture, 184–185; of peasant land, 183
Collinson, Patrick, 82, 85
The Coming of the French Revolution (Lefebvre), 43
commercial republicanism, 273n76
Committee of Public Safety, 111, 115, 120
communism, 37, 186
Communist Manifesto (Marx & Engels), 41
Communist Party (Russia), 156, 180, 191, 192; re-proletarianization of, 191
comparativists, 155
conspiracy theories, 23; English Revolution and, 11; Hughes on, 11

Constitution, French, 94; Article 2, Chapter II, 89–90; Article 5, Chapter II, 89–90
constitutional legitimacy, 160, 162
constitutional monarchy, 19
constitutions, written, 156–157
Conventionnels, 90, 97–98, 126, 256n49; Edelstein on, 127; trial blocked by, 90; Walzer on, 95
Cook, John, 87, 150
Cooper, Thomas, 146
Council of Elders, 169
Council of Five Hundred, 169
counterrevolutionary movements, 109, 117, 123, 128, 135, 243n82, 258n70; Louis XVI and, 94; Russian Revolution and, 37
coup d'etats, 170
Coursac, Pierrette Girault de, 14
Crawford, Patricia, 82, 85
Cressy, David, xxii; on English Revolution, 63
Crimean War, 34
crises of legitimacy, 155; of Bolsheviks, 180–195; constitutional, 160, 162; Cromwell, O., on, 157, 161, 163; in English Protectorate, 156–168; in Executive Directory, 169–180; in New Economic Policy Russia, 180–195; Robespierre on, 96–97; state, 194, 199
Critical Dictionary of the French Revolution, 122
Cromwell, Oliver, xxii, xxvi, 4, 12–13, 76, 160, 169, 171; conviction of, 86; on crises of legitimacy, 157, 161, 163; death of, 166, 167; on Drogheda, 147–148; Durston on, 270n25; Gaunt on, 160; Howell on, 158–159; Little on, 270n18; on monarchy, 83–84; Protectorate Parliaments of, 157; reforms of, 13; on regicide, 142–143; scholarly ambivalence towards, 159; as traditionalist, 159; Trevor-Roper on, 158; tyranny of, 90; Woolrych on, 151–152, 159, 166
Cromwell, Richard, xxvi, 156, 164, 169, 176; death of, 167; Hutton on, 165, 166; Woolrych on, 271n36
Croot, Patricia, 56

Cultural Revolution (Russian), 193

Daniel, Robert V., 155
Danilov, V. P., 184, 187, 188
Darnton, Robert, 44, 93
Daumard, Adeline, 43
Davies, Godfrey, 165
Debo, Richard K., 132–133
decentralization, 34
Declaration of the Rights of Man and the Citizen of 1789, 90
Declaration of Verona, 171, 243n82
deconstructionism, ix, xvii, 51, 125, 200; Russian Revolution viewed by, 63. *See also* postmodernism
democracy, 144; French Revolution and, 170–171; representative, 176; in Russia, 140
demographic change, xiv
Deniken, A. I., 38
Derrida, Jacques, xv, xvii
desacralization, of monarchy, 92, 93–94
Desan, Suzanne, 200; on the state, 201
developing world, revolutions in, 198
d'Herbois, Collot, 111
disequilibration of social systems, x
Donoghue, John, xxi, xxii
double trap, 190
Doyle, William, 42
Drogheda, 147–148, 151, 152
Dubois, Laurent, xx
Duma, 29, 68
Dunn, Susan, 98
Durston, Christopher, 161–162; on Cromwell, O., 270n25
Dzerzhinskii, Felix, 129–130, 135, 144–145, 146, 182

Eastern Association Army, 12
Edelstein, Dan, xiv–xv, 75, 89, 125, 258n79; on *Conventionnels*, 127; on Jacobin Terror, 126; on revolutionary authority, 110–111; on Robespierre, 97; on texts, xvii
Edward III (King), 77
Edwards, Lyford P., x
Eisenstadt, S. N., xxiv, 2–3
Elton, Geoffrey, 3
Emmons, Terence, 35

Engels, Friedrich, ix, 41
The English Atlantic in an Age of Revolution (Pestana), xxi–xxii
English Civil War, 8, 57
English Navy, 13
English Revolution, xxi, 1; bourgeoisie in, 53–63, 59; capitalism as factor in, 56; conspiracy theories and, 11; Cressy on, 63; cultural roots of, 149; elites after, 194; Hill on, 61–62; Malia on, 149; Manning, B., on, 58–59; Marxist interpretations of, 60, 62–63; mass-mobilization in, 12; modernizers in, 2, 12, 13; neostructuralist interpretations of, 61; revolutionary gentry in, 53–63; revolutionary terror in, 141–152; socioeconomic results of, 58; state modernization in, 195; traditionalism in, 2, 12, 13, 149; violence in, 145
Enlightenment, xxvi, 14, 45; Baker, M., on, 125–126
equality, 80
Evans, Richard J., xvi; on history, xv; on radical postmodernism, xvi; Southgate on, xvi
execution question, xxv
Executive Directory (France): crisis of legitimacy in, 169–180; First, 172; Livesey on, 177; political cultural conflict in, 177; *politique de bascule* of, 175; religion and, 172; Second, 172; transitions of, 178

Fairfax, Thomas, 12, 81, 144
famine, 71
fascism, 202
Feher, Ferenc, 89, 98
feminism, xviii
Fersen, Axel von, 88
feudalism, capitalism transitioned to from, 53–54, 56
Fifth Monarchists, 162
Figes, Orlando, xxiii, 34, 38, 71, 75, 145, 203; on *Cheka*, 140; on Red Terror, 135, 139; on regicide, 110; on Romanov Russia, 100–101; on Russian society, 72
finance capital, 63, 173

Index 283

Fire Under the Ashes: An Atlantic History of the English Revolution (Donoghue), xxi
First Balkan War, 30
First Coalition, 117–118, 119; geopolitical designs of, 119
First Directory, 172
Fitzpatrick, Sheila, xxiii, 73, 137, 155, 193; on Marxism, 67; on NEP, 180
Five-Year Plan, 182, 185, 191, 192
Fogelsong, David, 37
Foran, John, xviii–xix, 198
Foucault, Michel, xv, 200
Freeze, Gregory, 64, 193; on *soslovnost*, 65
French Constitution, Patrick on, 90
French Convention, 95, 117; Walzer on, 88
French Historical Studies (Desan), 200
French Revolution, xx, 273n82; bourgeoisie in, 42–53; Brown on, 176–177; democracy and, 170–171; Dubois on, xx; elites after, 194; Furet on, 122–123; furies in, 136; geopolitical factors in, 92; geostrategic factors in, 92; legitimacy of, reified, 76, 96; Miller, S., on, 22; modernizers in, 14–25; pre-revolution period, xx; revolutionary legal procedure in, 88–98; revolutionary terror in, 114–128; schizoid political culture leading to, 23; socially based resistance to, 91; state modernization in, 195; statism in, 94; theorization of process of, 76; traditionalists in, 14–25; wartime emergencies in, 92. *See also* Executive Directory
Frieden, Nancy, 68
Fructidor *coup*, 171, 172
Frumkin, M. I., 188, 191
Furet, François, xx, xxv, 43, 137, 264n34; on *ancien régime*, 121; Bien on, 123; on French Revolution, 122–123; on Jacobin Terror, 122, 124; Woloch on, 123–124
furies, 122, 123; defining, 113; in French Revolution, 136; gestation of, 136; in Russian Revolution, 138. *See also* revolutionary terror

Gainot, Bernard, 177, 178

Garrioch, David: on bourgeoisie, 50–51; on class formation, 50; on political behavior, 50
Gatrell, Peter: on Romanov Russia, 70; on WICs, 69
Gaunt, Peter, 157–158; on Cromwell, O., 160
Geertz, Clifford, 200
Gellner, Ernest, xvi; on postmodernism, xv
Gentles, Ian, 81, 86, 152, 255n23
gentry: Barry on, 57; in English Revolution, 53–63; intelligentsia, 252n92; major generals and, 162; revolutionary, 53–63; in Stuart England, 73. *See also* bourgeoisie
geopolitics, xii, 84–85, 102, 151, 174, 202; of First Coalition, 119; in French Revolution, 92; neostructuralists on, 108, 173; of Russia, 36, 104, 108
George V (King), 99, 104
geostrategy, 10; domestic affairs and, 61; finance and, 179; regicide and, 92–93; of Russia, 65, 132, 182, 189
Germany, 102–104; Romanov Russia and, 104; Russia and, 131–132
Girondists, 91, 94, 95
Glassey, Lionel K. J., 4
Gleason, Abbott: on class formation, 65–66; on industrialization, 66
Glorious Revolution, 1–2, 38
Godechot, Jacques, xx
gold standard, 27
Goldstone, Jack, xiv–xv, xix, 49–50, 59, 198
Goloschekin, Fillip, 100
Goodwin, Albert, 170
Goodwin, Jeff, 3
Gorsuch, Anne, 193
Gosplan, 181, 182
gosudarstvo, 68
Gravier, Charles, 14
Great Rebellion, 56
Great Reforms, 69
Great Terror, 123
Greer, Donald, 121; on Jacobin Terror, 115, 118–119, 120–121, 121–122; on Robespierre, 120–121
Guchkov, Aleksandr, 70
Gueniffey, Patrice, 125, 139

Gunpowder Plot, 11

Habsburgs, 156, 195
Hagen, Mark von, 193
Haimson, Leopold H., 65, 72, 193
Haitian Revolution, xx
Hardman, John, 14, 15, 18, 20, 94, 241n64; on Calonne, 17; on Louis XVI, 20, 25; on Necker, 16
Harris, Robert, 18
Haselrig, Arthur, 162
Haute Marne, 173
hegemony, 198
Heinzen, James, 187
Heller, Henry, xxi, 48; on Maza, 51–52
Henrietta-Maria, 144
Hill, Christopher, ix, 3, 11, 53, 59, 152; on English Revolution, 61–62
Hintze, Otto: Kimmel on, xii; on the state, xii
Hirst, Derek, 10, 157
history: as discipline, xvii; Evans on, xv; postmodernist description of, xvii; Southgate on, xvi, xvii
Hobbes, Thomas, 82, 177
Holles, Denzil, 78–79, 81, 91
Holquist, Peter, on Bolsheviks, 141
Hopper, Rex D., x
House of Commons, 76
House of Special Designation, 100
Howell, Roger, 158–159
Hudson, Hugh D., 187, 189, 190
Hufton, Olwen, 44
Hughes, Ann, 7, 8; on Charles I, 8; on conspiracy theories, 11
Huguenots, 82
Humble Petition, 157
Hunt, Lynn, 44
Huntington, Samuel, xxiv, 2–3
Hutton, Ronald, 141, 149, 152, 157; on Cromwell, R., 165; on Protectorate Parliaments, 165

identity politics, 193
ideology, 113
Imperia Duma, Stolypin on, 29
The Incidence of the Terror (Louie), 119
India, 116

industrialization: capitalism and, xi; Gleason on, 66; recasting effects of, 28; of Russia, 28–29, 66, 181, 195; Stalin on, 182; Witte on, 28. *See also* modernization
Intellectual Origins of the English Revolution Revisited (Hill), 61
Ireland, 11–12, 85, 147, 151
Irish Catholicism, 143, 152
Iudenich, N. N., 38
Ivnitskii, N. A., 184, 187, 188

Jacobins, 95, 256n49
Jacobin Terror, 24–25, 98, 114–115, 170, 171, 263n31; Baker, M., on, 126; driving forces of, 120; economic pressures in, 120; Edelstein on, 126; executions during, 118–119; Furet on, 122, 124; Greer on, 115, 118–119, 120–121, 121–122; Miller, M. A., on, 127; neostructuralist interpretations of, 128; official violence of, 127–128; Red Terror compared with, 138; sociological dimension to, 122
Jacobson, Jon, 183
Jainchill, Andrew, 177, 178
James II, 1, 90
Jansenists, 23
Jenkins, William, 146
Jenner, Robert, 84
Jessenne, Jean-Pierre, 52–53
Johnson, Chalmers, x, 197
Jones, Colin, 45–46, 47
Jones, Peter M., 21, 117–118
Jordan, David, 89, 91
Joseph II, 24
The Journal of Modern History, 125
July Days of 1789, 20
Justices of the Peace (JPs), 161

Kadet party, 103
Kaiser, Thomas E., xxi
Kassow, Samuel D., 68, 72–73
Kelsey, Sean, 84, 150–151
Kerensky, Alexander, 36, 99, 105, 107, 136, 139
Kerensky offensive, 131
Khrustalev, V. M., 105, 106

Kimmel, Michael S., x, 3; on Hintze, xii; on revolutions, xi; on the state, xi
kingship, 77–78, 80. *See also* monarchy
Kishlansky, Mark, xxi
Knox, Alfred, 33
Kokovstov, V. I., 27, 31, 244n101, 244n103, 245n104; policies of, 30–31
Kolchak, A. V., 38
Kolonitskii, Boris, xxiii, 102, 104
Komsomol, 191, 192
Konovalov, Aleksandr, 70
Kornilov, 37
Koslov, Denis, 184, 187, 188
kulaks, 184, 186, 192, 193

Lake, Peter, 3, 4
Lambert, John, 156–157, 157
Lameth, Charles de, 93
Lamoignon de Basville, 18, 19, 24, 241n58
landowners, 21
language, class formation and, 51
Laud, William, 5, 6, 7, 8, 13, 77
Lefebvre, Georges, ix, 18, 43, 44–45
legitimacy. *See* crises of legitimacy
Lenin, Vladimir, xii, 36, 97, 108, 194, 261n120; death of, 182; McDonald on, 189; in Red Terror, 99, 133–134; Robespierre compared with, 139; on state building, 138; successors, 180; Viola on, 191
Leviathan (Hobbes), 82
Levine, David, on Brenner, 56–57
Lewin, Moshe, 137–138; on NEP, 183; structuralism of, 266n73
Lewis, Gwynne, 174; on Cobban, 47–48
Lieven, Dominic, 26, 244n103
Lilburne, John, 80, 91
Linton, Marisa, 127
Little, Patrick, 160, 166–167; on Cromwell, O., 270n18
Litvin, Alter, 130; on Bolsheviks, 266n78
Litvinov, Maxim, 182
Livesey, James, 177, 178; on Executive Directory, 177
Loménie de Brienne, Etienne-Charles, 18, 19, 24
London Baptists, 83
Louie, Richard, 119

Louis XVI (King), xxiv, 1, 24, 28, 44, 143; absolutism of, 15; Calonne and, 16–17, 17; counterrevolutionary activity of, 94; execution of, 75, 90–91, 98; Hardman on, 20, 25; on modernization, 14, 19; Necker and, 16, 18, 19; Patrick on, 89–90, 94; reinstatement of, 93; revolutionary legal procedure and, 88–98; Robespierre on, 96; on social inequality, 15; socially based resistance to, 91; on state modernization, 19; traditionalism of, 14; trial of, 75, 90
Love, Christopher, 145, 146
Lucas, Colin, 171
Ludlow, Edmund, 162
Lyons, Martyn, 170, 172

Mailhe, Jean-Baptiste, 90
major generals, 161–162; gentry and, 162
Making Democracy in the French Revolution (Livesey), 177
Maklakov, N. A., 31
Malia, Martin, xv, 139; on English Revolution, 149; on Red Terror, 140
Mally, Lynn, xxiii, 201
Manning, Brian, 57, 58; on English Revolution, 58–59
Manning, Roberta, 69
Marie-Antoinette, 18, 24
Markoff, John, 119
Marx, Karl, ix, xi, xii, 41, 52
Marxism, 45, 59; capitalism-centered structuralism and, 45; English Revolution interpreted by, 60, 62–63; Fitzpatrick on, 67; Red Terror and role of, 137
Mason, Laura, 177
mass-mobilization: in English Revolution, 12; in Russian Revolution, 35
Mawdsley, Evan, 38, 136–137
Mayer, Arno, 113, 124, 134; on Bolsheviks, 182; on Red Terror, 129
Mayers, Ruth E., 165–166
Maza, Sarah: on bourgeoisie, 51; Heller on, 51–52
Mazauric, Claude, 48
McDonald, Tracy, 187, 189; on Bolsheviks, 189–190; on Lenin, 189

McPhee, Peter, xxi, 41, 53, 248n20; on bourgeoisie, 46, 52; on capitalism-centered structuralism, 45
Members of Parliament (MP), 157, 161
Mensheviks, 134
Merchants and Revolution: Commercial Change, Political Conflict, and London's Overseas Traders, 1550-1653 (Brenner), 53, 56
Mercy-Argenteau, Florimund, 116
Merrick, Jeffrey W., 93
middling sort, 57
Mikhailovich, Nikolai, 104
military employment, state modernization and, 19. *See also* major generals
Miliukov, Paul, 36, 103, 105
Miller, Mary Ashburn, 125; on Jacobin Terror, 127
Miller, Stephen, 21; on French Revolution, 22
Milton, Anthony, 7
Miromesnil, Hue de, 15, 16, 20
moderate postmodernism, xv, 1
modernity, 3; Pincus on, 5, 10
modernization, xxiv; authoritarianism and, 34; class consciousness and, 191; defining, 3; in English Revolution, 2, 12, 13; in French Revolution, 14–25; Lake on, 3, 4; Louis XVI on, 14, 19; Pincus on, 3–4, 38; in Romanov Russia, 33; in Russian Revolution, 25–38; state, 2–3, 3, 4, 19, 36, 195, 246n127; Stolypin as, 34; Stone, L., on, 5, 6; theoretical terms of, 4; traditionalists in conflict with, 13; Turgot's efforts towards, 15; Weissman on, 34; Witte as, 34
Moghadam, Valentine, xviii
monarchy: abolition of, 59; Cromwell, O., on, 83–84; desacralization of, 92, 93–94; preservation of, 87; Romanov Russia and worship of, 100–101; sacralization of, 101; Saint-Just on, 96. *See also* absolutism; regicide
monopolies, 63
Moore, Barrington, Jr., xiii
Morrill, J. S., 7, 81–82, 84
Muscovites, 70
muzhiki, 29, 35, 184, 187

Napoleon Bonaparte, 172
Napoleonic Empire, 178
Napoleonic Rule, 111, 169
Narkomzen, 187, 188, 191
narod, 68
National Convention, 88, 114
nationalism, 202
natural rulers, 111, 162, 171
Nechaev, Sergei, 101
Necker, Jacques, 15, 24, 241n54, 241n64; Hardman on, 16; Louis XVI and, 16, 18, 19; Price on, 18; reforms of, 16; reinstating of, 18
neo-Jacobins, 171
neostructuralism, xi–xii, 38, 41–42, 75; defining, 73; English Revolution interpreted by, 61; on geopolitics, 108, 173; insights of, 197; Jacobin Terror and, 128; on postrevolutionary states, 199; on revolutionary terror, 152; state modernization viewed by, 38; on Thermidorian crisis, 168
Nepmen, 192, 193
New Economic Policy (NEP), 155; abandonment of, 183; achievements of, 183; Bukharin on, 188; crises of legitimacy in, 180–195; Fitzpatrick on, 180; Moshe on, 183
New Model Army, 12, 76, 80, 86–87; criticism of, 13; delegitimizing, 160; saints of, 142–143
Nicholas II (Tsar), 1, 25, 75, 96, 244n93; dethroning of, 105; opposition to, 102–103; *raison d'etat* and, 99–112; Stolypin and, 29; traditionalism of, 31; Trotsky on, 105–106; Verner on, 25–26; on Westernization, 36; Witte and, 27–28; World War I and, 102, 108
nobility, Russian, 26
Norbrood, David, 150
Norfolk, 145
notables, 68; in Romanov Russia, 69

obschchestvo, 63, 72
October Days of 1789, 20
October Revolution, 182
Okhrana, 148
Origins of the French Revolution (Doyle), 42

Orr, D. Alan, 89, 92; on Charles I, 87; on law of treason, 77
Ouvrard, Gabriel-Julien, 174
Owen, Thomas C., 63; on class formation, 66; on Romanov Russia, 66
Ozouf, Mona, 89, 124

Paléologue, Maurice, 33
Palmer, Robert R., 119, 119–120, 123
papists, 11–12
Pares, Barnard, 244n100
Parker, David, 56; on the state, 202
Parker, Geoffrey, xxii
Parker, Noel, xix
patricians, 58
Patrick, Alison, 91; on French Constitution, 90; on Louis XVI, 89–90, 94; on Robespierre, 97
peasants, 184, 185; Altrichter on, 186; Bolsheviks and, 190; class consciousness of, 186; classes, 186, 190; collectivization of lands of, 183; the state and class formation of, xiii; *zemstvos* representing, 35. *See also kulaks*
Penser la Révolution française (Furet), 121
A People's Tragedy (Figes), 75
personal agency, xiii
Personal Rule, 6, 7, 21; Brenner on, 55–56
Pestana, Carla, xxi–xxii, xxii
Pestel, Pavel, 102
Peter and Paul Fortress, 100
Petrograd, 37, 69, 100
Petrograd Society of Factory and Mill Owners, 71
Pettee, George S., x
Pincus, Steve, xxiv, 1; on Catholic modernity, 4; on Charles I, 14; on modernity, 5, 10; on modernization, 3–4, 38; on state modernization, 4
Pipes, Richard, 99, 106, 109, 139; on Red Terror, 134, 265n61; on Romanov Russia, 111
Pitt, William, 116–117
plebeians, 58
polarization, 162, 163–164; social, 170–171
political behavior, Garrioch on, 50

Political Order in Changing Societies (Huntington), 2
Polivanov, Aleksei A., 27, 32, 33, 102
popery, Charles I on, 11–12
Popkin, Jeremy, xx–xxi
popular verdict, 107
populism, 202
postmodernism, ix, 273n69; affirmative, xvi; Brown on, 176; defining, 234n24; Gellner on, xv; on history, xvii; moderate, xv, 1; on Presbyterians, 79; radical, xv, xxiii; on Red Terror, 140–141; revolutions interpreted by, 38; Russian Revolution interpreted by, 138–139; split within, xv, xviii; structuralism on limits of, xviii; structuralism reconciled with, xix, 197
post-revisionism, 3, 5, 7, 9–11
postrevolutionary states, xiii, 202, 203; neostructuralist problematization of, 199
Potts. John, 79
power, balance of, 117
Preobrazhensky, Evgenii, 182
Presbyterian Right, 78, 143
Presbyterians, 79, 81, 146–147; postmodernists on, 79
prestructuralism, x
Price, Munro, 14, 18, 88, 94, 242n79; on Necker, 18
Pride's Purge, 79, 80, 144, 149
Privilege Russia, 34, 70
proceduralism, xxv
procedural justice, 107
Progressist Party, 70, 252n97
progressive militarization, 243n83
Protectorate Parliaments, 157, 160; crisis of legitimacy in, 156–168; failure of, 160–161, 165; First, 161, 163, 175; Hutton on, 165; Second, 157
Protestantism, 128
Provisional Government, 107
Pskov, 104
public sphere, 68
Putney debates, 83
Pym, John, 78, 79

Quakers, 162

radical centrism, 179
radical postmodernism, xv, xxiii; Evans on, xvi
Radischev, Aleksandr, 101
raison d'etat, 152; Nicholas II and, 99–112
Rappaport, Helen, 101, 106, 108–109, 261n120
Rasputin, 103
razmychka, 188, 192
Read, Christopher, xxii
recession, of early 1900s, 27
Red Army, 33
Red Terror, 111, 114, 124; Bolsheviks in, 135; chronology of, 129; duration of, 134; end of, 136; Figes on, 135, 139; Jacobin Terror compared with, 138; Lenin's role in, 99, 133–134; Malia on, 140; Marxism as factor in, 137; Mayer on, 129; Pipes on, 134, 265n61; postmodernist interpretations of, 140–141; social incidence of, 136; as systematic policy, 130; targets of, 133; Trotsky on, 129–130; victims of, 134
Reece, H. M., 167, 167–168, 168, 180
regicide, 91, 143, 255n23; Barber on, 111; Cromwell, O., on, 142–143; Figes on, 110; geostrategic roots of, 92–93; structuralist views on, 98
Regicide and Revolution (Walzer), 89
Reinhard, Marcel, 45
religion, 161–162; Executive Directory and, 172; intolerance and, 172–173. *See also specific types*
Remonstrance, 84
Renouvin, Pierre, 21
rentes, 42
republicanism, 94
Revel, Riot, and Rebellion (Underdown), xxi
revisionism, 52, 121, 158, 200; post-revisionism, 3, 5, 7, 9–11; social, 42, 44
Revolution and Rebellion in the Early Modern World (Goldstone), 49
Revolution and the Transformation of Societies (Eisenstadt), 2
revolutionary authority: Edelstein on, 110–111
revolutionary bourgeoisie, 45–46; in English Revolution, 53–63; state-centered structuralism and, 60
revolutionary gentry, in English Revolution, 53–63
revolutionary justice, 75, 89, 100, 111
revolutionary statism, 112
revolutionary terror, 113; in English Revolution, 141–152; in French Revolution, 114–128; neostructuralist interpretations of, 152; in Russian Revolution, 129–141
Revolutionary Tribunal, 115
Revolution: A Sociological Interpretation (Kimmel), xi
revolutions: Kimmel on, xi; postmodernist interpretations of, 38; Skocpol on, xiii; Wallerstein on, xi–xii; Weber on, xii
Riabushinsky, Pavel P., 68, 70, 71
Rieber, Alfred, 193
Roberts, George, 146
Robespierre, Maximilien, 88, 95, 110, 111, 159, 258n80; Edelstein on, 97; Greer on, 120–121; on legitimacy, 96–97; Lenin compared with, 139; on Louis XVI, 96; Patrick on, 97
Roche, Daniel, 44, 45
Roider, Karl, 116
Romanov Russia, 23; Figes on, 100–101; Gatrell on, 70; Germany and, 104; modernizers in, 33; monarch-worship in, 100–101; notables in, 69; Owen on, 66; Pipes on, 111
Roots, Ivan, 163, 163–164
Rosenau, Pauline Marie, xvi, xix, 139, 195
Rosenberg, William G., xxiii, 138–139, 266n82
Rousseau, Jean-Jacques, 123
royalists, 145, 146–147
Rump Parliament, 95, 146, 150, 164; Act of Oblivion, 147; quarreling in, 151; restoration of, 167
Rupert (Prince), 12–13, 144
Russell, Conrad, ix, 167
Russia, 63–71; capitalism in, 66; crisis of legitimacy in, 180–195; democracy in, 140; Figes on society in, 72; geopolitics of, 36, 104, 108; geostrategy of, 65, 132, 182, 189; Germany and, 32, 131–132; industrialization of, 28–29, 66, 181, 195; Privilege, 34, 70;

repopulation of urban, 185–186; state power in prerevolutionary, 33–34. *See also* Communist Party; New Economic Policy; Romanov Russia
Russian Revolution, xxii; counterrevolutionary movements and, 37; furies in, 138; honeymoon period in, 36; intragovernmental tensions leading to, 28; mass-mobilization in, 35; modernizers in, 25–38; postmodernist perspective on, 138–139; revolutionary terror in, 129–141; state modernization in, 195; structuralist perspective on, 138–139; traditionalists in, 25–38

Saint-Just, Louis-Antoine, 88, 95, 110, 111, 126; on monarchy, 96
Sanborn, Joshua, 141
sans-culottes, 91–92, 115, 171
Saul, John, 146
Scott, David, 83, 85
Scott, Jonathan, xxii
Scottish confederalism, 85
séance royale of June 23, 1789, 19, 24
Second Directory, 172
secularism, 179, 242n67
Selbin, Eric, xviii
self-awareness, of bourgeoisie, 51
September Massacres, 91, 125
Serbia, 30
seredniak, 190, 192
Serna, Pierre, xxi, 177, 178–179
Sewell, William H., Jr., 21
Shanin, Teodor, 186–187
Shapiro, Gilbert, 119
Sharp, Andrew, 80
Sharpe, Kevin, on Charles I, 7–8
Siegelbaum, Lewis H., 71, 181; on Stalin Revolution, 185
Sinnott, David, 148
1688: The First Modern Revolution (Pincus), 1–2, 5, 38
skeptical poststructuralism, xvi
Skinner, Quentin, 92
Skipworth, Ralph, 146
Skocpol, Theda: on revolutions, xiii; structuralism of, xiii, 200–201
Smith, David L., 160, 166–167

Smith, Steve A., xxii
smychka, 182, 188, 192
Soboul, Albert, 48, 91, 123
social hierarchy, 79
social inequality, Louis XVI on, 15
The Social Interpretation of the French Revolution (Cobban), 47
social participation, 21
social peace, 70
social revisionism, 42, 44
Sociological Theory (journal), xix, 198
sociopolitical transition, 46
Solemn League, 79
sosloviia, 64, 193; politicization of, 65
soslovnost, 64, 194; Freeze on, 65
Southgate, Beverley, xvii; on Evans, xvi; on history, xvi, xvii
sovereignty, 78
Sovnarkom, 130, 133
Sowerby, Scott, 4
Spanish Armada, 11
Stalin, Joseph, 181, 184; on industrialization, 182; Siberia visited by, 193
Stalinism, 193
Stalin Revolution, 185
the state, xxvii; authoritarian, 202; centralization of, xi; coercive power of, 199; enforcement of, xii; as geopolitical entity, xii; Hintze on, xii; Kimmel on, xi; Parker, D., on, 202; peasant class formation and, xiii; populism, 202; as sociopolitical entity, xii; structuralism and, xi; structuralism on formation of, 200; unitary, xiv; Weber on, xii
state-centered structuralism, xi–xiii, xiii, xxiii, 1, 75, 114, 125, 194; capitalism-centered structuralism and, 41, 49, 53, 198; revolutionary bourgeoisie and, 60
state failure, Campbell on, 52–53
state inadequacy, 71
state legitimacy, 194, 199
state modernization, 2–3, 3–4, 246n127; defining, 4; in English Revolution, 195; in French Revolution, 195; Louis XVI on, 19; military employment and, 19; neostructuralist view on, 38; Pincus on, 4; in Russian Revolution, 36, 195

state power, 19; in prerevolutionary Russia, 33–34
States and Social Revolutions (Skocpol), xiii
state-security, 156
state terror, 111
statism, 76; abstract, 93; in English Revolution, 93; in French Revolution, 94; revolutionary, 112; state-building, 138; ultra-statism, 97; violence and, 128
Steele, Ian K., xxii
Steinberg, Mark D., 105, 106
Stolypin, Peter, 27, 35–36, 185, 244n101; agrarian reforms of, 29; Ascher on, 29–30; death of, 30; on Imperia Duma, 29; as modernizer, 34; Nicholas II and, 29
Stone, Bailey, xiv, xix, 5, 11
Stone, Lawrence, 3, 20, 53; on modernization, 5, 6; on prerevolutionary regime, 7
St. Petersburg, 29, 68, 252n92
Strafford (Earl), 89
structural causes, of revolution, xiv
structuralism, ix; of Lewin, 266n73; on limits of postmodernism, xviii; postmodernism reconciled with, xix, 197; on regicide, 98; Russian Revolution interpreted by, 138–139; of Skocpol, xiii, 200–201; the state and, xi; on state formation, 200. *See also* capitalism-centered structuralism; state-centered structuralism
Stuart, Mary, 11
Stuart England, 10, 23, 53, 59, 239n23; Brenner on, 54; gentry in, 73. *See also* English Revolution
Stuart Restoration, 111, 155, 156, 194
Stürmer, Boris, 33
subvention territoriale, 17
succession, 82
Sukhomlinov, V. A., 32, 244n103
Suny, Ronald G., 186
surveillance committees, 115
Sutherland, Donald, 123, 124, 137
Sverdlov, Iakov, 134

Tackett, Timothy, 93, 128

Tanner, J. R., 6
Taylor, George V., ix, 52
Tereschchenko, M. I., 36
Thermidor, 121, 155, 156, 172; constitution drawn by, 169–170; neostructuralist interpretation of, 168
Thirty Years' War, 10, 144
Thomas, Keith, 3
Thugut, Baron, 116
Thugut, Franz Maria von, 116
Thurloe, John, 164
Tilly, Charles, xiii–xiv, 2
Tocqueville, Alexis de, 2
traditionalism, xxiv; of Charles I, 8, 14; of Cromwell, 159; in English Revolution, 2, 12, 13, 149; in French Revolution, 14–25; of Louis XVI, 14; modernizers in conflict with, 13; of Nicholas II, 31; in Russian Revolution, 25–38
traditional legal forms, Charles I and, 76–88
transient causes, of revolution, xiv
transitional politics, 175–176
treason, 145; law of, 77, 89; Orr on, 77; Walzer on, 89
Trevor-Roper, Hugh R., 160; on Cromwell, O., 158
Trotsky, Leon, 33, 97, 98, 109, 159, 180–181, 260n99, 261n112; on Nicholas II, 105–106; on Red Terror, 129–130
Tsereteli, Iraklii, 107, 136
Turgot, A.-R.-J., 14–15, 19, 24; modernization efforts of, 15
Turner, L. C. F., 31
Twelve Who Ruled (Palmer), 123

ultra-statism, 97
Underdown, David, xxi, 145, 149, 150
Union of Soviet Socialist Republics, ix
unitary state, xiv
United States, in World War I, 131
unity, 151
urban capitalism, 56
urbanization, 58

Van Kley, Dale, 23, 93
velikodushie, 107
Venning, Timothy, 164, 168

Verner, Andrew M., 28, 244n93; on Nicholas II, 25–26
Vesenkha, 181, 182
Vienna, 31, 116
vingtièmes, 17
Viola, Lynne, 184, 187, 188; on Lenin, 191
volosti, 106
voluntarism, xiv
Von Laue, Theodore H., xxiii, 187; on Witte, 27

Wade, Rex, 103
Wagner, William G., 68
Wahnich, Sophie, 125
Wallerstein, Immanuel, on revolutions, xi–xii
Walzer, Michael: on absolutism, 93; on *Conventionnels*, 95; on French Convention, 88; on treason, 89
War Industries Committees (WICs): Central, 71; Gatrell on, 69; role of, 253n101; Workers' Group in, 70
war *matériel*, 69, 70
Weber, Max, xi, 200, 203; on revolutions, xii; on the state, xii
Wedgwood, C. V., 84
Weissman, Neil, on modernization, 34
Wentworth, Thomas, 3, 7, 8, 13, 77
Westernization, 252n92; Nicholas II on, 36
Wexford, 147, 151, 152
What Is To Be Done? (Chernyshevsky), 102
Wheeler, James S., xxii

Wheeler-Bennett, John, 131
Why Lenin? Why Stalin? Why Gorbachev? (Von Laue), xxiii
Wickham-Crowley, Timothy P., xiii
WICs. *See* War Industries Committees
Wilder, Gary, xix, xx
Wildman, Allan, 104
Wilhelm II, 108
William of Orange, 143
Witte, Sergei, 185; on industrialization, 28; as modernizer, 34; Nicholas II and, 27–28; Von Laue on, 27
Woloch, Isser, 179, 180, 272n63; on Furet, 123–124
Wood, Ellen, 53
Woolrych, Austin, 150, 159, 160, 162; on Cromwell, O., 151–152, 159, 166; on Cromwell, R., 271n36
Worden, Blair, 146, 147, 148, 167
World War I, 69; Nicholas II and, 102, 108; United States in, 131
Wrightson, Keith, 57

Yakovlev, Vasili, 100
Young, Michael, 7; on Charles I, 8–9, 9
Young Russia (Zaichnevsky), 102

Zagorin, Peter, 11
Zaichnevsky, Pyotr, 102
Zaret, David, 150
zemstvos, 25, 29, 33–34; Atkinson on, 35; peasants represented by, 35

www.ingramcontent.com/pod-product-compliance
Lightning Source LLC
Chambersburg PA
CBHW031545300426
44111CB00006BA/186